VERGIL AT 2000

AMS ARS POETICA: No. 3

ISSN 0734-7618

VERGIL AT 2000

COMMEMORATIVE ESSAYS
ON THE POET AND HIS INFLUENCE

Edited by

John D. Bernard

AMS PRESS
New York

Library of Congress Cataloging in Publication Data

Main entry under title:

Vergil at 2000.

    (AMS ars poetica, ISSN 0734-7618; no. 3)
    Includes bibliographies and index.
      1. Virgil—Criticism and interpretation—Addresses,
essays, lectures.   2. Virgil—Influence—Addresses,
essays, lectures.   I. Bernard, John D.   II. Virgil.
III. Series.
PA6825.A3   1986b   883'.01   85-48005
ISBN 0-404-62503-7

Published by
AMS Press, Inc.
56 East 13th Street
New York, N. Y. 10003

VERGIL: 70–19 B.C.

Inter quae (ingenia) maxime nostri aevi emine[t] princeps carmium Vergilius. . . .
VELLEIUS PATERCULUS

THE EURYALUS FOUNDATION (SILACUSA-VENICE-NEW YORK) HAS
COLLABORATED IN THE PUBLICATION OF THIS VOLUME IN
RECOGNITION OF THE CONTRIBUTION TO EDUCATION IN THE
HUMANITIES OF THE HONORS PROGRAM
OF THE UNIVERSITY OF HOUSTON.

CONTENTS

ACKNOWLEDGMENTS

It is always a challenge as well as a pleasure to recognize the people who have made a book possible. But an editor's obligations, though no less pleasant or difficult than those of an author, are significantly different. For it is literally true, and not the usual authorly hyperbole, that the present book is a collaboration, a joint effort of many pens, minds, and aidant spirits. And while I am as certain as any other acknowledger that the words that follow are too few and too lame to do more than simply name the most prominent of those who really brought the book into being, I can at least indulge at the outset in the literal (but heartfelt) gesture of thanking the fifteen colleagues, now all old friends, who have shared the vicissitudes of this long-maturing project but who have, above all, furnished the substance of the volume.

Of these, I should particularly like to recognize Paul Alpers, Ralph Johnson, and Allen Mandelbaum, whose papers at the Houston symposium supplied both impetus and inspiration for the making of the book. I also want to acknowledge, at last in print, the support of others for that event: especially the then Provost of the University of Houston-University Park, George Magner, and the still Dean of the College of Humanities and Fine Arts, James Pickering; both of whom generously aided in putting it together. More than money (though that too) was provided by Ted L. Estess, Director of the University Honors Program, at that time as on countless occasions and in numerous ways subsequently, including his careful and critical reading of my introduction. One debt it is a special pleasure to pay; Paul Alessi, then an honored colleague at the University and much missed since, was the co-organizer of the symposium and would have been co-editor of this book had he not left for greener pastures. In a real sense this project is his too, and his help in the early stages of trying to turn the symposium into a book is deeply appreciated.

Throughout that arduous process, I have been beholden to the University for continuing support: in the form of Limited Grants-in-Aid for typing, and most of all in that of a generous subvention which helped allay the expenses of a large and costly book. For the latter I have to thank the university's Publications Committee and again (for this and for many other acts of kindness and support) Provost Magner, as well as his heroic and able assistant, Barbara Fasser. "Heroic" is almost too pale a word for the labors, under incredible pressure and amidst a welter of other professional demands, of Derrellyn Yates, who helped prepared the final draft of the manuscript.

Finally, a special word of gratitude to the editors at AMS, to Russell Till for his work in designing the book and preparing it for printing, and to Barry Moser for his generous donation of Aeneas and Anchises. No words could begin to acknowledge the myriad acts of help and encouragement by my wife, Artis — an editor long before I ever dared to try my hand, and gifted with an unfailing eye and ear for the false or extraneous, in prose as in other things. I owe her everything that has any value in my own contribution to this volume.

Strasbourg
November 1985

CONTRIBUTORS

ARCHIBALD W. ALLEN is Professor Emeritus of Classics at Wesleyan University. He has published articles on Latin elegy, especially Propertius.

PAUL ALPERS is Professor of English and Comparative Literature at the University of California, Berkeley. He is the author of books on Vergil's *Eclogues* and Spenser's *Faerie Queene*.

JOHN D. BERNARD, Associate Professor of Honors and English at the University of Houston–University Park, has written articles on Renaissance literature and is currently writing a book on pastoralism in the poetry of Spenser.

W.R. JOHNSON teaches Latin, Greek, and Comparative Studies at the University of Chicago. His books include *Darkness Visible, The Idea of Lyric*, and the forthcoming *Momentary Monsters: Lucan and His Heroes*.

JULIAN WARD JONES, JR., Chancellor Professor of Classical Studies at the College of William and Mary, is the co-editor of the *Commentary on the First Six Books of the Aeneid of Vergil Commonly Attributed to Bernardus Silvestris*.

ALLEN MANDELBAUM is a poet and scholar now residing in Venice, Italy. He is the National Book Award-winning translator of Vergil's *Aeneid* and has recently completed a translation of Dante's *Divine Comedy*.

GARY B. MILES is Associate Professor of History at the University of California, Santa Cruz. He is the author of *Vergil's Georgics: A New Interpretation*.

ROBERT S. MIOLA is the author of *Shakespeare's Rome* and of various articles and reviews concerning Renaissance literature. He is currently working on the New Variorum *Julius Caesar* and on a study of Shakespeare's classics.

RUTH MORTIMER, Curator of Rare Books and Lecturer in Art at Smith College, is author of *French Sixteenth-century Books* and *Italian Sixteenth-century Books*.

WILLIAM R. NETHERCUT is Professor of Classics at the University of Texas at Austin. He has published numerous articles on Vergil.

CHRISTINE G. PERKELL is Associate Professor of Classics at Dartmouth College. She has published several articles on Vergil and is currently working on a book on the *Georgics*.

MEYER REINHOLD is Visiting University Professor of Classical Studies at Boston University and Professor Emeritus, University of Missouri-Columbia. His books include *The Golden Age of Augustus, Diaspora, The Classick Pages, Classica Americana*, and *From Republic to Principate*.

STELLA P. REVARD, Professor of English at Southern Illinois University, Edwardsville, is the author of *The War in Heaven: Paradise Lost and the Tradition of Satan's Rebellion* and numerous articles on Milton and other subjects.

ALAN S. TRUEBLOOD, Adjunct Professor and Professor Emeritus of Hispanic and Italian Studies and Comparative Literature at Brown University, is the author of *Experience and Artistic Expression in Lope de Vega*, and has translated and edited works by Antonio Machado and Lope de Vega.

GORDON W. WILLIAMS is Professor of Classics at Yale University. His books include *Tradition and Originality in Roman Poetry, Change and Decline: Roman Literature in the Early Empire, Figures of Thought in Roman Poetry*, and *Technique and Ideas in the Aeneid*.

STEVEN N. ZWICKER is Professor of English at Washington University in St. Louis. He is the author of *Dryden's Political Poetry: The Typology of King and Nation* and *Politics and Language in Dryden's Poetry: The Arts of Disguise*.

BIBLIOGRAPHIC ABBREVIATIONS

AHMA	*Archives d'Histoire doctrinale et littéraire du Moyen Age.*
AJP	*American Journal of Philology.*
AL	*American Literature: A Journal of Literary History, Criticism, and Bibliography.*
ANRW	*Aufstieg und Niedergang der römischen Welt. Geschichte und Kultur Roms im Spiegel der neueren Forschung.*
Arethusa	*Arethusa. A journal of the wellsprings of Western man.*
ArtQ	*Art Quarterly.*
CB	*The Classical Bulletin.*
CIL	*Corpus Inscriptionum Latinarum.*
CJ	*The Classical Journal.*
CL	*Comparative Literature.*
C&M	*Classica et Mediaevalia. Revue danoise d'Histoire et de Philologie.*
CO	*Classical Outlook.*
CP	*Classical Philology.*
CQ	*Classical Quarterly.*
CritI	*Critical Inquiry.*
CSCA	*California Studies in Classical Antiquity.*
CW	*The Classical World.*
DNB	*Dictionary of National Biography.*
EAL	*Early American Literature.*
ELH	*ELH. A Journal of English Literary History.*
ELR	*English Literary Renaissance.*
G&R	*Greece and Rome.*
Gymnasium	*Gymnasium. Zeitschrift für Kultur der Antike und humanistische Bildung.*
Hermes	*Hermes. Zeitschrift für klassiche Philologie.*

Historia	*Historia. Revue d'histoire ancienne.*
HLB	*Harvard Library Bulletin.*
HSCP	*Harvard Studies in Classical Philology.*
ICS	*Illinois Classical Studies.*
JRS	*Journal of Roman Studies.*
Latomus	*Latomus. Revue d'études latines.*
Library	*The Library: A Quarterly Journal of Bibliography.*
MAAR	*Memoirs of the American Academy in Rome.*
MP	*Modern Philology: A Journal Devoted to Research in Medieval and Modern Literature.*
N&Q	*Notes and Queries.*
NEQ	*The New England Quarterly: A Historical Review of New England Life and Letters.*
NLH	*New Literary History.*
PAPS	*Proceedings of the American Philosophical Society.*
PBSR	*Papers of the British School at Rome.*
PCA	*Proceedings of the Classical Association.*
Ph	*Philologus. Zeitschrift für klassische Philologie.*
Phoenix	*The Phoenix. The Journal of the Classical Association of Canada.*
PL	Migne, *Patrologia Latina.*
PMLA	*Publications of the Modern Language Association of America.*
PP	*La Parola del Passato. Rivista di Studi antichi.*
PQ	*Philological Quarterly.*
Ramus	*Ramus. Critical Studies in Greek and Latin Literature.*
RE	*Paulys Real-Encyclopädie der classischen Altertumswissenschaft.*
REL	*Revue des Etudes Latines.*
RES	*Review of English Studies: A Quarterly Journal of English Literature and the English Language.*
RPh	*Revue de Philologie.*
SEL	*Studies in English Literature, 1500–1900.*
ShakS	*Shakespeare Studies.*
ShS	*Shakespeare Survey: An Annual Survey of Shakespearian Study and Production.*
SLJ	*Southern Literary Journal.*
SP	*Studies in Philology.*
Speculum	*Speculum: A Journal of Medieval Studies.*
SQ	*Shakespeare Quarterly.*
TAPA	*Transactions and Proceedings of the American Philological Association.*
Vergilius	*Vergilius.* The Vergilian Society of America
WMQ	*William and Mary Quarterly.*
YCS	*Yale Classical Studies.*
ZAnt	*Ziva Antika. Antiquité Vivante.*

VERGIL: "PRINCE OF SONG"

John D. Bernard

My title repeats that of the event which led to the publication of the present volume. On October 26, 1981, persisting in the fiction of a year 0, which would have confirmed in nature the purely mathematical verity that 19 + 1981 = 2000, the University of Houston-University Park sponsored a Vergil Bimillennial Symposium, a day's activities dedicated to remembering the Roman poet who, in this country, has often seemed in danger of being forgotten.

For as Meyer Reinhold's contribution to this collection makes clear, Vergil has always had an uncertain standing in the intellectual life of that America which John Crowe Ransom once called "this other Thrace." In his mock-ironic tribute to the classical muse, "Philomela," Ransom fancies that the poetico-tragical bird with the melodious name and "untranslatable refrain," having negotiated the migration from Greece to Rome, and from Rome to various other barbarian lands, never managed to find her way to the "cloudless, boundless, public" United States. Of course, the poet was being too literal-minded: even if we have heard no actual nightingales on these shores, we have learned to tune our ears to the "classic numbers" of the ancient singers. Yet in Vergil's case it has not been easy. Compared to our reception of Milton, perhaps his greatest son and rival, the rites of homage to Vergil have been honored here almost as much in the breach as in the observance. To this day, humanities curricula in our colleges that have nearly deified Homer dismiss Vergil as little more than a Latin conduit of the Greek *Weltanschauung* to the European vernaculars.

Reinhold's account of colonial schoolboys conditioned to hate Vergil, and Latin, by the enforcing pedagogy of the day would seem to be negated by the recollections of our own youth. On an occasion analogous to the

1

Houston symposium a mere Vergilian lifetime ago, Charles Grosvenor
Osgood observed that Vergil's song was "still alive, still passing into the
fiber and being of the young and susceptible soul,. . . forming, refining, and
sensitizing the susceptibilities of thousands of the undistinguished in every
generation who have determined and still determine the character and
texture of modern life."[1] Some of us may recall eagerly parsing the *Aeneid*.
But was our fiber being refined and sensitized in the process? If so, alas no
longer. Nor do we espy "the dogeared copy of the *Aeneid*, haled carelessly
homeward in a bookstrap . . . by loitering boy or girl." Not today the *Aeneid*,
not in a bookstrap, not even carelessly. *Our* boys and girls loiter to a
different drummer. Osgood's 1930 idyll, like Vergil's own in the *Eclogues*,
has been overtaken by history. Few of our greatest minds are—nor, if
Reinhold is right, have ever been—informed by Vergil's complex vision or
troubled by his song. We have heard Philomela infrequently, have only
rarely seen into the tears of things.

This aspect of our cultural history is surprising. On the face of it, few
great poetic *oeuvres* have been more suited to the American experience than
Vergil's. The very pattern of his itinerary, from pastoral to georgic to epic,
would seem to mirror that of our national dream: the search for Eden, the
pioneering ordeal by labor, the imperial expansion finding its limits at last
in the very nature of man. Is it possible that for Americans Vergil's time has
only now arrived? If our more optimistic forbears could respond only to
Vergil's pastoral myth or to his work ethic, while finding his epic vision
morally, theologically, and perhaps politically repugnant, our recent
travails may have made the message of the *Aeneid* more accessible. There are
signs—not the least of them the existence for more than a decade now of
Allen Mandelbaum's magisterial translation—that the *Aeneid* is at last
making its way among us. Since the beginnings of classical philology in this
country in the late nineteenth century, scholars have shown an interest in
Vergil that, according to William Nethercut's survey at the end of this
volume, has slowly shifted from philological questions to interpretive ones,
from the *Appendix* to (in that order) the *Aeneid*, *Bucolics*, and *Georgics*, once
again suggesting the voyage of our collective psyche. The tragically familiar
Vergil of W.R. Johnson, both in *Darkness Visible* and in the essay printed
below, may well give place, as Nethercut conjectures, to a more encouraging persona as the pangs of our protracted national adolescence
subside. But it is unlikely that we will ever again find the poem either too
grim or too simplistic for our taste.

Some such thoughts must have occurred to many of the teachers,
students, and others who gathered that warm autumn day in imperial
Houston to attend meetings and drink friendly toasts to the poet of frontiers
and empire, of restless dreaming and the severe impossible task. They were

encouraged in those reflections by the papers that form the core of the present volume, delivered by Johnson, Mandelbaum, and Paul Alpers. Alpers, speaking first, showed how Vergil teaches us, within the seemingly innocuous conventions of literary pastoral, something about constructing a human community. Johnson followed by warning of the strains imposed on such a community when it enters the arena of action. In compensation for those strains, Mandelbaum implied, the poets that follow find encouragement less in Vergil's political message than in the historical continuity of that original singing community. Clearly, whatever their differences, the three presentations demonstrated that even in these latter days help could be sought from our poet, not only in the dark truths about history so much to our present taste but in more enduring paradigms of culture and tradition as well. As the intense response to these papers confirmed, Vergil in Houston was much more than the object of formal gestures of commemoration: the second millennium of his death seemed an apt moment to reassess his meaning for a civilization—that of North America in the last decades of the twentieth century—which, it was evident, had much to learn from him. The terms that his poetry had articulated were once again useful for understanding our public and private lives.

This sense of Vergil's continuing importance prompted the present editor to expand the three Houston papers into yet another book-length homage to a long-dead poet. In doing so I hoped to produce not just a fuller tribute but an anatomy of the complicated relationship between our troubled times and the poet who has seemingly given us little more than a few national mottos. Moreover, I felt that the origination of the project in "Space City," the latest if not last frontier and certainly, in Ransom's words, "environ barbarous to the royal Attic," would especially qualify us to join the long line of outlanders to honor the gaunt provincial who had once given definitive voice to the Roman myth.

But to accomplish this synthesis meant more than simply gathering additional papers on topics variously Vergilian. It was, after all, not Vergil alone we wanted to conjure, nor even the Vergil of late twentieth-century America. Even that Vergil is a composite of any number of earlier ones. To understand what Vergil might mean, what he might be "saying," to us in the 1980s would require consideration of what he had meant and said to readers in A.D. 90, in 1310, in the 1490s or 1590s or 1690s, in 1882. This premise seemed to entail both an adequate challenge and an homage appropriate to the bimillennial moment. The book would attempt to follow Philomela, in her Vergilian incarnation, north by west, through good times and bad. It would pursue her divagations into the mazes of late-classical and medieval allegoresis, the splendors of Renaissance book illustration, even the democratic vistas of eighteenth-century American satire. Above all, it would seek out those junctures at which the Vergilian refrain rang with special urgency in an ephebe's ear and so begat a new song. By thus focussing on these moments of infusion and tracing the poet's migration down to the present it would try to summon again the ghostly presence, make audible once more the hoarse voice speaking to us what we hoped would be consoling words in our hour of need.

Finally, just because the need is so urgently ours, the effort I have described would rely mainly on our fellow-countrymen and -women, native or adoptive, despite the abundance of European talent devoted to Vergil studies in our time. I have sought the best Vergilians now working in this country and have let their interests dictate the high spots or sore points in that story. My hope is that whatever its weaknesses, this strategy, better than any possible survey of currently fashionable approaches to the poet, would add up to a substantial representation of the contemporary American Vergil. By contemplating what our predecessors have made of him we—the authors and myself—might gain a hold on what we must make of him, in the process defining an important part of the legacy from our European past.

The papers that follow reflect this strategy in ways partly predictable, partly serendipitous. Initial invitations for contributions matched the concerns outlined above roughly with those of several outstanding scholars in the field. As other intriguing possibilities came to my attention—some, alas, too late for the book to benefit by them[2]—these new interests gradually suggested the present organization into three parts instead of the two originally envisaged. The broader surveys of medieval, Renaissance, and American encounters with Vergil by J.W. Jones, Jr., Alan Trueblood, and Reinhold respectively, as well as Ruth Mortimer's selection and discussion of representative sixteenth-century Vergilian illustrations, implied that individual instances of appropriating Vergil might be viewed separately from his broad assimilation by the historical periods in which they occurred. Hence the purely convenient distinction between "Ages" and "Heirs." Of course the allegorization of the works detailed by Jones, whether in Servian or Silvestrian mode, does not exhaust the medieval reception of the poet—the subject occupies a relatively few pages of Comparetti[3]—any more than Mortimer's sampler of plates or Trueblood's of Spanish adaptations of the *Eclogues* can be said to do justice to Vergil's importance for the Renaissance. But even these limited studies of the poet's impact on historical epochs as a whole, along with Reinhold's more panoramic survey of two and a half centuries of his American *fortuna*, support the notion that the major phases of Vergilian influence constitute a significant and formally isolatable issue of the book, duly embodied in its middle section.

Yet the afterlife of a great poet still depends chiefly on those seminal acts of "translation" that, like Clytemnestra's beacons, beam the essence of his message down the centuries. The third section of the book acknowledges the peaks of this transmission from Statius to Dryden, that is, from sons sealed of the poet's tribe almost in his own lifetime to those enrolled more than sixteen centuries later. If this sequence is more unevenly represented here than the facts of the case require, the reader may ascribe this bias to the preoccupations I have noted. Gordon Williams demonstrates in the case of Statius that anxiety in the taking over of one's spiritual ancestor was already a factor in the first century of our era. And there are ways, as Mandelbaum suggests, that Dante can lead us to a Vergil more "contemporary" than the Renaissance one. But it is perhaps especially to the great English triumvirate of Shakespeare, Milton, and Dryden, in the papers by Robert Miola, Stella Revard, and Steven Zwicker respectively, that we look for guidance in our dual quest for the European adoption of Vergil and for Vergil himself.

Logically the search begins in the first century B.C. That Vergil's poetry is no naive register of Augustan values is the point of departure for Gary Miles and Archibald Allen in their paper on the poet and his times. What is peculiarly "Augustan" about Vergil's works turns out to be not the balanced elegance of their moral and rhetorical order but, quite the contrary, their precise mirroring of contemporary disorder. In fitting them to their historical context the authors argue that the major works progressively reflect the poet's meditation on those forces that repeatedly dissolve possibilities of stability. Further, his understanding of the origins of these forces widens to recognize how personal passions are projected into external events. Hence the historical cycle of "new beginnings" and failures appears to be rooted in the nature of man, particularly in *amor*, the source of both his creative vitality and his fateful lack of control. Such a paradigm would seem to be challenged implicitly by Alpers' idea that the pastoral convention may be a plausible basis of human community. Born of a separation from community in the usual sense, Vergilian pastoral, in Alpers' view, seeks to define a community of poets and readers in terms both problematical and less than fully open to complex realities. In Eclogue 5, convention emerges as the "form community takes in the absence of the hero," Daphnis. It is Vergil's convening or "composing" of Theocritus that establishes the pastoral convention. In advancing this thesis Alpers implies that in a historical world marked by violence and loss poetic practice may replace heroic action. The problem of actuality raised by Miles and Allen demands that the affirmative and negative elements in any situation be "held in suspension," as Nethercut observes later. Alpers' pastoral community accepts separation and loss as the condition of a poetry that withholds itself from both facile optimism and cynical despair.

Similar efforts to salve a familiar wound in the poet's world and ours mark the versions of Vergilian georgic and epic respectively in the essays by Christine Perkell and Johnson. Both reflect the strong anti-Augustan bias of current American Vergilians: Perkell's in the rejection of a "theodicy" of Jove in Georgic 1's account of the institution of *ars* or *techné* in human affairs, Johnson's in an anatomy of the sacrifice of Aeneas on the altar of "World Destiny." In both papers, not Juno as the obstacle to progress but Jove as its patron is the villain of the piece. As Perkell sees it, we—both Vergil's contemporaries and, implicitly, ourselves—live in an Iron Age in which a mechanized humanity is allowed little hope of any kind of community except that insinuated by the poet's own humane or passionate motives. Hence in the other frame of her diptych Perkell defends the vulnerable Orpheus in the fourth Georgic in his juxtaposition with another Iron Age deity, Aristaeus, the violence of whose art, the *bougonia*, is in implicit contrast with the warm if flawed humanity of the poet-hero's attachment to Eurydice. In Johnson's portrait of Aeneas one sees the same sympathetic humanity in the chosen victim of Jove's inhuman plan. *Dios d'eteleieto boulé*; but *this* plan imposes a burden of Stoic submission and ultimately of silence on a hero whose inner life harbors a richness undreamt of by Homer, while lending eloquence to Aeneas' tacit abhorrence of his fate. Prompted perhaps by Vergil's Epicurean resistance to his hero's historic mission, the death of Turnus, with his ordinary selfish loves, implies that of Aeneas himself as an effective moral agent.

It is easy to see that these four essays into what is peculiarly Vergilian in Vergil's major work constitute a marked revision of his traditional and (if Miles and Allen are right) unhistorical "Augustanism." This revision, as I have suggested, may well reflect the recent recoil of our own national psyche from an habitual optimism and self-confidence. Yet it is but one measure of the gap between the contemporary American Vergil and that of earlier times. The essays in the middle section of this book imply three distinct articulations of the intervening development. Despite the obvious impossibility of claiming that these articles in any way represent the medieval, Renaissance, and modern versions of the poet, I wish to urge the usefulness of viewing the "ages" of Vergilian influence under the three rubrics given here. In discussing the breakdown of European cultural unity Denys Hay cites Sir Kenneth Clark's observation of a shift around 1800 from a "Vergilian" to a "Wordsworthian" landscape.[4] For Hay this shift implies the crucial break with Renaissance culture that took place in the eighteenth- and nineteenth-century evolution of science and industry, leading him to view the period 1300–1800—that is, from the time of Dante and Petrarch to that of Wordsworth and Constable—as a reasonably distinguishable whole.

If we adopt this model for the moment, it becomes clear that the "Renaissance" thus loosely defined is quintessentially the Vergilian period in European civilization, in the sense that Vergil imparts to it a flavor and tone unavailable to earlier or later times. Clearly, what sets it apart is the concept of Antiquity, the effort to repossess which is the second chief focus of this book. In the broadest sense the Renaissance Vergil is represented in these pages equally by the contributions of Trueblood and Mortimer in the second section, and of Miola, Revard, and Zwicker in the third; that of the pre-Renaissance by Williams, Jones, and Mandelbaum; and the post-Renaissance, that is to say *our* Vergil, by Reinhold and Nethercut, for it is in America above all that post-Renaissance civilization abides. Although I have elected not to organize the book around this concept of periodization, it may still be useful to think of the Renaissance, thus defined as a period of relative cultural unity, as the central phase in the recovery of Vergil; and of the following centuries, the American centuries, as a wholly distinct phase, which has had little to say about Vergil, but which may now be coming to acknowledge his relevance. It is from the Renaissance in particular that we may learn how a culture very different in its informing premises can seek to assimilate an earlier one through the mediation of its strongest voices.[5] And while we are unlikely to repeat that epoch's naive fusion of pagan antiquity and Christianity, we would also do well to avoid the facile dismissal of Vergil in the nineteenth century, especially in this country, as unChristian, undemocratic, and therefore of no possible use to an enlightened technological civilization. The search for a usable past is likely to go on for as long as a future can still be imagined.

Of the Renaissance in the narrower sense one may note that Trueblood's three Spanish adaptors of Vergil's *Eclogues* represent three distinct stages: Humanism, High Renaissance, and (proto-) Counter-Reformation, with their respective classicizing, courtly, and quietist slants on the *Bucolics*. This paradigm underscores a potential for allegory inherent in Vergil that later readers could exploit in their own distinct ways.[6] In the Middle Ages, for example, it was possible to construct a typology even of the Vergilian *cursus*, in which the *Bucolics* signify the Aristotelian *vita contemplativa* (*bios theoretikós*), the *Aeneid* the *vita activa* (*bios praktikós* or *politikós*), and the *Georgics* the normally depreciated *vita voluptuosa* (*bios apolaustikós*) or life of pleasure.[7] The "medieval" allegorical tradition described by Jones remained substantially unchanged at least through Landino's *Disputationes Camaldulenses* (1475).[8] Yet despite the mode's resilience there is a distinct flavor to the pre-Dantean specimens of allegoresis. The now almost inconceivable status accorded the *sortes virgilianae* implies a widespread acceptance of Vergil as teacher and moral guide. The Stoic *physica ratio* echoed in Servius, extended by the moral allegory of Fulgentius, Bernardus, and their ilk, gives us a hint of the breadth of wisdom sought by Dante's predecessors and contemporaries from his *maestro* and *autore*. In our own time this allegorizing tendency expresses itself in the "heroic curriculum" discerned by Nethercut, as American scholarship shifts its attention from the *Aeneid* to the *Bucolics* to the *Georgics*. Glossing Nethercut, one might interpret our own critical odyssey as a revulsion from imperialism to a reflective, self-communing withdrawal and thence to a renewed interest in the fundamental proposition of Roman rhetorical culture, conveyed to us through Renaissance humanism and later through Vico and Goethe: namely, that we are what we do and make, and that it is by our physical, creative, and manifestly pleasurable activities (More's Utopian Epicureans are primarily farmers) that we project ourselves into the world as given.[9]

In turning from the Ages to the Heirs we come to the currently renewed fascination with *imitatio*. Once again, the five papers included do not pretend to be exhaustive. Moreover, questions of period and convention inevitably overlap in them with theoretical issues concerning imitation. But I should prefer to ignore these complications here and dwell instead on a few of the issues raised in this section of the book. First in order both of time and of our own critical priorities is the anxiety arising from "poetical oppression" discussed by Williams in his essay on Statius. Williams discerns a dilemma in the efforts of post-Augustan imitators like Statius to outgo their betters: the competition with one's admitted superior in open emluation challenges comparison with the original. More important, Williams suggests a radical change in the nature of "intertextuality" between Vergil's imitation of Homer and Statius' of Vergil, a kind of displacement of the evolving poetic community. Statius' anxiety results in "a constant extraction of the reader" from the imaginative world of the imitator to a shared perspective on the imitative act itself. In this way almost at the outset of Vergilian imitation a new variety of self-consciousness about *poesis* is effected. The moment invites careful comparison with Vergil's own relatively unproblematic imitation of Theocritus discussed in Alpers' essay.

Mandelbaum's study of Dante's abduction of Vergil in the *Commedia* entails a similar tension between tradition and innovation. But here the story implies a naive confidence in the imitating poet's ability to recapture antiquity. While his contemporary allegorizers were stressing Vergil's aid as guide and *psychopompos* in the heroic man's (or everyman's) odyssey through the moral life,[10] Dante follows the precursor himself into the Limbo of ancient makers and beyond, having first translated him from his silent tomb into a Christian otherworld virtually unimaginable without his example. Paradoxically, though, in appropriating Vergil Dante only becomes the more himself. He never forgets the pagan poet's limits, his refusal to "sit at the total table" like his Christian (or Neoplatonic) progeny. Mandelbaum sees this difference as the insuperable obstacle to Dante's "profoundest dream, . . . the resurrection of the father." To this reader at least, his essay also suggests why it is the pre-Romantic "Vergilian landscape" of the Renaissance tradition, and no longer the Wordsworthian sublime foreshadowed by the Dantean, that speaks most clearly to our present cultural predicament. If Dante has led many of us, including Mandelbaum, back to Vergil, some of us have found in him an Anchises more nurturing in his particularism than his totalizing offspring.

Considerations such as these are less likely to arise with respect to those master practitioners of Renaissance *imitatio*, Shakespeare and Milton, for whom three centuries of humanism gave Vergil and his contemporaries a virtually unchallengeable status. Nevertheless, the essays by Miola and Revard each give a special angle on familiar questions of influence. Against the Ovidian filiation of Shakespeare prevalent since Meres, Miola argues for a progressively organic repossession of Vergil in the plays from *Titus Andronicus* to *The Tempest*. This serial refinement of imitation results as well in a complex relationship of imitator to model. Gradually penetrating to the heart of Vergil's vision, Miola's Shakespeare arrives in the end at a more inward understanding of human action and contemplation, perhaps, one might infer, a post-Christian version of that Epicurean resistance to the Augustan ideal mentioned earlier. Revard's surprise comes not in the poet but in the poem nominated as the main influence on *Paradise Lost*, the *Georgics* rather than the *Aeneid*.[11] In Revard's reading, both prelapsarian Eden and postlapsarian world bear the imprint of Vergil's georgic rendition of man's "fall" into history and moral awareness. Perhaps less surprisingly, it is an essentially optimistic perspective on the future that Milton takes from Vergil, as against the problematical "tragedy of choice" in the *Aeneid*. With Zwicker's article on Dryden our attention comes to rest specifically on the politics of imitation. The 1697 *Virgil*, Zwicker shows, entails nothing less than the accommodation of the *Aeneid's* entire historical context to the translator-editor's personal and political circumstances. Dedication, subscription apparatus, plates, and translation all reveal the singleness of purpose with which Dryden's historical imagination reconstructs Vergil's Augustan moment and assimilates it to his own. In documenting this feat Zwicker indirectly raises an important critical issue in current Renaissance and seventeenth-century studies: the thin line separating poetry from propaganda, purely aesthetic from political intentions, in the act of literary creation; or, to shift the focus somewhat, the critical temptation to "textualize" social and other extraliterary events by ascribing to them the intentionality of poems. Although Zwicker himself stays well within the limits of this problematic, his very sensitivity to the implications lurking in every nuance of Dryden's Vergil will suggest to some readers his paper's affiliation with other, sometimes less skilled or cautious recent studies of the "politics" of literary production in an age of patronage.

The example of Dryden again reminds us how far certain assumptions of the early Renaissance have been undermined by the end of the seventeenth century. Two hundred years separate Juan del Encina's translation of the *Eclogues* into Castilian (1496) and Dryden's englishing of the *Aeneid* and other Vergilian works. Both Trueblood and Zwicker acknowledge a "program of misreading" (Trueblood) in their subjects, but Encina's carrying over of the fourth Eclogue retains at least a vestigial vocabulary of medieval typology: Vergil's mysterious child is a *figura* "fulfilled" in the Spanish Prince John. On the other hand the two Dedications, of 1496 and 1697, forcefully contrast the flattering style of a Renaissance courtier-poet with the self-assurance of a modern man of letters. As for Dryden's own un-typological reading of historical allegory into the *Aeneid*, this is a habit still perceptible in the twentieth century.[12] Like the "allegorical" criticism referred to earlier, it owes its persistence to qualities inherent, I believe, in the Roman poet himself.

Throughout this discussion I have alluded to Nethercut's concluding survey of American Vergilian scholarship in the twentieth century. Nethercut's thesis is emphatic: from the 1920s and 1930s to the 1960s and 1970s, American Vergilians have mirrored the great events of our national life, most particularly in the aftermath of World War II, the *crise de conscience* generated by Korea, Vietnam, and attendant domestic catastrophes. This view casts an interesting light on our collective Vergilian curriculum. As I have indicated, historically our scholarly encounter with Vergil seems to move from the irreconcilable divisions of the *Aeneid* through the aesthetic healing of the *Bucolics* to the renewed ecological hope of the *Georgics*. Following a period of substantial critical attention to the ironies of structure in the epic, doubts about our ability to find answers to the big questions raised there led, especially in connection with pastoral, to a habit of "suspension" between moral antinomies. This reaction in turn has given way to a qualified optimism as to man's capacity to "compose" his world, his past, and his political divisions through creative activity. Nethercut himself seems to favor recent interpretations of the *Georgics* that raise the possibility of escape from an imprisoning past, and we have noted some of the implications of the poem for Perkell and Revard.

In this perspective the American scholarly version of the *curriculum vergilianum* holds forth a certain promise even against the predominantly dark Vergil of recent years. Challenging the latter figure is the solitary gardener of Georgic 4, a symbol of that Epicurean core of the poet's sensibility intuited by Johnson and others. This alternative too, of course, has its dangers: the exhortation to cultivate one's private garden is a Siren song to a generation now facing the need (even in Academia) to choose between the civic and the private life. On reflection, the Epicurean option is a less tolerable avenue of escape from the nightmare of history than the bucolic community of singers. And in spite of his palpable attraction to it, Vergil himself seems to have resolved that an actual community of pleasures and pains in the strictest Platonic sense may provide the nobler challenge to human energy and art.

This dilemma, at any rate, may be the latest example of that balance or "suspension" of antithetical impulses it has been the special function of Vergil to provoke in American readers in our time. In this sense he aptly speaks to our present impasse. The essays in parts 2 and 3 below record the poet's importance for subsequent eras, either through the status accorded him in the culture of the day or through his personal impact on individual successors. Taken together with the readings of the works in the first part of the book, they may encourage us to hope that in the struggle to direct our national destiny Vergil will play an increasingly decisive role.

Notes

1. C.G. Osgood, ed., *The Tradition of Virgil* (Princeton: Princeton University Press, 1930), pp. 24–5.
2. It is a pleasure to acknowledge the cooperation of Professor Thomas Suits, organizer of the symposium on "Virgil and the European Tradition," held at the University of Connecticut at Storrs on May 8, 1982. Through his generosity we were able eventually to procure the papers by Gordon Williams and Alan Trueblood that appear in this volume.
3. D. Comparetti, *Vergil in the Middle Ages*, trans. E.F.M. Benecke (Hamden, Conn: Archon Books, 1966); see esp. pp. 104–18.
4. *The Italian Renaissance in its Historical Background* (Cambridge: Cambridge University Press, 1976²), pp. 209–10.
5. See now Thomas M. Greene, *The Light in Troy* (New Haven: Yale University Press, 1982).
6. For the suggestion that Vergil himself is aware of this possible hermeneutic from his familiarity with the Stoic scholiasts of Homer, see Robin P. Schlunk, *The Homeric Scholia and the "Aeneid"* (Ann Arbor: University of Michigan Press, 1974).
7. Quoted in Comparetti, p. 117n. Cf. A. Grilli, *Il problema della vita contemplativa nel mondo greco-romano* (Milan: Bocca, 1953). Cf. Robert Joly, *Le Thème philosophique des genres de vie dans*

l'Antiquité classique (Brussels: Académie des sciences de Belgique, 1956). The basic text on the three *genres* or "estates" is *Eud. Eth.* 1215–35, but cf. *Nich. Eth.* 1095b17–18.

8. See Thomas H. Stahel, S.J., *Christoforo Landino's Allegorization of the Aeneid* (Ph.D. dissertation, Johns Hopkins University, Baltimore, 1968), which includes a translation of books 3 and 4 of Landino's dialogue.

9. Ernesto Grassi, *Rhetoric and Philosophy: The Humanist Tradition* (University Park and London: The Pennsylvania State University Press, 1980).

10. See David Thompson, *Dante's Epic Journey* (Baltimore: Johns Hopkins Press, 1974), for Dante's relation to the allegorical tradition.

11. A similar application of the *Georgics* to Spenser is William Sessions, "Spenser's *Georgics*," *ELR* 10 (1980): 202–38.

12. D.L. Drew, *The Allegory of the Aeneid* (1922; reprt. New York and London: Garland Publishing Co., 1978).

VERGIL AND THE AUGUSTAN EXPERIENCE

Gary B. Miles and Archibald W. Allen

History has admired many Vergils: the supreme rhetorician, the *anima naturaliter Christiana* who foretold the birth of Christ, the magician whose wand (*virga*) helped change his name from *Vergilius* to *Virgilius*, the author of a pattern for Renaissance princes, the pale reflection of Greek splendor seen by Romantics, the "lord of language" and singer of "the doubtful doom of human kind" of Tennyson, the model for Eliot by which to judge what is a Classic. In his own lifetime he did not lack recognition; when the *Eclogues* and *Georgics* had appeared but the *Aeneid* had only been begun, Propertius wrote

> Cedite Romani scriptores, cedite Grai!
>   nescio quid maius nascitur Iliade
>
> (2.34.65-6)

> Give way, writers of Rome, give way, you Greeks!
>   Something greater than the *Iliad* is coming to birth.[1]

And yet it was Vergil's dying wish that the manuscript of the *Aeneid* should be destroyed, unpublished.

Such despair may have been caused by dissatisfaction with the unfinished condition of the poem. But the form which the work had reached was very near perfection. Therefore, the poet's dissatisfaction must lie somewhere deeper, and perhaps we can discover the reason by considering Vergil's relation to his own times. The durability of the Augustan Establishment, its stability and, on balance, salutary effect, were evident to subsequent generations; but when Vergil was writing, the catastrophic collapse of the old and honored world was far more certain

13

than were the hopes based on a new and untested creation. The purpose of this essay is to sketch the circumstances and ideas current in the period between the assassination of Julius Caesar and the death of Vergil, and to suggest that in them lie the causes of his desperate optimism and enigmatic melancholy at the time which the future was to look back on as the glory of the Augustan Golden Age.

Although Vergil was seven years Augustus' senior, the careers of the two men were closely parallel. Biographers agree that Vergil began the *Eclogues* either very shortly before or, more likely, shortly after the nineteen-year-old Octavian burst unexpectedly into Roman politics in 44 B.C.[2] Critics and historians who have written about Vergil and Augustus or Vergil and the Augustan Age have most often focused on the personal links connecting the two figures, or they have tended to discuss Vergil's poems in terms of direct responses to the new Caesar or to his policies. There is, however, another perspective from which we may characterize Vergil as an Augustan. We may see the poet as meditating upon changing experiences that would have been shared generally by all inhabitants of Italy from the time that Caesar, as he called himself and as we shall call him now, entered public life, through his initial consolidation of supreme power. From this perspective, each of Vergil's three major works corresponds not only to a distinct phase in Caesar's career, but also to a distinct historical situation as it was experienced by Vergil's contemporaries in Italy, for Caesar was early left in charge of Italy, while his fellow triumvirs and rivals established their bases of power elsewhere. The *Eclogues* comment on the sense of personal insecurity that permeated Italian life during the early years of the triumvirate; the *Georgics* address a widespread feeling of uncertain but hopeful anticipation; and the *Aeneid* gives voice to a fundamental ambivalence toward the Augustan Principate. Underlying those diverse perspectives is a common preoccupation with chaos, both in society and in the human psyche, and a progressive understanding of how these two aspects of disorder interact to form the basis of human experience.

I

Between the years 44 and 36 B.C. there could have been few inhabitants of Italy who did not feel that their well-being or their very lives were in jeopardy.[3] Three conditions stand out as contributing to this personal anxiety: the constant threat of full-scale civil war on Italian soil, the proscriptions of 43–42 B.C., and the confiscation of land for veterans. In each case the particular nature of the danger produced effects that reached far beyond those who were directly implicated. These indirect effects, even more than the specific dangers from which they originated, must have dominated life as most Italians experienced it in these years.

Civil war had threatened Italy ever since the assassination of Julius Caesar. Before Caesar, Antony, and Lepidus formed their triumvirate and imposed some order on chaos, armies and leaders shifted their loyalties with bewildering frequency. There were constant alarms at Rome; citizens changed from civilian to military dress and back repeatedly as the prospect of an attack seemed to approach or recede. At the same time a plague swept Italy. Then, for a while, the dreaded possibility of civil war became a reality when Antony besieged Decimus Brutus in the north Italian city of Mutina during the winter of 44/43 B.C. Both of the consuls for 43 B.C. died trying to raise the siege. Brutus eventually escaped but not until his troops were so weakened by famine that their effectiveness was diminished for some time thereafter. The condition of the city's civilians must have been even worse than that of Brutus' troops. These events offered early testimony of what awaited Italians, should widespread civil war break out anew.

When the triumvirs began to proscribe their fellow Romans in 43 B.C., their first object was to eliminate political enemies and potential rivals. An initial list of public enemies who were to forfeit their lives and property was supplemented with new names a day later; subsequent revisions of the list compounded initial uncertainty. No one could know how many would eventually find themselves, their relatives, friends, or associates among the proscribed. A further complication was the fact that relations among the triumvirs had changed so often that someone who had been the friend of one triumvir might for that very reason find himself proscribed as the political enemy of another. In contrast to the Sullan proscriptions of 82 B.C., past loyalties provided no guide for judging one's present security. Soon it also became apparent that some Romans were being proscribed solely because the triumvirs were short of money and land with which to reward their veterans.

The households, relatives, and associates of the proscribed or of those who might be proscribed were also implicated. All those who harbored one of the proscribed or, knowing of his whereabouts, failed to report him, were themselves threatened with the penalties of proscription. Personal loyalty became an act of heroism.[4] On the other hand, individuals who brought in the proscribed dead or alive, or even informed on them, were promised rewards. These included exemption from military service, a share of the proscribed's estate for free Romans, freedom for slaves. There are stories of sons turning against fathers, of wives turning against husbands, of slaves betraying masters. The entire order of Roman society was threatened. In some cases military patrols, even whole communities, joined in a man-hunt.[5] Dio and Appian agree that the guarantee of anonymity to informers led to abuses and that the general chaos provided a cover for private vengeance, so that many Romans never listed among the proscribed nonetheless shared their punishments. Many of the proscribed themselves brought rebellion and disorder as they fled through Italy. The situation encouraged almost universal distrust and suspicion.

The proscriptions came to an end sometime in 42 B.C., the year in which Caesar and Antony defeated Brutus, Cassius, and their Republican supporters at Philippi.[6] However, the loyalty of the triumvirs' armies had been secured by generous promises of land in Italy, and following the battle of Philippi many troops were ready to be discharged and to claim their rewards. Large-scale confiscations were necessary to obtain the land promised. The triumvirs had designated eighteen communities whose inhabitants were to be dispossessed in order to provide for the veterans. As a result, widespread anxiety continued. Complications began when representatives from the eighteen communities marched on Rome with a petition that the settlement of soldiers be distributed evenly over all Italy, or that communities should be designated for confiscation by lot. Although these petitions were denied, many whose land was not officially confiscated lost it nonetheless. Veterans took advantage of the general disorder and of the fact that the triumvirs' obvious dependence on their services discouraged strict discipline.

More ominous were the Perusine conflicts, which occurred when the communities selected for the confiscations joined in open rebellion and were met with force. Although the wars were limited to skirmishes at first, townspeople manned their walls against Caesar throughout Italy. Soon the city of Perusia became a focus for the conflict. Laid under siege by Caesar's troops, the defending soldiers did not surrender until they had been reduced to near starvation. They had initially gathered all food supplies in the city and allocated them on a graduated scale: the soldiers got the largest shares, slaves none. Before the siege was lifted, slaves could be seen foraging for grass outside the city walls. When they began to die in droves, they were buried in mass graves so that the smoke from funeral pyres would not reveal the extent of the defenders' distress. At Rome, in the meantime, the lawless behavior of Caesar's troops and their stockpiling of scarce food led to riots. Following the surrender of Perusia the city burned to the ground—whether the result of deliberate malice, at Caesar's command, was a matter disputed by contemporaries. Also uncertain was the actual number of citizens that Caesar executed. Some reports claimed that he sacrificed three hundred equestrians and senators on an altar to Divus Julius on the Ides of March. As long as the triumvirs continued to be responsible for large armies, the danger of renewed confiscations and rebellions was real. Perhaps even more unsettling was the fact that the Perusine rebellion had received support and leadership from Antony's wife and brother. There was the danger that this conflict or another like it might issue in an all-out civil war between Antony and Caesar. In 40 B.C. bad relations between Caesar and Antony led to skirmishes before full-scale war was averted at the last minute by the treaty of Brundisium. Three years later Brundisium was once again the focal point for hostility between the two rivals, hostility that again required the intervention of political inter-mediaries before the triumvirate was finally reaffirmed at Tarentum.

These uneasy truces brought no end to Italy's distress. Sextus Pompey, son of Pompey the Great, had established Sicily as his own base. His very existence as a rival to the triumvirs encouraged dissenters in Italy and perpetuated unrest there. Italians of every class, from the proscribed to runaway slaves, defected to him, rallying support and spreading disorder as they went. From Sicily Pompey harassed Italy's coast and was sometimes able to establish garrisons within Italy.[7] His disruption of Roman shipping caused repeated famine,[8] until the triumvirs were finally compelled to negotiate a treaty with him in 39 B.C., but this settlement did not last a full year.

The unstable relations among Caesar, Antony, and Pompey meant that Caesar had to keep Italy in a constant state of military preparedness, and this made unrelenting demands on the people. Successive taxes and special requisitions were not only unpopular, but disruptive. On occasion they led to resistance and open rebellion of such intensity that the army was required to suppress them. The constant presence and movement of troops in Italy must be reckoned as an even more widespread burden on the Italians. Lacking the elaborate supply systems of our own age, ancient armies had largely to live off the land. Italians were required to billet troops during the winters. On more than one occasion troops are reported to have ravaged the countryside as they passed through it. The triumvirs' soldiers, moreover, aware of their leaders' dependence on them, were often insubordinate and lawless. Dio twice says that the Italians regarded their presence as equivalent to that of hostile forces.[9] It was not long before the general level of disorder rose so high that Italy was overrun with brigands, both domestic and foreign, who were capable of laying siege to whole villages and towns. Italians were experiencing an almost complete break-down of order at the time when Vergil was writing the *Eclogues*.

The first Eclogue epitomizes the disorders caused by Roman civil strife in the experiences of two individuals, shepherds who are geographically and socially remote from the center of power. In this way, the poem emphasizes how completely these disorders had permeated Italian life. The fact that one of the shepherds, Meliboeus, suffers eviction from his home, while some special dispensation has allowed his companion Tityrus to stay on, conveys an appreciation of the fundamental randomness of events as they must have been perceived by innumerable Italians who found themselves caught up in the personal rivalries of Rome's leadership. This appreciation is heightened by vivid contrast between the distress of the one shepherd and the complacency of the other. Eclogue 9 evokes the larger sense of uncertainty and personal insecurity that such conditions entailed. In this poem we find that Menalcas, a shepherd who had won, or seemed to have won, immunity from confiscations for an entire region has failed to do so after all. Shepherds who thought that they were secure, like the Tityrus of Eclogue 1, now drive their flocks to the uncertain future that Meliboeus lamented. This unexpected turn of events casts doubt on Tityrus' own condition: was his salvation permanent or only temporary, real or illusory? Can we accept Meliboeus' emphatic characterization of him (*Ecl.* 1.46–58) as *fortunatus?* Is Tityrus' complacency naive? Must not all confidence in the security of the individual be naive? Within the framework of Eclogues 1 and 9, Vergil elaborates an ideal of private escape from the public disorders of his age and from the personal insecurity that they cause. His shepherds, it must be noted, are not without cares. When Tityrus explains to his companion why he went to the city,

> his account of his past enslavement, in all senses, is a narrative of ordinary pastoral unhappiness, which, now resolved, is set over against the exceptional distress of Meliboeus . . . it includes the various frustrations of age, social status, mistakes in love, the small farmer's normal activities, and the mysteries of one's own motives. (*Ecl.* 1.26–45)[10]

This freedom to devote oneself, as Tityrus does, to the mundane business of living without violent intrusions from the larger world is one of the great privileges of the pastoral world. When the larger world does bring itself to Tityrus' attention, he is able to view it with a certain aloofness. Thus, even though not indifferent to Meliboeus' distress or to the majesty of the city, Tityrus has seemed to some critics insensitive because he does not allow the anguish of another or the intrusion of Roman politics to overshadow his own preoccupations or to compromise his own pleasures.

Vergil gives no explanation for this extraordinary equanimity, but associates it, implicitly, with a more general freedom from violent passion. Eclogue 1 introduces the idea that freedom from destructive *amor* is as necessary to enjoyment of the pastoral idyll as is aloofness from public disorders. Tityrus' *libertas* depends not only on the beneficence of his young patron in the city, but also on a change in his romantic attachments:

> Libertas . . . sera tamen respexit inertem, . . .
> respexit tamen et longo post tempore venit,
> postquam nos Amaryllis habet, Galatea reliquit.

Namque (fatebor enim) dum me Galatea tenebat,
nec spes libertatis erat nec cura peculi.

                                                    (1.27–32)

Liberty . . . looked on me late, sluggard that I was, . . .
but looked on me nonetheless, and at long last has come,
now that Amaryllis possesses me and Galatea has left me,
because (I will confess it) as long as Galatea possessed me,
I had neither hope of liberty nor care for my savings.

Tityrus' meager profits were diverted from the accumulation of his *peculium*
to the satisfaction of Galatea; their relationship, not one of *amicitia* or of love
in a good sense, was rather one in which Tityrus' interests were sacrificed to
his mistress' desires. But somehow Tityrus was freed from that relationship,
just as he was exempted from the confiscations. With his new love he has
been able to think of his *libertas*. It is no wonder, then, that in the opening of
the poem we find him teaching the woods to echo Amaryllis' name.

For the most part, *amor* figures in the Eclogue not as the shepherds' own
experience, but as the subject of songs to which they listen or which they
sing to each other for amusement.[11] Corydon, the one lovesick shepherd
whom we do meet, is able to recall himself from an unrequited love to the
pleasures and preoccupations of pastoral life. Nonetheless, the prospect of
an existence free from destructive *amor* is no less problematic than that of
immunity to the effects of civil war. Among Corydon's consolations for the
loss of his unresponsive lover, for example, is the ambiguous expectation
that he'll find another—just like him. Just as Eclogue 9 reminds us that a
life secure from public conflict is uncertain, so Eclogues 6, 8 and 10 raise
questions about the possibility of a life free from disruptive *amor*. Silenus'
song in Eclogue 6 associates violent and perverted passion with the very
creation of the world. In Eclogue 8, *amor* is still the subject of song, but now
it is represented as a violent passion that has driven shepherds to suicide
and madness. In Eclogue 10 (26–30) no less a pastoral authority than Pan
himself acknowledges the insatiability of *amor*. In addition, we meet Gallus,
one of the leading figures of Vergil's age, who exemplifies the undeniable
reality of *amor* in the normal world of human affairs and who proclaims the
failure of the pastoral world to solace the furor that has overcome him.[12]
Thus the *Eclogues* suggest that an even more pervasive source of disorder
than Roman civil strife may be a propensity to uncontrollable passion that
is inherent in human psychology.

Within these larger speculations on the sources of disorder and the
possibility of a private escape from them, Vergil considers another kind of
response to the chaos of his times. The fourth Eclogue celebrates a return to
a Golden Age that involves not an escape from society, but its trans-

formation. When the return to the Golden Age is complete, not only will it be possible to enjoy the simple pleasures of the shepherds' modest life, the earth will pour forth its bounty everywhere. It will even be possible to enjoy all the luxuries of civilization without any of its evils: colored fleeces, a symbol of extravagant excess and decadence, will grow naturally on sheep and so be available for all to enjoy without the necessity for commerce and for the accumulation of private wealth, and will therefore be without value for vainglorious display. Vergil symbolically marks the distinctively collective, public nature of this alternative to civil disorder by placing it under the auspices of Pollio, a Roman consul (*Ecl.* 4.12).

But the possibility of this collective escape is no less doubtful than the secure private retirement of the shepherd. The poem opens with conspicuous understatement:

> Sicelides Musae, paulo maiora canamus!
> . . .si canimus silvas, silvae sint consule dignae.
>
> (4.1–3)

> Sicilian Muses, let us sing of somewhat greater things. . . .
> If we sing of woods, let the woods be worthy of a consul.

At the conclusion of the poem we are still waiting for the propitious infant smile on which the whole process of return to the Golden Age depends. The extravagant image of red, yellow, and scarlet sheep challenges our belief; the images by which Vergil characterizes the Golden Age have more to do with the classical tradition of *adynata*, "impossibilities," than with literary representations of the Golden Age.[13] Vergil acknowledges the desire for a completely new beginning and he conveys the attractiveness of that ideal forcefully, but not unreservedly.

Such conspicuous restraint is among the most striking features of the *Eclogues*. Vergil can acknowledge the chaos of civil strife and its cost to the spirit without dwelling on them; he can reflect both on the pleasures of retirement and on its uncertainty with appreciation of the one but without feelings of disillusionment at the other; he can contemplate the attraction of a Golden Age, but without giving himself up to longing. He can even accept without despair the universality of uncontrollable passion. The Gallus of Eclogue 10, who is a hopeless victim of unrequited love, whom the gods come to counsel, and whom the countryside cannot solace, is in all these respects modelled on the Daphnis of Theocritis' first Idyll (65–113). In one way, however, the two lovers are complete opposites. Daphnis is so unresigned to love's power that he calls down destruction on his beloved countryside and on himself (*Idyll* 1.115–36). Gallus accepts love's power: *Omnia vincit amor: et nos cedamus Amori* (10.69 "Love conquers all: let us too yield to love"). Gallus leaves the pastoral world with regret, but not with bitterness.

In the concluding lines of the *Eclogues* Vergil professes his own submission to love for Gallus,

> . . . cuius amor tantum mihi crescit in horas
> quantum vere novo viridis se subicit alnus.
> surgamus: solet esse gravis cantantibus umbra . . .
>
> (73-5)

> . . . for whom my love grows hourly as fast
> as the green alder thrusts itself up in early spring.
> Let us rise up: shade tends to be harmful for singers . . .

This is not mere acceptance, but positive affirmation. It does not deny the power of love to be violent and uncontrollable, but sees in it a vitality that is lacking in the protective but stunting shade of the pastoral idyll. The *Eclogues*, then, demonstrate that equanimity can be achieved in an age of disorder by regarding the extremes of human experience and hope with a kind of detached moderation that makes possible their rejection and the acceptance of a more complex reality. But even this ideal of equanimity is qualified. The poet withholds assurance that it can be sustained. His love is like a young tree in early spring, but spring is only one season of the year and young trees grow to produce shade of their own.[14] This final note of reserve is all the more foreboding inasmuch as the tenth Eclogue recalls the undefined interrelation between public and personal order in Eclogue 1. There, Tityrus' account of his salvation from eviction was mingled with an account of his improved fortunes in love. In Eclogue 10 the situation is reversed. The *insanus amor* that makes a pastoral existence impossible for Gallus also keeps him amidst arms and battles (44-5). Somehow, in a way that the *Eclogues* never make clear, public disorder is associated with that of the individual psyche.

II

There is general agreement that Vergil began the *Georgics* no earlier than 37 B.C. and no later than 35 B.C., and that he completed it around 29 B.C.[15] The composition of the *Georgics*, therefore, spans a critical period. It begins with Caesar as one of the hated triumvirs, perhaps the most hated of them, and ends with his receiving unprecedented powers and honors. This period, from a general Italian point of view, can be seen in terms of two crises: the decisive conflict between Caesar and Sextus Pompey in 36 B.C.

and the even more momentous battle of Actium in 31 B.C. In both instances, events led to a prospect of imminent disaster for Italy, and then to a miraculously swift and simple resolution which revived hope for a return to normality. It was a period, in other words, when specific events lent encouragement and immediacy to the desire for a new beginning that had been acknowledged in the fourth Eclogue.[16]

As long as Sextus Pompey controlled the seas around Italy and provided a rallying point for disaffected Italians, Caesar could not hope to consolidate his own position and to win popularity in Italy. In 37 B.C. he prepared to bring the war to Pompey, on the sea and in Sicily. He anticipated an invasion of Italy by erecting towers along the coast, a move that was not popular among Italians. When his initial campaigns ended in terrible naval disasters, Pompey's counterattacks "[threw] everything into confusion" (App. *BC* 5.11.10l). Caesar feared desertions from his cause and plots against his life. There was serious disaffection in Rome, and open rebellion in parts of Etruria.

Caesar's victory over Pompey was unexpectedly complete. Despite his initial reverses, he managed to eliminate not only Sextus Pompey, but his own rival triumvir, Marcus Lepidus—and he did this without bringing war to Italy. He returned a hero:

> The people of the capital unanimously bestowed upon him votes of praise, statues, the right to the front seat, an arch surmounted by trophies, and the privilege of riding into town on horseback, of wearing the laurel crown on all occasions, and of holding a banquet with his wife and children in the temple of Capitoline Jupiter on the anniversary of the . . . victory, which was to be a perpetual day of thanksgiving.
>
> (Dio 49.15.1).

We cannot dismiss this simply as the obsequiousness of a cowed populace fearful of reprisals. Rather, Caesar was the beneficiary of an overwhelming sense of relief and salvation. From Appian we learn that the removal of Pompey and Lepidus "seemed to be the end of civil dissensions. . . . Cities joined in placing [Caesar] among their tutelary gods" (*BC* 5.13.132). The literary evidence for an abrupt shift from intense popular anxiety to a correspondingly profound sense of relief is supported by the evidence of coins. Archaeological finds suggest that from 50–36 B.C. the number of coin hoards in Italy, Sicily, Sardinia, and Corsica reached totals equalled or surpassed only during the second Punic War and that the number of hoards then declined sharply in 35 B.C. and the years following.[17]

In addition to relieving numerous immediate sources of distress, such as exceptional taxes and brigandage, Caesar took steps to present himself as the champion of an imminent return to the traditional constitution. Following his victories over Pompey and Lepidus, he suppressed records of the recent civil strife and promised "that he would restore the constitution entirely when Antony should return from the Parthian war," whereupon, according to Appian, Caesar "was chosen tribune for life by acclamation, the people urging him, by the offer of this perpetual magistracy, to give up his former one" (*BC* 5.13.132). There is some uncertainty about specifics here, but if Appian's account is true to the general spirit of events, we have evidence that the urgent desire for a return to constitutional normality was widespread, not just a concern of the aristocracy.[18] This may also be the point at which Caesar finally dropped all reference to the triumvirate from his coinage.[19] More positively, he allowed magistrates to resume traditional functions that had hitherto been suspended, made conspicuous display of his respect for senatorial prerogatives, refused an unconstitutional offer of the office of Pontifex Maximus, and created new patricians.

The promise of a completely new beginning was, however, deferred, and it must have seemed increasingly problematic as awareness spread that tensions between Caesar and Antony were mounting. Nonetheless, the prevailing reality for most Italians from 36 to 32 B.C. was peace and order, with comparativey little fear of renewed hostilities. In 32 B.C., however, the pretense of *amicitia* between the two leaders was shattered. On February 1, the new consuls, both Antonians, denounced Caesar in the Senate; Caesar convened another meeting, where, surrounded by guards with concealed weapons, he denounced Antony. At this the consuls, soon to be followed by some three hundred senators, fled to Antony.[20] Preparations for war were begun on both sides. By May/June, when Antony divorced Octavia and Roman officials declared war against his ally, Cleopatra, those acts were mere formalities. Italians once more saw a general mobilization of troops; the imposition of harsh taxes provoked a renewal of dissension and rioting.[21] According to Plutarch, there were such disturbances throughout Italy that Antony was criticized for not taking advantage of them by pressing an immediate attack.[22] Once again, Dio reports, there were frightening portents and the donning of military cloaks at Rome, as though the enemy were actually at the gates.

Two circumstances gave to these familiar preparations an unprecedented urgency for Italians. The first was a product of Caesarean propaganda.[23] Taking advantage of Antony's protracted stay in the East, his colorful relationship with Cleopatra, his settlements of eastern kingdoms, and his extravagant gifts to the Egyptian royal family, Caesar claimed that Antony was no more than Cleopatra's slave. His declaration of war pointedly named her, not Antony, as the enemy. A natural extension of this policy was to encourage the fear that, if victorious, Antony and Cleopatra would transfer the seat of government from Rome to Alexandria. The proud conquerors of the world would become subjects of an Egyptian queen.[24]

The second circumstance that lent particular weight to the approaching conflict was that for the first time in a Roman civil war both leaders secured a personal oath of allegiance from their followers. With the exception of a few communities still loyal to Antony, all Italians swore their individual loyalty to Caesar.[25] Thus they were all directly implicated and forced to declare sides in this new civil war. While appeals to national pride and interdependence may have convinced many, others were less enthusiastic. Dio reports that before leaving Italy, Caesar

> assembled all his troops that were of any value, and likewise all of the men of influence, both senators and knights, at Brundisium, wishing to make the first cooperate with him and to keep the others from beginning a rebellion as they might if left by themselves, but chiefly with the purpose of showing to all the world that he had the largest and strongest element among the Romans in sympathy with himself.
>
> (50.11.5)

None of this assembled throng was to be left behind where they might create problems; all were instructed to accompany Caesar in his campaign. There would have been few Italian communities whose leading families were not represented in Caesar's retinue, whose young men of military age were not among his troops as he set out against the most distinguished general of the age, the veteran troops of the East, and the wealth of Egypt.

The decisive engagement, when it came, was anticlimactic. The battle of Actium was dominated by Caesar's forces from the beginning; Antony and Cleopatra were disgraced, their supporters alienated. Caesar had fought the battle under Apollo's auspices, and some years later Propertius (4.6.67–8) could reduce the entire episode symbolically to the firing of a single shaft from Apollo's bow. Horace (*Odes* 1.37.17–20) likened Cleopatra's flight to that of doves before a hawk. Once again Italy had, contrary to reasonable expectation, been spared war on its own soil. In his celebration of Cleopatra's defeat, Horace gave famous expression to what must have been an almost universal sense of release:

> Nunc est bibendum, nunc pede libero
> pulsanda tellus . . .
>
> (*Odes* 1.37.1–2)

Now is the time to drink, now with unfettered foot
to beat the earth . . .

When Caesar had to return home to quell unruly veterans, he was met with such an outpouring of spontaneous, popular enthusiasm that the troops gave up their demands. From then through his spectacular triumph of 29 B.C. honors were heaped upon him, his achievements were acknowledged by public holidays and thanksgivings that were to become fixed celebrations in the religious calendar. When news arrived in 29 B.C. that Caesar had reached an accommodation with the Parthians, the Senate voted many new honors, among which was that "his name should be included in their hymns equally with those of the gods" (Dio 51.20.1).

Once again, Caesar sought to win favor and forestall opposition by encouraging Romans to believe that a return to the traditional constitution was imminent. Those who had received amnesty during the civil wars were now permitted to return to Italy to live. Caesar appointed new members to the Senate and again enrolled new families in the depleted patrician class. His closing of the gates of Janus in 29 B.C. was a clear turning point; the first such closing since the end of the first Punic War, it marked the end of civil war at Rome and was thus a formal announcement that the time for a new beginning was finally at hand. What exact form that new beginning might take would not be clear at least until the constitutional settlement of 27 B.C.

In the *Georgics* it is the prospect of new beginnings, a subordinate concern in the *Eclogues*, that Vergil takes as his point of departure and his chief point of reference. The first 70 lines of the poem suggest a parallel among three different kinds of beginnings. The introduction evokes the tutelary gods of the farmer's work, including Liber, who added wine to water; Ceres, who taught men to cultivate grains; Minerva, who is *inventrix oleae*, "discoverer of the olive"; Triptolemus, who demonstrated the use of the plow; and Aristaeus, who is identified here only as *cultor nemorum*, "cultivator of groves," but is celebrated in Georgic 4 as the discoverer of a technique for generating new swarms of bees. Together these gods take us back to the very origins of civilization.

The second beginning evoked in the poem brings us abruptly to the immediate present of Roman politics. Caesar is addressed as one who will soon become a god and whose special realm is still undecided. This address acknowledges the political reality between 31 and 27 B.C., when Caesar had eliminated the last of his rivals but had not yet made explicit his own role for the future. He is poised at a moment of immense possibility for himself and the world. His power is awesome, the choices available to him virtually

limitless: patronage of the earth, of the seas, or of the heavenly con-
stellations (1.24–35). The alternatives suggest mastery of the very elements
of the universe: earth, air, fire, and water:

> da facilem cursum atque audacibus adnue coeptis,
> ignarosque viae mecum miseratus agrestis
> ingredere et votis iam nunc adsuesce vocari.
>
> (1.40–42)

> grant an easy course: assent to bold beginnings,
> and pitying, with me, the rustics who are ignorant of the way
> come forward and become accustomed even now to be
>   addressed with prayers.

We may take him to be asking Caesar's blessings for the *Georgics*, but his
prayer is equally relevant to Caesar's larger responsibilities: now is the time
for the statesman, as for the poet, to commit himself to "bold beginnings."

The initial exposition of the poem evokes a third kind of beginning:

> Vere novo, gelidus canis cum montibus umor
> liquitur et Zephyro putris se glaeba resoluit,
> depresso incipiat iam tum mihi taurus aratro
> ingemere et sulco attritus splendescere vomer.
> illa seges demum votis respondet avari
> agricolae, bis quae solem, bis frigora sensit;
> illius immensae ruperunt horrea messes.
>
> (1.43–9)

> When spring is new and cold damp on white mountains
> melts and the loose clod of earth crumbles under the
>   West Wind,
> then, as I press down the plow, let my bull begin
> to groan, the plowshare to be burnished to a shining by the
>   furrow.
> That crop will respond at last to the prayers of the eager
> farmer, that twice has felt the sun, twice the cold;
> his are the immense harvests that burst the barns.

Here the beginning of the year brings with it the beginning of the farmer's
work. Like the initiation of Caesar's rule, this is a time of immense promise.
Vergil relates this annual opening of the farmer's year to the origins of
civilization: the farmer must conform to natural laws that were laid down

when Deucalion created a new human race by casting stones on the earth (1.60–63). Thus, the farmer's annual beginnings reenact the earliest work of civilization. They are a reminder that civilization must be repeatedly begun anew. The new beginning that faces Caesar may be on a far grander scale than the farmer's, but it is part of a common pattern which has been presented on three levels: divine, political, and natural.

This dramatic emphasis on beginnings recurs at the conclusion of the *Georgics*. The second half of book 4 introduces Aristaeus, who discovered how to generate new swarms of bees. His discovery, following the total annihilation of his bees by disease, offers hope that even the most extreme disasters, though apparently irremediable, may be overcome. But the bees are not like other animals: their swarm is analogous to Roman society. Vergil describes the bees as Quirites (4.201), the traditional title for Roman citizens, and attributes to them "civil wars" (*discordia*, 4.68). Vergil does not ignore significant differences between the bees and Roman society, but there are sufficient similarities so that the dissolution of the bees' swarm brings to mind the recent disturbances that threatened to destroy Rome. Correspondingly, the generation of a new swarm of bees suggests the possibility that Roman society may likewise be reconstructed. In this way we are recalled to the new beginnings that Vergil had urged Caesar to undertake in the introduction of the *Georgics*. Just as the pastoral world of the *Eclogues* is framed by violent intrusions of civil war, so in the *Georgics* rustic life is framed by emphasis on the possibility of new beginnings.

This new emphasis corresponds, as we have seen, to a change in the historical circumstances of Vergil and his contemporaries: it does not signal a retreat from the complex point of view suggested by the *Eclogues*. Quite the reverse. That point of view is now elaborated and grounded in a more formal conception of human nature and its relation to the larger order of things. The possibility of new beginnings and the promise that they hold are reasons for hope, but they represent only one part of reality. Behind them is the fact that new beginnings are always necessary. The farmer's work is determined by the natural order. He must renew his work each spring; he must regulate it according to the seasons of the year, the stages in the growth of his crops and animals, even the time of day. Natural disasters are a part of this order. They may be uncontrollable, but they are not unpredictable: storms are announced by reliable signs (1.351–463), and plague follows a strict pattern (3.440–566).

The Roman civil wars are identified with these natural disasters and presented as conforming to the same universal patterns. When Vergil introduces the civil wars at the end of book 1, it is as the last and greatest in a series of destructive storms that prove the utter reliability of the sun as a weather sign (1.463–514). Vergil repeats the analogy between natural and civil disturbances in Georgic 3. There he describes a plague that is comparable to the civil wars because it too is a violent disturbance that is beyond human control, overturns the normal order, and drives the farmer off the land. Those essential similarities are underlined by structural parallelism of the two passages.[26] The idea that civil war is a kind of natural phenomenon is brought to our attention once more in Georgic 4, where Vergil describes the *discordia* within a swarm of bees. His mock-heroic description (4.67–87) reminds us that Roman civil wars differ only in scale from the kind of internecine strife that the bees experience "frequently" (*saepe*, 4.67).

Although Vergil gives no explanation for this implicit identity of natural and civil violence, he does point to one source of disorder that humans and animals share: *amor*.[27] In the conclusion to his discussion of breeding livestock (3.209–83), he develops the paradox that *amor*, the impulse to procreation, leads also to violence and madness. The tremendous energy unleashed by *amor* is not only destructive to the animals' masters but exceeds the animals' own control, so that it may result in behavior that is self-destructive and obstructs the fulfillment of *amor* itself. The contention of two bulls for a heifer, for example, becomes a mock-heroic struggle in which personal honor and revenge come to assume at least as much importance as the original object of their rivalry (3.224–9). The influence of *amor* and Venus on mares manifests itself in the animals' "signal madness" (*furor . . . insignis*, 3.266). Vergil claims that this destructive aspect of *amor* is universal and explicitly includes humans within its scope: *Omne adeo genus in terris hominumque ferarumque / . . . in furias ignemque ruunt . . .* (3.242, 244 "so does every race on earth both of humans and of wild beasts / . . . rush into burning rage . . .") Leander's suicidal attempt to swim across the Hellespont to his beloved Hero is evoked as a specific instance of the way *durus amor* affects humans (3.258–63).

Above all, the story of Orpheus and Eurydice in Georgic 4 reaffirms the dual nature of *amor*. On the one hand, Orpheus' love for Eurydice leads him to heroic achievements: he not only descends to the Underworld and returns; he wins permission to bring his Eurydice back with him. On the other hand, his love for Eurydice leads him to look back at her and thus to violate the one condition that Proserpina placed upon his success. Vergil generalizes the meaning of Orpheus' failure by describing it in the language traditionally used by Latin authors to express the irresistible madness that love inflicts upon its victims: Orpheus is seized by madness (*dementia cepit*, 4.488) and his mind is overcome (*victusque animi*, 4.491); Eurydice is made *misera* (4.494) by their separation and attributes her lover's failure to *furor* (4.495).[28]

Humans, then, share in an elemental vitality that makes new beginnings possible, but the power of that vitality is beyond human control and can therefore lead to destruction as well as to creation. As agents of that vitality, humans themselves become part of the pattern of disorder inherent in the world. The irrationality of human passion, like storms and plagues, assures that the promise of new beginnings is never certain, its realization never lasting. History, therefore, must be an endless cycle in which the hopefulness of new undertakings alternates with the despair of failure. So we must understand the hopefulness that Vergil expresses in the introduction of the *Georgics*. After the suffering and chaos of civil war a new beginning is possible, but there is no comforting assurance of lasting peace and prosperity.

III

The magnificent triple triumph (for victories in Illyria, at Actium, and in Egypt) held in August, 29 B.C., had clearly demonstrated Augustus' power (Caesar soon received the title Augustus and we may now begin to use that name).[29] But within a year of the triumph Propertius published an elegy expressing sorrow for his family's loss in the crushing of Perusia twelve years before:

> Si Perusina tibi patriae sunt nota sepulcra,
> Italiae duris funera temporibus,
> cum Romana suos egit discordia civis . . .
>
> (1.21.3–5)

> If you know the Perusine graves of my country,
> deaths in the cruel days of Italy,
> when Roman discord drove her citizens . . .

Though he soon learned to praise the victor, Propertius bears witness to bitterness which still survived and is not completely absent even from his last poems. There must have been much grief and anger remaining in the many Italian municipalities that had suffered so severely in the civil wars. As usually happens, it is largely through the eyes of the victors that we see the decade of the twenties, but signs of a hostile or ambiguous attitude are not lacking. There were plots against the life of Augustus on three occasions before the death of Vergil: by M. Lepidus in the year of Actium, by Fannius Caepio and Terentius Varro in 23 B.C., by M. Egnatius Rufus in 19 B.C.[30] These men were all members of the senatorial class: Lepidus was the son of the triumvir; Terentius Varro was probably consul at the time of the plot in which he became involved; Egnatius Rufus had been praetor and formed his conspiracy when he was denied permission to run for the consulship. We know very little of these conspiracies, which may have been provoked by the ambitions of a few individuals; there were no popular uprisings against Augustus.

Nostalgia for the old days before the civil wars certainly did exist.[31] Praise of the Republic and its heroes was freely allowed. Livy, Pollio, and Messalla all lauded the *libertas* of the past. Popular talk, as Seneca tells us Livy reported, could even question whether the birth of Julius Caesar had benefitted or harmed his country: *utrum illum magis nasci an non nasci reipublicae profuerit* (Sen. *QNat.* 5.18.4). Cremutius Cordus told of the civil wars with sadness and went so far as to proscribe everlastingly the authors of the proscriptions: *proscribentis in aeternum ipse proscripsit* (Sen. *ConsMarc.* 26.1). More direct criticism of Augustus was not permitted. Instead, criticism of the present would be veiled in praise or blame of the past. The burning of books did not come until years later.

We can see evidence of lingering criticism and doubts mainly through Augustus' actions, the steps he took to allay fears and give comfort to those who regretted the Republic. Julius Caesar, by his patent contempt for the traditional Roman constitution had alienated Republicans and as a result failed to establish a new order. Augustus, while expressing full respect for tradition in government, religion, and morality, succeeded in creating a new state and society. In the twenties the measures taken were still tentative, subject to change and experiment, and must have been observed with a mixture of skepticism and hope.

Postquam bella civilia exstinxeram . . . rem publicam ex mea potestate in senatus populique Romani arbitrium transtuli (*Res Gestae* 34 "After I had extinguished the civil wars . . . I transferred the republic from my power to the judgment of the Senate and Roman people"). With these words Augustus stated the fulfillment of his promise of a return to normality, by the Restoration of the Republic in 28 and 27 B.C. But it was a very different *res publica* from that of the past. The senators, fearing chaos and acknowledging Caesar's pre-eminence, begged him not to desert the republic, and it was agreed that he should exercise proconsular command over those provinces which were most threatened by disturbances, chief among them Gaul, Spain, and Syria. The great majority of the legions therefore remained under his command. At the same time he received many honors and the name Augustus, meaning "possessing moral authority" and implying divine approval through its connection with augury.[32] The name Romulus had been considered, to mark him as Rome's second founder, but was rejected as suggesting a king—whatever the reality, the appearance of monarchy was to be avoided. Power rested on the command of most of the legions, moral authority, and the great wealth Augustus had acquired, particularly by the conquest of Egypt.

Among the honors voted to Augustus was a gold shield *virtutis clementiaeque et iustitiae et pietatis causa* ("for courage, clemency, justice, and piety"). It has recently been argued that these four virtues were not a conventional canon, and that the inclusion of *clementia* is unusual.[33] It is ironic that in the first year after the bestowal of the shield, Augustus, who was trying to live down his early reputation for ruthlessness, felt himself forced to a refusal of clemency which he later regretted. Cornelius Gallus, a knight who had served in the campaigns of Actium and Alexandria, an elegiac poet and friend of both Augustus and Vergil, was the first Roman prefect of Egypt. He was boastful in inscriptions on Egyptian monuments and evidently disrespectful toward Augustus. Even after his recall from Egypt, other unspecified charges were reported. Augustus renounced friendship: Gallus was condemned by the senate and committed suicide. Augustus lamented that he alone could not indulge in anger toward a friend (Suet. *Aug.* 66).

Italy, however, was now at peace. Half the legions, including those of Antony, had been discharged with generous bonuses. Interest rates had fallen drastically, and a long period of prosperity was in fact beginning. In Italy and most of the senatorial provinces the Augustan Peace meant actual freedom from conflict, but elsewhere foreign policy was designed to encourage the belief that Rome had turned finally from internecine strife to the foreign conquests of a more glorious past. On the periphery of the empire peace again was to mean pacification—reduction of rebellious people and extension of Rome's control. Augustus, while continuing to hold one of the consulships, as he had done every year since 33 B.C., went to Gaul in 27 B.C. and spent the years 26–24 B.C. in Spain, where there were hard campaigns against the Cantabri and Astures. When victory seemed won in 25 B.C., the gates of Janus were closed for the second time by Augustus' orders, but war soon broke out again.

The foundations of the Augustan establishment were severely tested and almost collapsed in 23 B.C., after his return from Spain at the end of 24. At the trial of M. Primus for exceeding his authority as governor of Macedonia, Augustus gave witness against him and was roughly treated by the advocate for the defense; "not a few" (Dio 54.3.4) voted for acquittal. Soon afterward came the conspiracy of Caepio and Murena, brother of Maecenas' wife. They were convicted and put to death, but even in this case some jury members voted (secretly) for acquittal (Dio 54.3.5–6). Augustus then became so ill that his death seemed very possible. His precarious health was a source of particular concern in men's minds because there was great uncertainty as to who would succeed to his power if he died. On his recovering he made a concession to senatorial feelings by resigning the consulship which he had held for ten consecutive years, so that henceforth two consulships could be open for ambitious senators. But he assumed two important and unusual additional powers: *imperium maius*, an authority superior to that of the governors even in the senatorial provinces, and full *tribunicia potestas* for life. This tribunical power made him the representative and protector of the common people and probably marks the moment when he became their accepted leader.[34] When the Tiber overflowed its banks in 22 B.C. and there were plague, famine, and riots, the people demanded that Augustus be appointed dictator and take charge of the grain supply. He refused the dictatorship, but did relieve the food shortage. Clearly the mass of the population of Rome now placed more confidence in him than in the Senate.

This trust was the culmination of a long series of actions aimed at attracting the favor of the people and inspiring renewed self-confidence in them. In addition to distributions of cash to some 250,000 Romans on several special occasions (*Res Gestae* 15) and regular grain doles, he gave frequent public games and shows. In doing so he made a point of showing that he shared in the pleasure of the crowd, particularly enjoying boxing matches (Suet. *Aug.* 45.2).[35] His building program reawakened pride in the city, emphasized traditional religious practices, and associated Augustus and his family with the greatness of Rome. In the year 28 B.C. alone he claimed to have restored eighty-two temples (*Res Gestae* 20), completed the Forum Iulium, begun construction of the Mausoleum for his family, dedicated the temple of the deified Julius in the Forum Romanum on the spot where Julius Caesar's body had been burned, and on the Palatine (near his own home and the Hut of Romulus) built the Temple of Palatine Apollo, whom he regarded as his protector and the guide to victory at Actium. He was planning a new forum with a temple to Mars Ultor, the Avenger, adjacent to Julius' forum with its temple to Venus Genetrix, mother not only of the Aeneadae, but also of the Julian family (Suet. *Caes.* 6.1). Near the end of his life he could claim that he had received a city of brick and left it built of marble (Suet. *Aug.* 28.3). But during Vergil's lifetime completion of this building program lay in the future.

In 22 Augustus went to the East, stopping in Sicily, Greece, Asia Minor, and Syria, exercising his *imperium maius*. His great success was a diplomatic one, the surrender by the Parthians of the surviving prisoners and the standards of the legions captured over thirty years before at Carrhae. The fact that he made this rather modest diplomatic success a central element in his program to restore Roman self-confidence and pride suggests that a popular desire for return to the glorious past of the Republic had not yet been satisfied and was still a force to be reckoned with. Augustus surely hoped that Vergil's new poem, "greater than the *Iliad*," would also contribute to this restoration of Roman pride in her past: in the winter preceding his trip to the East he had heard Vergil read books 2, 4, and 6 of the *Aeneid* in his house on the Palatine.

But Augustus' hopeful plans were not to be so easily fulfilled. When he was returning to Italy in 19 B.C., he was joined in Greece by Vergil, who became ill on the journey and died at Brundisium on September 21. The poet's final wish was that his unfinished epic be destroyed. Shortly before Augustus reached Rome in October, the plot of Egnatius Rufus to assassinate him was discovered. Even at the time of Vergil's death the new order was not yet firmly established. If his poem had voiced pure optimism, Vergil would have been whistling in the dark.

The background and implied subject of the *Aeneid* are escape from the disasters of recent history and the effort to begin reconstruction. The central concerns of the earlier poems persist: the sense of insecurity arising both from the external world and from the passions of the soul, and the longing to escape into either an ideal world or a stable society based on a just and rational order. But now the field of vision has expanded. It is a whole people whose existence has been put in jeopardy—in the remote past of the poem's setting, the Trojans; in the present mirrored in that past, the Romans. Aeneas' story, the pursuit of a goal always escaping his grasp like the ghosts of Creusa and Anchises, is paradigmatic of Roman historical experience and, by implication, of all human experience. His successes and failures represent the range and limits of human capacity. The value of his final achievement is rendered problematical by the price he must pay and by the means he must use, means which, because of the ambivalence in human nature, may contain the seeds of future failure.

The success of Rome in conquering the world is foreseen early in the *Aeneid* in Jupiter's prophecy to Venus (1.257-96). It seems unqualified and climaxes in the closing of the gates of Janus, marking the establishment of peace. The gates had been closed by Augustus in 29 B.C., yet Vergil's readers knew that this was a transitory moment, not a final act. The gates were soon opened again, closed once more in 25 B.C., but before long opened yet again. The rage (*Furor impius*) of war could not long be controlled. Juno opens these gates in the *Aeneid* (7.620-22), chronologically long before the events to which Jupiter's prophecy points but subsequent to them in the order of Vergil's narrative, and in any case the time of the poem is mythological, not historical: what happens once happens over and over again. Even when the prophecy reaches its glorious climax, the reader, knowing how soon *Furor impius* will again be set loose, must doubt the security of the promised success and reflect on its cost. Rome's success is also foreseen by Anchises in Elysium, promising that Augustus Caesar will restore the Golden Age in Latium, where Saturn once ruled (6.791–5); but when Aeneas visits the site of Rome we are reminded that the rage for war (*belli rabies*) and the love of wealth (*amor habendi*) had destroyed that Golden Age (8.326–7).[36]

Immediately after Jupiter's prophecy the episode of Dido and Aeneas begins. As a study of the way the destiny of nations is determined by public action under the influence of private passion it is a key to the interpretation of the whole poem. Into the love story Vergil weaves memories of both the wars with Carthage in the distant past and the civil wars now barely ended. In Dido there is a fusion of identities: at the moment before her suicide she is *pallida morte futura* (4.644 "pale with coming death"), and on the shield of Aeneas Cleopatra is depicted as fleeing from Actium to her suicide in Egypt *pallentem morte futura* (8.709). In Aeneas there are traits of both Antony and Augustus. The relationship of Dido and Aeneas, like that of Cleopatra and Antony, combines sexual *amor* with political *amicitia*.[37] And in Carthage there is a likeness to Rome. When Aeneas looked down on Carthage for the first time, he saw the Tyrians building a new city. A visitor in the years 29–19 B.C. would have seen the same activity at Carthage, but the actors would have been Romans: among the many colonies established by Augustus was the Colonia Iulia Concordia Carthago, replacing the old Carthage totally destroyed by Scipio Aemilianus in 146 B.C. at the end of the Third Punic War. Now Carthage was being rebuilt, and Rome was being transformed from the city of brick to the city of marble; both were making new beginnings under Augustus. Contemporaries could say, like Aeneas:

O fortunati, quorum iam moenia surgunt!

(1.437)

Happy are these, whose walls now are rising!

For Aeneas the settlement in Carthage is a relief from conflict and suffering. With Dido he finds a peace and happiness that we have not seen him enjoy before and that he will never enjoy again. He has found an escape from his *labores* by relinquishing the dream of founding a new state of his own, his "destiny." Instead, for a little time, Dido's offer is accepted: *urbem quam statuo vestra est* (1.573 "The city I am building is yours"). Carthage could be built by Trojans and Tyrians in concord like the *concordia* of the city building in Vergil's own day. Aeneas is renouncing the task enjoined on him by Apollo, to seek out the Trojans' ancient mother (*antiquam matrem*, 3.96); all the fresh beginnings—from Troy, Thrace, Delos, Crete, the Strophades, Actium, Buthrotum, Aetna—can end in the calm of helping Dido build Carthage (4.260). Aeneas has found love, and Arcadia, in Carthage.[38]

But Mercury comes to charge that Aeneas has rejected *gloria*, public achievement, for *otium*, private peace and contentment (4.271-2). We are reminded of Tityrus in the first Eclogue (1.6) and of the end of the *Georgics* (4.559-66), where Vergil is enjoying his *ignobile otium*, his "inglorious leisure," under the protection of Caesar's power.[39] This call to glory, Aeneas' *pietas*, his sense of duty to his people and his family, and his ambition to found a new Troy, induce him to leave Dido. His overriding love is love for his country: *hic amor, haec patria est* (4.347). That Vergil recognized fully how dreadful can be the consequences of such love of country is shown by words of Anchises in the same vision of the future in which he foresaw the triumph of Augustus. Among the souls awaiting birth by the shores of the river Lethe is L. Junius Brutus, who will expel the Tarquins and be the first consul of the Roman Republic, but whom *amor patriae* (6.823) will cause to order the execution of his own sons when they conspire against the Republic—*infelix! utcumque ferent ea facta minores* (6.822 "unhappy man, however future generations may regard his acts").

Now Dido's love turns to rage and hatred. Aeneas must suffer her curse on him and his people (4.607-20). This curse is put into effect as soon as Juno accepts her death (4.693-705), for her suicide is like the *devotio* which a Roman commander performs so that the gods will be obligated to fulfill his curse on the enemy; it will reverberate through time and be fulfilled in Rome's coming wars.[40] The departure from Carthage is another fresh start faced with ambivalent emotions: the Trojans receive their sailing orders with joy (*laeti* 4.295), but they go with gloomy omen (*triste per augurium* 5.7) and a new storm threatens.[41] Jupiter—and history—have forbidden fulfillment of the dream of escape into an ideal of peace.

When Aeneas comes to Latium, where Saturn had once established a Golden Age, he, like Augustus after him, hopes to re-establish that Golden Age, but his initial hope for settlement in justice and peace with understanding among peoples is shattered by the outbreak of conflicting passions. Love and ambition again lead to hatred and enmity. When Aeneas and Turnus meet in their decisive duel, they are likened to two bulls struggling to determine which will rule the herd and possess the cows (12.715-22). This simile is an unmistakable echo of *Georgics* 3.209-41, where, as we have seen (above, p.28), Vergil illustrates the destructive power of love by describing two bulls who join battle for a heifer. In the *Aeneid* the rivalry is for leadership in Latium and possession of Lavinia. Her figure, shadowy for us, has been vital for Turnus. Denial of marriage to her played its part in arousing his first rage against the Trojans (7.423, 433); the sight of her blinded him to the wise advice that he forego the hopeless duel with Aeneas (*illum turbat amor*, 12.70); and he enters the fatal combat, to which the fighting bulls are compared, influenced by shame, madness, grief, rage-maddened love (*furiis agitatus amor*), and courage (12.667-8). Passion as irrational as that of animals in combat is an inevitable element in human action: *amor omnibus idem* (*G.* 3.244 "love is the same for all").

But it is not enough to see Aeneas only in terms of private passion. He is a public figure, the prototype of Roman magistrates, a figure of majesty and power—to be honored and feared. In the tenth book there is a revealing vision of Aeneas the leader of his people, both as savior and as destroyer. At the moment of his landing in Latium, when he has returned from Etruria, "Standing in the lofty stern, he raised his blazing shield." *Stans celsa in puppi* (10.261) is a phrase which has come to carry multiple associations. It had been used of Anchises in the joyful moment when Italy first came in sight (3.527). Aeneas himself was *celsa in puppi*, his mind fixed on departure, when Mercury brought his final command to leave Carthage (4.554). And Augustus at the battle of Actium as depicted on the shield of Aeneas (8.680) is "standing in the lofty stern" leading the Italian peoples to war, with fathers and people, penates and the great gods, while twin flames gleam from his brow and his father Julius' star rises over his crest. When Aeneas approaches the hostile shore of Latium *stans celsa in puppi* we see him in the foreground, but behind him are the images of Anchises greeting the promised land of Italy, Aeneas himself sacrificing the possibility of private happiness in Carthage, and Augustus leading his fleet to victory at Actium. Aeneas is greeted by the besieged Trojans with a shout of joy and rage for battle; but for the Italians of Turnus' army the flame gleaming from his crest and the fire pouring from his shield are an omen of terror, "as when blood-red comets gleam mournfully or the heat of the Dog Star rises, bringing thirst and disease to suffering mortals" (*mortalibus aegris*, 10.274): the Julian star, which on the crest of Augustus appears as an omen of victory, is now an omen of suffering for humanity. Opening on the proud and hopeful note established by *stans celsa in puppi*, the lines pass through joy to anger to terror to unrelieved despair. All these are emotions aroused by the man who is to be the new leader of the Italian peoples.

Aeneas exemplifies the ambivalence Vergil found in human nature. He loves Dido and he loves his people, yet he causes her death and everlasting war for Rome. He hopes to act with justice and to confirm the peace he finds in Latium, but he brings with him war. Vergil saw in his own time hope for justice, order, and peace, but he also saw clearly the drives in human character which thwart such hope. In the *Aeneid* the most just of men die casually—Galaesus the Ausonian (7.535-7), Ripheus the Trojan (2.426-7). The judgments of the gods are different—*dis aliter visum* (2.428).

A perfectly just and rational order of society is an impossible ideal, like the dream of a pastoral Arcadia.

The complexity of human nature exists also in Vergil's gods. All that happens in Carthage happens with their approval. Jupiter sends Mercury to insure that Dido will give kindly reception to Aeneas (1.297-304). Venus, goddess of passionate love, and Juno, goddess of passionate anger, together plan the union of Dido and Aeneas (4.90-128). Jupiter again sends Mercury, this time to command Aeneas' desertion of Dido (4.219-37). Juno, by accepting Dido's *devotio*, insures fulfillment of her curse. And in book 10 Jupiter, while condemning the *discordia* of Trojans and Italians, gives his blessing to war with Carthage (10.11-14). These Vergilian gods embody a human perception of reality, an inextricable mingling of good and evil, reason and passion, order and chaos, in which a measure of stability in society can be achieved only by controlled violence. The Jupiter who prophesied Rome's triumph is the ruler of the Iron Age, who has willed that men must live by labor—toil and suffering (*G.* 1.118-46). Hercules, who bore so many *labores* (8.291-3), is held up as a model to Aeneas by Evander (8.362-5), and Evander tells Aeneas how Hercules saved his people from the monster Cacus (8.185-267). In doing so he had acted with rage: *furiis exarserat* (219). . . *furens animis* (228). . . *fervidus ira* (230) ("he had caught fire with fury . . . furious in spirit. . . hot with anger"). This capacity for suffering the hot passion of rage is demanded of those who will succeed in the competition of Jupiter's world, and it is demanded of Aeneas. He requires constantly to be reminded to honor Juno; he shows that he has finally learned the lesson, both in his battle rage after the death of Pallas (10.510-605) and in the chilling final scene when Turnus pleads for his life in the name of Anchises, who had spoken the command to spare the vanquished (*parcere subjectis*, 6.853). We expect mercy and remember Augustus' claim to imitate the *clementia* of Julius Caesar, but among Caesar's assassins had been recipients of that clemency. Aeneas does not spare Turnus. Violence, the *furor* and *ira* of Juno, have become part of his nature.[42]

In Aeneas Vergil presented a man who tried to justify in his conduct Ilioneus' tribute that no man was more just than he in fulfilling his duty (1.544-5). The strains of the responsibility he faced in peace and war were greater than human nature could bear with equanimity. As we saw Dido in rage in Book 4, so we see Aeneas by the end of the poem yielding to passion. Vergil was too honest to flatter Augustus with a false assurance that the dangers known in the past had been overcome by the Augustan settlement. He looked to the future as did Anchises when he interpreted the omen of the four white horses seen on the Italian shore (3.537-43): they threaten war, *bellum minantur*; . . . there is also hope of peace, *spes et pacis*.

IV

The *Eclogues* announce themes that were to occupy Vergil throughout his life: civil war, the longing for escape, the hope for a new beginning. These concerns were a direct response to the disorders that Vergil and his countrymen experienced during the early triumviral period. For Vergil these immediate concerns raised more fundamental questions about the sources of disorder in the world and how to come to terms with them. In the *Eclogues* he looks at the origins of the universe and at *amor*, the vulnerability of humans to uncontrollable passions, but his speculations are tentative; it is not clear whether Roman civil war and the inherent susceptibility of humans to *amor* are related or simply analogous phenomena, and in the end it is this very tentativeness that defines Vergil's perspective in the *Eclogues*: he admits neither immediate despair nor confidence in the future.

The violent and repeated alternation of anxiety and hopefulness brought by the events of 36–29 B.C. seems to have suggested to Vergil that the concerns of the *Eclogues* could never be finally set aside. In the *Georgics* he ascribes the alternation of destruction and renewal, of despair and hope, to the universal pattern of nature. Although he still asserts no causal relations, Vergil now emphasizes a formal parallelism between impersonal disasters, such as storm and plague, the collective disaster of civil war, and the private disasters caused by violent passion. All are presented as inherent and inescapable aspects of nature. The tentativeness and reserve of the poet in the *Eclogues* is now formalized in a view of the natural order that emphasizes its variety and complexity.

But it is in the *Aeneid* that Vergil's thought is most fully integrated. Roman destiny becomes intelligible as the interaction between the larger course of history and the individual propensity for violent passion. History brings the Trojans into contact with other peoples, but it is human passion, above all the madness induced by *amor*, that precipitates conflict and leads to excesses of violence. There can be no sure escape from disorder, because history has shown that it is the Romans' character to extend their *imperium* endlessly (*imperium sine fine dedi*, as Jupiter proclaims it 1.279) and because humans in conflict will never be proof against their own passions. It is paradoxical that Vergil should arrive at such conclusions at the time in his life that appears to us to be the most peaceful and secure; but the interpretation of Rome in the *Aeneid* presents the elaboration and evolution of ideas that were deeply rooted in Vergil's thought, and our retrospective view of the Augustan Principate was not available to him. Nor is it certain that Vergil would have modified his ideas, even if he could share our perspective on his age.

Notes

1. All translations are the authors' own except for those of Appian, where we have used Horace White, *Appian's Roman History*, vol. 4 (Loeb, 1913, repr. 1968); and those of Dio Cassius, where we have used Ernest Cary, *Dio's Roman History*, vols. 5 and 6 (Loeb, 1917, repr. 1955).

2. For a recent review of the dating of Vergil's works, see Rudolf Rieks, "Vergil und die römische Geschichte," *ANRW* II 31.2 (1981): 846–52.

3. The following survey of events from 44–36 B.C. is based primarily on Appian, *Bellum Civile* bk. 3 through bk. 5.9.80, Dio Cassius bks. 45–48, and Suetonius, *Divus Augustus*.

4. Even allowing for invention and exaggeration in Appian's numerous stories of loyalty and betrayal (*BC* 4.3.13–6.51), they must have a considerable basis in fact. Appian (*BC* 4.3.16) says that there were many such reports in many Roman historians; the well-known epitaph in which a husband recalls in grateful detail the risks his wife and her family took for him during the proscriptions (the *Laudatio Turiae, CIL* VI, 1527,31670-Dessau, 8393) provides independent corroboration.

5. For a community that united to protect a benefactor, see App. *BC* 4.6.47.

6. The actual loss of life in battle should not be neglected in assessing the cost of civil wars to Italy. Appian (*BC* 4.14.112) estimates 24,000 dead among the troops of Cassius and Octavian alone at the battle of Philippi. Even allowing for the exaggeration typical of ancient historians, the implications of this estimate for the total dead in the civil wars are sobering.

7. Pompey's efforts were augmented for a while by Lucius Domitius Ahenobarbus in the Adriatic.

8. Again, Ahenobarbus' piracy exacerbated the problem.

9. Michael H. Crawford, *The Roman Republic* (Atlantic Highlands, N.J.: Humanities Press, 1978, repr. Cambridge, Mass.: Harvard University Press, 1982), pp. 189–90, suggests that Cornelius Nepos' comments (*Eumenes* 8.2) on the arrogance and insubordination of the troops of Alexander the Great after his death were informed by Nepos' own perception of the army's role in generating disorder at Rome during the late Republic. Cf. Appian, *BC* 5.17.68–71.

10. Paul Alpers, *The Singer of the Eclogues: A Study of Virgilian Pastoral* (Berkeley and Los Angeles: University of California Press, 1979) p. 81.

11. Ibid., p. 201.

12. *Ecl.* 10.44–51, 58–69, and for *furor* see also v. 38.

13. See Ernest Dutoit, *Le thème de l'adynaton dans la poésie antique* (Paris: Société d'édition "Les Belles Lettres," 1936); the chief examples of the Golden Age theme before Vergil are Hesiod, *Erga* 109–201, Aratus, *Phaenomena* 96–136, and Catullus 64.384–408.

14. Alpers calls attention to the poet's "self-conscious diffidence" in the *Eclogues* (p. 8), but he does not connect it, as here, with the poet's profession of his own susceptibility to the universally uncontrollable power of passion. Thus, he avoids our conclusion that not only the limits of the pastoral perspective, but the poet's capacity to sustain his own larger, more complex perspective are opened to question. For a reading of Eclogue 10 similar to our own but with a much more unqualified emphasis on Vergil's "pessimism," see A.J. Boyle, "A Reading of Virgil's Eclogues," *Ramus* 4 (1975): 195–9.

15. See above, n. 2.

16. The following survey of events from 36–29 B.C. is based primarily on Appian *BC* 5.9.81–end and Dio 49–51.

17. Five hoards discovered for the years 55–51 B.C., 14 for 45–41, 13 for 40–36, but only six for 35–31 and 2 for 30–26. The figures are taken from Michael Crawford, "Coin Hoards in the Late Republic," *PBSR* (1969): 76–81. He suggests that the general correspondence

between the high number of known coin hoards and civil disturbances during the late Republic is significant. He does not comment on the specific contrast between the numbers of known hoards for the decades immediately preceding and following Caesar's defeat of Pompey in 36 B.C.

18. Cf. a slightly different version of events in Dio 49.15.5-6 according to which Caesar was offered not the tribunate but only tribunician *sacrosanctitas*.

19. Lily Ross Taylor, *The Divinity of the Roman Emperor*, American Philological Association Monographs, vol. 1 (Middletown, Conn., 1931), p. 131.

20. On the actual number, see Sir Ronald Syme, *The Roman Revolution* (Oxford: Clarendon Press, 1939, repr. with corrections, 1952), p. 278n3.

21. In addition to Dio 50.6.2, 10.2-6, see Pliny *NH* 37.10.

22. Plutarch, *Antonius* 58.

23. Kenneth Scott, "The Political Propaganda of 44-30 B.C.," *MAAR* (1933): 7-49, remains the standard discussion.

24. Besides Dio 50.4.1 and 5.1-4, see L.R. Taylor, p. 127 and n. 55, who concludes from examination of Alexandrian coins that Antony and Cleopatra sought to represent their city as the New Rome from 34 B.C.

25. Suet. *Aug.* 17.2 and Augustus *Res Gestae* 25. Dio (50.6.6) reports that *both* leaders received personal oaths of allegiance from their respective followers.

26. For fuller discussions see the observations of D.L. Drew, "The Structure of Virgil's *Georgics*," *AJP* 50 (1929): 242-54 (although we do not agree with the conclusions based on those observations), and Herta Klepl, *Lucrez und Vergil in ihren Lehrgedichten* (Diss. Leipzig, 1940, repr. Darmstadt: Wissenschaftliche Buchgesellschaft, 1967), pp. 95-7. On verbal comparisons of storm and plague in the *Georgics* see Gary B. Miles, *Virgil's Georgics: A New Interpretation* (Berkeley: University of California Press, 1981), pp. 219-20.

27. This discussion of *amor* is developed more fully in G.B. Miles, "*Georgics* 3.209-94: *Amor* and Civilization," *CSCA* 8 (1975): 177-97, and Miles, *Virgil's Georgics*, pp. 186-205, 275-81.

28. See Archibald W. Allen, "Elegy and the Classical Attitude toward Love: Propertius 1.1," *YCS* 11 (1950): 255-77, esp. 258-64.

29. The chief historical sources for the period from the triumph to the death of Vergil are Dio 51.21-54.12, Suetonius *Divus Augustus*, Velleius Paterculus 2.89-93, and the *Res Gestae Divi Augusti* (*Monumentum Ancyranum*). For the last, the brief introduction and commentary by P.A. Brunt and J.M. Moore (London: Oxford University Press, 1967, repr. 1970) is particularly helpful on constitutional questions.

30. Suetonius (*Aug.* 19) also tells of several later plots.

31. See J.H.W.G. Liebeschuetz, *Continuity and Change in Roman Religion* (Oxford: Clarendon Press, 1979), pp. 101-8, "The Ambivalent Acceptance of the Principate."

32. This is indicated in Ennius' phrase *augusto augurio* (Enn. *Ann.* 502 V³). See Suet. *Aug.* 7.2 and Dio 53.16.6-8.

33. See Andrew Wallace-Hadrill, "The Emperor and his Virtues," *Historia* 30 (1981): 298-323.

34. See Zvi Yavetz, *Plebs and Princeps* (Oxford: Clarendon Press, 1969), p. 91. In a later article, "The *Res Gestae* and Augustus' Public Image," in *Caesar Augustus: Seven Aspects*, ed. Fergus Millar and Erich Segal (Oxford: Clarendon Press, 1984), pp. 1-36, Yavetz argues that the favor of the aristocratic, educated, and wealthy classes was gained more slowly, and that the *Res Gestae*, "carefully drafted and redrafted between 23 and 2 B.C.," was intended to influence them.

35. In this he differed from Julius Caesar, who often engaged in correspondence while the games were in progress (Suet. *Aug.* 45.1).

36. For the elusive character of the Golden Age see Charles Paul Segal, "Aeternum per Saecula Nomen, The Golden Bough and the Tragedy of History: Part II," *Arion* 5 (1966): 49–50, and Sara Mack, *Patterns of Time in Vergil* (Hamden, Conn.: Archon Books, 1978), pp. 72 5. See also Gerhard Binder, *Aeneas und Augustus* (Meisenheim am Glan: A. Hain, 1971), pp. 102–5.

37. See Richard C. Monti, *The Dido Episode and the Aeneid: Roman Social and Political Values in the Epic* (Leiden: E.J. Brill, 1981).

38. Viktor Pöschl, *The Art of Vergil*, trans. Gerda Seligson (Ann Arbor: University of Michigan Press, 1962), p. 15, suggests that the *Aeneid* could be called the "epic of love."

39. See Miles, *Virgil's Georgics*, pp. 289–94, and idem, "Glorious Peace: The Values and Motivation of Virgil's Aeneas," *CSCA* 9 (1976): 148.

40. For Dido's suicide as the equivalent of *devotio* see A.-M. Tupet, "Didon magicienne," *REL* 48 (1970): 229–58.

41. Wolf-Lüder Liebermann, "Aeneas—Schicksal und Selbstfindung," in *Studien zum antiken Epos*, ed. Herwig Görgemanns and Ernst A. Schmidt (Meisenheim am Glan: A. Hain, 1976), pp. 173–207, interprets Aeneas' decision in existential terms as self-assertion, a freeing of himself from passive submission to circumstances. By his decision to leave Dido he comes to be in harmony with divine purpose, but at the same time he must accept his guilt toward Dido. Aeneas is "responsible" and, in Karl Jasper's words, "Verantwortung heisst die Bereitschaft, die Schuld auf sich zu nehmen" (p. 198).

42. The final scene of the *Aeneid* and the element of violence in the character of Aeneas have been much discussed and very differently judged. Recent opinions incline to avoid extremes of condemnation or approval. So R. O. A. M. Lyne, "Vergil and the Politics of War," *CQ* (1983) 188–203, recognizing Vergil's realistic evaluation of human nature, concludes: "The wars that gain empire involve ugly violence, and less than perfect motivations will sometimes direct even the greatest hero." And Viktor Pöschl, "Das Befremdende in der *Aeneas*," in *2000 Jahre Vergil: Ein Symposium* (Wiesbaden, 1983) 175–88, who is firm in his defense of the conduct of Aeneas as justified by the standards of Vergil's time, nevertheless grants that: "Es tun sich Wiederspruche auf, die der Dichter gesehen hat und die man nicht hinvegschieben kann. . . . Der Dichter urteilt nicht, sondern stellt dar. Er zeigt die Probleme, aber lösst sie nicht. An uns est es, zu urteilen" (p. 185).

COMMUNITY AND CONVENTION IN VERGILIAN PASTORAL

Paul Alpers

Vergil's poems are the fountainhead of much European poetry, and one learns to turn back to them for insight into the procedures and concerns of their descendants in the various vernacular literatures. But it is also true that later poems can shed light, retrospectively, on their Vergilian models. I want to begin with a section of Milton's *Lycidas*, one of the last great examples of Vergilian pastoral, and use it to open up the problem of community and convention in the *Eclogues* themselves. Unlike most of the pastoral elegies that consciously derive from Theocritus and Vergil, *Lycidas* is not at first represented as the song or utterance of a shepherd. The opening lines use pastoral images, but seem to be spoken in the poet's own voice. Only after twenty lines does a fully pastoral world appear:

> Together both, ere the high lawns appeared
> Under the opening eye-lids of the morn,
> We drove a-field, and both together heard
> What time the grey-fly winds her sultry horn,
> Battening our flocks with the fresh dews of night,
> Oft till the star that rose, at evening, bright,
> Toward heaven's descent had sloped his westering wheel.
> Meanwhile the rural ditties were not mute,
> Tempered to the oaten flute,
> Rough satyrs danced, and fauns with cloven heel,
> From the glad sound would not be absent long,
> And old Damaetas loved to hear our song.
>
> (25–36)

These lines represent a pastoral community in the most literal sense: from the opening words, "Together both," everything is held and experienced *in common*. As a consequence, we find that no individual singer is represented. The passage is full of sounds, but the human figures are represented as listening to them: "both together heard" the grey-fly; "old Damaetas loved to hear our song"; "Meanwhile the rural ditties were not mute"—no doubt sung by shepherds, but the locution suggests that they simply occur, like the sounds of nature. Hence when the satyrs and fauns are said to dance to the glad sound, it is a sign not of the poet's power, but rather of a shared joy. The shepherd who is the singer of this poem finally emerges in the next verse paragraph:

> But O the heavy change, now thou art gone,
> Now thou art gone, and never must return!
> Thee shepherd, thee the woods, and desert caves,
> With wild thyme and the gadding vine o'ergrown,
> And all their echoes mourn.
> The willows, and the hazel copses green,
> Shall now no more be seen,
> Fanning their joyous leaves to thy soft lays.
> As killing as the canker to the rose,
> Or taint-worm to the weanling herds that graze,
> Or frost to flowers, that their gay wardrobe wear,
> When first the white-thorn blows;
> Such, Lycidas, thy loss to shepherd's ear.
>
> (37–49)

The pronoun is no longer "we," but "thou," and where there is a "thou" there is an "I." At the same time, the sound has changed not only its character but its source: it does not come from nature and the pastoral community, but is the strongly vocalized utterance of an individual speaker. Separation and loss have given this speaker his voice. This moment of individuation, of separation from community, might seem to be equally a separation from the conventional, for a convention is what members of a group have in common and know each other by. Yet it is precisely in this passage that we first encounter some of the familiar conventions, the identifying marks, of pastoral elegy—the landscape and its echoes mourning the dead shepherd, the landscape devastated by his loss, and the serial listing conveying the dead shepherd's worth by analogies from nature. The paradox of this development in *Lycidas*—that the relevant poetic conventions emerge as the represented community disappears—suggests that ideas of community and convention are not wholly interchangeable. This is as much a matter of connotation as denotation. A convention is something a group of humans have in common: it can even be constitutive of the group. No one will find it odd for Thomas Kuhn to say of scientists that "A paradigm is what the members of a scientific community, and they alone, share. Conversely, it is their possession of a common paradigm that constitutes a scientific community of a group of otherwise disparate men."[1] Similarly, one could say that the readers for whom Milton wrote *Lycidas* shared a knowledge of classical poetry and specifically of Vergilian pastoral; for the purposes of the poem, this shared knowledge, which specific conventions manifest and transmit, constitutes the community of readers. Nevertheless, the word "community," with its implications of a permanent and cohesive shared life, makes larger claims than poetic conventions can be counted on to sustain. To speak, as I do in my book on the *Eclogues*,[2] of a "community of song" is at best to be ambiguous. The legitimate question, "What kind of community is constituted by poetry?" is not adequately separated from the claim that poetry constitutes a full human community, with all the implications of *Gemeinschaft* that come naturally to humanists in the twentieth century. I therefore think it useful, for our understanding both of Vergil and of poetic convention, to ask what sense of pastoral community is manifested when shepherds come together, *convenire*, to sing, and thus renew or give rise to the conventions of pastoral poetry.

I

In Vergil's fullest representation of the circumstances of pastoral singing, convening and community are closely identified. Eclogue 7 begins:

> Forte sub arguta consederat ilice Daphnis,
> compulerantque greges Corydon et Thyrsis in unum,
> Thyrsis ovis, Corydon distentas lacte capellas,
> ambo florentes aetatibus, Arcades ambo,
> et cantare pares et respondere parati.
>
> (7.1–5)

> Under a whispering holm-oak, Daphnis sat,
> Corin and Thyrsis drove their flocks together,
> Thyrsis his sheep, Corin goats swollen with milk,
> Both in the flower of youth, Arcadians both,
> Equal in song and eager to respond.[3]

The line which describes the meeting of Corydon and Thyrsis begins with the word *compulerant* and ends with the phrase *in unum*, which fully establishes the force of the prefix *com-*. In one line, then, convening becomes community. The passage concludes by describing Corydon and Thyrsis as, so to speak, identical twins, and Vergil bestows on them what was to become the title of all literary shepherds, *Arcades ambo*. The representation of community in Eclogue 7 becomes more complex with the emergence of the narrator Meliboeus, whose relation to the group is more problematic than that of the others: he is seeking a goat who strayed, and he feels a conflict between the play of the song contest and the work that awaits him at home (lines 14–17). It is clear that Vergil means these fictional complications to represent complexities of poetic utterance, for he puts the entire singing contest between Corydon and Thyrsis into Meliboeus' mouth. But in Eclogue 7 such complexities do not compromise the full sense of union. When Daphnis invites Meliboeus to join the group, he begins, like a pastoral lover, *huc ades* ("come hither," cf. 2.45 and 9.39), and he fills in the "here-ness" of the spot in the following terms:

> huc ipsi potum venient per prata iuvenci,
> hic viridis tenera praetexit harundine ripas
> Mincius, eque sacra resonant examina quercu.
>
> (7.11–13)

> To drink here, willing bullocks cross the fields;
> Here slender reeds border the verdant banks
> Of Mincius, and the cult-oak hums with bees.

These lines show why Vergil is the father of what T.G. Rosenmeyer calls the *locus uberrimus*, as distinguished from the Theocritean *locus amoenus*.[4] There is a sense of plenitude here and even of magical powers: nature is resonant with song, and the bullocks seem to come to drink not driven by herdsmen but, as in the fourth Eclogue, of themselves (4.21). Such a harmonious, magically responsive landscape guarantees and is part of the community of shepherds. Similar harmonies, quite explicitly magical, appear at the beginning of Eclogue 8—in which two more pastoral twins exchange songs—and in Eclogue 3, where the shepherd Palaemon transforms a quarrel into a singing match by representing the setting as a *locus uberrimus* (3.55–7). These three eclogues—3, 7, and 8—are the ones in which Vergil most directly follows the pattern of Theocritean singing matches, and what we have said of them suggests why critics have viewed normal Vergilian pastoral as dependent on a privileged landscape and why they have regarded eclogues like 1 and 9, in which landscape is flawed and meetings are problematic, as critical of pastoral. In Vergil, true pastoral convenings would seem to be dependent on an unproblematic, even magical sense of community, which by its very nature is vulnerable to the stresses and complexity of reality.

But so neat and simple an account, however much it accords with our usual notions of pastoral, will not survive a reading of Eclogue 5. From its opening line with the key word *convenimus*, the poem is concerned with convention and community. It is an imitation of Theocritus' first idyll, and mainly consists of a double song for the dead shepherd-hero Daphnis. But its central interests are shown by the way it differs from its model. In Theocritus, Daphnis speaks to herdsmen and gods, resists their taunts and urgings, justifies himself, and bids a grand farewell as he dies. In Vergil, Daphnis' death has already occurred, and it is precisely his absence that dominates the poem and motivates the songs of the shepherds Mopsus and Menalcas. Mopsus' song laments the loss of Daphnis and its effects on the pastoral world; Menalcas restores that loss by celebrating Daphnis as a new god who will bestow favor on and be honored by the world he has left. Menalcas' song is based on an idea of community, and Mopsus', I shall argue, is based on an idea of convention.

Menalcas' song (56–80) describes the whole pastoral world united by the deification of Daphnis. There are magical effects, more directly claimed indeed than in the other passages we have noted, but magic is no longer a sign of fragility. The singer's confidence in the restoration of a heroic presence enables him to represent a much fuller pastoral world than that of singers in a *locus amoenus*. He begins with the woodland world of Pan, Dryads, and hunters, wolves, deer, and mountains, and then confirms its magical expressions of joy by recounting the ceremonies and celebrations with which the shepherds will honor the hero who has been restored to them. This passage is full of the details and atmosphere of Roman country life, and by the end of the passage the inhabitants of this world are called farmers (*agricolae*, 80). The concluding lines, in which vows and honors are promised for as long as fish love streams and bees love flowers, assume a community in the full sense—a coherent world and a permanent way of life.

It is obvious why one speaks of community in Menalcas' song, but it may not be clear why convention is central to Mopsus'. His song opens and closes with scenes of mourners gathered around the dead Daphnis. It begins:

Exstinctum Nymphae crudeli funere Daphnin
flebant (vos coryli testes et flumina Nymphis),
cum complexa sui corpus miserabile nati
atque deos atque astra vocat crudelia mater.

(20–23)

Snuffed out by cruel death, Daphnis was mourned
By nymphs—you streams and hazels told their grief—

While clasping her son's pitiable corpse,
His mother reproached both gods and cruel stars.

By the end of the song, this immediate mourning at the actual scene of
death has become a commemorative gathering at Daphnis' tomb:

Spargite humum foliis, inducite fontibus umbras,
pastores (mandat fieri sibi talia Daphnis),
et tumulum facite, et tumulo superaddite carmen:
"Daphnis ego in silvis, hinc usque ad sidera notus,
formosi pecoris custos, formosior ipse."

(40–44)

Strew foliage on the ground and shade the springs,
You shepherds—Daphnis calls for rites like these.
Build him a mound and add this epitaph:
"I woodland Daphnis, blazoned among stars,
Guarded a lovely flock, still lovelier I."

The convening implicit in these scenes is not actually described, but related
verbs of motion are important elsewhere in the passage. The first effect of
Daphnis' death is that no one drove herds to water at the streams (24–5).
One of the deeds for which Daphnis is praised is teaching the shepherds to
lead Bacchic dances (30). Most important, his death is described in terms of
departures:

postquam te fata tulerunt,
ipsa Pales agros atque ipse reliquit Apollo.

(34–5)

After the fates took you,
Pales herself and our own Apollo left the fields.

Such verbs of purposeful movement do not occur in Menalcas' song: in the
expressions of joy and harmony, verbs—except for those representing
utterances—are rather underplayed.[5] The only verb of motion occurs near
the end and is, significantly, a ritual action:

haec tibi semper erunt, et cum sollemnia vota
reddemus Nymphis, et cum lustrabimus agros.

(74–5)

These be your ceremonies, when we offer
Vows to the nymphs and purify the fields.

Here the phrase *lustrabimus agros* refers to rites which involve processions or ceremonial perambulations.

The final vignette of Mopsus' song does not directly represent shepherds coming together. But the idea of convening is important in it, and we can see how it underlies and leads to poetic convention. The idea of convening appears in the first line of Mopsus' address to his fellow shepherds: *Spargite humum foliis, inducite fontibus umbras* (40). The second phrase has troubled commentators. It literally means, in T.E. Page's words, "draw shade over the fountains," and from Servius on commentators have explained it by replacing Vergil's active verb with a static image. But the sense of purposeful motion towards a spot or gathering at or over it is crucial to the phrase. It makes the celebration of Daphnis an act on and for an occasion, not an instance of a ritual that is predetermined or otherwise guaranteed by a stable context or setting, like the grove dedicated to a hero that Servius thought Vergil intended here. The phrase, however, does have its own kind of stability, which Page suggests in his delicate rephrasing, "o'ercanopy the fount with shade." This stability has three sources. First, the phrase is firmly parallel to the opening injunction, *spargite humum foliis*— which, despite the uncertainty over whether leaves or flowers are meant, is clearly a ceremonial action. Second, the verb *inducite* is repeated from the account of Daphnis' deeds, ten lines earlier:

> Daphnis et Armenias curru subiungere tigris
> instituit, Daphnis thiasos inducere Bacchi
> et foliis lentas intexere mollibus hastas.
>
> (29–31)

> Daphnis instructed us to harness tigers
> On chariots, to lead on Bacchus' revels
> And intertwine tough spears and delicate leaves.

When the hero was alive, the verb *inducere* represented a real ceremony; here, in the absence of the hero, it opaquely refers to an action and draws attention to itself as a locution. This displacement from represented action to poetic practice is characteristic of the whole passage and is confirmed by the third source of stability in this phrase, the word *umbras*. In this eclogue and in Vergilian pastoral generally, this word is neither funereal nor sacred, but suggests a locus for meeting and singing.[6] *Inducite fontibus umbras* begins to show us the nature of pastoral convention in Vergil: in the absence of the hero, represented action gives way to poetic practice.

We can now take notice of another way in which convening is central to this passage. In these lines, Mopsus convokes his fellow shepherds (this is, indeed, one sense of English "convene," though not of Latin *convenio*). This

act of convening makes a real difference to the passage. The imperatives
give a different sense of projected action from the future tenses with which
Menalcas tells how Daphnis will be honored. Menalcas' mode—I shall pour
wine, we shall purify the fields, the farmers will make vows—assumes a
continuing world and way of life; indeed Menalcas himself gradually
disappears from the scenes he foresees. The greater urgency with which
Mopsus speaks reflects the ways in which imperatives are less secure than
simple futures: by their very nature, they draw attention to what is not yet
done, and the actions they envisage depend for their completion on the
compliance of one or more auditors. Like the phrase for shading the
fountains, the grammatical mood of these lines gives an occasional
character to a celebration which might well have been represented as a
ritual. By the same token, the authority for this celebration is very different
in character from what it is in Menalcas' speech, where the promised rituals
are authorized by the flat statement *amat bonus otia Daphnis* (61 "the good
Daphnis loves peace") and by the shouts emanating from and filling the
natural world. In Mopsus' speech too Daphnis authorizes the celebration,
but his authority is dependent on the shepherd's convening his fellows:

> spargite humum foliis, inducite fontibus umbras,
> pastores (mandat fieri sibi talia Daphnis).
>
> (40–41)

> Strew foliage on the ground and shade the springs,
> You shepherds—Daphnis calls for rites like these.

On the model of Menalcas' speech, we would say that Mopsus here
attributes the force of his own imperatives to his heeding of Daphnis'
commands. But the rhetorical force of these lines—with *mandat* coming on
the heels of Mopsus' own imperatives in the preceding line—makes it seem,
unavoidably, that Mopsus is speaking for Daphnis, has taken on some of his
powers. We accept Daphnis' commands because of the shepherd's urgent
tones. When the woods and mountains hail Daphnis as a god, Menalcas
becomes an auditor: *deus, deus ille, Menalca!* (64). In Mopsus' speech,
Daphnis' authority is dependent on the speaker, the shepherd who is left to
celebrate the dead hero.

 The poetic mode of these lines is based on ideas of convening, but it
may not be clear why we should speak of this mode as conventional in the
ordinary sense. The *Oxford English Dictionary*'s treatment of the word is quite
unhelpful, so I quote the relevant definitions from a desk dictionary:

1. A formal meeting of delegates or members
2. The persons attending such a meeting.

3. An agreement or contract.
4. General consent or approval; accepted custom, rule, opinion, etc.
5. A rule or approved technique in conduct or art; a custom or usage.

The last two definitions, which are the ones most germane to literary convention, have a characteristic and misleading bias. The other definitions, which involve agreements and meetings, keep in view individuals' coming together either literally or in their attitudes and commitments. This element is evaded or buried in the definitions that concern us: "a rule or approved technique," "general consent" (the least evasive), "accepted custom or rule." Such definitions represent literary conventions as prior, impersonal realities. Thus the relevant definition in the *OED* runs, "A rule or practice based upon general consent, or accepted and upheld by society at large; an arbitrary rule or practice recognized as valid in any particular art or study." In the light of such definitions, it is not evident why the lines we have been examining should be called conventional. But when we recognize that convening is of the essence of convention, we can see that the usages of these lines are conventional in a precise sense: they depend on the presence and sometimes the consent of other persons than the speaker himself. We have already noted the dependence of the imperatives on their auditors. There is a similar dependence on another's presence in the line *mandat fieri sibi talia Daphnis*. We have said that Daphnis' authority depends on Mopsus' presence as speaker, but there is a mutual dependency here. Mopsus does not flatly claim to be a heroic spokesman for Daphnis; rather, this emphasis is held in suspension with the sense that Mopsus is simply one more shepherd who heeds the injunction of the dead hero. The urgency with which he speaks thus depends on the implied presence of Daphnis.

Let me now propose a definition of literary convention that I think these lines exemplify. At the heart of Vergilian pastoral is the idea of singing a song *for* someone. This idea is most fully presented in the opening lines of the tenth eclogue:

Extremum hunc, Arethusa, mihi concede laborem:
pauca meo Gallo, sed quae legat ipsa Lycoris,
carmina sunt dicenda: neget quis carmina Gallo?

(10.1–3)

Grant this, my final effort, Arethusa:
A song for Gallus—but may Lycoris read it—
Is to be sung: who would not sing for Gallus?

Pauca meo Gallo . . . carmina sunt dicenda can mean either "A few songs must be sung *for* my Gallus" or "*to* my Gallus" or "*by* my Gallus." The final phrase has the same range of meanings. *Carmina Gallo* can mean songs for his benefit (with Lycoris) or sung to him as a listener or, construing more loosely, sung on his behalf or instead of him. The poem proceeds to play out all these meanings. Vergil represents it as an act of friendship, to benefit Gallus; it begins with a scene in which various Arcadians, concerned about his woes, speak solicitously to him; its main passage is a monologue in which the poet impersonates his lovelorn friend. Vergilian pastoral coordinates all possible meanings of the English phrase, "a song for Gallus," or of Milton's version, "Who would not sing for Lycidas?"[7] Seen in the light of this motto, a conventional song is a song sung for you (this is our usual notion of convention) and that you in turn sing or sing back: this is the particular emphasis or inflection of Vergilian pastoral, with its emphasis on convening. The line *mandat fieri sibi talia Daphnis* exemplifies this structure exactly, as Daphnis' injunction is both heard and restated by Mopsus.

Everything that makes these lines conventional appears in the last three lines of Mopsus' song:

> et tumulum facite, et tumulo superaddite carmen:
> "Daphnis ego in silvis, hinc usque ad sidera notus,
> formosi pecoris custos, formosior ipse."
>
> (42–4)

> Build him a mound and add this epitaph:
> "I woodland Daphnis, blazoned among stars,
> Guarded a lovely flock, still lovelier I."

Again the rhetorical basis is the shepherd calling upon his fellows, and the concluding inscription depends on convening all the persons hitherto involved: the shepherds, who are to hear and inscribe the epitaph; Daphnis, in whose person the words are spoken; and Mopsus, on whose voice everything depends. The epitaph has the same doubleness as the earlier line about Daphnis' commands: we can feel Mopsus' identification with the hero for whom he speaks, while at the same time we can imagine a certain distance between Mopsus and these words, which may be simply an epitaph he tells others to inscribe. These two aspects of the epitaph involve two different meanings of singing a song "for" Daphnis—singing in his stead and on his behalf. But a conventional song, we have said, is not simply one you sing for someone, but one that is in the first place sung for you. These lines fulfill this condition precisely—not simply because, as with Daphnis' first command, we can imagine a prior utterance of the dead shepherd, but because there is in fact a prior utterance which produces

Vergil's and Mopsus' and Daphnis' words here. These lines imitate the moment in Theocritus' first idyll when the shepherd Thyrsis represents— that is, both depicts and takes on the character of—the heroic shepherd as he dies:

> I am that Daphnis, he who drove the kine to pasture here,
> Daphnis who led the bulls and calves to water at these
>   springs.

(Idyll 1.120–21)[8]

To the presences essential to Vergil's lines—the shepherds, Daphnis, Mopsus—we must add that of Theocritus. By doing that, we bring our definition of convention in these lines in contact with the ordinary, even casual sense in which one would say they are conventional.

II

I now want to use the preceding analysis and definition to give a larger account of convention in this passage and particularly its relation to Theocritus' idylls—for it is the joint action and presence of these two bodies of poetry that give rise to pastoral conventions as we know them. Thomas Greene has said, "One might define a convention as a set of allusions. A convention exists when the full literary meaning of a word or a line requires a knowledge of many past works in order to be wholly understood."[9] This definition seems to me eminently sensible, but I want to put a little pressure on the relation between allusion and convention. In a brilliant essay entitled "Allusion: the Poet as Heir,"[10] Christopher Ricks argues that for the greatest allusive poets in English—the so-called Augustans, notably Dryden and Pope—the proper model for the relation between predecessor and successor is not Harold Bloom's anxiety of influence, with its drama of rivalry and repression, but a more benign parental-filial relation, for which inheritance is the appropriate metaphor. Ricks' mode of analysis and his definition of allusion, though historically specific, pose the appropriate questions for Vergilian pastoral. Ricks says that in an allusion, the poet "creates his own meanings by bringing into play the meanings of other poets,"[11] and he notices that many of the most powerful allusions in Augustan poetry are explicitly concerned with parental-filial relations. Thus, to give one example, the satiric butt of Dryden's *MacFlecknoe*, Thomas Shadwell, is given a blessing by his poetic parent in the following terms:

> Shadwell alone my perfect image bears
> Mature in dullness from his tender years.

(15–16)

The phrase "my perfect image" alludes to a line in *Paradise Lost* and engages its relation to two others. "Whereas the Son of God is 'the radiant image of his Glory' (*PL* 3.63), and Adam and Eve shine with 'The image of their glorious Maker' (4.292), the 'perfect image' is that which Satan narcissistically loved in his daughter Sin: 'Thy self in me thy perfect image viewing / Becam'st enamourd' (2.764-5)." "Dryden," Ricks says, "here writes as a true son of a true poet, about a false son of a false poet, and the words 'perfect image' bear a perfect image of this filial allusion." It is not just that *MacFlecknoe* is about poetic inheritance, but that, in Ricks' words, "its allusions are at once given point and protected against too easy a pointedness by themselves continually being engaged—as a matter of principled literary procedure—with that paternity, succession and poetic inheritance of which they speak."[12]

I want to ask two questions about Vergil's use of passages in Theocritus. First, are such passages allusions in Ricks' sense? that is, do they create their meanings by bringing into play Theocritus' meanings? Second, in such passages, what is analogous to the thematic emphasis on paternity and inheritance that in the Augustan poets engages and reveals the structure of allusion? The opening passage of Mopsus' song gives us a full view of Vergil's use of Theocritus:

> Exstinctum Nymphae crudeli funere Daphnin
> flebant (vos coryli testes et flumina Nymphis),
> cum complexa sui corpus miserabile nati
> atque deos atque astra vocat crudelia mater.
> non ulli pastos illis egere diebus
> frigida, Daphni, boves ad flumina; nulla neque amnem
> libavit quadripes nec graminis attigit herbam.
> Daphni, tuum Poenos etiam ingemuisse leones
> interitum montesque feri silvaeque loquuntur.
>
>   (20-28)

> Snuffed out by cruel death, Daphnis was mourned
> By nymphs—you streams and hazels told their grief—
> While clasping her son's pitiable corpse,
> His mother reproached both gods and cruel stars.
> No one, in those days, drove his well-fed cattle,
> Daphnis, to cooling streams; no wild steed tasted
> The running waters, or touched a blade of grass.
> Daphnis, the very lions groaned at your
> Harsh death, which mountains and wild woods resound.

We recognize here what everyone calls the conventional mourning of pastoral nature. But the convention was not prior to Theocritus and Vergil.

They created it, and the question is what is entailed in a poetic invention or creation of this sort. If we think of convention as an automatic procedure and recall the extravagances of some later poets, we may be surprised to discover how finely gauged and grounded in human realities is Vergil's representation of nature's sympathetic grief. He begins with human mourning—the weeping of the nymphs and the bereaved mother's accusation of the heavens. The only suggestion of nature's mourning is in the cunning line, *vos coryli testes et flumina Nymphis*. *Testes* means those who bear verbal witness, who testify,[13] and this hint of active response is justified by the speaker's directly addressing the hazels and streams, as if to acknowledge that it is his voice and sense of relation that endow them with theirs. This delicate giving voice to nature emerges fully in the mourning of the lions and the wild woods. These lines are saved from extravagance by the fact that their representations are enclosed in an address to the dead shepherd. The full presence of the speaker and the grounding in the human relationship that is most at issue—companionship and its violation—makes humanly plausible the hyperbole (as Servius calls it) of the final lines, as if the laments of fierce and inanimate nature could be regarded as an extension of the speaker's own voicing of grief. The effect is clinched by the last word, *loquuntur*. The unexpected present tense brings to life the interaction between man's voice and nature's. The word does not simply render something external; the present tense makes us hear it as utterance, and it therefore suggests, "My present speech is what you now hear and is what endows nature with her voices."

Now let us turn to the passage Vergil is imitating or recalling here—the opening lines of Thyrsis' lament for Daphnis, in Idyll 1:

> Lead now I pray, dear Muses, lead you the pastoral song.
> Thyrsis am I of Etna; and sweet is the voice of Thyrsis.
> Where were ye then, while Daphnis pined away, where were ye,
>   Nymphs?
> Haunting Peneios' lovely valleys, or the glens of Pindos?
> For not by the great river of Anapos were you dwelling,
> Nor upon Etna's heights, nor yet by Akis' holy stream.
>   Lead now, I pray, dear Muses, lead you the pastoral song.
> For him the jackals howled, for him the wolves: the lion even
> Came forth from the thicket to lament him when he died.
>   Lead now, I pray, dear Muses, lead you the pastoral song.
> Many a cow and many a bull stood round him where he lay,
> Many a heifer and young calf, lowing for misery.
>
> (64–75)

In this passage, as in Vergil's, there is an artful blending of human speech and the mourning attributed to nature. This is due not only to the fact that two of the three words used of the animals are terms for human mourning, but also because of the way their lament becomes associated with human song. Thyrsis begins by identifying himself by his "sweet voice," which he immediately displays in an appeal to the nymphs who should have protected Daphnis ("Where were ye, nymphs?"). The "pastoral song" which the muses are asked to lead is thus explicitly vocalized and emotional. When the refrain is then followed by the account of the animals' wailing, one naturally takes them to be participants in this song, not merely figures described in it. Thyrsis (or Theocritus) does not impersonate the animals: there seems to be no onomatopoeia, certainly not as much as in Vergil's imitation, *Daphnis, tuum Poenos etiam ingemuisse leones* (5.27). Yet one effect suggests how readily this mode of representation can lead to the identifications found in later versions of sympathetic nature. The first line of the scene (71) ends with the verb *ōrusanto*, which means "howl" and is properly used of wolves and dogs. The last line (75) ends with the word *ōduranto*, which means "lament" or "bewail" and is only used of humans. Each word consists of two spondees and occupies the last two feet of its line. It seems certain that some kind of echo is to be heard here, and its significance is twofold. First, it suggests a likeness between animal howling and human lamenting. Second, there is no separating this effect from the speaker's vocalization, which is decisively felt here. Thus, without directly imitating the animals, Thyrsis' voice enters into a pastoral consort with them.

There are a number of things we can say about these two passages taken together. We can see, for example, that they exemplify Schiller's distinction between naive and sentimental poetry. Theocritus' appeal to the nymphs and his account of the animals mourning are discrete and in the mode of direct representation: for all the sophistication with which he deploys the words for mourning, they occur in accessible formulas which one takes at face value. Vergil's lines, by contrast, are self-conscious not only about justifying what they claim to represent but also about effects like the full voicing of *etiam ingemuisse leones*. If we ask, beyond comparing the passages, what Vergil has done with his source, we can see that this is a characteristic instance of the way in which he "composes" Theocritus—that is, interprets and unifies what in his predecessor are self-sufficient and heterogeneous details and elements. Where Theocritus separates the appeal to the nymphs and the animals mourning, Vergil's handling of the nymphs and of the speaker's mode of address is such that his opening lines render the foundation in human grief of the mourning later attributed to nature. These two passages not only exemplify the naive and the sentimental; Vergil can here be said to turn a naive into a sentimental passage.[14]

None of this, however, answers the question raised by Christopher Ricks' essay: to wit, what difference does it make to recognize, as we read, that Vergil's lines are based on Theocritus? (Let us remind ourselves that our awareness cannot be that Vergil is using a convention; we are seeing a convention in the process of being established.) It seems to me that this is not an instance of allusion in Ricks' sense. Vergil does not create his own meanings by bringing his predecessor's meanings into play, the way Dryden exposes Flecknoe's arrogance by his own understanding of what "perfect image" means in *Paradise Lost*. At the level of meaning, Vergil's lines seem more self-sufficient than Dryden's, less dependent on an allusion. (It is perhaps more accurate to say that an allusion is precisely that kind of imitation in which a passage *is* dependent on its predecessor.) Vergil's act of composing Theocritus, with its attendant self-consciousness, might be described as an interpretation of his predecessor, but if so it does not seem to be with any thought of differing significantly from him. Rather, Vergil's purpose seems to be to repeat Theocritean lines. The repetition is under different poetic and cultural circumstances, and therefore Vergilian emphases and meanings are new and specific to him. But insofar as his use of Theocritus involves prompting our conscious awareness of his predecessor, the main effect is of repetition. The opening passage of Mopsus' lament moves toward a distinct point of contact with Theocritus, the howling of the lions from the thickets. Mopsus' statement of Daphnis' epitaph brings to life, in Vergil's sentimental mode, the naive self-assertion of Theocritus' hero. In the ninth Eclogue, Vergil's most explicit treatment of the way he uses his predecessor, it is precisely repetition of song that is at issue. If repetition seems the reverse of what we want in poetry, that is because we see it, as we often see convention, in the light of Romantic poetics, as the opposite of what is authentically individual. But the poem we are examining and Vergilian pastoral in general give us a quite different model of repetition—that of one voice not merely mimicking but responding to another, in the exchanges of which the singing contest is the purest example.

Let us now ask the second question prompted by Ricks' account of allusion: what is the thematic emphasis in passages with an important connection to a predecessor? In Vergil's pastorals this emphasis is convening for the sake of song or other utterance. Mopsus' lament begins and ends with mourners gathered for Daphnis, and the speaker's addressing first the hazels and streams and then Daphnis becomes, in the final passage, a direct act of convoking. Furthermore, the Theocritean sources of these passages themselves involve ideas of convening. To ask "Where were ye, nymphs?" is in effect to invert the act of convoking, and the serial listing of the mourning animals gives a suggestion of convening which is reinforced by the statement that some of the animals, at least, mourned "at his feet" (74). Daphnis' self-declaration, "I am that Daphnis," comes between his bidding farewell to beasts, woods, and streams—an act of departure—and his calling on Pan to come hither and take his shepherd's pipe from him (lines 115–30). Vergil, then, is responding to Theocritus as one shepherd answers another in a pastoral singing match: he gives his own version, in his own accents, of what his predecessor sings. The one difference, of course, is that the first shepherd is not literally present in these later pastorals. Under these conditions—which are precisely analogous to the conditions of Eclogue 5, in which Mopsus and Menalcas restore the absent Daphnis to their presence—responding to Theocritus takes the form of calling him into the presence of the shepherds and other creatures said to be gathered together in the poem. The conventions of Vergilian pastoral arise from acts of convening, and what makes them conventions in the literary sense is the act of convening Theocritus.

III

The conditions under which Vergil convenes Theocritus show why we should distinguish community and convention in Vergilian pastoral: convention is the form community takes in the absence of a hero. This thematic emphasis emerges in yet another passage in Mopsus' lament that we recognize as conventional:

> vitis ut arboribus decori est, ut vitibus uvae,
> ut gregibus tauri, segetes ut pinguibus arvis,
> tu decus omne tuis.
>
> (32–4)

> As vines adorn the trees and grapes the vine,
> Great bulls the herds and harvests the rich fields,
> So you adorned us all.

This is what Rosenmeyer calls a priamel, "a series of brief statements or propositions which are felt to be based on an underlying pattern, and which usually lead up to a terminal proposition of somewhat greater weight."[15] The closest Theocritean prototype is in Idyll 8:

> As acorns are a pride [*kosmos* = *decus*] to the oak, to the
>   apple-tree its apples,
> So to the heifer is her calf, to the cowherd his kine.
>
> (79–80)

Vergil adapts these items so as to emphasize natural connections. The imagery of the list provides a compendium of rural well-being, and the sense of community is augmented by the common element of the vine, in the first two items, and by the plural numbers of the last two. But the community represented here lies under the shadow of an absence, which is adumbrated in the final item in the list. *Tu decus omne tuis* ("[so] you [were] the whole glory of your comrades") is a strong phrase, the force of which is brought out by Dryden's expansion of it:

> As vines the trees, as grapes the vines adorn,
> As bulls the herds, and fields the yellow corn;
> So bright a splendor, so divine a grace,
> The glorious Daphnis cast on his illustrious race.

In the listed phenomena to which Daphnis is compared, the glories—the grapes, the bulls, the rich crops—grow out of, are the product of what they in turn adorn. On these analogies, the final phrase should be *tu decus omnibus tuis*. By saying *tu decus omne tuis*, Vergil represents Daphnis as, in Dryden's words, casting splendor on his people. To emphasize the hero's priority is to acknowledge his separateness, which is also intimated by the rhetorical placement of *tu decus omne tuis* at the end of the list and at the beginning of a new line. Separateness, in turn, is an augury of separation. It is therefore fitting that the line which begins *tu decus omne tuis* ends with the fates removing Daphnis and the departure of the gods:

> postquam te fata tulerunt,
> ipsa Pales agros atque ipse reliquit Apollo.
>
> (34–5)

> After the fates took you,
> Pales herself and our own Apollo left the fields.

These separations and departures reveal the true force of the priamel which lists rural goods: its authority comes not from fullness of representation, but from the verbal formalities which are precisely what is left to ordinary shepherds when separate from the hero. Once more an English Augustan provides a valuable piece of creative interpretation. John Martyn, in his edition of 1734, says of the departure of Pales and Apollo:

> This desertion of the fields by the goddess of shepherds and the god of music and poetry is a figurative expression of the grief of the shepherds for the loss of Daphnis. They were so afflicted, that they neglected the care of their sheep, and had not spirits to sing, in which their chief diversion consisted.[16]

The priamel can be seen as the form song takes when the shepherds recover their voices. The idea of convention, then, is crucial to it: not only the idea of gathering for song on a specific occasion, but also the idea of a usage that implicitly convenes an absent predecessor—the poet who instituted the practice of these priamels, as Daphnis, in the immediately preceding lines, is said to have instituted ceremonial practices.

Even in Menalcas' song—which we have hitherto treated as a foil to Mopsus'—the representation of community occurs under the conditions and in the mode of the conventional. Neither song claims, as *Lycidas* does, to be prompted directly by the shepherd's death. Like the lament in Theocritus' first Idyll, these are performed songs. Their occasion is like that of Eclogue 7, the gathering of shepherds to sing. The embedding of the songs for Daphnis in the circumstances of pastoral singing becomes clear in the middle of the poem, when Menalcas responds to Mopsus' song:

> Tale tuum carmen nobis, divine poeta,
> quale sopor fessis in gramine, quale per aestum
> dulcis aquae saliente sitim restinguere rivo.
> nec calamis solum aequiperas, sed voce magistrum:
> fortunate puer, tu nunc eris alter ab illo.
> nos tamen haec quocumque modo tibi nostra vicissim
> dicemus, Daphninque tuum tollemus ad astra;
> Daphnin ad astra feremus: amavit nos quoque Daphnis.
>
> (45–52)

> Your song, inspired poet, is like slumber
> On soft grass to the weary, or a brook
> Of sparkling water, quenching noontime thirst.
> Piping and singing both, you are his equal,
> Fortunate lad, his one and true successor.
> But in response to you, as best I can,
> I'll sing and raise your Daphnis to the stars:
> Yes, to the stars—for Daphnis loved me too.

On the one hand, the effect of Mopsus' lament, particularly the way he takes on the character of Daphnis, has been to give a heroic cast to the representation of pastoral song. Not only is he called *divine poeta* and said to be Daphnis' equal and true successor; Menalcas attributes to his song restorative powers that seem to reverse the effects of the first hero's death.

But if Mopsus appears as Daphnis' successor, it is only because the dead shepherd has been turned from a heroic leader to a master singer and, in the final lines, an object of song. Menalcas' song for the new god, taken in isolation, seems to make him more present than in Mopsus' lament. But this transitional passage makes it clear that the sense of presence depends on pastoral convention and is conditioned by its assumption of separation from what it represents and sings for. As opposed to Thyrsis' direct representation and impersonation of Daphnis in Theocritus 1—of which, as we have said, Mopsus gave a "sentimental" version—Menalcas here responds less to Daphnis than to his fellow singer. His inspiration comes not from the new god he will celebrate, but from the spirit of eager rivalry in song that pervades this eclogue.

Menalcas' song itself shows that Vergil was much more aware of the conditions of celebrating a hero than are some of his recent interpreters. One of them, for example, says, "Vergil's fictional Daphnis is not a beautiful, ineffectual Adonis figure, a hero of pastoral withdrawal, but an inspirational leader who brings peace and harmony to the agricultural world."[17] This sounds as if Menalcas represents the dead Daphnis as doing, in his new form, what he did when alive—harnessing wild beasts, instituting Bacchic dances, and the like. But what is striking in Menalcas' song is that Daphnis is not an active agent or even influence. From the initial scene of his wondering at the unaccustomed threshold of Olympus—rather like a shepherd dazzled by a new place—his presence is rather passive. The crucial phrase about him—which makes Brooks Otis say that "Daphnis, become immortal..., *reverses* nature"[18]—is *amat bonus otia Daphnis* (61 "good Daphnis loves peace"). The suggestion, reinforced by the preceding verb, *meditantur*, is that *otia*, the benign peacefulness of the countryside, is not what Daphnis creates or empowers, but what he loves to contemplate, what he enjoys. The active energy in this scene of peace is the keen desire that seizes the shepherds and the woodland demi-gods. Moreover, the active verbs in Menalcas' song represent utterance, song, and cognate activities—beginning wth *voces iactant* (62) and *sonant* (64) in the opening scene, and going on to the ceremonies and convivialities that end in the vignette which suggested to Milton his own opening scene of pastoral community:

cantabunt mihi Damoetas et Lyctius Aegon;
saltantis Satyros imitabitur Alphesiboeus.

(72-3)

Palaemon and Damoetas will sing to me,
Alphesibee mimic the leaping fauns.

Rough satyrs danced, and fauns with cloven heel,
From the glad sound would not be absent long,
And old Damaetas loved to hear our song.

(*Lycidas*, 34-6)

The concluding pledge to Daphnis reflects this emphasis on ceremony and song:

> dum iuga montis aper, fluvios dum piscis amabit,
> dumque thymo pascentur apes, dum rore cicadae,
> semper honos nomenque tuum laudesque manebunt.
>
>   (76–8)

> While boars love mountain ridges, fish the streams,
> Bees feed on thyme and grasshoppers on dew,
> Your honor, name, and praises will endure.

The difference between these lines and Mopsus' priamel reflects the difference between the two songs. Daphnis is not separate, as he was in the phrase *tu decus omne tuis*: his honor and praises are absorbed into the natural activities which represent their permanence. Similarly, the speaker is absorbed into the representation of external processes: what looks like a pledge, for which the appropriate verb would be in the first person, is here conveyed by the third person, *manebunt*. Finally, this list has no specific Theocritean antecedent. Just as the shepherds in Menalcas' song are not convened, but simply are together, so this priamel does not convene Theocritus. It presents itself simply as conventional utterance in our usual sense, the accepted practice of a community. In its freedom from the self-conscious rhetoric and thematics of Mopsus' song, it bears witness to Menalcas' sense of community. Nevertheless, the priamel cannot be thought to be free of the conditions of conventional song in the sense we have defined it. However much it elides the fictional and textual separations relevant to it, it is emphatically a rhetorical performance, an instance of poetic practice. What remains of Daphnis is not represented action or presence, but precisely what is due to human utterance—honor and praise. Menalcas' song continues the work of Mopsus' and exemplifies the form community takes in the absence of the hero. Just as it begins as a response to Mopsus' song, so its conclusion shows how thoroughly it is grounded in pastoral convening. Menalcas' last words—*damnabis tu quoque votis*, which speaks to the farmers' obligation to give in return when the god has favored them—are transformed by Mopsus' response into a similar obligation between singers:[19] *Quae tibi, quae tali reddam pro carmine dona?* (81 "What can I give in return for such a song?")—where *reddo*, "give in return," is the word used earlier for offering vows to the nymphs (75). On the one hand, we might say that Mopsus is obliquely praising Menalcas as Menalcas praised him, in effect calling him *divine poeta* and a surrogate for Daphnis. But any such implications are colored by, indeed subject to, the conditions of pastoral convention. Mopsus' question returns us to the world of pastoral rivalry and exchange, and of occasion and variety in song and nature. The gifts exchanged at the end of the poem are attractively problematic symbols: the frail reed, which represents the power of song, and the artfully decorated crook, which represents pastoral work (85-90). Eclogue 5 less concerns the restoration of the hero than human continuity—the way in which men continue their lives after and sometimes in spite of a loss. The ending of the poem, with its recollections of Theocritean language and practice, shows that Vergil here conceives continuity in terms not of represented community, but of conventional practices that ensure repetition and therefore commemoration.

IV

The eclogue-book begins and ends with poems which draw our attention to convening and its implications. Of these eclogues, the ninth most fully engages the issues that have concerned us here. It treats as problematic all those aspects of pastoral convention that are central to the poetics of Eclogue 5. Like the earlier poem (to which it more than once alludes), it begins with a meeting of shepherds whose discourse dwells on loss—the absent master-singer Menalcas, the diminished countryside, and the threatened homestead and community. But in this poem the shepherds do not settle down to performing songs, and there is a diminished confidence that poetic practice can restore presences or reestablish connections. Rather, poetic practice and the power of poetry are explicitly at issue, and in terms that will now be familiar to us: the pressing questions are whether songs can be repeated and whether Menalcas, who (like the absent Daphnis) is directly addressed, will return to his companions and enable them to resume normal pastoral singing. When the poem is described this way, one can see why many critics regard it as an ironic anti-pastoral. At the same time, there are reasons for the more positive readings that Klingner and others have given it. These find their justification in the marked increase in poetic richness and political confidence of the songs the shepherds quote to each other in the course of the poem. We can augment and support this account in the terms provided by Vergilian convention. The quoted songs are successful repetitions (two are direct reworkings of Theocritus), and each of them begins with and is informed by direct address to another person. In the action of the poem, addressing Menalcas may not assure that he will rejoin his companions; in the quoted songs, on the other hand, absent persons are adequately addressed and even celebrated, and thus in some sense made present.

This last observation confirms our formula that in the face of loss heroic acts and fully represented worlds give way, in Vergilian pastoral, to poetic practice. Eclogue 9 displays the shift explicitly. The first half of the poem is marked by scenes of disruption and disturbance in the world of the poem. These give way to the quoted songs, the last of which foretells a period of fruitful Caesarean peace; it engages some of the Roman themes of Eclogue 5 and in its last line rewrites, in positive terms, one of the bitterest utterances of the displaced Meliboeus in Eclogue 1.[20] Our awareness of pastoral convention should enable us both to understand the poetic self-consciousness of this shift in the poem, and to acknowledge the force of all its modes of representation. Critical disagreement about the poem comes from treating one or another of its aspects as dominant, whereas what is remarkable is that its ironic and affirmative elements are held in suspension. As I have tried to show elsewhere, this poise is largely due to Vergil's sense of the community of shepherds—the relations between shepherds within the poem and the analogous relation between Vergil himself and Theocritus.[21] This pastoral community is neither as fragile as it has seemed to critics like Snell and Putnam nor as adequate to the realities of the Roman world as it has seemed to Otis and others. Vergil's shepherds regularly come together for song, and song is what unites them. But they and their creator understand that separation and loss are the conditions of their utterance, and the human connections their songs establish are felt to be real precisely because of this poetically self-conscious and sometimes sobering awareness.[22]

Notes

1. *The Essential Tension* (Chicago: University of Chicago Press, 1977), p. 294.
2. *The Singer of the Eclogues: A Study of Virgilian Pastoral* (Berkeley and Los Angeles: University of California Press, 1979). One sympathetic auditor at the Houston symposium congratulated me for having the courage to "renounce" a position so recently stated in print, so perhaps I had better say that in my view the endeavor of this paper is to clarify, not contradict, the emphasis in my book on the human community implicit in Vergilian pastoral song. This clarification does involve a degree of correction—what might be considered a modest "deconstruction" of such a statement as (concerning 5.32-34, discussed below) "as a poetic convention [the priamel] is the product of a whole community" (p. 197).
3. The Latin text is based on that of R.A.B. Mynors, *P. Vergili Maronis Opera*, Oxford Classical Texts (Oxford: Clarendon Press, 1969); the translation is mine, from *The Singer of the Eclogues*. In discussing individual lines and details, I sometimes give more literal renderings than are possible in a verse translation.
4. *The Green Cabinet: Theocritus and the European Pastoral Lyric* (Berkeley and Los Angeles: University of California Press, 1969), p. 190.
5. In lines 60-61 and 73, it would even appear that vivid verbs are evaded.
6. Cf. Eclogue 1.4 and 7.10. The shepherds of Eclogue 5 choose between two shady settings for their singing: *sive sub incertas Zephyris motantibus umbras / sive antro potius succedimus* (5-6 "whether we go under the shade that trembles at the breezes or enter that cave").

7. I discuss the idea of "singing for someone" at various points (noted in the index) in *The Singer of the Eclogues*.

8. Trans. R.C. Trevelyan (New York: Bond, 1925).

9. "Spenser and the Epithalamic Convention," *CL* 9 (1957): 219.

10. In *Studies in the Eighteenth Century III*, ed. R.F. Brissenden and J.C. Eade (Toronto: University of Toronto Press, 1976), pp. 209-40.

11. Ricks, p. 231.

12. Ricks, pp. 229, 228.

13. As opposed to those whose witness is visual, for which the Latin would be *arbitri* or *spectatores*.

14. On the general relevance of Schiller's distinction to Theocritus and Vergil, see *The Singer of the Eclogues*, pp. 204-10. On Vergil's "composing" Theocritus, see pp. 210-22.

15. *The Green Cabinet*, p. 338.

16. *The Bucolicks of Virgil*, note on 5.35. I quote the fourth edition (London, 1834).

17. Eleanor Winsor Leach, *Vergil's "Eclogues": Landscapes of Experience* (Ithaca: Cornell University Press, 1974), p. 182.

18. *Virgil: A Study in Civilized Poetry* (Oxford: Clarendon Press, 1964), p. 140, italics mine.

19. Robert Coleman translates the phrase, "you too will hold them to their vows," and explains: "the petitioner made his vow to the god; if the petition was granted, then the god obliged him to keep the vow." Vergil, *Eclogues* (Cambridge: Cambridge University Press, 1977), *ad loc*.

20. *Insere nunc, Meliboee, piros, pone ordine vitis* (1.73 "Go graft your pear trees, Melibee, plant your vines!") becomes *insere, Daphni, piros: carpent tua poma nepotes* (9.50 "Graft pear trees, Daphnis; your sons will pluck the fruits").

21. See *The Singer of the Eclogues*, pp. 136-54.

22. Some of my discussion of the first half of Eclogue 5 repeats some paragraphs in my article, "Convening and Convention in Pastoral Poetry," *NLH* 14 (1982-83): 277-304.

VERGIL'S THEODICY RECONSIDERED

Christine G. Perkell

The celebrated "theodicy of labor"[1] at Georgic 1.121–46 is a description of Jove's dissolution of the Golden Age, of his establishment of the Iron Age, and of man's consequent development of technology, the *variae artes* (1.133, 145). The familiar interpretation of this passage, reflected in the very term "theodicy," is that Vergil is here affirming his faith in the beneficence of Jove, in the spiritual value of *labor*, and in the technical progress which man has achieved.[2] According to this view, Jove's intervention in human affairs was beneficent in that by compelling man to activity he saved him from an inevitably tedious and inconsequential lethargy.[3] Rescued from sloth, man experienced the challenge of ennobling *labor*[4] and contrived the various arts. Essentially, then, Vergil would be adhering to the Stoic position here, i.e. that the world's challenges reflect divine providence.[5] The famous verses

> labor omnia vicit
> improbus et duris urgens in rebus egestas
>
> (1.145–46)

> Labor has conquered all things, immoderate labor, and need pressing in harsh circumstances

are accordingly taken to signfy that *labor* is the means by which man has triumphed over difficulty.[6]

If Vergil were expressing faith in Jove's providence and in the value of technological progress, the significance of this passage would corroborate the interpretation of the *Georgics* overall as a reflection of Vergil's faith in the revitalization of Rome under Octavian.[7] Indeed, many critics suggest that it

67

was the poet's political purpose in this poem to support Octavian's new regime by recalling the Roman people to the putative peacefulness and morality of rural life.[8] They argue that Vergil's faith in Rome's future under Octavian, although expressed most emphatically in the miracle of rebirth which concludes Georgic 4, is reflected also in the optimism of his picture of man's discovery of technology (*artes*) in Georgic 1.[9] Because of this perceived relationship to the *Georgics'* central purpose, the theodicy passage is critical to an understanding of the poem as a whole. Further, through its description of the creation of culture, the passage suggests the poet's attitude towards the character and value of civilization, which he calls the product of *ars* (1.133, 145) and *labor* (1.145, cf. 1.150) as he reflects on the nature of civilization and the real character of technology and man's work. Thus he suggests his attitude towards the Iron Age, that is, his present reality,[10] and toward Jove, whom we may envisage as the creator of the Iron Age and in many ways its epitome.

This important passage is unfortunately marked by difficulties of interpretation. Although the critics cited above feel that the poet considers Jove's intervention in human affairs to be beneficent, others have questioned such an unambiguously positive reading.[11] First, as La Penna comments, the justification of Jove's intervention is either absent or very weak.[12] If man is indeed benefited by Jove's intervention, the poet has neglected to point out how. Second, the use of the adjective *improbus* to modify *labor* seems unaccountable if the poet intends to show *labor* as a good thing. (*OLD*, s.v., offers "unconscionable," "shameless," "presumptuous," "relentless," for the verse under discussion, more generally "of poor quality," "inferior," "morally unsound.")[13] Third, there is the inconcinnity of this passage, approving as it purportedly is of Iron Age technology and experience, with other passages in the poem (notably 2.458ff., 2.492ff.) which seem to endorse Golden Age life and to deplore Iron Age immorality.[14] Another difficulty is that of reconciling the positive view of Jove here with the more ambiguous portraits of him elsewhere in the poem. Putnam, for example, comments on several passages in which Jove is clearly implicated in the world's moral deficiencies.[15]

Various solutions have been offered for these long-acknowledged difficulties. For the problems of inconsistency or confusion in the poet's attitude towards the Golden and Iron Ages, it has been suggested that Vergil simply failed to integrate successfully the austere Hesiodic tradition, his major source for book 1, with the tradition of pastoral idealization of country life which inspired him in book 2.[16] In a similar vein, it has been suggested that Vergil, thinking his portrait of the Iron Age too grim, may have wanted to lighten the overall effect of his poem by incorporating Golden Age visions into it—but without thinking it necessary to harmonize them with the rest of his text.[17] With respect to *improbus*, it has been thought that—uniquely here—it may have a positive sense.[18] Thus the verse as a whole would mean that indomitable or ceaseless labor has made all things tractable.[19] One critic, for example, feels that in this context we must interpret the verse as expressing the ultimate "victory of human effort."[20]

These explanations, as it seems to me at least, have flaws: the former because they leave us with the implausible notion of Vergil as negligent or as an incompetent synthesizer;[21] the latter because all attested uses of *improbus* (including those in *Georgics* 1.119, 1.388, 3.431) are pejorative, making a singular positive use of the word here improbable.[22] I would like to propose an alternative reading of the theodicy passage, one which eliminates the problems described above and which also may help to clarify the importance of the passage for the *Georgics* overall. To pursue this latter goal particularly, I will conclude with an examination of the Iron Age god Aristaeus as he appears in the epyllion of Georgic 4. From a comparative study of Jove and Aristaeus we will see that Vergil's representation of these Iron Age gods and of the values which they embody constitutes an ironic and provocative commentary on what is worshipped in the Iron Age world.[23]

I

The interpretive difficulties of Georgic 1.121–46 center, I suggest, in the ambiguity of its famous closing (*labor omnia vicit*, etc.) and in the irony of its opening description of Jove.[24] These particular difficulties can be productively dealt with by a reader-response criticism, which emphasizes the reader's continuous experience of a text rather than the search for a single correct reading. That is to say that another way of reading this passage is to decline to seek a single correct reading, which excludes all others, and simply to acknowledge the effects on the reader of the cruxes in the passage which have always made interpretation difficult.

Let us consider the closing first. As the reader comes to verse 145 he reads: *labor omnia vicit*. Making a closure here, taking the words as they stand, the reader conceives an initial interpretation of the meaning of this verse as: *labor* or work conquered all things, that is, made all things tractable (cf. the "victory of human effort," cited above). As he reads on to 146, however, *improbus et duris urgens in rebus egestas*, he must make a new sense, realizing that his initial understanding of the words must comprehend a different, even an opposite, meaning. The translation now becomes: "Relentless toil/suffering and need, pressing in harsh circumstances, have dominated all things." Here *labor*, modified as it is by *improbus* and in conjunction with *egestas*, calls forth the common meaning of *labor* as "suffering" rather than "toil."[25] The reader remembers that *opus*, not *labor*, is the usual word for farmwork in Cato and Varro.

How is a reader to interpret a text which seems to present two (here opposed) meanings? Reader-response criticism would have us acknowledge and interpret both these experiential structures. As both contribute to a reader's continuous experience of a text, both constitute its "meaning." Concerning a similar crux in Milton, Stanley Fish has written: "To clean the line up is to take from it its most prominent and important effect—the suspension of the reader between the alternatives its syntax momentarily allows."[26] The ambiguity of these lines is a fact, as long controversy over them shows, and it is this ambiguity which is their meaning. The significant effect of this ambiguity, of these opposing senses, is that Vergil makes two opposing views present in the reader's mind: the one that technology is man's universal solution to problems, the other that technology epitomizes the suffering of a material age. The reader, then, in his search for consistency, seeks to comprehend this opposition in a larger structure. His imagination is engaged in a debate, the poles of which the poet himself has established through syntactical ambiguity. The crucial point is that the poet has made both views present in a dynamic tension which challenges the reader's interest and imagination. This inconsistency or opposing of views, which leads ultimately to new perspectives and synthesis, is the poet's characteristic mode in this poem. Therefore we can say that the ambiguity which readers have always experienced is not the difficulty of the passage, but rather may be perceived as its meaning.

The second interpretive crux of this passage involves what I see as the irony of the term *veternus* (lethargy) in 124. In whose opinion is it a *veternus*? Jove's? the poet's? Critics have consistently identified these two points of view; but we must see the possibility of a discrepancy. The obstacle, I suggest, to a more workable reading of this passage has been the common and unexamined assumption that the poet endorses Jove's actions and shares his attitudes.[27] Let us look at the verses in question:

> pater ipse colendi
> haud facilem esse viam voluit, primusque per artem
> movit agros, curis acuens mortalia corda
> nec torpere gravi passus sua regna veterno.
>
> (1.121–4)

But the Father himself wished that the way of agriculture not be easy, and he first stirred the fields through art, sharpening mortal spirits with cares, not enduring that his realms should become sluggish with lethargy.

From the assumption that the poet approves Jove's action follows necessarily the interpretation that Jove's intervention must have been legitimate, for man's good. One critic, for example, writes representatively: "Like Prometheus, Jupiter benefits human beings by freeing them from a dull-witted, torpid existence."[28] My contention, however, is that the poet is making a reflective, subtly ironic comment on Jove's values and on the character of the Iron Age which he both founded and epitomizes. This is to say that in reading Vergil's poetry we should understand that no one single character necessarily represents at all times standards which the poet himself endorses. Rather Vergil may be presenting his characters' behavior with ironic distance and in such a way as to invite readers continually to assess its merit.[29]

How does one determine that irony exists here? The most useful test for irony is the presence of discrepancy or disparity.[30] The disparity which one might observe here is that between the Iron Age, which Jove institutes, and the Golden Age, that is, the period which preceded it. We learn that *veternus* is ironic because juxtaposition with the previous Golden Age passage suggests that the Golden Age is morally and spiritually superior to the Iron Age.

When we look at the description of the period preceding Jove's intervention, we see that it is a period which, although not explicitly so described, clearly recalls the Golden Age. Since the Golden Age is described entirely positively, the effect here is to allow or invite the reader to wonder in whose opinion the term *veternus* is appropriately applied to it. If Jove's, then the reader must question his ethical judgment. That is, this passage permits us to wonder if *veternus* is not ironic and if, indeed, the Iron Age as a whole is not the object of ironic comment.

In approaching this thesis I would like to look first at the description of the period preceding Jove's intervention, a period which, although not explicitly so described, clearly recalls the Golden Age:[31]

> ante Iovem nulli subigebant arva coloni,
> ne signare quidem aut partiri limite campum
> fas erat: in medium quaerebant, ipsaque tellus
> omnia liberius, nullo poscente, ferebat.

> (1.125–8)

Before Jove's time no settlers subdued the land; it was not right even to mark the fields or to divide them with boundary-lines. All sought the common gain; and earth, of her own accord, brought forth all things more freely, when no one was asking.

These few verses suggest the traditional Golden Age, characteristic features of which, throughout antiquity, were: eternal spring, easy feasting, abundant food, and freedom from war, toil, and unhappiness.[32] What Vergil singles out as significant features of his Golden Age are harmony between man and nature (nature, unasked, gives all things more freely, 1.127–8) and harmony amongst all men equally (they look to the common good, 127). The poet does not, as does Hesiod (*Op.* 109–15), describe this Golden Age as a period of inconsequential or thoughtless merriment, such as might legitimize divine intervention in order to direct man to a higher moral plane. Neither is there mention here (as opposed to 1.501–2 or 2.537) of some primal crime which would have justified divine wrath. The significant result of these omissions is that Jove's intervention at this point appears unmotivated or arbitrary from any moral viewpoint.[33] Above all, in this Golden Age we note the deeply solemn moral quality of *fas* (127): "right" of absolute or divine (as opposed to human) origin. Plowing the earth, represented as a kind of aggression against (*subigebant*) nature by man, is not allowed (125); neither is the possession of earth by man (127)[34] nor, consequently, the pursuit of inequitable private interest.

The irony of the poet's vision here is that in this age of sharing, harmony, and morality, Jove saw only torpid lethargy (*torpere . . . veterno*, 124), thinking simply that men should be productive. If Jove has concern for moral conscience or spiritual purpose in man, this is not stated here; neither is it reflected in Iron Age reality, since a necessary consequence of Jove's intervention in mortal affairs is that man's moral relationships become compromised. Merely for survival man must now be aggressive towards nature:

> tunc alnos primum fluvii sensere cavatas;
> navita tum stellis numeros et nomina fecit,
> Pleiadas, Hyadas, claramque Lycaonis Arcton;
> tum laqueis captare feras et fallere visco
> inventum et magnos canibus circumdare saltus;
> atque alius latum funda iam verberat amnem
> alta petens, pelagoque alius trahit umida lina;
> tum ferri rigor atque argutae lammina serrae
> (nam primi cuneis scindebant fissile lignum),
> tum variae venere artes.

> Then first did rivers feel the hollowed alder; then the sailor numbered the stars and called them by name, Pleiades, Hyades, and Arctos, Lycaon's gleaming offspring. Then men found how to snare game in toils, to cheat with bird-lime, and to circle great glades with hounds. And now one lashes a broad stream with casting net, seeking the depths, and another through the sea trails his dripping drag-net. Then came iron's stiffness and the shrill

saw-blade—for early man cleft the splitting wood with wedges; then came the various arts.

The verbs *captare* and *fallere* (139), *verberat* (141), and *scindebant* (144) suggest the assault on nature which Iron Age civilization entails.[35] That agriculture requires destruction and domination of natural things becomes a leitmotif of the poem as the farmer's mode is the vanquishing of nature through a technology whose aggressive character is expressed in the military terms which Vergil applies to agriculture throughout the *Georgics*.[36] Further, such a usage as *arma* (160) for agricultural tools is not at all conventional but rather is original with Vergil[37] and hence illuminating of his purpose.

As man becomes aggressive towards nature, he becomes competitive with other men. Where once there was sharing (1.127), now the individual, envying another's private plenty, is left to starve alone:

> quod nisi et adsiduis herbam insectabere rastris
> et sonitu terrebis aves et ruris opaci
> falce premes umbram votisque vocaveris imbrem,
> heu magnum alterius frustra spectabis acervum
> concussaque famem in silvis solabere quercu.
>
> (1.155-9)

> Therefore, unless your hoe, time and again, assail the woods, your voice affright the birds, your knife check the shade of the darkened land, and your vows invoke the rain, vainly alas! will you eye your neighbor's big store, and in the woods shake the oak to solace hunger.

While the Golden Age is described positively, the poet's austere picture of the Iron Age is unrelieved by any hint of a benefit resulting for man from Jove's intervention. It is represented as the withdrawal of Golden Age harmony and plenty, its technology an end in itself and not directed toward the achievement of a greater goal:

> ille malum virus serpentibus addidit atris,
> praedarique lupos iussit pontumque moveri,
> mellaque decussit foliis, ignemque removit,
> et passim rivis currentia vina repressit,
> ut varias usus meditando extunderet artis
> paulatim et sulcis frumenti quaereret herbam
> ut silicis venis abstrusum excuderet ignem.
>
> (129-35)

It was he that in black serpents put their deadly venom, bade
the wolves to plunder and the ocean to swell; shook honey from the
leaves, hid fire from view, and stopped the wine that ran everywhere in streams, so that practice, by taking thought, might little
by little hammer out the various arts, might seek the corn-blade in
furrows, and strike forth from veins of flint the hidden fire.

Suffering extends also to the natural world:

> prima Ceres ferro mortalis vertere terram
> instituit, cum iam glandes atque arbuta sacrae
> deficerent silvae et victum Dodona negaret.
> mox et frumentis labor additus, ut mala culmos
> esset robigo segnisque horreret in arvis
> carduus; intereunt segetes, subit aspera silva,
> lappaeque tribolique, interque nitentia culta
> infelix lolium et steriles dominantur avenae.
>
> (1.147–54)

> Ceres was the first to teach man to turn the earth with iron, when
> the acorns and arbutes of the sacred wood began to fail, and
> Dodona denied men food. Soon, too, on the corn fell trouble
> (*labor*), so that the baneful mildew fed on the stems, and the
> unfruitful thistle bristled in the fields; the crops die, and up grows
> a prickly wood, burrs and caltrops, and amid the shining corn
> the luckless darnel and barren oats reign.

To summarize: the poet never states that the current age is better for man.
While he represents the past in terms traditionally ascribed to the Golden
Age,[38] he merely enumerates man's Iron Age accomplishments without
qualifying them.[39] The fact that man's skills thus remain with no specific
qualification or evaluation (since the poet uses no adjectives at all) allows
the ambiguous potential of *labor* and *ars* to suggest itself. Many modern
readers, however, have missed the irony here because, in fact, the surface
meaning of the text, with its positive attitude towards technology, fits well
with their thought. As Booth points out, readers have greatest difficulty
sensing ironies directed at their own values and beliefs.[40] Vergil's intent,
however, his mission (2.176), is to turn us into an audience which would see
the irony in *veternus* and have an apprehension and appreciation of non-
competitive peace, harmony, and sharing, that is, of "Golden Age"
values.

Comparison of this passage with Manilius *Astronomica* 1.66–98 makes
Vergil's reticence very plain. Manilius, while obviously familiar with Vergil's
poem, is unambiguously enthusiastic about the development of civil-

ization. His admiration of the arts and his conviction of their usefulness is clear. He describes the early stages of man's history in negative terms: earth is empty, uninhabited, the sea unmoved; men are miserable, their languages barbarous. Civilization, however, has brought about wise practice, contributes to the common good, makes the fields fruitful. *Omnia conando docilis sollertia vicit* (95) is unambiguous in its faith in man's supple ingenuity and persistence. *Docilis sollertia* is in clear contrast to *labor improbus*, both terms of which are ambiguous (as we have seen above).

Besides being morally ambiguous, the arts which man has been compelled to contrive are all aimed at material survival and therefore lead to visible and quantifiable, but not to moral or esthetic, progress. This theodicy includes the material and practical, but omits *fas* and art, a suggestive and emphatic omission for a poet to allow. Wilkinson states that we have here a general theodicy, that Vergil "has in mind all the arts, not merely agriculture."[41] Since the poet, however, has entirely omitted the fine arts from his description of civilization's progress, we must doubt that this is so. Vergil's passage differs significantly in this respect from those of his two major models, Lucretius and Hesiod. Lucretius includes poetry, painting, and sculpture in his history of civilization:

> Navigia atque agri culturas moenia leges
> arma vias vestis et cetera de genere horum,
> praemia, delicias quoque vitae funditus omnis,
> carmina picturas, et daedala signa polire,
> usus et impigrae simul experientia mentis
> paulatim docuit pedetemptim progredientis.
>
> (*DRN* 5.1448-53)

> Ships and agriculture, fortifications and laws, arms, roads, clothing and all else of this kind, life's prizes, its luxuries also from first to last, poetry and pictures, the shaping of statues by the artist, all these as men progressed gradually step by step were taught by practice and the experiments of the active mind. (W.H.D. Rouse)

Equally in Hesiod we find that Zeus likes poetry and is, indeed, the father of the Muses (e.g. *Th.* 36-43, 53ff.). In the *Georgics*, however, Jove, like the farmers of Georgic 2 or the Romanized bees of Georgic 4, is indifferent to art. In this he is typical of traditional Romans (cf. Hor. *Ars Poet.* 323ff.).[49] Significantly, the poet's mission is to bring Greek song to Italy:

> ubi res antiquae laudis et artem
> ingredior, sanctos ausus recludere fontis,
> Ascraeumque cano Romana per oppida carmen.
>
> (2.174-6)

'Tis for you I try the theme of ancient praise and art; daring to unseal the sacred founts, I sing through Roman towns the song of Ascra.

Thus the poet attempts to redress the omission of Jove.

In sum, I would like to suggest that this passage is not a true theodicy ("a justification of the existence, justice, and goodness of God in light of the existence of evil," Webster, s.v.), but rather a distanced, ironic reflection on the present material age and its supreme god—indifferent to spirit, morality, and art. The poet is not uncritically praising the new age and its various arts, but rather is commenting, with subtle and fresh attention, on the character and quality of the Iron Age and its presiding divinity. The effect of the passage is to subvert the reader's even confidence in Iron Age values, to hold them up to critical evaluation. The poet's method of achieving this effect is to generate poles of debate or tension in the reader's mind by bringing to the fore both positive and negative views of the Iron Age and its technology. The reader, attempting to resolve this opposition, becomes consequently a critic of Iron Age values himself. He becomes, in sum, capable of seeing the irony of *veternus*.

II

A corroborating impression of Iron Age divinity in the *Georgics* emerges from the portrait of Aristaeus, who, in Georgic 4, is represented as becoming a god (implicit also in his invocation at 1.14, and cf. 4.314–16). In addition, the association of Aristaeus with Zeus in myth throughout Greek tradition suggests that we may legitimately find in his experience an analogue for that of Jove in this poem.[43] In accounts of Aristaeus outside the *Georgics* he appears as a culture hero through his teaching of agriculture, cattle-breeding, hunting, and bee-keeping.[44] Vergil's portrait of Aristaeus in Georgic 4, however, diverges significantly in several features from other extant accounts. These innovations, departures from the tradition familiar to his readers, become the emphatic features of his portrait of Aristaeus and hence of Iron Age divinity as well.

The portrait of Aristaeus in the *Georgics* is unique both in its attribution to him of the fantastical *bougonia* and in its association of him with the tale (and most particularly with the deaths) of Orpheus and Eurydice. While in other poets' accounts Aristaeus is always an exemplary figure and true benefactor of mankind, here alone is he represented with negative qualities and as the founder of a delusive technology or *ars*. Querulous and petty, he blames his mother for the evil consequences of what we learn were his own actions (4.321-2). His inclination to violence[45] (as in his behavior toward Eurydice and Proteus) results in his becoming inadvertently responsible for the death of Eurydice as well as of his own valued bees.

That Aristaeus is made to be guilty of the attempted rape of Eurydice, a dryad and hence a natural creature, is consonant with his role as tutelary god of agriculture in this poem. As has been indicated above, it is a leitmotif of the *Georgics* that agriculture requires destruction and domination of natural things. Aristaeus' pursuit of Eurydice (4.457-9) and his attack on Proteus, a creature of the sea, exhausted and old (*defessa senem . . . membra* 4.438), reveal that violence against nature is characteristic of him (4.398-400; cf. 4.450). Aptly Proteus addresses him as *iuvenum confidentissime* (4.445 "most audacious of youths"). In each instance of aggression Aristaeus pursues his own desires without expressing—and hence perhaps without feeling—regret for the consequences of those actions upon others.[46] In this connection we may think not only of Orpheus and Eurydice, both of whom perish, but also of the calf, four bulls, four heifers, and black ewe which have to be sacrificed in order for Aristaeus to acquire new bees (4.534-47). Aristaeus appears committed to success regardless of its cost.[47]

Aristaeus' major contribution in this poem is the *bougonia*, an *ars* of unmistakable brutality[48] and dubious reality. The *bougonia*, a fabulous procedure for generating bees, requires that a calf, its ears and nostrils stopped up, be pounded to death and its carcass left to putrefy in an enclosed place. Some time later, as the story goes, a swarm of bees emerges from the slain calf's body:

tum vitulus bima curvans iam cornua fronte
quaeritur: huic geminae nares et spiritus oris
multa reluctanti obstruitur, plagisque perempto
tunsa per integram solvuntur viscera pellem.
sic positum in clauso linquunt, et ramea costis
subiciunt fragmenta, thymum casiasque recentis.
hoc geritur Zephyris primum impellentibus undas,
ante novis rubeant quam prata coloribus, ante
garrula quam tignis nidum suspendat hirundo.
interea teneris tepefactus in ossibus umor
aestuat, et visenda modis animalia miris,
trunca pedum primo, mox et stridentia pennis,
miscentur, tenuemque magis magis aera carpunt,
donec ut aestivis effusus nubibus imber
erupere, aut ut nervo pulsante sagittae
prima leves ineunt si quando proelia Parthi.

(4.299-314)

Then a bullock is sought, one just arching his horns on a brow of
two summers' growth. Spite of all his struggles, both his nostrils
are stopped up, and the breath of his mouth; then he is beaten to
death, and his flesh is pounded to a pulp through the unbroken
hide. As thus he lies, they leave him in the enclosed room, and
strew beneath his sides broken boughs, thyme, and fresh cassia.
This is done when the zephyrs begin to stir the waves, ere the
meadows blush with their fresh hues, ere the chattering swallow
hangs her nest from the rafters. Meantime the moisture, warmed
in the softened bones, ferments, and creatures of wondrous wise
to view, footless at first, soon with buzzing wings as well, swarm
together, and more and more take the light air, until, like a shower
pouring from summer clouds, they burst forth, or like arrows
from the string's rebound, when the light-armed Parthians enter
on the opening battle.

The ritual of atonement which Cyrene prescribes to Aristaeus, although not
identical in all respects to that described above, has the same substance and
character:

hic vero subitum ac dictu mirabile monstrum
aspiciunt, liquefacta boum per viscera toto
stridere apes utero et ruptis effervere costis,
immensasque trahi nubes, iamque arbore summa
confluere et lentis uvam demittere ramis.

$$(4.554-7)$$

But here they espy a portent, sudden and wondrous to tell—
throughout the paunch, amid the molten flesh of the oxen, bees
buzzing and swarming forth from the ruptured sides, then trailing
in vast crowds, till at last on a tree-top they stream together, and
hang in clusters from the bending boughs.

Whether or not the ancients believed in the reality of *bougonia* is perhaps
an arguable point.[49] The essential point is that we can assert that the quality
of its reality for them could not have been routine, but rather at most a
matter of faith since no one could ever have witnessed it. As an *ars*, though,
it is a powerful image for the poet of Iron Age technology, another image
expressing the motif of destruction of nature for man's progress. Although
some critics, perhaps influenced by Christian tradition, have suggested that
bougonia is an image of resurrection, of death restored to life, we may
perhaps more accurately view it as a picture of death exchanged for life
since the soul of the slain calf, upon leaving its body, is then thought to
animate the bees.[50] We see that in this poem *bougonia* is made to require that
a sentient and individual creature be sacrificed or exchanged for the

impersonal swarm of bees. Certainly it is difficult to assign appropriate values to the terms of this equation,[51] and thoughtful people could hold opposed views. However, it is without apparent reflection upon the relative value of what is lost and what is gained that Aristaeus pursues and acquires new bees for himself and achieves his desired divinity. In the apotheosis of this particular figure, then, and in the history which Vergil attributes to him, we have a provocative comment on what is worshipped in the Iron Age.

Vergil's treatment of Aristaeus, an Iron Age god, in its suggestions of violence, lack of sentiment, and delusive progress recalls certain qualities of Jupiter in Georgic 1 and hence lends credence to my contention that the "theodicy of labor" is not, in fact, a theodicy. The passage reflects rather the poet's vision of the Iron Age as it is expressed in its technology (*variae artes*), a technology which aims at material goals and remains largely indifferent to such matters of spirit as morality and art. Art is reasonably excluded from this particularly Roman "theodicy" since it serves no practical or material purpose (cf. *Aen.* 1.464: *pictura inani*). Such a provocative view of the Iron Age is implicit not only in the poem's Golden Age passages (especially 1.125-8; 2.336-42, 535-40), which reflect a nostalgic desire for a purer, humane time,[52] but also in the *bougonia*, which epitomizes the character of Iron Age culture in the *Georgics*. The moral quality of the *bougonia* parallels the moral status of Jove and of the technological advances which he instigates. In each of these cases, success is achieved through the destruction of something natural and innocent (cf. *Aen.* 8 and the innocence of early Italy, untouched). In this passage, then, Jove cannot be seen to represent an absolute moral standard which the poet uncritically endorses. Rather, as a characteristically Roman god, he reflects a relative standard. The poet is not seeking simply to justify the ways of God to man, but is reflecting on contemporary Rome and its values, which are (to use Parry's phrase in another context) in need of a "lesson of poetry."[53]

To summarize, it has not been my intent here to exchange one simplistic reading (Vergil praises technology and Rome) of this passage for another (Vergil deplores technology and Rome), merely its opposite. Rather my intent has been to show that the poet's method is to effect a tension in the reader's mind by means of ambiguity and irony. He allows oppositions to arise, the poles of which he himself determines. Thus he engages the reader's imagination in the problems which the poem poses. In terms of the passage under consideration here, these poles are the values of a naturally moral and sustaining Golden Age versus those of a materially productive but spiritless Iron Age. These oppositions function within what I see as the larger oppositions of the poem: harmony with nature versus manipulation of it; artistic mission and sensibility versus material and martial success.

Within these oppositions, however, and deepening their complexity, move the artist (Orpheus) and the farmer (Aristaeus), both flawed in their relation to Eurydice, a natural figure who dies once for each.[54] Thus Orpheus and Aristaeus pursue different goals, but with similar failures. Aristaeus by his self-assertion (*iuvenum confidentissime*) achieves his desired divinity, while Orpheus, whose sorrow we are invited to share (4.489-90. 504-5), is the eventual victim of Aristaeus' passion and of his own. If ultimately the reader is led, by his whole experience of the poem, to sympathize more deeply with one figure or set of values than with the other, this does not mean that he is to sympathize simplistically. Rather the poet has shown both sets of values to be in dynamic, present tension with each other. These contrasting values signify most importantly as poles of unresolvable oppositions. The poem presents a vision of how life is, not a solution to its conflicts. The poem is, therefore, not the didactic work it initially claims to be (1.1-5), for truly didactic works are not characterized by ambiguity.[55] Rather it falls into the category of tragedy, which perceives and aims to reveal conflicts of human experience as inevitable and unresolvable.[56] Vergil's poetry proposes no facile solutions, careless of perceived reality. His poetry is dialectical and polemical, not partisan.

Notes

I wish to thank Professors Zeph Stewart, Michael Putnam, John Van Sickle, James Tatum, and the editors of this volume, whose generous help greatly improved this paper.

The following works will be referred to by author's name alone: H. Altevogt, *Labor Improbus: Eine Vergilstudie* (Munster: Aschendorffsche Verlagsbuchhandlung, 1952); K. Büchner, "P. Vergilius Maro," *RE* 8a.2 (1958); J. Conington, H. Nettleship, and F. Haverfield, edd., *The Works of Vergil* (London 1898[5]; repr. ed., Hildesheim, 1963); Patricia A. Johnston, *Vergil's Agricultural Golden Age: A Study of the Georgics* (Leiden: Brill, 1980); F. Klingner, *Virgil: Bucolica, Georgica, Aeneis* (Zurich: Artemis Verlag, 1967); A. La Penna, "Esiodo nella cultura e nella poesia di Virgilio," in *Hésiode et son influence*, Fondation Hardt Entretiens 7 (Geneva, 1960); Gary B. Miles, *Virgil's Georgics: A New Interpretation* (Berkeley: University of California Press, 1980); Brooks Otis, *Virgil: A Study in Civilized Poetry* (Oxford: Clarendon Press, 1963); Michael C.J. Putnam, *Virgil's Poem of the Earth: Studies in the Georgics* (Princeton: Princeton University Press, 1979); Will Richter, *Vergil: Georgica* (Munich: Hueber, 1957); L.P. Wilkinson, *The Georgics of Virgil* (London: Cambridge University Press, 1969). Translations of the *Georgics* are those of H. Rushton Fairclough (London, 1935; repr. 1965), with certain modifications as seemed necessary to clarify my arguments.

1. This title is taken from L.P. Wilkinson, "Virgil's Theodicy," *CQ* n.s. 13 (1963): 75–84. Miles, pp. 79, 85, uses the phrase "Jupiter's theodicy."

2. Richter, p. 137; Büchner, p. 1271; Klingner, p. 189-91; Wilkinson (1963), p. 81. Miles, p. 79, speaks of "positive consequences" for man, although he discusses also the negative potential of man's technology.

3. Johnston, pp. 71, 58; Wilkinson (1963), p. 80.

4. Jacques Perret, *Virgile* (Paris: Hatier, 1965), p. 81. Cf. Eva M. Stehle, "Virgil's *Georgics*: The Threat of Sloth," *TAPA* 104 (1974): 347–70.

5. See Wilkinson (1963), p. 77, who cites, e.g., Sen. *Dial.* 1.2.6: *Patrium deus habet adversus bonos viros animum et illos fortiter amat; 'operibus,' inquit, doloribus, damnis exagitentur, ut verum colligant robur'* ("God has a fatherly spirit towards good men and loves them powerfully. 'Let them,' he says, 'be roused up by labors, pains, and hurts so that they may acquire true strength' ").

6. Miles, p. 81. (But cf. p. 79 for a more ambivalent view.) Putnam, pp. 33f., notes that these lines can be and have been taken positively; he, however, is dubious of such a reading. See pp. 33-6 for his thoughtful discussion of this passage.

7. Cf., e.g., Wilkinson, pp. 74-5; Otis, p. 151; Klingner, p. 194; and Perret, p. 86.

8. Cf. Wilkinson, p. 183, on Vergil's belief "that a return of Rome's ruling class to the old values symbolized by country life could cure a sick generation." Similarly Otis, p. 145, and E. Burck, "Drei Grundwerte der römischen Lebensordnung: *labor, moderatio, pietas*," *Gymnasium* 63 (1951): 166.

9. E.g. Otis, pp. 154-5, 213; Perret, p. 86; Klingner, p. 194. For a different view of the optimism of Georgic 4, see my "A Reading of Virgil's Fourth *Georgic*," *Phoenix* 32 (1978):

10. Miles, p. 81, well notes that the present tense of *verberat* (and cf. *trahit*, 142) shows the truth of the passage continuing into the present.

11. Cf. Putnam, pp. 32ff., and Miles, pp. 78ff., for sensitive comments on troubling implications of this passage.

12. La Penna, p. 238.

13. These difficulties are well set forth by Wilkinson (1963), pp. 75, 78-9, 83.

14. As Wilkinson (1963), pp. 82-3, observes.

15. Putnam, pp. 22n9, 22-3, 32ff., 79, 253, 322.

16. La Penna, pp. 239-40. Miles, p. 79, finds "alternation of tone" within the passage itself.

17. Wilkinson (1963), p. 84.

18. See Otis, p. 157 n.1, for a useful bibliography of scholars who take *labor improbus* in a "good sense."

19. See notes 2, 4, 6 above.

20. Miles, pp. 81, 82. Another possible reading, however, might be that *labor* has dominated or overwhelmed man's existence—as has need: *labor omnia vicit / improbus et duris urgens in rebus egestas*. This reading is compatible with the use of *labor* in 1.150. For this latter interpretation see Altevogt, p. 7. Cf. Putnam, p. 34, who writes persuasively of the significance for this verse of the proximity of *egestas* to *labor* and also its negativity, even elsewhere in Virgil.

21. We must not forget that the ancient *Lives* of Vergil tell us that he devoted seven years to composing the *Georgics'* 2000 lines.

22. Cf. Conington, *ad loc.*, and Altevogt, p. 6.

23. Cf. Wolfgang Iser, *The Act of Reading: A Theory of Aesthetic Response* (Baltimore: Johns Hopkins University Press, 1978), p.3: "For, in general, literary texts constitute a reaction to contemporary situations, bringing attention to problems that are conditioned though not resolved by contemporary norms."

24. Barbara Herrnstein Smith, *Poetic Closure: A Study of How Poems End* (Chicago: University of Chicago Press, 1968), p. 254: "Both irony and ambiguity are 'pluralistic' ways of speaking, evasions of committed speech."

25. Altevogt cites Caes. *BGall.* 7.67.4; Hor. *Carm.* 2.9.6; Tib. 1.1.3; Ov. *Pont.* 2.6.22, *Met.* 2.296; Sen. *Ben.* 2.27.2, as well as *Aen.* 6.277. Cf. Dieter Lau, *Der lateinische Begriff "labor"* (Munich: Fink, 1975) p. 19; see also p. 11 for its frequent metonymic use amongst Augustan writers.

26. Stanley E. Fish, "Literature in the Reader: Affective Stylistics," *NLH* 2.1 (1970): 126; reprinted in Jane P. Tompkins, ed., *Reader-Response Criticism: From Formalism to Post-Structuralism* (Baltimore: Johns Hopkins University Press, 1980), pp. 70–100.

27. Similar interpretive problems ensue for a reader of the *Aeneid* who assumes that Vergil endorses all of Aeneas' actions.

28. Johnston, p. 71. Similarly, pp. 48, 50.

29. Cf. Iser, pp. 196–7, on the different possible perspectives in a text—hero's, narrator's, author's. The meaning of a text does not lie in any single one of these perspectives, but rather is "a product of interconnections." Similarly Stanley E. Fish, "Interpreting the *Variorum*," *CritI* 2 (Spring 1976): 472; reprinted in Tompkins, pp. 164–84, concerning a verse of Milton's: "Does the poet appropriate these lines or share them or simply listen to them, as we do?" The reader's inability to know to what degree the speaker participates in the affirmation contributes to the "continuing instability" of the text.

30. Quintilian, *Institutio Oratoria* 8.6.54; Wayne C. Booth, *A Rhetoric of Irony* (Chicago: University of Chicago Press, 1974) p. 183.

31. Johnston, p. 52, well points out that Vergil never actually uses the term "Golden Age."

32. See A.O. Lovejoy and George Boas, *Primitivism and Related Ideas in Antiquity* (Baltimore: Johns Hopkins Press, 1935; repr. New York: Octagon Books, 1973), pp. 23ff., for an exhaustive collection of passages describing the Golden Age.

33. See Otis, pp. 158ff., on the lack of a fall in this passage. Contrast Hes. *Op.* 47ff., where Zeus' taking away of fire is a punishment for crime.

34. Contrast 2.162 (*indignatum . . . aequor*) and 2.163 (*Iulia . . . unda.*)

35. Cf. Otis, p. 157n1.

36. Cf. Conington *ad* 99, 104–5, 125, 155, 160. See also G. 2.207–11, 277, 367–70, 3.468–9, 4.106–8. Altevogt, p. 24, notes the "military character of agricultural labor."

37. Wilkinson, p. 80.

38. Cf. Hes. *Op.* 109–20; Aratus *Phaen.* 96–114; Tib. 1.3.35–50, 1.10.1–12, 2.3.35–46; Ov. *Met. 1.94–211, Am.* 3.8.35–6. Similar versions in Pind. *Pyth.* 10.38f., *Ol.* 2.68f.

39. They are, however, *topoi* for the origin of vice in the world. Cf. e.g., Tib. 1.3.35–52.

40. Pp. 81, 221–4.

41. Wilkinson (1963), p. 78.

42. Jasper Griffin, "The Fourth *Georgic*, Virgil, and Rome," *G&R* 26 (1979): 64–6, is important on the bees of *G.* 4 as embodiments, in part, of traditional Romans' indifference to art. Cf. *Aen.* 6.847–50.

43. Wilkinson, p. 108n1; Stehle, p. 363n24 and 25.

44. Cf. Wilhelm Heinrich Roscher, *Ausführliches Lexikon der griechischen und römischen Mythologie* (Leipzig: Teubner, 1884–1890), s.v. "Aristaeus," and Hiller v. Gaertringen, "Aristaios," *RE* 2 (1896): 852–9; Miles, p. 258n14; and n. 43 above for sources on Aristaeus.

45. Cf. W. Richter, p. 388, who takes a milder view: "Aristaeus is also not without energy and power."

46. Miles, p. 270, is excellent on Aristaeus' indifference to others. Cf., however, Putnam's cautionary note on Aristaeus' being "an easy character to depreciate" (p. 314n61).

47. Cf. Miles, p. 271. John Van Sickle, *The Design of Virgil's Bucolics* (Rome: Edizioni dell' Ateneo Bizzarro, 1978), p. 227, puts it another way: Aristaeus is "concerned above all about property . . ."

48. Büchner, p. 1310.

49. See, e.g., A.J. Boyle, "In Medio Caesar: Paradox and Politics in Virgil's *Georgics*," *Ramus* 8 (1979): 85n26, for a useful note.
50. B.G. Whitfield, "Virgil and the Bees: A Study in Ancient Apicultural Lore," *G&R* 3 (1956): 117: "The Main Idea seems to be that the life of the bull passes into that of the bees; the closing of the ears and nostrils, as well as the insistence on death by slow contusion, seem to aim at preservation of the soul within the carcass."
51. Cf. Van Sickle, *Design*, p. 228.
52. Contrast Altevogt, Stehle and Johnston, who believe the Golden Age will return through man's *labor*.
53. Adam Parry, "The Idea of Art in Virgil's *Georgics*," *Arethusa* 4 (1972): 51, regarding Aristaeus.
54. I intend to treat these oppositions more fully elsewhere. On polarities between Aristaeus and Orpheus, see Perkell, pp. 216ff.
55. Iser, p. 189.
56. James M. Redfield, *Nature and Culture in the Iliad* (Chicago: University of Chicago Press, 1975), p. 219.

THE FIGURE OF LAERTES:
REFLECTIONS ON THE
CHARACTER OF AENEAS

W.R. Johnson

I'll be your foil, Laertes. In mine ignorance
Your skill shall, like a star i' the darkest night,
Stick fiery off indeed.

Hamlet 5.2.256-8

I

sum pius Aeneas, raptos qui ex hoste penatis
classe veho mecum, fama super aethera notus . . .

(Aen. 1.378-9)

I am pious
Aeneas, and I carry in my ships
my household gods together with me, rescued
from Argive enemies; my fame is known
beyond the sky.

Sum pius Aeneas. That seems a rather unusual way of introducing
oneself. Granted, the scene smacks of Strauss operetta: a naughty, teasing
mother, wittily disguised as her arch-rival (the goddess of chastity) in sports
attire; her stalwart, stolid, middle-aged son—querulous, earnest, naive.
Vergil is here at his wittiest, his most purely Alexandrian. Granted, too, that
on the surface at least Vergil is not very far from the Homeric model he here
uses and abuses: Odysseus, when finally revealing himself to Alcinoos, had
claimed that his *kleos* reached to heaven (he did not, however, suggest that
his fame transcended heaven), and he too had boasted of his distinctive
quality—his razzle-dazzle conman style and guile. But it is one thing to say:

85

I'm a tricky kind of guy; quite another to say: I'm loyal, filial, patriotic, reverent and compassionate. Odysseus, moreover, speaks wholly in character, a character we have seen in dramatic action for four books by the time he speaks these words. But up to this point in the *Aeneid*, we have seen Aeneas only briefly, and we have heard him speak only twice before (the first monologue at sea; his first address to his comrades). For him to identify himself with his essential epic epithet, I am pious Aeneas—that takes one's breath away. Why has Vergil inflicted this studied indecorum on his hero, on Homer, on us?

If this were the single apparent indecorum in Vergil's representation of his hero, we might feel justified in passing it off as a mysterious lapse in characterization or as a charming, if misleading, arabesque. But even readers of the poem whom Aeneas' character doesn't bother—those, for instance, who feel that he grows steadily as a character from his initial, baffled *aporia* to, after his ascent from hell, perfection of Stoic obedience and flawless patriotism—even these admirers seem at times somewhat uncomfortable with their hero's characteristic deportment, seem ill at ease not so much with flaws or inconsistencies of his character, but rather with something that verges on the absence of personality. In what follows, I want to try to describe what seems to me Vergil's central strategem in rendering his hero obscure, implausible, unsatisfying; and I want then to try to go on to suggest what seem to me possible reasons for Vergil's having elected this difficult and dangerous mode of characterization. We will look first at the ways in which Aeneas speaks, how he reveals or fails to reveal himself, what he wants, what he values when speaking to himself or to other characters; having done this, we will examine how Vergil uses contrasting personality, the foil-figure, to illumine the figure of Aeneas.

II

The scene between Aeneas and Venus that I've just recalled ends with a moment in which what seems to me one of Aeneas' most typical situations of discourse is vividly drawn. Venus, in her huntress disguise, has asked Aeneas and Achates whether they happen to have seen one of her missing companions anywhere about. Aeneas replies that he has seen no one answering to this description and goes on to ask for information about his whereabouts, and then, though he fails to recognize his mother in her unusual costume, goes on to express his intuition of divine presence. Venus, coyly denying any claim to divinity, offers, as answer to his question, a quick but thorough sketch of Dido, her perils and her founding of Carthage: this by way of preparing him for his fatal encounter with the Punic queen. She then asks him who he is and receives the reply we have just glanced at. Finally, she calls his attention to an omen that signals the salvation of his fleet, and then, perhaps having grown bored with the small ironies of her masquerade, she disappears in a stunning, enchanting burst of naked and perfumed glory:

> ille ubi matrem
> agnovit tali fugientem est voce secutus:
> quid natum totiens, crudelis tu quoque, falsis
> ludis imaginibus? cur dextrae iungere dextram
> non datur ac veras audire et reddere voces?'
>
> (1.405–9)

> And when Aeneas recognized his mother,
> he followed her with these words as she fled:
> "Why do you mock your son—so often and
> so cruelly—with these lying apparitions?
> Why can't I ever join you, hand to hand,
> to hear, to answer you with honest words?"

This scene shows, I believe, Aeneas' most sustained effort at conversation anywhere in the poem: two whole interchanges, but the third interchange is broken off—*cur . . . non datur ac veras audire at reddere voces?*[1] Aside from grappling with Juno's grand designs, from dreaming and enacting historical destiny, his trouble with communication is perhaps Aeneas' central problem, and the scene, the broken scene, we have just witnessed is a recurrent experience for Aeneas throughout the first half of the poem. Indeed, it is so recurrent that one is tempted to classify this as a Vergilian type-scene.

Nor is it limited to the *Aeneid*. Vergil had first experimented with it, and superbly, in *Georgics* 4, where Orpheus, having won Eurydice back from Hades, loses her again and forever:[2]

> dixit et ex oculis subito, ceu fumus in auras
> commixtus tenuis, fugit diversa, neque illum
> prensantem nequiquam umbras et multa volentem
> dicere praeterea vidit. . .
>
> (499–502)

> So she spoke, and suddenly, like smoke mingled with the
> fragile air, she fled in the opposite direction, and saw
> him no more, as he grasped in vain at the shadows, wishing
> to say much to her. . .

This scene is repeated, recreated, and hardly less poignantly, at the terrible

moment when the ghost of Creusa appears to Aeneas in the dark dawn of
ruining Troy:

> haec ubi dicta dedit, lacrimantem et multa volentem
> dicere deseruit, tenuisque recessite in auras.
> ter conatus ibi collo dare bracchia circum;
> ter frustra comprensa manus effugit imago,
> par levibus ventis volucrique simillima somno.
>
> (2.790–94)

> When she was done with words—I weeping and
> wanting to say so many things—she left
> and vanished in transparent air. Three times
> I tried to throw my arms around her neck;
> three times the Shade I grasped in vain escaped
> my hands—like fleet winds, most like a winged dream.

So, with less poignancy perhaps, but with more genuine dramatic force
(because Dido is a fully realized dramatic character), the final earthly
interview between Dido and Aeneas finds abrupt termination:

> his medium dictis sermonem abrumpit et auras
> aegra fugit seque ex oculis avertit et aufert.
> linquens multa metu cunctantem et multa parantem
> dicere . . .
>
> (4.388–91)

> Her speech is broken off; heartsick, she shuns
> the light of day, deserts his eyes; she turns
> away, leaves him in fear and hesitation,
> Aeneas longing still to say so much . . .

So in Book 5 the vision of Anchises orders him to depart from Sicily and
head for Italy. Then:

> dixerat et tenuis fugit ceu fumus in auras.
> Aeneas quo deinde ruis? quo proripis?' inquit,
> quem fugis? aut quis te nostris complexibus arcet?'
>
> (740–42)

> He spoke, then fled like smoke into thin air.
> "Where are you rushing now, where hurrying?"
> Aeneas cries. "Whom do you flee? Or who
> keeps you from my embraces?"

Aeneas here again confronts the failure of speech. Here, as in the scene with Venus, Aeneas is not quite speechless, not *multa volens-parans dicere*; but his brief desperate questions cannot rescue him from the by now familiar moment: a sense of isolation, of swift, mystifying transitions, of baffling advice and warnings—his is a world where *veras audire et reddere voces* becomes increasingly impossible. Finally, there are those two moments in the underworld when the fact of loss, separation, isolation finds its perfect form. When Aeneas encounters Dido in the Field of Mourning, he is at last able to speak to her as he could not (could not bring himself to do) in their last fatal interview in the upper world. But just as he has got to the heart of the matter, she turns and moves away:

> tandem corripuit sese atque inimica refugit
> in nemus umbriferum . . .
> nec minus Aeneas casu percussus iniquo
> prosequitur lacrimis longe et miseratur euntem.
>
> (6.472–3, 475–6)

> At last she tore herself away; she fled—
> and still his enemy—into the forest
> of shadows . . .
> Nevertheless, Aeneas, stunned by her
> unkindly fate, still follows at a distance
> with tears and pity for her as she goes.

Again the respondent flees (but why doesn't he continue to follow her, to speak to her?). This is the most terrible silence, for Dido is at once the object of his purest love and of his deepest compassion, and she is also the source, the single source—until the poem's final moment—of his only guilt. *Lenibat, ciebat* (468): the imperfects are very expressive here; he was trying to solace her, was himself on the verge of tears, was beginning to weep, was desperate to show his feelings—if ever, then now, from the heart. The laconic, tongue-tied hero, whose feelings are too deep for words, almost finds his tongue at this pitch of sorrow, but cannot, and fails, fails yet again. He speaks with difficulty at best everywhere; worse, he moves in a world where the occasions of discourse are rare and at last illusory, where speech is, for him by its very nature, aborted, tragic.

In the last scene of this kind, the grief of imperfect communication is somewhat mitigated, for speaking with Anchises and hearing him are, in this their last encounter, almost possible. Almost, but not quite. In the Homeric model for this scene, where Odysseus meets with his mother, Anticleia, in their leisured conversation *about* their grief their grief finds solace. In place of solace, Aeneas receives from his father some rather confusing instruction in metaphysics and history. The emotional content of the scene is rooted in an anguish in which all his previous moments of isolation are recalled and confirmed:

> da iungere dextram,
> da, genitor, teque amplexu ne subtrahe nostro.'
> sic memorans largo fletu simul ora rigabat.
> ter conatus ibi collo dare bracchia circum;
> ter frustra comprensa manus effugit imago,
> par levibus ventus volucrique simillima somno.
>
> (6.697–702)

"O father, let me hold your right hand fast,
do not withdraw from my embrace." His face
was wet with weeping as he spoke. Three times
he tried to throw his arms around Anchises'
neck; and three times the Shade escaped from that
vain clasp—like light winds, or most like swift dreams.

Da iungere dextram here recalls the *cur dextrae iungere dextram / non datur?* of the scene with Venus, even as, perhaps, *tua tristis imago* here (695) stirs memories of *crudelis tu falsis ludis imaginibus* in the scene with his mother. Certainly the emphatic verbatim repetition of *ter conatus* from the Creusa scene suffuses this meeting with a sadness which, despite its partial joy, the remainder, and particularly the close, of book 6 will do little to alleviate. The lost father is here recovered, yes—but he is also irremediably, eternally lost; their reunion and their speech, lacking wholly the warmth and the interchange of the scene between Odysseus and Anticleia, are embarrassed, stilted.

But let us look at Aeneas as speaker from a slightly different angle. By way of analogy only, as sheer metaphor, not in an effort to beshrink Vergil or his hero, suppose we say, borrowing Jung's model, that Aeneas is something of an introvert feeling-type for whom the desperate need to shape his feelings vocally, a problem greatly exacerbated by his having to increasingly adopt an extravert persona, is oppressive to him almost to the point of agony.[3] He tries to speak, but he speaks almost always (as against Achilles, say, or Odysseus) too little and too late. This is not because, having nothing to feel, he has nothing much to say. Rather, his taciturnity derives from his having too much to feel and to say. What he feels so powerfully and so intensely is invariably at odds with what he feels himself called upon to do, what he feels himself called upon to say, what he is trying, consciously and archaically, to think. The splendid self-revelations of Achilles (particularly in book 9 of the *Iliad*), the ebullient improvisations of

Odysseus, or even the awkward, somewhat disingenuous, yet passionate efforts at expression of Turnus in *Aeneid* 11—none of these finds any shadow of a counterpart in Aeneas' narrow verbal repertoire. He is a man with everything to say and no way to say it.

When he encounters Andromache in book 3, the powerful utterances of Hector's widow reduce him, by his own admission, to virtual silence:

> vix pauca furenti
> subicio et raris turbatus vocibus hisco:
> 'vivo equidem vitamque extrema per omnia duco;
> ne dubita, nam vera vides.
> heu! quis te casus deiectam coniuge tanto
> excipit, aut quae digna satis fortuna revisit,
> Hectoris Andromache? Pyrrhin conubia servas?'
>
> (3.313–19)

> She is so frenzied, I —
> disquieted—must stammer scattered words:
> "Indeed, I live and drag my life through all
> extremities; do not doubt—I am real.
> But you, what fate has overtaken you,
> divided from so great a husband, or
> what kindly fortune comes again to Hector's
> Andromache? Are you still wed to Pyrrhus?"

Astonished, greatly moved at finding her so suddenly, he tries to be rational, to be kind, but stumbles into the brutal tactlessness of *Pyrrhin conubia servas?* Are you still the concubine of Pyrrhus? Then, in answer to Andromache's tender, anxious question about Ascanius—a dreadful moment when we remember, as we are supposed to, Astyanax—Aeneas, the man of few words, says nothing. Helenus arrives, and Aeneas spares himself, is spared by Vergil, the pain of speech. So in his relatively brief response to Dido's first impassioned outburst in book 4, the spare difficulties of his speech are emphasized:

> dixerat. ille Iovis monitis immota tenebat
> lumina et obnixus curam sub corde premebat.
> tandem pauca refert . . .
>
> (331–3)

> Her words were ended. But Aeneas, warned
> by Jove, held still his eyes; he struggled, pressed
> care back within his breast. With halting words
> he answers her at last.

And he himself says, at a pause towards the beginning of his response: "I'll speak / brief words that fit the case," *pro re pauca loquar*. Nothing could be simpler or more Roman, or more pathetic and inadequate.

On diplomatic and ceremonial occasions, and in addressing his troops, although he still favors brevity, Aeneas can speak with clarity and force; but when he must talk with father or mother, wife or mistress, as later when in book 10 he kills and hates killing, his words are forced, cramped, groped after—or words burst into or are wholly replaced by a dead, anguished silence. When it matters most he cannot speak, and the pain of silence is almost invariably a signal for movement. He moves away from the sorrows of his isolation and of bad ineffabilities to action, to the blind quest and the mission: *gressumque ad moenia tendit* (1.410), after Venus leaves him; *sic demum socios consumpta nocte reviso* (2.795), after Creusa leaves him; *iussa tamen divum exsequitur classemque revisit* (4.396), after Dido leaves him.

In addition to speech frustrated or total silence or muffled impatience with words, Aeneas has another way of dealing with loss, baffled feelings, isolation. Like his creator, he is, at his core, something of a lyric poet in the modern, Romantic sense of that word. Again and again, it is to the extended cry, to the spontaneous apostrophe, that he is driven. It is, I think, in these lyrical apostrophes that we get our best glimpse of who Aeneas is, what he values most. Indeed, our very first encounter with him, in the storm at sea in book 1, defines Vergil's and Aeneas' lyrical apostrophe— another substitute for genuine dramatic discourse—with precision:

> extemplo Aeneae solvuntur frigore membra;
> ingemit et duplicis tendens ad sidera palmas
> talia voce refert: o terque quaterque beati,
> quis ante ora patrum Troiae sub moenibus altis
> contigit oppetere!'
>
> (92–6)

> At once Aeneas' limbs fall slack with chill.
> He groans and stretches both hands to the stars.
> He calls aloud: "O, three and four times blessed
> were those who died before their fathers' eyes
> beneath the walls of Troy."

The groan quickly gives way to a spontaneous gesture of prayer, but though he tries to pray (out of fear for himself, for his companions) the prayer dissolves into lamentation. Those who died in battle at Troy were blessed because they died honorably martial deaths and so won glory—that is the *topos* of the scene (so, in the Homeric model, *Odyssey* 5.356ff.); but it is overwhelmed here by something that is Vergil's and Aeneas' own: this meaningless catastrophe recalls, inevitably, that other meaningless catastrophe. In the midst of the wild waters of the sea, another vision of fatal water flashes against him—the bloody river with its shields and helmets and corpses:

> '. . . ubi tot Simois correpta sub undis
> scuta virum galeasque et fortia corpora volvit!'
>
> (100–101)

Beyond his fear and the present danger, it is the death of Troy, it is the human condition, that he here calls out against. Beyond his despair and wish to die, this speech resounds with Aeneas' unique and passionate intuition of human suffering: *sunt lacrimae rerum*.

The same intuition of the prevalence and primacy of human suffering (I have elsewhere called Vergil's grasp of it distinctively Epicurean, and I stick by that) also informs later apostrophes that are, most of them, more nearly personal than the one we have just looked at.[4] At the end of book 3, when Anchises dies, in closing the tale of his wanderings Aeneas cries out:

> hic pelagi tot tempestatibus actus
> heu, genitorem, omnis curae casusque levamen,
> amitto, Anchisen. hic me, pater optime, fessum
> deseris, heu, tantis nequiquam erepte periclis!
>
> (708–11)

> It is here [Drepanum] that—after all
> the tempests of the sea—I lose my father,
> Anchises, stay in every care and crisis.
> For here, o best of fathers, you first left
> me to my weariness, alone—Anchises,
> you who were saved in vain from dreadful dangers.

In book 5, once more at the closure, comes the brief, haunting apostrophe to Palinurus: *o nimium caelo et pelago confise sereno / nudus in ignota, Palinure, iacebis harena* (870–71 "O Palinurus, / too trustful of the tranquil sky and sea, / you will lie naked on an unknown shore"). In this apostrophe the isolations, vulnerabilities and unintelligibilities of human experience find a lapidary form that perfectly answers Aeneas' profoundest intuitions about life. The deaths of Anchises and, in a lesser degree, of Palinurus represent personal losses to Aeneas, and in this regard they are connected with the earlier scenes of grief loss-silence that we first looked at. Those scenes, too, are clustered in the first six books of the poem where encounters with loved ones, with loved ones lost, are frequent. After book 6, with the exception of

Ascanius, to whom we will presently turn, Aeneas has no loved ones. He is, by the time he issues from hell, a man of destiny—with a vengeance. And his tendency to repress his feelings, powerful though this was before, becomes increasingly marked from the end of book 6 until the end of the poem. Nevertheless, even when he arms himself in a *gravitas* that unremitting suffering has made increasingly attractive, his innate compassion, his enormous sympathies, his hatred of what breaks life, still struggle against the destructive contingencies that he has become ever more enmeshed in, whose servant he has finally become. In book 8, just at the moment when he accepts, now unambiguously, now irrevocably, the call of destiny, his thoughts—let us say, more accurately, his feelings—veer instantly to the human suffering, the waste, the carnage, the demonic lunacy that his mission will bring in its wake:

> heu quantae miseris caedes Laurentibus instant!
> quas poenas mihi, Turne, dabis! quam multa sub undas
> scuta virum galeasque et fortia corpora volves,
> Thybri pater! poscant acies et foedera rumpant!
>
> (537–40)

> What slaughter menaces these sad Laurentians!
> What penalties will Turnus pay to me!
> What shields of men and helmets and brave breasts
> will roll beneath your waves, o father Tiber!
> Now let them ask for battle, break their treaties!

The entire speech is one of his noblest and comes very close to defining him. The reprise of the lines from his first speech underlines fiercely what kind of man he is and signals the tragedy that snatches him up when he tries to become, and finally in fact becomes, what *gravitas* and ruthless purpose demand that he become. Here he grieves for the Italians, and he grieves also for Turnus, his rival and his enemy; it is a grief that this admixture of anger and despair make almost unbearable, for him, for us. Thus, what might have been the glory of *ego poscor Olympo* (533 "I am summoned by Olympus") in another context is here utterly consumed by the bitter, sorrowing, furious apostrophe to the Latins, to Turnus, and, finally, to Father Tiber: yet another bloody river, another image of murderous water—repetition, the determinism of historicist fate, its illusions and satanic mechanisms.[5] Aeneas is now in the trap of History; he certainly feels this, and he almost manages to say it.

Some of the central qualities of this trap are revealed in his next apostrophe, to the corpse of Lausus, the young warrior who has attacked him and whom he has just killed:

At vero ut vultum vidit morientis et ora,
ora modis Anchisiades pallentia miris,
ingemuit miserans graviter dextramque tetendit,
et mentem patriae subiit pictatis imago.
'quid tibi nunc, miserande puer, pro laudibus istis,
quid pius Aeneas tanta dabit indole dignum?
arma quibus laetatus, habe tua; teque parentum
manibus et cineri, si qua est ea cura, remitto.
hoc tamen infelix miseram solabere mortem:
Aeneae magni dextra cadis.'

(10.821–30)

But when he saw the look and face of dying
Lausus—he was mysteriously pale—
Anchises' son sighed heavily with pity
and stretched out his right hand; the image of
his love for his own father touched his mind.
"Poor boy, for such an act what can the pious
Aeneas give to match so bright a nature?
Keep as your own the arms that made you glad;
and to the Shades and ashes of your parents
I give you back—if Shades can care for that.
But, luckless, you can be consoled by this:
You fall beneath the hand of great Aeneas."

The hand that has taken the young man's life now reaches out to him in compassion, almost in supplication. In this scene, a sinister, ironic adumbration and reversal of the poem's final scene—for there will be, at last, no pity for Turnus there, nor promise of burial—Epicurean, or simply humane, feeling struggles against but finally gives way to epic code, and *pius* Aeneas becomes, almost for good and all, *magnus* Aeneas. But before the genuine and typical feelings of Aeneas are mastered by the exigencies of this new, this neo-Homeric, neo-Stoic *gravitas* and *virtus* and their rigid persona, we have a clear vision, almost the last, of Aeneas' troubled, powerful humanity; and once again we see him, now tragically, checking those feelings, repressing them, against the grain, in the interests of goals and values that are alien to him.

In Aeneas' final apostrophe, which is shared by the dead Pallas and his father, Evander, lyric compression and lamentation for the dark forces that threaten humankind are replaced by a leisured meditation on the chances of war and the complexities of statecraft: what concerns Aeneas chiefly in this speech is his failure to keep to Evander the promise that he made him in exchange for the alliance that he desperately needed, namely, that he would bring Pallas back to him, safe and sound:

'tene,' inquit, miserande puer, cum laeta veniret,
invidit Fortuna mihi, ne regna videres
nostra neque ad sedes victor veherere paternas?
non haec Evandro de te promissa parenti
discedens dederam . . .'

(11.42–6)

"Poor boy, when Fortune came with happiness,
was she so envious as to grudge me this:
not let you live to see my kingdom or
return in triumph to your father's city?
For this was not the promise that I gave
Evander when I left with his embrace . . ."

Although Aeneas speaks these words with tears (*lacrimis ita fatur obortis*, 41),
gone now are the old lamentations, gone the grief for the human being, the
person. Pallas will miss the grandeurs of victory, Evander will be
disappointed in his hopes, and Ascanius will lack a formidable ally when he
grows to manhood and to power (57–8).

This moment in book 11 recalls a more famous and more haunting
image of young soldiers cut down in the first flowering of their glory; it
comes just at the poem's center, at the end of book 6. In answer to Aeneas'
question as to the identity of the young man who accompanies the great
Marcellus, Anchises laments the early death of Augustus' heir apparent and
bewails the fortunes of Rome, now bereft of its best and brightest hope. But
this lament ends with a deeply personal apostrophe in which political
tragedy dissolves into something less exact and more disturbing:

heu, miserande puer, si qua fata aspera rumpas,
tu Marcellus eris. manibus date lilia plenis,
purpureos spargam flores animamque nepotis
his saltem accumulem donis, et fungar inani
munere.

(882–6)

O boy whom we lament, if only you
could break the bounds of fate and be Marcellus.
With full hands, give me lilies; let me scatter
these purple flowers, with these gifts, at least,
be generous to my descendant's spirit,
complete this service, although it be useless.

Munus inane? An empty ritual? This, in a celebration of the golden age
reborn in eternal Rome? The ruined glory is nothing. The ruined life, this

one, all the young ruined lives, here and throughout the poem—that is everything, and also nothing. Here the voice of the poet overwhelms the voice of Anchises, and, towards the close of the *Aeneid*, it overwhelms the entire poem in Vergil's great, final apostrophe:

Quis mihi nunc tot acerba deus, quis carmine caedes
diversas obitumque ducum, quos aequore toto
inque vicem nunc Turnus agit, nunc Troius heros,
expediat? tanton placuit concurrere motu,
Iuppiter, aeterna gentis in pace futuras?

(12.500–504)

What god can now unfold for me in song
all of the bitterness and butchery
and deaths of chieftains—driven now by Turnus,
now by the Trojan hero, each in turn
throughout that field? O Jupiter, was it
your will that nations destined to eternal
peace should have clashed in such tremendous turmoil?

This is, indeed, *aporia* and invocation—but of a most sardonic variety. And the second question is not rhetorical, nor is it a genuine question that the poem anywhere, in any way, answers—not a question, but a cry. The essential Vergilian apostrophe which Aeneas uses up to the time when he views the corpse of Pallas, which Anchises uses, which Vergil himself uses— to prepare us for the closure, for the catastrophe, of his epic—that apostrophe is not sad, gentle, tender; rather, it is informed by a profound concern for, a love of, humanity, and by a passionate anxiety about and hatred for what warps humanity, destroys it. This complex configuration of love, fear, hate, pain, and grief is fierce, tough, implacable; is, at its core, as the final outcry to and against Jupiter shows, compounded of rage and something like despair. So, thwarted at every turn, Aeneas' love becomes anger; and the feelings that hid themselves in muttering or in silence or in heartbroken, heartbreaking cries issue at last in the terrible speech to Turnus. At the end of the poem, his humanity shattered, Aeneas' feelings are archaic, confused, dishonest. He projects onto Turnus the guilt he feels for Pallas' death and for his own betrayal of his dreams, blames Turnus for what Juno has done, can no longer face her nightmare world of nihilism against which he has valiantly struggled throughout the poem. And so he punishes what there is to punish—Turnus and himself. For in killing Turnus he kills himself, and once again, now for the last time, what he says is inadequate to and seeks to hide what he feels; and the person, Aeneas, disappears, with his poem, into the mask of rage, into the frozen persona.

Before we move to Vergil's use of the foil figure, there is one last speech that we should consider. It is in book 12, just after Aeneas' wound has been miraculously cured, just after he has fitted on his divine armor for battle. Aeneas loves his son, Ascanius, as much as he has loved and grieved for all of humankind. This *patrius amor* is clearly manifested in book 1 and in scattered moments throughout the poem, but until now it has been only fleetingly alluded to, not really pictured, not dramatized. Here there is, if not drama, a vivid picture of that love, and this representation of Aeneas' paternal love reveals with unusual clarity not only who Aeneas is (and is becoming), his virtues and their defects, but also the aims and the problems that Vergil had when trying to imagine Aeneas' conflicts and sufferings. Aeneas needs at this moment to tell his son that he loves him, to give him a sense of living, of values and of purpose that will, in case Aeneas should die in battle, sustain him through his growth to manhood and beyond it. This he tries to do. But the words, when they come, are severely restrained, almost embarrassed; are tinged with Stoic moods, perhaps, but are most certainly informed by Roman *gravitas*:

> postquam habilis lateri clipeus loricaque tergo est,
> Ascanium fusis circum complectitur armis
> summaque per galeam delibans oscula fatur:
> disce, puer, virtutem ex me verumque laborem,
> fortunam ex aliis. nunc te mea dextera bello
> defensum dabit et magna inter praemia ducet.
> tu facito, mox cum matura adoleverit aetas,
> sis memor et te animo repetentem exempla tuorum
> et pater Aeneas et avunculus excitet Hector.'
>
> (432–40)

>   Then to his flank
> his shield is fitted; to his back, his corselet;
> and dressed in mail, he hugs Ascanius
> and through his helmet gently kisses him:
> "From me, my son, learn valor and true labor;
> from others learn of fortune. Now my arm
> will win security for you in battle
> and lead you toward a great reward: only
> remember, when your years are ripe, your people's
> example; let your father and your uncle —
> both Hector and Aeneas —urge you on."

Virtus and *verus labor*.[6] Nothing could be more Roman than that, and epic decorum, in this regard, is flawlessly served. But Aeneas is, or rather was, until just recently, more than Roman, more than epical; he was profoundly

human and humane; was, in his generous courage and wide sympathies, a
son of the Graeco-Roman Enlightenment stumbling in a dark world. The
appeal here to *disciplina* and to *mos maiorum*, then, answers the needs of a
Roman foundation epic beautifully at a crucial moment (and this poem,
which is many poems, is a Roman foundation epic); but it fails here,
radically, of the needs of the larger, more complex, more universal, more
ambitious and ambivalent poems that Vergil was writing under and beyond
the Roman poem. The telling detail here lies not in what Aeneas says or fails
to say to Ascanius, but in what he does; *summaque per galeam delibans oscula
fatur:* their lips barely touch because his helmet obstructs the father's
farewell kiss. Until the mention of the *avunculus*, of Hector as an *exemplum* of
virtus, we may not remember that other helmet and that other father's kiss
(*Iliad* 6.466ff.), but with the name of Hector we remember it all—the
father's laughter, Astyanax (again obliquely evoked), and the smile of
Andromache, that most beautiful smile in all of Western literature. We
remember these things, that eternal moment, because Vergil wants us to *feel*
what is, especially at this moment, utterly absent from his poem, because he
requires us to imagine this absence. Again, in his action as always before in
his speech, Aeneas' feelings are checked, his effort to show emotion is
frustrated, by Aeneas himself and by this loveless hellish world: by the
warrior's mask which has become Aeneas' face.

III

In the first part of my discussion, I have suggested that in literature, as
to some extent in life, character is usually revealed by speech and gesture,
by what a character says or does not say about himself, about what he likes
and dislikes. But if identity is most directly revealed by what a character says
or does not say about what he values (call this, perhaps, identity-as-value), it
is also the case, I think, that identity-as-value itself, in literature at any rate,
is most vividly glimpsed (I want to say, sensed, felt—not really understood)
in what a character does: in conflict and crisis, in comparison and contrast,
in what one might call identity-as-difference. This critical principle (or
metaphor) is, of course, familiar enough and obvious enough. Certainly it
has been frequently employed when students of the *Aeneid* have undertaken
the task of describing the character of Aeneas; but many such efforts—I will
not rehearse them here—end by defining Aeneas' goodness or nobility or
piety in terms of Turnus' brutality or arrogance or cowardice or depravity.
To behave in this fashion is not to contrast character but to coddle it on the
one hand and to assassinate it on the other.

To suggest, for example, that Achilles is a monster, as compared with
Hector, a paragon of the patriot and the family man, is to miss the curve of

the complex tragedies that these two mutually illuminating identities-in-difference gradually reveal. The responsibilities of Hector, and what one might call his normal self-esteem and normal aggressions, light up the extraordinary freedom of Achilles, together within his extraordinary temptations and his irresponsible power. Hector's values, his loves, beautifully reflected in the triple threnody at the epic's close (Helen, Hecuba, Andromache), foil the dynamic imbalance and the furious striving for balance in Achilles even as they foil—for Hector is fully brother, father, son and husband—Achilles' radical loneliness, his *Einsamkeit*. Where Hector is totally absorbed into and committed to mortality (birth, procreation, nurture, death) Achilles is driven, both by his peculiar nature and by his strange circumstances, to renounce the solace and the burdens of mortality and to elect the bitter glory of his uniqueness and its immortality. Finally, the anger of Achilles, who is neither quite man nor quite god, is a luxury that Hector, the protector, cannot afford; but Achilles, who is not truly responsible to or for anything—or so he thinks, for a while—who need not care for anything, learns to define, through his terrible guilt and its sufferings, the limits of his fate: he is not fully human but neither is he a god, is something betwixt and between, with a place neither on earth nor in the heavens. Because of this tragic antinomy in his being, because of his massive, intolerable guilt, his dreadful frustrations, his inhuman, inevitable selfishness, he is not only able to accept, finally, his fate but also to tell himself and us something about the misery of greatness, and about anger and discord and limit, that we find nowhere else more subtly or more passionately uttered (*Iliad* 18.107–11):

> O how I wish that discord might perish away from the world of gods and men, and with it anger, which drives even the wisest man to hatred—and it is sweeter than dripping honey, billows like smoke in the hearts of men. So now, Agamemnon, king of men has forced me to fury.

This is not merely self-knowledge, nor does Achilles really become a wiser, better person because he has seen this truth—as no one except a not quite human human could see it—face to face. Achilles comes to, is forced to, see things as they are; then he accepts them and with them, his destiny. What Achilles does and says throughout the poem enables us to believe him as he speaks these somber, unpersuadable words; he is the kind of man, we have come to see, to feel, who might say, might be able to say, such things. But part of our ability to believe him here has its roots in the elaborate contrast that the figure of Hector constantly affords him. Hector mediates between Achilles and us; like Achilles, he is very great, but he has not the supernal grandeurs and miseries of Achilles, and in his more limited chances and choices he is more nearly like us. He could no more come upon and blurt out that raw, dreadful, necessary wisdom than could you or I.

I'm not interested in propounding a law, a structure, of foil-figures,[7] but before I turn to the role of Turnus as Aeneas' foil, I think it might be worthwhile to glance for a moment at Hamlet and his Laertes, since I think that the tension-reflection between them more nearly resembles the contrast between Aeneas and Turnus than does that between Achilles and Hector. For where Homer gives nearly equal space and emphasis throughout the *Iliad* to Achilles and Hector, where Achilles and Hector are almost interdependent in their movement toward their fused yet separate destinies, both Laertes and Turnus are essentially foils, settings in which and against which the characters of Hamlet and Aeneas, respectively, are brilliantly revealed.

At this point I can hardly hide the fact that I have painted myself into a rather disagreeable corner. If, in offering Laertes as a kind of metaphor for how Turnus functions in the *Aeneid*, I undertake to describe how Laertes foils Hamlet, I am of course constrained to say something about the character of Hamlet. This, naturally, I am loathe to do. Permit me—in the interests of brevity and of prudence—to say that, essentially, Hamlet is crazy. Not in the way that his fellow characters think him crazy, not quite in the way that he may suspect himself of being crazy. With your extreme indulgence, then, he is a crazy intellectual who makes a mess of everything he lays a hand to.

What is Laertes, then? He is a nice young fraternity boy who loves his father and sister and who likes having a good time. On learning that his father has been murdered, he wants to kill his father's killer. Then, on learning that his sister—crazed by her father's death and, as Laertes thinks, abandoned by her seducer—has gone mad, he wants to kill her seducer, who happens also to be his father's killer. I fail to see anything remarkable or objectionable in his responses or in his behavior. He is a normal, healthy male (or, if you like, human being). He is, to be sure, headstrong, and he has a silly father and happens to live in a rather peculiar time and place. But he is a fairly sane, rather decent, pretty average young man. That such a person collides with Hamlet is unfortunate, but that is the way that Shakespeare's imagination and reality work.

What do these two have in common, and how does Laertes foil Hamlet? They both want revenge. Or rather, Laertes both needs and wants revenge, Hamlet only needs it. To put it crudely, when Laertes goes off to college he majors in wine, women and song; and minors in fencing, at which he is really good. Hamlet, however, for reasons that are neither supplied nor necessary, hits the books when he gets to Wittenburg; he becomes, while the folks back home are downing their wassails, civilized, refined, interested in the theory of language. Language and life become problematic for him; and they become superproblematic when the need for revenge is suddenly thrust upon him. Hamlet tumbles in his mind the problems and possibilities of appearance and reality, doubts everything, including, apparently, doubt. Laertes is so incapable of doubt that—and here perhaps he is naughty—he descends to poison. Hamlet is a creature of inwardness on whom the chores of revenge ought never to have been inflicted; Laertes is an extravert of the intuitive type who sees True and False in neon lights, and, as the world goes, he sees things pretty clearly (but not, as it turns out, quite clearly enough). He shoulders revenge readily and rightly and is thereby destroyed.

Nowhere perhaps in poetry is the anguish of inwardness and isolation better imagined, recreated in plausible yet ideal forms, than it is in Hamlet's great soliloquies. But our sense of this inwardness, of its crystalline shape, of its precise intuitions of the alien, outer world, gains most of its clarity from the careful contrast which the figure of Laertes proffers it. The disbelief of Hamlet, his radical withdrawal from a world in which he must but cannot act, takes hold of us in proportion as we become persuaded of, as we feel, Laertes' belief in himself and in the world, as we witness and admire the extraordinary zest of his loves and hates, the unequivocal, unreflecting quality of his desire to greet life, embrace it.

What of Turnus? For our immediate purposes, it is perhaps enough to say that he resembles Laertes both in his youthful vigor and in his uncomplicated trust in his powers and perceptions. He has, it is true, been incited to challenge Aeneas by the fury from hell that Juno sets upon him, but there is no question, I think, of his sanity, or of the purity, indeed of the justice, of his motives. He sees Aeneas—how could it be otherwise?—as a ruthless interloper come to conquer Latium and to steal away his betrothed. It is hardly impious in him to disallow the validity of oracles that proclaim the divine, fateful sanctions for Aeneas' presence in Italy: oracles are, in the ancient as in the modern world, notoriously ambiguous when they are not simply wrong or misunderstood at best or, at worst, purchased fabrications. His challenge to Drances, moreover, whom he rightly regards as an envious, loathesome Quisling, is nothing if not admirable. If there is more than a touch of arrogance in his words to the dying Pallas, that arrogance is not unmatched in the speeches of Aeneas to those whom he kills in book 10. His loves are not selfless, but what human love can be wholly selfless? Turnus is, in short, to my mind an attractive figure (allowing for the conventions of war and the poetry of war), whose gallantry is matched by his guilelessness. Like Laertes, he trusts life and himself; in Isak Dinesen's great phrase, he is a proud man "in love with his destiny"[8]—that is, of course, a romantic utterance, but it is very far from being romantic hogwash. That his perceptions of right and wrong turn out to be inadequate and even ruinous (to himself, to Latium), that the world he trusts is by no means as simple as he believes it to be—these things are nothing against him. When he claims to be *sancta . . . anima atque istius inscia culpae* (12.648), a spirit vowed to heroic death, innocent of the crime of cowardice, he is hardly boasting and he is not far from the truth. The near purity of will that leads him into jeopardy, that makes him at once Juno's final pawn and Aeneas' final victim, also makes him, no less than Dido, who had also trusted Juno and was betrayed by her, a tragic sacrifice to the nightmare of historical determinism.

How does he foil Aeneas? Again, we see the introvert's inwardness and isolation against a contrasting extraversion and singleness of will. Turnus both needs and wants Latium and Lavinia, Aeneas only needs them: because his destiny requires this of Aeneas (and it is a destiny he does not love), because his experience of life, his tragic experience of life, has confirmed his intuitions of desolation and has divested him of desire (he is not, that is to say, a Stoic saint who deliberately and systematically denudes himself of his natural emotions and his natural humanity). *Verus labor*: his life becomes, by the time he leaves Carthage and arrives in Italy, pure toil, in John Passmore's splendid formulation, "care without enjoyment,"[9] almost without love and without hope (though there is always, but very unemphatically, the figure of Ascanius which we have already pondered). His heart becomes radically divided between its initial, essential instinct for compassion and peace and the ruthless, snarled mechanism of World Destiny whose instrument he imperceptibly, almost unconsciously becomes. To imagine, to recreate this extreme inwardness and sensitivity and, simultaneously, the public persona into which it is slowly absorbed was no easy task, and for its execution the usual stratagems of realistic narrative were all but useless. We have seen that Vergil, in the first half of his poem, where sensitivity is of the essence, had rendered inwardness and its intensities through silence or through failed and broken speech or through *cris de coeur*. In the second half of the poem, from the first appearance of Turnus, Aeneas, the dogged, middle-aged, weary warrior, is contrasted with the vigorous and vocal young man. It is in book 12 that this contrast is, naturally, most extensive and most powerful. There the figure of Aeneas enters the poem rarely; the angle of vision shifts, as it had in book 4, from the hero to Juno's victim. What we watch in book 12, steadily, is the disintegration of Turnus. As Turnus tries to summon all his courage; as he becomes, magnificently, in his great speeches to Juturna (632–19, 676–80), thoroughly aware of himself, watching himself move to his doom; as he talks about this, acts against it, submits to it; we see dimly yet feel vividly another picture, another disintegration that takes shape beneath the figure of Turnus in its frightening decomposition. We see the figure of Aeneas, the gentle, suffering introvert, now himself dispossessed of self, ferocious, frozen in his iron mask. Each the other's destiny, each the other's doom. The death of Dido signals the first death of Aeneas, that of the "merely personal," the human being; the death of Turnus signals Aeneas' second death, that of his humanity: what remains, terrible, unintelligible, rendered only by the strictest apophatic decorum, is the dead persona, the servant of Roman History and its manifest destiny. *Corruptio optimi pessima.*

IV

Sum pius Aeneas. Looked at from the perspectives I've been trying to fashion, the phrase seems not arrogant or absurd, but poignant, baffled, naive, and utterly convincing. Aeneas is not at home in his skin, cannot communicate, either to himself or to others, the powerful feelings, the rich intuitions of good and bad, the desire to solace and to save, that crowd his mind and his heart. In that same speech to Venus he had described himself as *ignotus* and *egens*, meaning thereby "unknown" and "destitute" in the wilds of Libya. But, in fact, he *is ignotus* and *egens*, here and throughout the poem. He is *profugus* as well, the very first epithet given him in the poem's invocation; and even after arriving in Italy he remains *profugus*—a man driven, a suppliant, having no home. He is the wanderer, the outcast, the supreme imagination of *Einsamkeit* in classical literature.[10] (For Achilles *is* redeemed, not by the lying dialectic of History, but by the grace of Zeus and the kiss of Priam.)

Aeneas haunts the imagination of the West, not merely because his sufferings and his sacrifices, his dreadful self-sacrifice, helped to shape, or until recently helped to shape, our sensibilities, but also because he is, this quintessential founding father, as unintelligible to himself as he is to us; because he is an elliptical, obscure inwardness whose griefs and loves and humanity—and their fragility—only the shaping of silence and the tragic figures of Dido and Turnus can indirectly yet unforgettably reveal:

> infert se saeptus nebula (mirabile dictu)
> per medios, miscetque viris neque cernitur ulli.
>
> (1.439-40)

> Then, sheltered by a mist, astoundingly,
> he enters in among the crowd, mingling
> together with the Tyrians. No one sees him.

Notes

1. For statistical (and other) descriptions of Aeneas' speeches, see Gilbert Highet, *The Speeches in Vergil's Aeneid* (Princeton: Princeton University Press, 1972) pp. 25, 29–43.
2. All translations in this paper, except from the *Aeneid*, for which I use the Mandelbaum translation, are my own.
3. C.G. Jung, *The Collected Works*, Bollingen Series 20, vol. 6: *Psychological Types*, (Princeton: Princeton University Press, 1971), pp. 387–91.
4. W.R. Johnson, *Darkness Visible* (Berkeley: University of California Press, 1976), pp. 149–54.
5. See the eloquent attack by Sir Karl Popper, *The Open Society and its Enemies* (Princeton: Princeton University Press, 4th ed., 1963), *passim* and especially vol. 2, pp. 60–80. See also C.S. Lewis, *The Discarded Image* (Cambridge: Cambridge University Press, 1964), pp. 174–7.
6. For precise and imaginative comments on *virtus* and other Roman virtues, see Montesquieu's *Considerations on the Causes of the Greatness of the Romans and their Decline*, trans. David Lowenthal (Ithaca: Cornell University Press, 1968), *passim* and especially pp. 16, 34–6, 44–5, 170. The book is nowadays somewhat neglected, but no student of Vergil or Rome should ignore it.
7. That is to say, I make no effort to contribute to a "systematic poetics." For the phrase and the notion, see Jonathan Culler, "Beyond Interpretation: The Prospects of Contemporary Criticism," *CL* 28 (1976): 244–56 (reprinted, in a revised version, in his *The Pursuit of Signs* [Ithaca: Cornell University Press, 1983], pp. 3–17). How gross misreadings of scientific method nourish this unfortunate delusion are explained with the greatest clarity and vigor by Sir Isaiah Berlin in his essay, "The Concept of Scientific History," in *Concepts and Categories: Philosophical Essays*, ed. Henry Hardy (New York: Penguin Books, 1978), pp. 103–42.
8. *Out of Africa* (New York: Random House, 1937), p. 261.
9. *The Perfectability of Man* (New York: Charles Scribner's Sons, 1970), pp. 295–303, 306–25; see also Passmore's *Man's Responsibility for Nature* (New York: Charles Scribner's Sons, 1974), pp. 88, 90, 93n., 126.
10. This aspect of Aeneas is beautifully evoked by Christa Wolf in her *Cassandra*, trans. Jan van Heurck (New York: Farrar, Strauss and Giroux, 1983.) See in particular the closing page of the novella, "Soon, very soon, you will have to become a hero," p. 138.

THE ALLEGORICAL TRADITIONS
OF THE *AENEID*

J. W. Jones, Jr.

When Vergil's contemporary Propertius proclaimed (*Elegies* 2.34.66) that something greater than the *Iliad* was being produced, he became the first recorded critic of the *Aeneid*. Since his time there have been hundreds of others. Succeeding generations have added, sometimes copiously, to the mass of Vergilian exegesis, so that today the serious student labors against a mountain. We shall not be so presumptuous as to attempt to discuss the various forms of interpretation, but shall focus on one type—the allegorical. Even here we are faced with complexity, for there are not one, but two, allegorical traditions of the *Aeneid*: the Classical and the Medieval. The Classical is represented, in its ripest form, by the fourth-century *Commentary* of Servius. The Medieval culminates in the twelfth-century commentary commonly attributed to Bernardus Silvestris of Tours. In this study we shall, so to speak, set these two traditions side by side, so that the reader may perceive their basic forms. We shall describe and summarize the interpretations, suggest how they originated or what inspired them, and try to separate out those explanations which, we believe, are truly perceptive and apt.

What follows is meant to be a small contribution to the history of the allegorizing of the *Aeneid*. To date, there has been written no single book which comprehensively surveys this subject, indicating both continuing trends and new developments. In fact, even now such a book cannot be written. The editing and publication of a number of primary Latin texts must come first.[1] Current literary taste hardly favors the allegorical treatment of classical authors and the present writer does not wish to be regarded as a proponent or defender of such exegesis. However, we do wish to argue that the various allegorical interpretations of the *Aeneid* are worthy of close scrutiny and dispassionate analysis. They constitute an important aspect of Vergil's *fortleben*, and they have a rightful place in the history of literary thought.

I. The Classical Tradition

The great commentary of Servius contains thousands of notes and runs to more than thirteen hundred printed pages in the edition of Thilo and Hagen (Leipzig, 1884). The work is obviously a repository of the explanations of many schoolmasters and other scholars from Vergil's time to late antiquity. Sometimes, Servius simply explains Vergil's meaning; sometimes he notes a peculiar grammatical point; sometimes he gives an etymology or explains a proper name; sometimes he identifies a source; sometimes his comment treats a mythological or historical or antiquarian point. No perceptive person, having examined Servius, would categorize his commentary as allegorical. However, scattered here and there are approximately one hundred eighty-five notes of the allegorical type. These notes constitute a highly significant part of the exegesis, for if we accept their assertions, our understanding of the *Aeneid* will be profoundly affected. Not unexpectedly, we find in Servius examples of all the forms of *allegoresis* evolved by the Greeks and Romans; we also find some allegorical notes that are unique.[2]

Vergil's *Eclogues* must have prepared ancient readers to look for covert allusions to historical persons and events in the poet's other works. That Vergil intends such allusions at times in the *Aeneid* is incontrovertible. Servius discovers them in more than fifty places. Vergil, he contends (*ad Aen.* 1.382), touches history in passing (*per transitum*) because, by the laws of the poetic art, he cannot treat it openly. Some of Servius' historical explanations seem quite apt and have definite value for us. King Priam is slain in his palace by Pyrrhus; yet Vergil speaks of his huge body as lying on the shore. Servius (*ad Aen.* 2.557) rightly suggests that Vergil wishes to call to mind the fate of Pompey the Great, who was slain on the Egyptian shore. King Latinus' house at Laurolavinium is styled *augustum* (venerable) by Vergil (*Aen.* 7.170). This epithet does not appear elsewhere in the *Aeneid* other than as the title of the emperor, and Servius plausibly concludes that Vergil wishes to bring to mind Augustus' house on the Palatine. Lastly, in *Aeneid* 8 (184–369) Hercules, driving the cattle of Geryon upon his return from one of his labors, stops in Italy and kills the fire-breathing monster Cacus. Vergil speaks of the *victor Alcides* (lines 362–3), who comes up to the palace of Evander and is received there. Servius believes that Vergil designates Hercules as *victor* here because he wishes to allude to a temple in Rome, built by Augustus, in which the hero was worshipped under this title. Servius' comment, again, is quite appropriate. Various details throughout the passage in question show that Vergil consciously intends to draw analogies between Augustus and Hercules.[3]

The figure in the *Aeneid*, of course, with whom we expect Servius to associate Augustus is the protagonist Aeneas himself. Servius does not outrightly identify the two anywhere, but he makes comparisons in a number of places. He does not debate whether Aeneas may be a model for Augustus or whether, on the other hand, Augustus may be a model for Aeneas, but his comments suggest that he takes the latter view.[4] Thus, the games which Aeneas holds at Actium are connected by Servius (*ad Aen.* 3.274, 276, 280) with those held there by Augustus after his victory over Antony and Cleopatra; the temple of Apollo in which Aeneas hangs the shield of Abas is identified with the one built in the same vicinity by Augustus; the small city that Aeneas and his band approach on first landing on the Actian promontory is declared to be Ambracia, rebuilt by Augustus after his victory at Nicopolis. In order to honor Augustus, says Servius (*ad Aen.* 3.274), Vergil attributes to his legendary ancestor things which the first emperor actually did. Presumably, in this manner these imperial acts may be incorporated into a story set in the Heroic Age.[5]

Surveying all the allegorical notes of the historical type, we may wish to berate Servius on two counts. First, some of these notes will surely seem bizarre and far-fetched. There is a recognizable tendency, for instance, to find a preternatural significance in numbers. Dido, dying, rolls over on her couch three times, thus presaging the three Punic Wars (*ad Aen.* 4.691); Mezentius' breastplate is dented and pierced in twelve places as a sign that the Etruscans were divided into twelve tribes (*ad Aen.* 11.9–10). Secondly, appropriate interpretations that might be offered are not. Historical comment is sporadic, and in no episode is there a well-elaborated allegorical interpretation that proceeds point by point. Servius recognizes a parallelism (*ad Aen.* 5.45) between the games given by Aeneas in honor of Anchises and those given in honor of Julius Caesar by Augustus in July, 44 B.C. However, he does not spell out the details of this parallelism.[6] Though highly conscious of supposed allusions to Caesar's star (cf. *ad Aen.* 1.287, 3.158, and 6.790), he passes over the most obvious explanation of Acestes' flaming arrow (*ad Aen.* 5.524). None of the allegorical possiblilities for the characters of Dido and Aeneas in *Aeneid* 4 are recognized.[7]

Many of Servius' allegorical notes derive from philosophic sources.[8] Greek philosophy early found it desirable, by the device of allegory, to equate the gods and goddesses of traditional religion with physical forces or natural phenomena or to discover in them and in the stories about them moral ideas or truths. An extension of the latter tendency led, more broadly, to the ascription of moral significance to human actions and situations not ostensibly ethical. In Servius, somewhat more than fifty notes illustrate the physical interpretation, while approximately twenty-two are examples of moral allegorism.

Servius assumes that Vergil has a *physica ratio* (a physical system or conception) which he leaves and to which he returns (cf. *ad Aen.* 1.78), so that in the *Aeneid* the gods are to be construed sometimes as anthropomorphic beings, sometimes as natural phenomena. The philosophic explanation of such a dual portrayal is that the gods, though incorporeal, may take to themselves human bodies if they wish to appear to mortals (*ad Aen.* 7.416).

At *Aeneid* 10.18, Jupiter is declared to be truly the ruler of the gods because he is the *aether*, or fiery upper air, which enjoys the chief place among the elements. The fire which burns continuously in the temple of Jupiter Ammon is said (*ad Aen.* 4.201) to be an image of Jupiter, the ethereal fire. An everglowing flame is to be found also in the temple of Minerva since she, too, is an ethereal power. As a matter of fact, she resides above the *aether*, and this is why she is thought to have sprung from Jupiter's head.

Juno is frequently presented by Servius as *aër*, the lower air. Not without reason, says the commentator (*ad Aen.* 1.71), does Vergil portray the queen of the gods as having the nymphs in her power, for she herself is *aër* from which clouds are created and from the clouds come the waters which are the nymphs. She promises a nymph to Aeolus (*Aen.* 1.71ff) because he is king of the winds which are created by the movement of the water. At *Aeneid* 1.47, Vergil calls Juno both the sister and wife of Jupiter. Juno, the commentator notes (*ad loc.*), may be said to be the sister of Jupiter because the elements *aër* and *aether* are both tenuous. She may likewise be considered the wife of Jupiter because the *aër* is located beneath (is subject to) the *aether*. Jupiter's name, understood as derived from *juvare* (to help), is very appropriate since nothing "helps" a person so much as heat from the *aether*.

Other divinities that figure in Servius' *physica ratio* are Janus (as air or as the entire universe),[9] Iris (as a watery cloud inflamed by the sun's rays), Venus (as sexual power or energy), Vulcan (as lightning), Neptune (as the sea and moisture in general), Vesta (as earth, the container of fire), Proserpina (as earth), Cybele (also as earth), and Ceres (as earth, consumer of dead bodies). Cerberus, the Hound of Hades, is rationalized in the same way as Ceres (cf. *ad Aen.* 8.297).

The sensitive modern reader will likely be repulsed and revolted by Servius' physical interpretations. They seem in the main to be an inappropriate display of philosophic lore. In effect, they reverse the usual poetic process in places by "depersonifying" natural forces. We shall, however, in fairness ask to what extent the Vergilian contexts seem to invite or provoke such interpretations. Servius attributes a number of his comments to the *physici* (*ad Aen.* 10.18, *ad Aen.* 5.801), and we know that this is a name by which Stoic philosophers were known in Servius' day.[10] A likely Latin source for Servius would be Varro, who in his *Libri divinarum rerum* introduced the chief gods of the Roman state according to the allegorical principles of Stoic philosophy.[11] Vergil, himself a student of philosophy, would surely have heard of Stoic physical interpretation and would probably have glanced at Varro's work (published 47 B.C.). We would not expect him as a poet to be subservient to the Stoic *physica ratio*, but we might expect him to be influenced by it. It has long been recognized that Vergil, much more than Homer, tends to associate gods and goddesses with natural realms and to confine them to these realms. Vergil's descriptions are often brilliantly ambiguous, so that divinities and natural elements are skillfully confused or blended. This is notably so in the storm scene in *Aeneid* 1 and in the description of the "marriage" of Dido and Aeneas in *Aeneid* 4. Atlas (4.246–51) is at once god and mountain. A clear sky is at the same time the serene face of Jupiter (1.255). Aurora is both the dawn's early light and a goddess leaving the bed of Tithonus (4.584–5). Pandarus hurls his spear at Turnus, but "the breezes catch it and Juno [the *aër*?] turns it aside" (9.745). In at least one place Vergil may be consciously using the philosophic *physica ratio*. Aeolus, in *Aeneid* 1, informs us that Juno grants to him whatever kingdom he possesses (1.78). No known ancient myth explains this situation. Perhaps we can do no better than accept Servius' explanation (*ad Aen.* 1.71, summarized above) that Juno as *aër* "is ultimately the source of the winds Aeolus rules."

Most of the moralizing allegorical interpretations given by Servius are concentrated in book 6. While one might expect to discover more of these interpretations in other books, it is not surprising that there is such a large number here. We cannot imagine any theme in literature that would be a better inspiration for moralizing comments than the theme of a journey to the nether world. Furthermore, Servius is convinced that of all the books of the *Aeneid* book 6 is richest in those "deeper meanings" one might term allegorical. In his preface the commentator declares:

> All of Vergil is full of knowledge, but in knowledge this book holds first place. The greater part of it is from Homer. Some things are said plainly, but many things are drawn from history and many things are said with reference to the deep science of the philosophers, theologians, and Egyptians, so that many have written whole treatises on the individual facets of this book.[12]

The conception of the universe which Servius finds in book 6, in effect, defines the whole underworld scene as an extended moral allegory and asserts as a corollary that Vergil is simply using the traditional representations of Tartarus and of the underworld in general as poetic forms to clothe profound moral truths. The universe of book 6, says Servius (*ad Aen.* 6.127), should be understood as geocentric. Surrounding the earth are nine concentric circles (or spheres). The seven closest to the earth are the orbits of the planets—which are the Moon, Mercury, Venus, the Sun, Mars, Jupiter, and Saturn. The two outermost spheres are known as the great circles. Considered from any point outside such a universe, the earth is *infima* (lowest). Earth and the place of the *inferi* (i.e., the inhabitants of the infernal region) are therefore the same, and Tartarus is a poetic fiction. The nine circles girdling the earth are symbolized by Vergil in the nine circuits of the Styx. The spirits of the *inferi* of which Vergil offers a description in book 6 in reality are to be found in their proper places in these circles. When Vergil says that the descent to Avernus is easy and the door of grim Pluto lies open night and day, but the return to the upper air is difficult, he may be referring to the philosophic tenet that the souls of those who live well return to the upper circles which are their origin, while the souls of those who live badly are compelled to linger for a longer time in the body on earth.

From this conception there follows, quite expectedly, Servius' interpretation of the fabled punishments of Tartarus and of the golden bough. The punishments of Tityos, the Lapiths, Ixion, Pirithous, and others, as described in book 6, symbolize earthly situations, as the poet Lucretius maintained (*De rer. Nat.* 3.980–1023). Tityos is said to be spread out over nine acres because he was a lover and lust is rampant far and wide. The Weeping Fields spread out in all directions because the number of those in whom lust dominates is always the greater (*ad Aen.* 6.596, 6.440). The golden bough, Aeneas' passport to the netherworld, is compared with the symbol of the letter "Y." Pythagoras, says Servius (*ad Aen.* 6.136), used this letter as a sort of diagram of human life, which at the earliest age is given over to neither vice nor virtue but beginning with adolescence follows either the path of vice on the left or the one of virtue on the right. The bough is concealed in the forests just as in this life integrity and virtue are concealed by confusion and vice. Some would say that the *inferi* are sought by a bough of gold because mortals are easily corrupted by riches.

We must not leave book 6 without seeking further to explain Servius' comment. We must try to account for the interpretation which he makes at line 127 since Vergil's words do not invite it.[13] The germ of Servius' interpretation would seem to be the multiplicative *novies* (nine times) found later in book 6 at line 439. Servius again responds to a "magic" number.

Assisted by this number, he is able to foist upon Vergil a cosmology of nine circles and spheres—a cosmology which will strike the knowledgeable reader as strongly Neoplatonic. We may speculate that the Servian interpretation of *Aeneid* 6 is a bow to the *Zeitgeist*. In the fourth century Neoplatonic doctrine was employed by pagan writers as a countervail to Christianity, and Servius clearly belongs in this company as his presence as an interlocutor in the *Saturnalia* of the Neoplatonist Macrobius shows.[14]

Outside the commentary on book 6, there are found in Servius only eight notes which may be discussed under the heading of moral allegorism. Most of these tend to fall into the class of philosophic generalization rather than strict moralistic interpretation. Some may reflect the commentator's personal view of some facet of human nature. For example, Vergil, says Servius (*ad Aen.* 1.57), assuages the spirits of the winds (*mollitque animos*) in order to show that the vices of nature can be mitigated somewhat, but not changed. The fact that Venus, addressing Aeneas in the guise of a huntress, expresses momentary doubt in the augural art taught her by her parents (*Aen.* 1.392) is construed by many as a reference to those parents who by excess of tender affection teach their children things superfluous. The Fury Allecto hurls a serpent into the bosom of queen Amata, showing that in women venom always thrives (*ad Aen.* 7.456).

As we have seen, Servius sometimes rationalizes divinities as physical forces. Ancient exegetes also at times rationalized gods as deified heroes. To this practice—and to the practice of explaining any mythical story on a historical basis—is given the name euhemerism, a term derived from the name of Euhemerus, a Greek of the third century B.C.[15]

Servius is an eager euhemerizer, who resorts to this method of explanation on forty-one different occasions. Sometimes he is quite thoroughgoing as when, for example, he offers three euhemeristic interpretations in close succession (*Aen.* 6.287, 288, and 289). In his view, the mythical stories are often fabrications contrived by the poets and others (cf. *ad Aen.* 1.52, *ad Aen.* 5.824). By recognizing their euhemeristic nature, one may occasionally penetrate the shield of poetic and popular fancy and arrive at the germ of truth underlying the particular myth under consideration.[16]

Servian euhemerism concentrates on mythical monsters and other superhuman creatures, not upon divinities. However, in the notes on *Aeneid* 8.319 and *Aeneid* 9.561 is found the commentator's version of the "original" euhemerism. When Vergil writes that Saturn (Cronus in the Greek version), expelled by Jupiter (Zeus), came down from airy Olympus to Italy, he is, says Servius, expressing himself poetically. In reality Saturn was a king of Crete who was forcibly driven out by his son Jupiter. Fleeing his island, he came to Italy and was received by king Janus, who had a city on the site of the Janiculum hill. After teaching Janus the culture of the vine and the use of the sickle and after introducing him to a more civilized diet, he was admitted into a share of the rule and built for himself a town at the foot of the Capitoline Hill. Later, he resought his own kingdom. Thus, Servius explains in a euhemeristic story the role of Saturn in Italy and his connection with the founding of Rome.

Every familiar mythic cycle seems to be affected by Servius' euhemeristic interpretation. Homeric monsters or superhuman beings mentioned by Vergil are thus explained. Scylla was really a rock which to those gazing from a distance seemed to possess the well-known form described by Vergil (*Aen.* 3.426–8). The notion that dogs and wolves grew from the body of the mythical creature was due to the fact that the places where she was said to live were full of marine monsters and the roughness of the sea sounded like the barking of dogs (*ad Aen.* 3.420). The Cyclops Polyphemus was in actuality a very wise man, and because through his prudence he saw more than the normal person, he was said to have an eye in the center of his head near the brain. Ulysses surpassed him in prudence and therefore was reported to have blinded him (*ad Aen.* 3.636). The Sirens were actually prostitutes. Leading wayfarers to the point of poverty, they gave rise to the story that they were the cause of shipwreck (*ad Aen.* 5.864). Circe was believed to be the daughter of the sun because she was a very "brilliant" courtesan and nothing is more brilliant than the sun. By her lustful nature and her blandishments, she turned men to a more savage, beast-like existence and hence occasioned the story that she could turn human beings into animals (*ad Aen.* 7.19).

Euhemeristic explanations are supplied for stories centering on the hero Hercules. Hercules was in reality a philosopher and for this reason was said to have conquered certain monsters. It was believed that he received the sky from Atlas and supported it for a time on account of the knowledge of astronomy which he transmitted (*ad Aen.* 1.741). The Hydra should be understood as a place which poured forth water and laid waste the neighboring state. Whenever one stream of water was dammed up, many others burst forth. Hercules burned the area around this place and thus stopped the flow of water (*ad Aen.* 6.287). Geryon was a king of Spain, commonly believed to have three bodies because he ruled over three islands (*ad Aen.* 7.662). Cacus was not really a son of Vulcan who spewed forth fire and smoke from his mouth and thereby devastated everything around himself. As historians and philologists know, he was a very base servant of Evander and a thief who set fire to citizens' fields. The name Cacus is an obvious index of his character (*ad Aen.* 8.190).[17]

One lengthy note (*ad Aen.* 6.14) offers euhemeristic interpretations for several Minoan-Cretan myths. If truth is considered, says Servius, the monster known as the Minotaur never existed. Taurus was a palace secretary whom Pasiphae loved and with whom she had adulterous relations. In time she gave birth to twins, one sired by Minos and one by Taurus. The name applied to the mixed offsping was *Minotaurus*. Daedalus escaped from Crete, not by wings attached to his body, but by the wings of his ship, i.e. its sails.

For Servius euhemerism seems to be almost a habitual mode of thought. That Vergil himself shares the commentator's disbelief in mythological representation is now widely supposed. As J. Wight Duff observes, Vergil at times turns critically upon his own account with a saving clause like *si credere dignum est* ("if it is worth believing") at *Aeneid* 6.173 or with a question like *tantaene animis caelestibus irae* ("Is there such great anger in celestial minds?") at *Aeneid* 1.11.[18] And Servius points out that Vergil likes to use such expressions as *ut fama est* or *fama est* to excuse or apologize for a mythical story.[19] Furthermore, Vergil himself definitely suggests euhemeristic meanings for the figures Faunus, Janus, and Saturn. These gods appear in his account as members of a dynasty of early Latin kings (cf. *Aeneid* 7.48 and 7.177-82). Nevertheless, sophisticated and urbane as our poet may be, he carefully measures his overt rationalizing. He makes no effort, for example, to rationalize the tale of Cacus (*Aen.* 8.184-279) even though the name is the most obvious invitation to do so. Vergil knows, as Servius does not, that the habit of detached analysis may spoil a good story by constantly breaking the dramatic illusion. We may marvel at the cleverness and ingenuity of Servius' euhemerisms, but surely we shall wish to have little recourse to them as we read Vergil's epic.

The forms of allegorism thus far discussed—the historical, the physical, the moral, and the euhemeristic—are all traditional, with well-known antecedents in antiquity. A fifth type is something new and something quite bizarre. It is based upon Roman religious ritual and is represented by approximately twenty notes. Most of these notes have to do with the ritual of the flamens, who were special priests attached to particular divinities to attend to sacrifices and burnt offerings.

A notable concentration of religious notes occurs in the commentary on *Aeneid* 4, and we shall confine our discussion to these. In this book Aeneas and Dido are said to represent a flamen and a flamen's wife, or flaminica, respectively. Vergil, asserts the commentator (*ad Aen.* 4.103), by having Juno propose a marriage in which Dido will be "subservient to a Phrygian husband" alludes to the ceremony known as *coemptio* as a result of which the bride passed into the power of her husband in the capacity of a free slave. Juno's promise to grant the Tyrians as a dowry to the "right hand" of Venus is a reference to the rite of *conventio in manum*, which was a part of the *confarreatio*, the marriage ceremony ordained for a flamen and flaminica. Dido, Servius maintains (*ad Aen.* 4.29), should have remained true to the dead Sychaeus because it was not permissible for a flaminica to remarry. A flamen could marry again if his first wife had died. Accordingly Aeneas, in wedding Lavinia, was guilty of no sinful act since Dido was no longer alive.

The garb Dido wears as she goes forth to the hunt is said to typify that of the flaminica. The flaminica, it is explained (*ad Aen.* 4.137), was required by ceremonial regulations to be covered with a dyed garment. Thus, Dido wears a Sidonian (i.e., purple) mantle. When Mercury flies down to Carthage with a message from Jupiter, he finds Aeneas dressed in a purple garment called a *laena* and wearing a sword studded with yellow jasper. In these particulars, notes Servius (*ad Aen.* 4.262), Vergil subtly alludes to pontifical rite. The flight of Mercury and the poet's comparison of him to a bird represent the augural ceremony by which the flamen was installed. The *laena* was a tunic of double thickness which the flaminica wove for her husband after his installation. Aeneas' elegant sword corresponds well with the long knife used by the flamens for sacrificial purposes. When Aeneas tells Dido that he has not proffered to her the torches of marriage, his meaning is that he and the Carthaginian queen have not been joined by the ceremony of *confarreatio* as would be proper for a flamen and flaminica.[20] The marriage torches he mentions represent the fire which was a necessary element in the confarreate marriage (*ad Aen.* 4.339). In complaining that in her madness she "placed" (established) Aeneas in a part of her kingdom, Dido has in mind the fact that during the confarreate marriage ceremony, the flamen and flaminica were "placed" side-by-side in two chairs joined together by the skin of the sheep that had been the sacrificial victim (*ad Aen.* 4.374). While addressing the gods in the course of the magic rites which she executes just before her death, the rejected queen has one foot bare and her garments ungirdled. This is quite proper since the flaminica was not permitted to have shoes or any type of sandal made from the skin of an animal that had died of itself, nor was she allowed to gird herself above the knee (*ad Aen.* 4.518).

Some might wish to suggest that these comments are examples of defensive allegorism. In book 4 Aeneas is reprehensible from the Roman point of view since he forgets his mission and dallies with Dido. Furthermore, Servius believes (*ad Aen.* 4.1) that the style of this book is, incongruously, almost comic (*paene comicus*) since it turns wholly on machinations and subtleties and the theme is love. Religious allegorism imparts a seriousness to the narrative and turns Aeneas and Dido into a dignified flamen and flaminica. Nevertheless, Servius' comments do not reflect a wish to explain away nor to disparage the literal account. We cannot detect in his words a defensive position.

Perhaps Servius' religious notes are, like his moralizing comments on *Aeneid* 6, a reflection of the spirit of the times in which he lived. In the fourth century the pagan reaction to Christianity took two different forms. On the one hand, there was a recourse to something new—Neoplatonism; on the other, a return to something old—Roman rite and ritual.[21] The Servian commentary, with its vast mixture of notes, may illustrate both tactics. We should add that the authority of Vergil on matters religious was well established by the fourth century. In the *Saturnalia* (1.24.16), Macrobius has the interlocutor Vettius say:

> Among all the subjects in which the glory of Maro shines bright, I, surely, his constant reader, admire this—that in many diverse parts of his work he has very learnedly preserved pontifical law just as if he had followed this profession, and if this conversation were not unequal to so great a disquisition, I promise that our Vergil would be declared the greatest of pontiffs.[22]

One Servian note is in a class by itself and deserves separate treatment. At the end of his commentary on *Aeneid* 3, Servius declares:

> It is to be noted that in the manner of controversies Vergil gave epilogues to these first six books, which he also wished to be mirrors of life. For he gave individual themes to the individual books. Thus, the theme of the first book is prophecies; of the second, suffering; of the third, wanderings; of the fourth, character; of the fifth, festivity; and of the sixth, knowledge.[23]

Servius does not pursue at all the assertions of this note. As a matter of fact, no ancient commentator known to us, following the lines suggested by this note or employing some other principle, wrote a treatise which, in effect, generalized or universalized the meaning of the *Aeneid*. As we shall see, it remained for the exegetes of the Middle Ages to do this.

II. The Medieval Tradition

The commentary attributed to Bernardus Silvestris of Tours (fl. ca. 1150) is quite different from the Servian. It is much briefer, extending in the latest printed edition to a mere one hundred fourteen pages.[24] The reason is readily apparent: this commentary pursues resolutely just one line of interpretation, the allegorical. So single-minded is it that if we meet an occasional grammatical or antiquarian note in one of the manuscripts, we may as a rule exclude it as a spurious intrusion. As is well known, allegory was the prevailing interpretive mode of the European Middle Ages. Bernardus' *Commentum* is thus a typical piece of Medieval literary exposition and analysis. It is the only allegorical commentary on the *Aeneid* to survive from this period.

How popular was this work in its time? The manuscript tradition is not rich, comparatively speaking, and this would tend to indicate a limited appeal.[25] However, the four manuscripts that survive (and two others that do not) show that the commentary was known not only in France, the home of the presumed author, but also in Germany, Italy, and Poland. One manuscript, *Ambrosianus* G 111 *inf.*, provides dramatic proof of the use of the commentary in scholastic environments. This manuscript is actually a summary of Bernardus, made by a master or tutor, who at the end of his summary of *Aeneid* 5 promises a still briefer recapitulation to his students: "In order that all these aforesaid matters may be better entrusted to memory, I shall summarize them in a compendium, giving heed commonly to history, fable, and philosophy."[26]

Bernardus begins (p. 1) with the assumption that Vergil is primarily a philosopher and secondarily a poet: "We consider that Maro in his *Aeneid* taught two things at the same time, as Macrobius witnesses: he both taught the truth of philosophy and he did not overlook poetic fabrication."[27] As a poet, Vergil writes of the fall of Troy and the subsequent adventures of Aeneas and his Trojan followers. As a philosopher, he describes the nature of human life. Specifically, under an *integumentum*—an allegorical cover or veil—he describes what the human spirit does or suffers when placed temporarily in the human body (p. 3). From this allegorical representation the reader may take great utility because in it he may perceive himself and consequently acquire a truer knowledge of himself (p. 3).

Having stated his basic assumptions, Bernardus proceeds to interpret the books of the *Aeneid* in order. For the first five, he typically presents a summary of the literal account (the *continentia fabulosa*) and then presents his allegorical explanation (or *expositio*) of it. Each of these books, he supposes, represents allegorically an age, or physical period, of human life.[28] Thus, book 1 is infancy. The birth of a person entails the death of the soul, since the soul must at that moment descend from its divinity, be oppressed by the weight of the flesh, and consent to carnal desire (pp. 4–5). Aeolus is human birth or the destroyer of life, his name being etymologically analyzed as the Greek *aion* (life or lifetime) and *ollus* (destroying). Aeneas (spelled E-N-E-A-S) is *ennos* (that which dwells in), or the human spirit dwelling in the prison of the body (p. 10).[29] His mother is Venus, who is the harmony of the world or the even proportion of worldly things (p. 9). His father Anchises is *celsa inhabitans* (Greek *anō skēnōn*), "the one dwelling on high," the father of all, the heavenly father, presiding over all things (p. 9). Thus, Aeneas is said to be the son of Venus and Anchises because the human spirit coming from God ("the one dwelling on high") begins through "harmony" to exist in the body (p. 10).

Books 2–4 take us from boyhood to the threshold of maturity. Book 2 is boyhood, or *pueritia*, when natural speech begins (p. 14). The story Aeneas begins to tell Dido results from his wish to satisfy an inclination to express himself in words (p. 15). Book 3 expresses the nature of adolescence (p. 15). From Troy Aeneas goes to the city of Antandros (p. 16), a name to be analyzed as *anti* (Greek for "against" or "the opposite of") and *andros* (man). Antandros represents instability, the primary quality of the adolescent and "the opposite of" the manly virtue of constancy. The adolescent is quick to anger and quick to lay his anger aside. He changes from one hour to the next, and quickly abandons what he cherished just now. From Antandros, Aeneas sails to Thrace and from Thrace to Delos (pp. 17–19). On Delos, the oracle of Apollo admonishes him "to seek his ancient mother" (p. 28). Actually, he has two ancient mothers: Crete, the mother of his body or temporal nature, and Italy, the mother of his soul or divine nature. He misinterprets the oracle and goes to Crete because he supposes at first that happiness is to be sought in the pleasures of the flesh. Eventually, Aeneas reaches western Sicily and there buries his father at Drepanum (p. 23). Drepanus is, as it were, the Greek *Drimus pais* (bitter child) and stands for childish acerbity or the anger which plagues the young. In the heat of anger God the father is forgotten for the moment, and to be forgotten is to be buried. Book 4 both manifestly (*manifeste*) and mystically (*mistica narratione*) describes the nature of young manhood (p. 24). At this stage, the young male devotes himself to the hunt and other useless pursuits and indulges the propensity of the flesh for sexual experimentation (p. 24). Eloquent entreaty and censure, represented by Mercury, eventually recall him from his lust, or *libido*, represented by Dido (p. 25).

Book 5 represents the beginning of full manhood, or the *virilis aetas* (p. 25). The games celebrated in honor of the dead Anchises symbolize the exercise by the mature man of the four cardinal virtues (p. 26). By the guiding and control of the ships in the boat race is to be understood temperance, which is the moderator of all pleasures. The boat race precedes the other contests because temperance checks the vices and this necessarily precedes the operation of the other virtues. Through the boxing match, for which the contestants wear gauntlets to which plummets of heavy lead are attached, is figured bravery by which the weight of labor is borne, for bravery is nothing else than the premeditated undertaking of dangers and the enduring of toils. In the foot race and the equestrian exercise, from which the swiftness of men and horses may be perceived, we should understand prudence, which enables us to recognize the course and instability of mutable things. Also, in these races some seem to pursue, others to flee. Likewise, prudence teaches us what we must pursue and what we must avoid. The archery contest, in which arrows are shot to a distance, symbolizes the fourth virtue, justice, by which harmful things are removed from us.

The commentary on book 6 differs in form from the preceding. From the allegorical standpoint, it is Bernardus' most spectacular achievement. When the famous Florentine chancellor, Coluccio Salutati, refers to Bernardus as the *diligens allegorizator* (the assiduous allegorizer),[30] he almost certainly has in mind this part of Bernardus' work. Even though the comment on *Aeneid* 6 breaks off abruptly at line 636 (the point at which Aeneas is about to enter Elysium), it nevertheless takes approximately eighty-seven pages in the latest edition.[31] Bernardus explains that in *Aeneid* 6 Vergil declares philosophic truth more profoundly than elsewhere. Therefore a summary of the allegorical meaning will not be sufficient: it is necessary to change procedure and to expound this part of the epic word-by-word (p. 28).[32]

Actually, Bernardus does not alter his approach immediately and his failure to do so is puzzling. He begins by summarizing the first thirty-six lines of the literal story and then offering an allegorical *expositio* in the same running text to which we have become accustomed (pp. 30–31). After this, he goes back to *Aeneid* 6, line 1, and proceeds to expound the first thirty-six lines and the rest of the book (to line 636) *ad litteram*, or word by word. We should like to suggest that Bernardus did not initially plan a different, minute interpretation of Vergil's *nekyia*. Rather, having begun his interpretation, he was overwhelmed by the profundity of this episode and decided to change his method accordingly. However, he did not discard the interpretation, already made, of the first thirty-six lines.

Aeneid 6, notes Bernardus, describes the descent of Aeneas to the *inferi*, this term having roughly the same significance as in the Servian note on *Aeneid* 6.127 discussed above. There are, however, says Bernardus (p. 30), four descents to the *inferi*: the first of nature (*natura*), the second of virtue (*virtus*), the third of vice (*vitium*), and the fourth of artifice (*artificium*). The first, or natural, is common to all since it is the birth of man. By this descent the soul begins to exist in this fallen (*caduca*) region and thus to descend to the *inferi*. It recedes from its divinity when it enters the body and gradually inclines to vice and to the pleasures of the flesh. The second, or virtuous, descent occurs when a wise man descends through contemplation (*consideratio*) to worldly things, not that he may set his heart upon them, but that having perceived their fragility and rejected them, he may turn himself completely to invisible matters and through a knowledge of His creatures come to know more evidently the Creator. Orpheus and Hercules were wise men who made this descent. The third, or vicious, descent is that of the vulgar throng. By it, one comes to temporal things, sets his whole heart upon them, is a slave to them with all his mind, and is never diverted from them. This was the descent of Eurydice; from it there is no recall. The fourth descent, the artificial, takes place when a necromancer, by the necromantic art, through an execrable sacrifice seeks conversation with demons and consults them about his future life.

The *Aeneid*, at the literal level, describes the fourth descent (p. 30). Aeneas sacrifices Misenus to demons and along with the Sibyl, the Cumaean prophetess, seeks conversation with them and questions them about the fortunes of his future life. At the allegorical level, through the device of the *integumentum*, Vergil represents the second descent; this descent, says Bernardus, will be the subject of his comment (p. 30).

During the descent of virtue, what does Aeneas contemplate? Among other things he contemplates knowledge and its divisions. Approaching Italy, Aeneas brings his ships to the Euboean shores and Cumae. Euboea, explains Bernardus, is a region having many cities (p. 32). Mystically, the name Euboea is to be analyzed as the Greek *eu* and *boe*, "that which sounds good," and Euboea represents the branches of knowledge (*scientia*). There are in fact four principal branches: philosophy (*sapientia*), poetry (*poesis*), eloquence (*eloquentia*) and mechanics (*mechania*). Each of these has a role to play in the war against the four evils that plague human nature: ignorance, vice, lack of skill in speaking, and want. To each of these vices is opposed a good: to ignorance, wisdom; to vice, virtue; to lack of skill in speaking, the ability to speak well; to want, sufficiency. For obtaining wisdom philosophy was invented; for acquiring virtue, poetry; for learning to speak well, the discipline of eloquence; for having a sufficiency, mechanics (pp. 32, 36).

Aeneas also thinks about teachers and students and the educational process. Achates, Aeneas' close companion, is, so to speak, *a-chaire-ethos*, or "grim habit." He represents study, which is both grim and a habit. Aeneas sends Achates ahead through the groves of Trivia to fetch the Sibyl (6.13, 34-5). The Sibyl represents understanding (*intelligentia*). Trivia is eloquence with its three divisions of grammar, dialectic, and rhetoric; the groves are the arts or books in which eloquence is contained. Achates, sent through the groves, brings back the Sibyl when study exercised in the arts produces understanding (p. 31). The leaves on which the Sibyl ordinarily writes her prophecies (6.74) stand for unstable and wandering teachers through whom the understanding (i.e., the Sibyl) educates us in its precepts (p. 49). The cypress trees which Aeneas places before the tomb of Misenus (6.216) signify knowledge (*scientia*). As the cypress tree often planted inside the tomb penetrates the rocky matter to emerge on the outside, so knowledge, sown in the person by instruction, emerges through the mouth and voice

(p. 66). Aeneas gains the entrance (*aditum occupat*) to the Underworld after the Sibyl has thrown Cerberus a honeyed cake (6.419-26). Here Cerberus, with his three heads, is eloquence with its three divisions; the honeyed cake is the sweetness of wisdom; thus, the Sibyl (i.e., understanding) in tossing the cake to Cerberus joins wisdom and eloquence. This has to be achieved before one can be a good teacher. If one teaches without wisdom, he knows how to speak, but not what to say. If he teaches without eloquence, he has in his mind what he wishes to say, but he cannot artfully express it (pp. 90-91). In Tartarus, Aeneas sees those who hated their brothers during life (6.608). Figuratively, "brothers" are colleagues (*fratres*) in disciplines and offices. The reference here, then, is to those who envy their colleagues during their active careers (p. 111).

Ever and again, Aeneas focuses his mind on virtues and vices. As ferns and brushes are removed from a field by fire, so by reflection may noxious passions and vices be cleared from the mind (p. 66). Vices should be buried in oblivion, but virtues should be stored in the memory (p. 80). Vergil writes that Aeneas meets the shade of his dead companion Leucaspis in the Underworld (6.334). Leucaspis' name means "enclosure of whiteness or beauty" and he represents natural virtue. Natural virtue "encloses beauty" because it protects the beauty of the soul against the contamination of vice (p. 82). A prerequisite to admission to the underworld is the sacrifice of seven bullocks and seven sheep (6.38-9). The bullocks that plow the earth represent the seven virtues that vex the flesh: abstinence, moderation, sobriety, chastity, sparingness, modesty, and verbal restraint. The seven sheep, or *bidentes* (animals with two teeth) represent the seven virtues that pertain to the two qualities of simplicity and mildness: innocence, friendship, concord, devotion to relatives, religion, affection, and sympathy (pp. 39-40). Among the monsters that infest the entrance to the Underworld are the Gorgons (6.289). According to the story, the Gorgons—Sthenno, Euryale, and Medusa—were three daughters of Phorcys, a god of the sea. They had only one common eye which they shared among themselves.[33] Perseus killed the third one with the aid of Pallas and Mercury. Figuratively, Phorcys is that spirit which rules in the flesh, conceived as a sea. His three daughters are wicked desire (Sthenno), wicked speech (Euryale), and wicked deed (Medusa). The single, common eye which Sthenno gives to Euryale, and Euryale to Medusa, is bad conscience, which is present in wicked desire, then in wicked speech, and finally in wicked deed. Perseus, who represents virtue, kills the third wicked sister (wicked deed) with the help of his sister Pallas and his brother Mercury (wisdom and eloquence). He uses the sword of Mercury, which is the written law. He does not kill the other two sisters because by no law can wicked desire or wicked speech be restrained (pp. 72-3).

Since Aeneas reflects seriously about both knowledge and virtue, the perceptive reader may wish to interrupt to ask whether the two ends are bound together in Bernardus' mind. We may answer positively that they are. *Virtutes* (virtues) and *scientiae* (knowledge) are paired again and again in the *Commentum*, and in at least six places (pp. 46, 84, 85, 95, 105, and 113) they are allegorical glosses for the words *di, deae,* or *divi* (gods, goddesses, divinities). According to Bernardus (p. 82), the soul has by nature three volitional faculties, which are the beginnings (*initia*) of virtue: *irascibilitas* (revulsion against evil), *concupiscentia* (appetite for the good), and *animositas* (boldness in opposing guile and defending the good). These three volitional faculties are ruled by three intellectual faculties: *ingenium*, the faculty for discovering things; *ratio*, the faculty for differentiating among the things discovered; and *memoria*, the faculty for preserving those things differentiated.[34] Bernardus would seem to reaffirm the Socratic and Platonic notion that virtuous action is dependent upon and ensured by true knowledge.

In regard to Bernardus' discussion of vices, we must interject one further point: in places we detect the same uncomplimentary and biased view of the feminine sex which is to be found also in some Servian comments (see above, p. 113, *ad Aen.* 7.456). The Weeping Fields (*Lugentes Campi*) in Vergil's Underworld (6.440–76) are inhabited by those who have died for love. These people, asserts Bernardus (p. 93), figuratively represent those who are devoted to the lecherous life. The individuals named by Vergil are all women—Phaedra, Procris, Eriphyle, Evadne, Pasiphae, Laodamia, Caenis, and Dido. This is quite proper in the commentator's opinion: everywhere the woman designates weakness and softness, and the vice of lechery is especially dependent upon such weakness and softness.

During the virtuous descent, Aeneas also contemplates temporal goods and their qualities. In Tartarus, writes Vergil (6.547–51), is the stronghold of Dis or Pluto, set under a cliff and encircled by a triple wall. Allegorically Dis, "the rich one," is the earth which contains various riches, or *divitiae* (p. 51). His stronghold is comprised of the five temporal goods: sufficiency, power, dignity, glory, and mirth. It is surrounded by a triple wall, i.e. by ignorance, poverty, and weakness. It is set under a cliff because temporal goods are subject to the weight of fortune (p. 106). The groves of Avernus (6.118) also represent temporal goods, which share three qualities with groves. As groves are dark on account of the absence of the sun, so are temporal goods obscure because of the lack of reason. As woods are impassable because of the multitude and variety of paths, so are temporal goods impassable because of the various paths that seem to lead to the highest good but do not. As Avernus is a grove without the season of spring (*sine vere*)—that is, without delight—so temporal goods lack true delight, or *vera delectatio* (p. 53).

Aeneas reflects, too, upon the vicissitudes of earthly life. The sea (*pelagus*) over which the Trojans have sailed to Italy (6.83) and which is disturbed by the winds is, by one interpretation, temporal life. The winds are the two temporal fortunes, prosperity and adversity, which quickly come and quickly go and snatch ships (i.e., human wills) in various directions and draw the minds of men sailing on this sea to the shipwreck of vices (pp. 49–50). In Tartarus some of the condemned hang stretched on the spokes of wheels (6.616–17). These wheels are images of fortune, which spins like a wheel, now raising us up only to thrust us down, now thrusting us down only to raise us up (p. 113).

Naturally, Aeneas on occasion contemplates his past life. In the literal account Aeneas descends to the *inferi*, and the experiences he has had and companions who are dead are led back before his eyes. This means allegorically that when the rational spirit (Aeneas) inclines itself to contemplate "fallen things" (*caduca*), the mortified vices of the first ages of life are brought back to it by a certain imaginary representation. Thus the shade of Dido and the shade of Deiphobus return when there is recollection of past lust and fear (p. 83). Dido is the image of former passion and lust. Aeneas speaks to Dido's shade (6.455) when the rational spirit contemplates through recollection the nature of lust (p. 95). Dido also represents the typical lecherous person. She flees from Aeneas (6.465–6) because the lecherous person does not pay attention to the learning of the wise man (Aeneas). Aeneas recalls the fleeing Dido to a conversation when the rational spirit invites the embarrassed lecherous individual to instruction (p. 96). Finally, Dido withdraws into a grove and the arms of her husband Sychaeus (6.473–4). This is to be expected because Sychaeus symbolizes gluttony and intoxication, and as everyone knows, lust (Dido) and gluttony and intoxication complement each other (p. 96). Deiphobus, whose name is analyzed as *demos* and *phobos*, symbolizes fear (p. 99). Aeneas sees Deiphobus in the Underworld without hands, feet, ears, and eyes (6.494–7) because the rational spirit sometimes contemplates fear, which does not know what to do, where to go, what to listen to, or what to see (p. 100).

At this point we must again interrupt our description, this time to note a significant parallelism between Bernardus and Vergil. Throughout his exegesis Bernardus, we think, conveys to us his own intention, not Vergil's. However, no allegorizer can depart altogether from his original. Therefore, even in such a writer, we expect to find some interpretations, which, if not precisely to the point, nevertheless resemble closely those that the original seems to suggest. In Bernardus' virtuous descent to the *inferi*, Aeneas reviews his past, as represented by Dido, Deiphobus, and others, in order to evaluate it and to reject its errors (p. 30). Similarly, in the Vergilian original, Aeneas encounters his past in order to see it in final perspective and to dismiss it, thus ending its traumatic power over him. Louis A.

MacKay's statement is excellent:

> The primary importance of the journey [through the Underworld] is that it
> represents a spiritual purification and illumination that fit him [i.e.,
> Aeneas] for his mighty task. To this development belong, as might be
> expected, the three episodes in which Aeneas is personally involved, the
> meetings with Dido, with Deiphobus, and with Anchises. For the last of
> these, the culminating illumination which fits him for his historic mission,
> he is prepared by the recall and dismissal of two great traumatic
> experiences, the tragedy of Dido and the disasters of Troy.[35]

The virtuous descent as described by Bernardus culminates, not
unexpectedly, in contemplation of the Creator (Anchises). This has always
been the final objective of Aeneas' descent. According to Vergil's narrative,
the old ferryman Charon rebukes Aeneas and the Sibyl when they approach
the River Styx and tries to stop them. The Sibyl responds that Aeneas has no
malevolent design, but is only descending to see his father (6.387–404).
Figuratively, Charon is a prudent old man who, when he sees someone
following the path of contemplation, fears that that person may be
"descending" only because of curiosity or love of temporal goods. He is
reassured if he learns that the person is descending in order to know the
Creator (pp. 86–7). One may know the Creator more fully through his
creations, but knowledge in this life means only contemplation of Him, not
the attainment of a vision.[36] Only in the next life may the Creator be seen
face to face (p. 52). Active curiosity about the temporal world is to be
condemned. Tityos, the giant whose liver and intestines are forever
consumed in Tartarus by a huge vulture (6.595–600), is a symbol of the
curious person. Such a person, as long as he seeks after the arcane nature of
things with the energy of laborious study, consumes his mind insofar as its
immortal nature permits (p. 110).

The substance of Aeneas' reflection on the Creator is not revealed to us
by Bernardus since his commentary ends at *Aeneid* 6.636. It is after this
point that Vergil tells of Elysium and its inhabitants, including Anchises
(allegorically the Creator). We might suppose that Bernardus has played a
cruel joke on his readers. He takes his account to a point of climax, but then
fails to provide one. We are given no hint of the reason for the
incompleteness of the *Commentum*. Clearly, Bernardus planned to continue,
and there are some signs in the extant interpretation of the way the
remainder of the commentary on *Aeneid* 6 would have been developed.
Before entering Elysium, Aeneas and the Sibyl approach the walls of the
Cyclopes, or the palace of Pluto (6.630–31). The rational spirit (Aeneas),
says Bernardus, having surveyed visible things, may proceed now to inquire
about the invisible: *Visibilibus peragratis, restat invisibilia perquirere* (p. 114). The

Cyclopes are, as it were, *policiculos*, or "multitudes of circles." By circles, which lack an endpoint and which focus on an indivisible and immobile center, are figuratively represented spirits that are immortal and that cling to an indivisible and immutable creator. The "walls" of the Cyclopes are the heavens, which are the natural regions of spirits (p. 114). Elsewhere (p. 29), Bernardus seems to subscribe to the notion that our universe is divisible into upper and lower regions, the upper region being called Paradise by the Greeks and Eden by the Hebrews. He also declares that the Creator (Anchises) is elevated over all (*super omnes excelsus*) and that angels are an order intermediate between man and the Creator (p. 52). I think we may conclude that Aeneas' contemplation of the Creator would have involved contemplation of a celestial Elysium and its inhabitants.

We have now completed our review of the content of Bernardus' *Commentum*. From this review the moral and religious focus of the commentary will be evident. It should be further observed that Bernardus supposes that one may profit morally from the reading of Vergil's poetry even if he cannot remove the *integumentum* and perceive the allegorical meaning. The literal narrative offers examples of correct and incorrect behavior. Thus, in the labors of Aeneas, we have an example of endurance. His affection for Anchises and Ascanius is an example of familial devotion. By his veneration of the gods, his consultation of oracles, his offering of sacrifices, and his making of vows and prayers we are invited to the practice of religion. On the other hand, by the immoderate love of Dido we are called away from appetite for illicit things (pp. 2–3). As Bernardus asserts, poetry (*poesis*) was discovered for the inculcation of virtue.

A comprehensive study of Bernardus' sources has yet to be accomplished. Such a study may not be possible until more of the writings of the twelfth century are published. Our judgment is that when this study is made, Bernardus will be seen to be more original than most academic commentators. Of course, whatever the extent of Bernardus' originality, he has obvious debts to other writers, several of whom we should mention here. For the notion that the *Aeneid* is a mirror of human life Bernardus is indebted to Fabius Fulgentius Planciades (ca. A.D. 467–532). It was Fulgentius who, in his *Continentia Vergiliana*, first generalized the meaning of Vergil's epic, changing it by allegory from the "epic of Rome" to the "epic of man."[37] According to Fulgentius, the first five books of the *Aeneid* recount the physical and moral progress of the individual from infancy to manhood. Book 6, the descent to the *inferi*, tells of the penetration of the obscure and secret mysteries of knowledge by means of study. The last six books recount the war that the individual (now a *vir sapiens*) wages against a host of vices and eventually wins. Bernardus cites Fulgentius twice (pp. 60,

87) and takes from him not only the general notion of the *Aeneid* as a Christian pilgrim's progress, but also specific interpretations and etymologies. We do not find in Fulgentius the identification of the place of the *inferi* with our world or the idea that the soul descends at birth from its heavenly origin to the prison of the body. These Platonic and Neoplatonic notions Bernardus draws from Macrobius' *Commentary on the Dream of Scipio*.[38]

Bernardus does not acknowledge by name a single contemporary author or source, but contemporary strains are recognizable in his commentary. He displays in places a great interest in the workings of the physical body, and we know that such interest was kindled in Western Europe in the twelfth century by the translation into Latin of Greco-Arabic medical treatises by Constantine the African and others. Bernardus, for instance, expounds the theory (pp. 67–8) that the malfunctioning of the soul when placed in the body is to be connected with the digestive process. Man has in him, he explains, the four elements: fire or vital heat, water, air, and earth. In an infant the vital heat is excessive and large amounts of food and drink are required to satisfy it. The continual ebb and flow of matter in digestion produces a dense vapor (*fumus*) which rises to the head and there seriously beclouds the intellectual faculties. As man matures, the power of the vital heat lessens, and digestion consequently decreases along with the beclouding *fumus*. He becomes more and more capable of knowing, and through knowledge, of attaining virtue. This same theory is enunciated in the *Philosophia Mundi* (4.35, 36) of William of Conches, an older contemporary of Bernardus, and William may be Bernardus' immediate source.[39] William is probably also to be credited with the differentiation of four descents to the *inferi*. In any case, reference to these descents seems to occur for the first time in his commentary on the *Consolation of Philosophy* by Boethius.[40]

Conclusions

The description which we have now offered of the allegorical comment of Servius and of the interpretation of Bernardus has, we hope, served to indicate that there are two different traditions. The reader may well ask, however, whether there are not some points of contact between them. In fact there are, perhaps, enough to justify a study of some length. We shall content ourselves here with noting two examples. First, at *Aeneid* 6.288, Bernardus discusses the Chimaera, a triform monster having the foreparts of a lion, the midsection of a goat, and a posterior extremity of serpents. According to the historians (*historici*), writes Bernardus, the Chimaera is nothing other than a mountain having lions on its peak, goats in its middle areas, and snakes at its feet. This same rationalization of the monster is found in Servius (*ad loc.*). Bernardus goes on to say that philosophers (*philosophi*) recognize the Chimaera as a symbol of lust, which in the beginning, in gaze and in speech, exhibits the ferocity of a lion, in mid-course has the "goat-like and stinking" practice of sexual intercourse, and at the end is marked by the stings of a serpent (i.e., the goads of penance and a bad conscience). Bernardus' long comment illustrates the use by him, probably indirectly or from a common source,[41] of explanations also found in Servius. It also illustrates well the difference in emphasis and direction between the two commentaries. Secondly, Bernardus' notion that *Aeneid* 6, at the literal level, describes a necromantic or artificial descent probably has an ancient origin. As we have seen (above, p. 111), Servius in his preface to his comment on this book states his conviction that Vergil's account imitates Homer closely. In *Odyssey* 11, Odysseus goes to the stream of Ocean and calls up the shade of Tiresias and others by sacrificing sheep and letting their blood pour into a trench. Similarly, says Servius (*ad Aen.* 6.149), Aeneas in the vicinity of Baiae accomplishes an *evocatio umbrae*, "a calling up of a shade," presumably the shade of his father. Ordinarily, this rite would require a blood sacrifice. Aeneas does not have to undertake this because Misenus has already been killed on the waves and may serve as such. Again, Servius is probably not Bernardus' immediate source. In any case, the latter insists, Servius to the contrary notwithstanding, that Aeneas actually kills Misenus as a sacrifice (p. 30).[42]

For Servius and Bernardus and indeed for all commentators on the *Aeneid* the crucial question must be: To what extent do they truly expound Vergil's meaning?[43] Typically, modern annotators of Vergil now and again quote with approval some comment of Servius. On rare occasions, they consider one of Servius' allegorical comments worthy of repetition. Seldom, if ever, do they notice the medieval allegorizers, Fulgentius or Bernardus.[44] The situation that obtains in these modern editions implies a judgment: a few pieces of Servian allegorism may contribute to our understanding of the *Aeneid*; the medieval comments have no such value.

After careful—and we hope dispassionate—study of Servius and Bernardus we find ourselves agreeing with this judgment. Some of Servius' historical comments are appropriate and relevant and probably should be accepted. Some of his physical comments deserve careful study since they may lead us to a better appreciation of the way Vergil represents gods and goddesses in certain contexts. The remainder of his allegorical interpretations probably may best be characterized as misapplied erudition. The *Commentum* of Bernardus is not really an illumination of the *Aeneid*. It does not respond to or derive from the suggestion of Vergil's text; rather it is imposed upon the poem. It sets aside completely the Vergilian cultural context, imperial Rome, and substitutes another, medieval and Christian Europe. Most important, it seeks to make the *Aeneid* a vehicle for a particular form of ethical or philosophical teaching. It amounts, in the final analysis, to a piece of moral instruction through misapplication.

We shall not, then, expect any great assistance from the allegorizers in our effort to comprehend Vergil's epic. This should not keep us, however, from having some positive appreciation of them. It will not do to read Servius or Fulgentius or Bernardus, describe them as nightmares, and forget about them.[45] Many of the comments of Servius that today seem to us irrelevant made Vergil relevant to men of the fourth century. We cannot claim that the *Aeneid* would have perished utterly in the Middle Ages without Fulgentius and Bernardus, but we can claim that their interpretations probably made the *Aeneid* acceptable and valuable to many who otherwise would have been hostile or unmindful. Furthermore, the prodigious achievement of Bernardus in imposing a continuous, line-by-line and sometimes word-by-word, allegorical interpretation upon an inherently foreign context must be re-stressed. Bernardus' imagination may be perverse, but it is unfailingly adaptable and unceasingly fertile. Many of his disquisitions we can read with sympathy and interest if we can just forget for the moment they are being applied to the *Aeneid*.

To these conclusions we append two further observations. First, those who would be inclined to ridicule ancient and medieval allegorizers must be sure they have no beam in their own eyes. Allegory at present has no dignity, but its kinsman, symbolism, does. The modern scholar must be very careful that in his mad search for symbols he does not seek to claim special significance for every rock, tree, bird, and bee in Vergil. Secondly, while we reject the particular generalized meaning that Fulgentius and Bernardus assigned to the *Aeneid*, we reassert the view of many modern scholars that Vergil's epic deals, always in a Roman setting, with themes of universal significance. Surely these give the *Aeneid* its timeless appeal. Recently, Robert Deryck Williams, one of the most sensitive and sensible of Vergilian scholars, described the *Aeneid* as a work which at the deeper level treats the themes of man and his gods, man and the state, and man and himself.[46] In our view, about these fundamental matters and others the *Aeneid* raises important questions; in some instances, it also provides answers.

Notes

1. Meanwhile, the reader is referred to the great classic by Domenico Comparetti, *Vergil in the Middle Ages*, trans. E.F.M. Benecke (London: Sonnenschein, 1895). Comparetti discusses, in a general way and *inter alia*, the allegorizing of Vergil.

2. For an authoritative discussion of the varieties of ancient allegorism, see Konrad Müller, "Allegorische Dichtererklärung," in *Real-Encyclopädie der klassischen Altertumswissenschaft*, sup. vol. 4, 14–22. We consider to be allegorical any interpretations which are clearly "other than" or "different from" the ones which might be suggested by a literal rendering of Vergil's text.

3. See William A. Camps, *An Introduction to Virgil's Aeneid* (London: Oxford University Press, 1969), pp. 98–100.

4. Another commentator of the fourth century, Tiberius Claudius Donatus, concludes that it is Vergil's great labor to make Aeneas worthy of Augustus Caesar. See *Interpretationes Vergilianae*, ed. H. Georgii (Stuttgart: Teubner, 1905), Vol. 1, p. 2.

5. We shall perhaps be pardoned for parenthetically stating our own view here: we take Vergil's Aeneas to be both model and copy. In the *Iliad* the Trojan hero is already a figure of notable religious piety (cf. 20.297–9). In respect to this trait, he may be a model for Augustus and other Romans. On the other hand, the *pietas* which Aeneas displays in the *Aeneid* reflects the broad definition given to this virtue in the Augustan Age, when it implied much more than religious devotion.

6. Douglas L. Drew, in *The Allegory of the Aeneid* (Oxford: Blackwell, 1927), pp. 42–59, tries to do so.

7. See Arthur S. Pease, ed., *Aeneid IV* (Cambridge: Harvard University Press, 1935), pp. 23–8.

8. On the early development of physical and moral allegorism, see Eduard Zeller, *The Stoics, Epicureans, and Sceptics* (London: Longmans, Green, 1880), pp. 354–69.

9. By Servian "logic," the same divinity may represent now one physical phenomenon, now another, and the same physical phenomenon may be associated at different times with different divinities. Servius makes these points explicit in his note on *Georgics* 2.325.

10. See Ernest G. Sihler, "Serviana," *AJP* 31 (1910): 9.

11. See Georg Wissowa, *Religion und Kultus der Römer* (Munich: Beck, 1912), p. 61. Cf. also August., *De civ. Dei* 6, 7 *passim*.

12. "Totus quidem Vergilius scientia plenus est, in qua hic liber possidet principatum, cuius ex Homero pars maior est. Et dicuntur aliqua simpliciter, multa de historia, multa per altam scientiam philosophorum, theologorum, Aegyptiorum, adeo ut plerique de his singulis huius libri integras scripserint pragmatias."

13. See Sir Frank Fletcher, *Aeneid VI* (Oxford: Clarendon Press, 1941), p. xxvii.

14. Herbert Block, in *Paganism and Christianity in the Fourth Century*, ed. Arnaldo Momigliano (Oxford: Clarendon Press, 1963), p. 210, suggests that Servius and Macrobius intend to present the *Aeneid* as a pagan Bible. On Servius' philosophic views see Sihler (above n. 10), pp. 11–14.

15. Euhemerus, who supposedly originated this form of allegorical interpretation, was a Greek and a close friend of King Cassander of Macedon (316–297 B.C.). He was often compelled by his sovereign to attend to certain affairs of state and to make great journeys abroad. On one of these journeys he claimed to have sailed southward from Arabia into the Indian Ocean to the island of Panchaea. Here there was, according to Euhemerus, a sanctuary of Zeus Triphylius, which was established by Zeus himself when he was king of the inhabited world and was still living among men. In the temple there was a stele on which were inscribed briefly the deeds of Uranus, Cronus, and Zeus. Zeus, it seems, before his death, had visited many peoples who honored him and publicly proclaimed him a god (Diodorus Siculus, *Hist.* 6.1.3–10).

16. Servius is fond of recounting a mythical story and then presenting a euhemeristic rationalization, introduced by *re vera* (in actual fact), *secundum veritatem* (according to the truth), or a similar phrase.

17. Cacus is the Greek *Kakos*: the evil one, the villain, the rascal.

18. *A Literary History of Rome from the Origins to the Close of the Golden Age*, 3rd ed. (New York: Barnes & Noble, 1960), pp. 335-6. On *Aeneid* 6.173 see also John W. Mackail, ed., *The Aeneid of Virgil* (Oxford: Clarendon Press, 1930) and Roland G. Austin, ed., *P. Vergili Maronis Aeneidos Liber Sextus* (Oxford: Clarendon Press, 1977).

19. See *Aeneid* 6.14 and *Aeneid* 3.578 and the Servian notes thereon.

20. The confarreate marriage ceremony was the stateliest and most solemn known to Rome—a far cry from the sexual union of Dido and Aeneas in the cave in *Aeneid* 4. Vergil, in what amounts to his own disclaimer (line 172), tells us that Aeneas and Dido have been joined by no legitimate or civilized marriage.

21. See Sihler (above, no. 10), pp. 6-7. Also, John Conington, ed., *P. Vergili Maronis Opera* (London: Whittaker, 1881), 1:cv.

22. "Equidem inter omnia quibus eminet laus Maronis hoc adsiduus lector admiror, quia doctissime ius pontificium tamquam hoc professus in multa et varia operis sui parte servavit et, si tantae dissertationi sermo non cesserit, promitto fore ut Vergilius noster pontifex maximus adseratur."

23. "Notandum sane quia controversiarum more epilogos dedit sex istis prioribus libris, quos et esse bioticos voluit. Nam singulis res singulas dedit, ut primo omina, secundo pathos, tertio errores, quarto ethos, quinto festivitatem, sexto scientiam."

24. *Commentum Quod Dicitur Bernardi Silvestris Super Sex Libros Eneidos Virgilii*, ed. J. W. Jones and E.F. Jones (Lincoln: University of Nebraska, 1977). All references to Bernardus' *Commentary* will be to the pages of this edition.

25. Jones and Jones discuss this tradition in their introduction, pp. xiv-xx.

26. "Ut hec predicta melius memorie mandentur omnia sub compendio repilogabo communiter ystorie, fabule et philosophie deserviens."

27. "Gemine doctrine observantiam perpendimus in sua Eneide Maronem habuisse, teste namque Macrobio: et veritatem philosophie docuit et ficmentum poeticum non pretermisit." The Macrobian reference is *In Somn. Scip.* 1.9.8.

28. The resumé I present here is not thoroughgoing. Some of the points made by Bernardus I omit. My aim is to indicate in a general way the nature of the development.

29. *Ennos* is Bernardus' rendering of the Greek present participle *ennaion*.

30. *De Laboribus Herculis*, ed. B.L. Ullman (Zurich: Artemis-Verlag, 1947), p. 536.

31. As mentioned above, the entire commentary runs to only one hundred fourteen pages.

32. All allegorizers of the *Aeneid* accord a special treatment to *Aeneid* 6. The process begins with Servius, whom we have quoted (above, p. 111).

33. Bernardus obviously confuses the Gorgons with the Graeae.

34. Bernardus nowhere declares that the intellectual faculties rule the volitional, but his system implies and demands it. The best discussion of this whole subject is that of Daniel C. Meerson, *The Ground and Nature of Literary Theory in Bernard Silvester's Twelfth-Century Commentary on the Aeneid* (doctoral dissertation, University of Chicago, 1967), pp. 23-49.

35. "Three Levels of Meaning in *Aeneid VI*," *TAPA* 86 (1955): 184.

36. "Contemplation" here is the Latin *contemplatio*. Bernardus uses *contemplatio* and *consideratio* with no appreciable difference in meaning.

37. The most recent edition of the *Continentia* is that of Rudolphus Helm (Leipzig: Teubner, 1898). Fulgentius' work is a summary and description of the "contents" (*continentia*) of the *Aeneid*, not an extended commentary. The *Continentia* is translated into English by Leslie George Whitbread in *Fulgentius the Mythographer* (Columbus: Ohio State University Press, 1971), pp. 105-53.

38. Cf. *In Somn. Scip.* 1.12.8 and Bernardus' *Commentum*, p. 67. Bernardus cites Macrobius six times (pp. 1, 3, 36, 51, 67, 113).

39. The *Philosophia* is edited in Migne's *Patrologia Latina*, 172:39-102. It is wrongly attributed there to Honorius of Autun. Cf. Meerson (above, n. 34), pp. 36-7.

40. See Edouard Jeauneau, "L'usage de la notion d'integumentum *à travers les gloses de Guillaume de Conches,*" *AHMA* 24 (1957): 42. A printed edition of the commentary on Boethius has not yet appeared.

41. Bernardus never names Servius and never seems to quote him directly. Some comments may derive from Servius through an intermediary like the Vatican Mythographers, ed. George Heinrich Bode (Celle: Schulze, 1834).

42. Since Bernardus refuses to expound what, in his view, is Vergil's literal narrative, he does not satisfy our curiosity with respect to this shocking detail. What may be a standard medieval amplification is found in an anonymous *expositio* of *Aeneid* 6, now in the Ambrosian Library in MS G 111 *inf*. Here, the author alleges that Aeneas does sacrifice his trumpeter, but Vergil conceals this fact out of respect for Augustus, who disapproved of such rites. We have prepared an edition of the *expositio*.

43. See the statement of Rosemond Tuve on imposed allegory in *Allegorical Imagery* (Princeton: Princeton University Press, 1966), pp. 219-20. We agree with her assertions wholeheartedly.

44. The writer has close familiarity with the annotated editions of John Conington (London: Whittaker, 1881), A.P. Sidgwick (Cambridge: Cambridge University Press, 1890), T.L. Papillon and A.E. Haigh (Oxford: Clarendon Press, 1892), T.E. Page (London: Macmillan, 1900), Charles Knapp (Chicago: Scott Foresman, 1928), John W. Mackail (Oxford: Clarendon, 1930), and Robert D. Williams (London, 1972, 1973).

45. So Edward K. Rand in "Life and I," *Speculum* 3 (1928): 286: "Nor must we forget the medieval allegorizers and what they had done to the ancient poets. Fulgentius had led the way with his amazing exposition of the 'Contents of Vergil,' a work that I am tempted to call a nightmare, being confident that the ancient poet would have called it by some term at least as strong."

46. "Vergil's *Aeneid*—The First 2,000 Years," *PCA* 78 (1981): 7-16. See also Theodore J. Haarhoff, *Vergil the Universal* (Oxford: Blackwell, 1949).

VERGIL'S *ECLOGUES*
AND THE SPANISH RENAISSANCE

Alan S. Trueblood

When the Renaissance reaches a culmination in late fifteenth-century Italy, its effects become variously manifest in the Spain of the Catholic Monarchs, Ferdinand and Isabella.[1] One noteworthy manifestation is an extraordinary vernacular version of Vergil's *Eclogues* by a rising dramatic poet, Juan del Encina (1469-1529/30). With this version the pastoral Vergil is established as an important presence in the Spanish Renaissance. He will remain such in the succeeding reign of the Emperor Charles V, when the Renaissance achieves a literary flowering in the poetry of Garcilaso de la Vega (1501-36). Subsequently, when persisting currents of Renaissance culture increasingly contend with the developing spirit of the Counter-Reformation and the incipient baroque, Vergil remains a presiding presence in the poetry of the humanist friar Luis de León (1528-91), who translates the *Eclogues* afresh at the outset of his writing career. A fair picture of the impact of Vergil as a pastoralist on Spanish literary expression may be gained by considering these three different stages in the absorption of the *Eclogues* into the literary culture of the Spanish Renaissance.

In the plays of Juan del Encina a fusion of Castilian literary strains with Italian and classical currents gives the nascent genre of the Spanish secular drama a vigorous start. It is no accident that Encina entitles "eclogues" the fourteen musical dramas for which he is best remembered: their beginnings in the 1490s are coincident with his translation and adaptation of Vergil's *Bucolics*. The most striking aspect of these translations and the focus of my present concern is not their evident exploitation of the dramatic potentiality Encina saw in the *Eclogues* but his procedures for adjusting the texts to his own time and place. With Garcilaso de la Vega the emphasis falls on the first of the three eclogues composed in Naples at the end of his life which constitute his masterpieces. In them the modern Spanish lyric attains majority in one leap. In the odes of Luis de León, it is the Vergilian tone and tempering, diffuse but unmistakable, that impress themselves on the sensitive reader. These are demonstrably foreshadowed in the early translations of the *Eclogues*. The significance of the pastoral Vergil is enhanced by the fact that the demands which the classical text placed on the vernacular sensitized Luis de León to the expressive resources of his native tongue, enabling the critic to catch early indications of progress toward the poet's mature style.

I

Although Juan del Encina in his translations of the *Eclogues* is the first Spanish writer ever to render a classic of Latin poetry into Castilian metrical form, his interest in the poems is scarcely that of a literary artist. To be sure, he finds it appropriate to model his literary beginnings in the traditional way on those of Vergil. Yet it is not Vergil's accomplishment as craftsman and stylist that draws him but the adaptability of the *Eclogues* to his extra-literary purposes. He particularly wishes to highlight the civic dimension of the Vergilian pastoral, best exemplified in the fourth Eclogue, on which I shall accordingly concentrate. An important result of Encina's emphasis is a triumphant application of the millenarian vision of this eclogue to his own age.

Though as a Latinist Encina never attained the level of rigor and refinement of the Italian humanists of the fifteenth century, he was clearly the beneficiary of a renewal of *latinitas* carried out in Spain, in the manner advocated by Lorenzo Valla in his *Elegantiarum linguae latinae libri sex*, during the reign of Ferdinand and Isabella. This meant a turning toward Cicero and Quintilian as mentors of style and rhetoric and a reversion from the practices of medieval grammarians and lexicographers. This thorough-going reform of Latin studies was largely the work of a single figure, Antonio de Nebrija (1444-1522), the greatest Spanish humanist of the age. Encina's teacher at Salamanca and mentor thereafter, Nebrija in all likelihood suggested to him the translation of the *Eclogues* and remained associated with the enterprise.[2] The mood created in Spain by Nebrija's activity as well as by the accomplishments of Ferdinand and Isabella helps one to understand the tone and tenor of Encina's translations of Vergil and will bear a moment's notice.

Nebrija had spent some ten years in Italy, mostly at the Spanish College of the University of Bologna, developing there into a versatile classical philologist. Following his return, he spurred a revival of learning during the rest of his long life. Twenty years were spent at the University of Salamanca, then entering upon one of its most brilliant periods as a center of new learning and old, thanks to the enlightened support given the universities by Ferdinand and Isabella. Nebrija reformed the study of ancient and modern languages and of classical philology with his Latin grammars, Latin lexicons, Spanish grammars and dictionaries, and grammars of Greek and Hebrew. In 1486 he translated into Spanish for the benefit of Isabella and the ladies of her court his Latin grammar, *Introductiones latinae* (1481). In middle age, the Queen became proficient and made the study of Latin de rigueur at court.

The revival of classical learning is not achieved at the expense of the vernacular. To the contrary, the modern tongue is now first viewed as capable of developing into a vehicle of learning and literary expression in no way inferior to Latin. In a famous passage of the Dedication of his Spanish grammar to Queen Isabella (1492), Nebrija affirms his intention of "subjecting this Castilian language of ours to orderly rules so that whatever is written in it now or hereafter may acquire a uniform character and endure throughout all time to come. As we see has been the case with the Greek and Latin tongues. . . . "[3] The passage reflects in a linguistic context a new sense of national destiny, sometimes characterized as messianic, which marked the heady atmosphere of rebirth, both political and cultural, in this dynamic age. Isabella had fought a five-year war of succession to secure her right to the Castilian throne in 1479. (Ferdinand had been King of Aragon since 1474, five years after their marriage in 1469). During their twenty-five years of rule as joint sovereigns—Isabella died in 1504—the rebellious nobility, veritable warlords, were put down by the Crown, the last Moorish kingdom was conquered in 1492 with the taking of Granada, the system of justice was reformed, and the power and prestige of the joint monarchy were immeasurably enhanced. Isabella's piety, however, also created an atmosphere of religious zealotry: the Inquisition had been established in 1478 to examine the firmness of the faith of "New Christians"—mostly converts from Judaism. In 1492 the important Sephardic and Moslem segments of the population had been given the choice of conversion or exile. Meanwhile Isabella's patronage of the new learning continued unabated; the Court supported artists and craftsmen of every kind.

Coming to maturity in this age of expanding horizons, Juan del Encina was well equipped by an energetic temperament, abundant talent, boundless ambition, and evident social skills to take fullest advantage of the opportunities it offered. Encina's humble origins—his father had been a Salamanca shoemaker—help account for his peculiar strength as a poet and playwright in a popular or rustic vein. Overlaying but not smothering this talent is his classical training at the University of Salamanca with Nebrija and the Italian humanist Lucio Marineo Siculo. Training at the Cathedral in Salamanca will eventually also make of him the leading composer of his age, a cantor, and a choirmaster, while his savoir faire as a courtier will make him a music director to princes and a table-companion to popes.[4]

We need not follow the steps by which Encina acquired the patronage of the Duke of Alba and, with the Duke's favor, bid for that of Ferdinand and Isabella. His translations of the *Eclogues* appear to date from the mid-1490s; they were published in his *Cancionero* in 1496. A consideration in undertaking them was evidently the function which bucolic poetry, with its supposedly low stylistic register, had acquired as the starting-point for an aspiring poet. In a cultural climate clearly favorable to translation, Encina would prove his competence as a Latinist and practice his hand in the vernacular. More striking is the fact that for the first time in Spain he presented a translation for which patronage had not been arranged in advance. His rendering of the *Eclogues* in fact constitutes a bold personal stroke, an unabashed bid for royal favor. It is in the service of this aim that he adapts the poems freely, indeed forcibly, to the circumstances of the age and to the persons of King Ferdinand and Queen Isabella; more surprisingly, he applies the messianic and millenarian typology of the fourth Eclogue to their heir apparent, Prince John. Encina feels constrained to point out to the sovereigns, almost apologetically, that "there will be many passages impossible to apply to [my] purpose" and adds that such passages, "as Servius says," will have to be taken as "pastoral talk simply uttered," noting that "ecclesiastics will often go through a whole psalm for the sake of a single verse applicable to the feast day" (*OC* 223–4). This almost sounds like an apology for an involuntary adherence to the text in the midst of what, in contemporary terms, could be called a program of misreading.

Encina makes quite plain that the translations are his first serious endeavor. In the Proem to Ferdinand and Isabella he explains, predictably, that he wants "to try myself out first in a low style most suited to my natural abilities and later to write something of your histories in a higher style, if you should be so pleased," proceeding to cite the habitual example of the three stages of Vergil's career (*OC* 219). Yet quite aside from his conflicting motivations, and despite his training as a Latinist, Encina proves ill-equipped to penetrate, let alone recapture, the craftsmanship, the tonality, and the lyric power of Vergil. Nor can he forego indulging his talent for rustic dialect and dialogue and for broad humor. For all this, as a translator Encina is far from assuming unthinkingly a medieval offhandedness or capriciousness in dealing with the text. "As far as his learning and ability will allow," he says, as translator "he will always try to follow the letter" of the Latin (*OC* 223). There is probably less convention, more genuine perplexity in his complaints about "the great deficiency of words" in Castilian than in those of earlier fifteenth-century translators. He feels called upon to explain that meter, to which he has bound himself, will force him to spin out and condense (*OC* 223).

Unfortunately his metric repertory, which consists mainly of octo-syllables intermingled with their hemistichs, essentially a medieval heritage, precludes almost from the start his capturing the subtle phrasing and rhythms of the *Eclogues*.[4a] The effect is often trivializing and can become choppy as well. Despite his awareness that within what he calls the "rough bark and plainness" of the low style "the poet set very lofty sentiments and allegorical meanings," his discomfort at addressing the highest personages in the realm in the lowest style leads to repeated protests that he is not in violation of decorum (*OC* 228 and, e.g., 230). In short, stylistically speaking, Encina fails to discriminate adequately between the rustic and the pastoral.

An examination of the rendering of Vergil's first seventeen lines will serve to bring out characteristic tendencies in Encina's handling of the civic pastoral. Following this we will see how subsequent parts of his version reflect the euphoric millenarianism of the Argument, and how his none-too-delicate touch alters the tone of Vergil's ending.

It takes Encina a whole stanza to unburden himself of the inferences he draws from Vergil's first two lines:

Sicelides Musae, paulo maiora canamus.
non omnis arbusta iuvant humilesque myricae;

Muses of Sicily let us sing of a somewhat loftier theme. Hedge
and lowly tamarisk do not delight everyone.

Musas de Sicilia dexemos pastores,
alcemos las velas del nuestro dezir,
razón nos combida aver de escrevir
misterios más altos de cosas mayores,
ni a todos agradan los grandes primores
ni a todos tan poco las cosas palpables,
cantemos estilo notable a notables
y suene el menor allá con menores.

(1–8)

Sicilian muses, let's drop shepherds, let's hoist the sails of our style. Reason invites us to write of higher mysteries involving greater things. Great refinements are not pleasing to all, but neither are palpable things. Let's sing in a noteworthy style to people of note and relegate the lesser style to lesser people.

The tone is offhand but it reveals some defensiveness in regard to the anticipated reactions of certain possible audiences.[5] There are those who may be inclined to criticize him for aspiring too high, personally and stylistically, Encina seems to be saying. Let them confine their interest to its sphere—the more "palpable" earthy parts of his translations, the unavoidable "pastoral talk simply uttered."

Vergil's third line carries Encina halfway through his second stanza:

si canimus silvas, silvae sint consule dignae.

If we sing of woods, let woods be worthy of a consul.

Si silvas cantamos, las silvas merecen
de rey tan notable gozar fe y dar gloria,
pues reyna tal rey de tanta vitoria
los grandes triunfos a él se enderecen.

(9-12)

If we sing of woods, woods are worthy of enjoying the confidence of so notable a king and of glorifying him. Since so victorious a king reigns, may great triumphs come his way.

The courtier sees his opportunity for flattery, but Encina also takes refuge in the authority of his text and converts the succinct optative of Vergil's justification of the civic pastoral ("let woods be worthy of a consul") into a slightly defiant indicative ("woods are worthy . . .," 9).

The final four lines of Encina's second stanza adjust fairly smoothly to Vergil's lines 4–6. In his third stanza Encina manages to make the returning "Virgo" of Vergil's sixth line (*iam redit et Virgo*)—i.e., the virgin Astraea (Justice)—do double duty as justice (in process of reformation by the Catholic Sovereigns) and the Virgin Mary. The Christian Virgin additionally stands in for the Lucina (Juno as goddess of childbirth) of Vergil's eighth and tenth lines:

tú da perfeción
al príncipe don Juan ya nacido . . .

(19-20)

grant fulfillment to Prince John, born already.

This last adaptation enables Encina to slip by the awkward fact that Prince John is rapidly maturing into young manhood as he writes: the Virgin is to grant fulness of years to the "already born" prince.

Two stanzas follow, addressed to the sovereigns, in which Encina manages, none too smoothly, to equate the enterprising and optimistic spirit of his own times, created by the monarchs' rule, with Vergil's vision of an imminent Golden Age. Encina's need to observe proprieties by addressing the two monarchs simultaneously lies behind some variation on Vergil's successive addresses to father and son. At one point—*tenéys él y vos y assí vos como él, / con Dios tanta fe* (29–30 "He and you, you as well as he, keep such faith with God")—he is evidently underscoring the Catholic sovereigns' motto, *Tanto monta, monta tanto, Isabel como Fernando* (i.e., Ferdinand is just as sovereign as Isabella, Isabella just as sovereign as Ferdinand). He then derives from Vergil's *te duce, si qua manent sceleris vestigia nostri, / insita perpetua solvent formidine terras* (13–14 "Under your leadership, any traces of our guilt that remain will become void and release the earth from everlasting fear") an allusion to Moslems, Jews, and the Inquisition:

> . . . que sus deservicios
> avéys destruydo y todos los vicios
> y alguno, si queda, daréis cabo dél.
>
> (30–31)

> . . . that you have undone wrongs done Him and all vices, and if any remains, you'll put a stop to it.

The aggressive zeal of Encina's tone carries him far beyond Vergil's imperturbability. On the other hand, he can on occasion smoothly Christianize his original. His lines

> avréys con los santos su mesmo consuelo
> gozando en presencia la vista de Dios . . .
>
> (37–8)

> you will share the recompense of saints, rejoicing in the direct sight of God . . .

hark back to Vergil's

> ille deum vitam accipiet divisque videbit
> permixtos heroas et ipse videbitur illis.
>
> (15–16)

> He will accept the life of the gods and will see heroes consorting with gods and himself will be seen by them.

After reproducing with earthy touches—e.g. in the "palpable" detail of the goats' swollen udders (Vergil's line 21)—the Latin poet's evocation of Nature's coming bountifulness, Encina eventually reaches the climax of his version of the millenarian vision, in his adaptation of Vergil's final invitation to the *cara deum suboles* ("dear offspring of the gods") to enter into his birthright (lines 49-52):

> O claro linage, vitoria escogida!,
> los grandes triunfos y mucha alabança
> a vos que se deve se dé, sin dudança,
> ya vienen los tiempos de gloria crecida;
> mirad toda España que estava perdida,
> las tierras y el mar, la fe no constante:
> alégranse todos por lo de adelante,
> que el bien se nos viene con vuestra venida.
>
> (97-104)

Oh bright family line, select victory! May triumphant acclaim and great praise be given you, as is your undoubted due. The times of increased glory are now upon us. Behold all Spain, which had been lost, lands and sea, tottering faith: all rejoice in what lies ahead, for all good is coming to us with your coming.

If the cosmic dimensions of Vergil's exalted look into the future are missing here and the *caelumque profundum* of line 51 is reduced to "tottering faith" (102), the insertion of an allusion to the past, to a Spain "which had been lost" (101) but is now rejoicing in the promise of the age to come, effectively captures the buoyancy of Vergil's tone.

While Vergil avoids sustaining the note of exultation to the end, Encina has no thought of a similar relaxation:

> incipe, parve puer, risu cognoscere matrem
> (matri longa decem tulerunt fastidia menses)
> incipe, parve puer: qui non risere parenti,
> nec deus hunc mensa, dea nec dignata cubili est.
>
> (60-63)

Begin, baby boy, to recognize your mother with a smile (your mother endured ten long months of trial). Begin, baby boy. Those who do not smile on their parents no god honors with his table, no goddess with her couch.

Fin

Mostradle comienço de bienes estraños,
pues deven los hijos gran deuda a las madres,
que a los que no toman plazer con sus padres
aquéllos da Dios trabajos y daños;
comiencen verdades, feneçan engaños,
feneçan pesares, comiencen plazeres,
o reyna tan santa, primor de mugeres!,
o rey ecelente, biváys dos mil años!

(121–8)

End

Show her [i.e., Prince John show Isabella] the beginnings of rare blessings, for children are much in their mothers' debt, and upon those who don't take pleasure in their parents, God visits toils and harm. Let truths begin, deceptions end; troubles end, pleasures begin. Oh most saintly queen, flower among women, oh most excellent king, may you live two thousand years!

Encina is decorous in adapting to Christian and royal circumstances Vergil's allusions to gestation and to the consorting of humans with goddesses. In contrast to the gentle intimacy of Vergil's ending, however, Encina makes the amphibrachs of his final four lines pulsate almost dithyrambically in a triumphant coda. His display of energy is far less refined than the lightness of Vergil's touch.

II

History, in her unaccountable fashion, fulfilled Encina's hopes far otherwise than he had envisaged. When Garcilaso de la Vega turns to Vergil some forty years after the publication of Encina's *Cancionero* of 1496, Ferdinand and Isabella's Castile and Aragon have become the imperial Spain of their grandson Charles V, born in 1500. The hopes centering in the person of Prince John have long since been dashed: he had died without issue in 1497. As heir to the throne of the Holy Roman Empire, following the death of his father, Philip the Fair, Charles unites in his person the destinies of Spain with those of Hapsburg Austria.

Throughout Garcilaso's short life, the development of his exceptional artistic gifts had constantly to contend with his discharging of duties as courtier and soldier to the Emperor whose nearly exact contemporary he was. There are Vergilian echoes in his poetry prior to 1533 but it was only after a happy turn of fortune took him to Naples in that year to serve at the court of the Emperor's viceroy, the Duke of Alba, that he was able, in the three years remaining to him, to bring his art to plenitude in his three eclogues. The Vergilian pastoral model, Vergilian paradigms and imagery, sometimes mediated by intervening Italian voices, led him into the expression of a voice indisputably his own and an achievement that was to set the future course of poetry in Spain.

This would not have been possible had it not been for the thorough humanistic education which Garcilaso had enjoyed as the second son of a noble family of Toledo, his training in Latin according to the prescriptions of Nebrija, and his exposure to fresh currents of Erasmian humanism, then strongly flowing in Spain. Two other occurrences, one a personal experience, the other a literary development, played a decisive role in the maturation of Garcilaso's art. The first is the deep, unreciprocated passion he conceived for Isabel Freyre, a lady-in-waiting to the Portuguese princess, Leonor, who came to Granada in 1526 to marry her cousin, Charles V. The second is the metrical revolution which came about through an encounter, during this same Granadine sojourn of the court, between Garcilaso's intimate literary confrère, Juan Boscán, and the Venetian ambassador, Andrea Navagero. The latter strongly urged the adaptation of Italian meters and strophes to Spanish poetry, counsel of which Garcilaso would be the chief beneficiary. It is primarily this metrical revolution which opens a chasm between the art of Juan del Encina and that of Garcilaso. Despite the former's long sojourns in Rome and the composition there of his finest dramatic eclogues, he had remained impervious to Italian metrical practice. Garcilaso, on the other hand, had attained by 1526 a mastery of the Spanish courtly lyric and of Spanish metrics which left him more than ready for an expansion of his artistic horizons. He was not long in mastering the supple Italian hendecasyllable with its several prosodic types and their variants. Of the new verse-forms and strophic patterns from the Italian, the operative one in the case of Garcilaso's *First Eclogue*, from which my illustrations are drawn, is that of Petrarch's fifth canzone: *Ne la stagion che 'l ciel rapido inchina* ("At the time of day when the sky [sc., the sun] rapidly declines"). Garcilaso reproduces Petrarch's fourteen-line stanza of intermingled seven- and eleven-syllable lines but strengthens its impact by turning the final line of each stanza into a forceful and unvarying one-line refrain: *Salid sin duelo, lágrimas, corriendo* ("Well, tears, unstintingly, and flow").

A final factor in the blossoming of Garcilaso's talent in Naples was his frequentation of the humanists of the Accademia Pontaniana, where the recently deceased Sannazaro (d. 1530) was still a revered presence. In the *Egloga primera* an art sprung from native Spanish tradition has assimilated the humanistic heritage, modes, and pregnant conventions of Italian literature, most evidently of Petrarch, the Petrarchists, and Sannazaro.

Behind them one discovers Vergil, Ovid, Horace, and other Latin poets, who are both mediated for Garcilaso by Sannazaro and his countrymen, and perceptible in direct resonance, Vergil most of all. While it is the poet of the *Bucolics* who furnishes the major subtexts for the *First Eclogue*, no overview of Garcilaso's art would be complete that did not take into account the interplay and the blending of ancient and modern voices and, in the present connection, the particular role of Sannazaro vis-à-vis Vergil.

The frame of the *Egloga primera* was clearly Vergilian, as any reader acquainted with Vergil's eighth Eclogue would have recognized. But it would soon have become evident that Vergil's pattern was undergoing expansion and readjustment in being fitted to a new situation. In Vergil's five-line introduction and in Garcilaso's first six lines, an intention is announced to sing of two shepherds whose own songs transfix the dumb creatures of the natural world. But whereas Damon and Alphesiboeus are presented as competing in song (*certantis*, 3), Garcilaso's shepherds are simply lamenting jointly, as their opening lines declare:

> El dulce lamentar de dos pastores,
> Salicio juntamente y Nemoroso,
> é de cantar. . .
>
> (1-3)

> Of two shepherds' sweet laments,
> at once Salicio's and Nemoroso's,
> shall be my song. . .

Expansion of a Vergilian paradigm is particularly evident at the "hinge" between the ending of the first shepherd's song and the beginning of that of his companion:

> Haec Damon; vos, quae responderit Alphesiboeus,
> dicite, Pierides: non omnia possumus omnes.
>
> (62-3)

> Thus Damon. Do you, maids of Pieria, sing what Alphesiboeus answered. We are not all capable of all things.

> Aquí dio fin a su cantar Salicio,
> y sospirando en el postrero acento,
> soltó de llanto una profunda vena;
> queriendo el monte al grave sentimiento
> d'aquel dolor en algo ser propicio,
> con la pessada boz retumba y suena;
>   la blanda Philomena,

casi como dolida
  y a compassión movida,
dulcemente responde al son lloroso.
Lo que cantó tras esto Nemoroso,
dezildo vos, Piérides, que tanto
    no puedo yo ni oso,
que siento enflaquecer mi débil canto.

(225–38)

Salicio stopped his singing with these words,
subsiding in a sigh that soon
became a stream of copious tears.
The mountain sought to show it had a share
in the deep pain that song expressed:
with heavy voice it rumbles and resounds.
    The gentle nightingale
    as if she knew the pain
    and felt the pity,
softly takes up the tearful strain.
What following this was sung by Nemoroso,
is yours to tell, Pierians; I cannot,
    I lack the art and daring,
I feel my slender song deserting me.

More is involved here than a Renaissance literary artist's emulative variation on an older paradigm. The lacrimosity of Garcilaso's shepherds, in the first place, evidently owes more to Petrarch and his followers and to Sannazaro than to Vergil. As for their non-competitiveness, it is true, of course, that the song contest in Vergil is only embryonic: there is no one to award a prize and the competitive situation of the singers is quietly passed over at the end. Nevertheless, the relationship in which the songs of Salicio and Nemoroso stand to each other is significantly different from that obtaining between the songs of Damon and Alphesiboeus. Of Eclogue 8, Michael Putnam notes that "The whole poem—both its constituent parts—is a hymn to that power in song capable of molding nature, animate or inanimate, to its will. The two songs are individual variations on the theme."[6] In Damon's song Nyssa's deception, through the rent it makes in the pastoral fabric, propels the shepherd toward death.[7] In the song of Alphesiboeus, Amaryllis regains her lover Daphnis by her *carmina*—song-spells—bringing about his re-integration into the pastoral world.

    Garcilaso's *First Eclogue* is less a celebration than a demonstration; what it demonstrates is only incidentally the Orphic power of song. Its emphasis is on the cathartic or therapeutic value of singing for the individual singer-composer. (This in a far more thoroughgoing manner than in the *boutade* of

Corydon at the end of Vergil's Eclogue 2 or in the Polyphemus of Theocritus.) In the interpretation most convincing to me, Garcilaso relives in Salicio's song the emotional cycle of his responses to what he saw as a defection on the part of Isabel Freyre, her marriage to an unworthy suitor.[8] In the second part, the song of Nemoroso, he pours out his grief at the news of Isabel's death, which reached him shortly before he wrote the *Egloga primera*. Both personae and both voices are Garcilaso's own. The *dédoublement* gives his art a wholly different cast from that of Vergil, let alone from Sannazaro's lovingly assembled mosaics of classical *loci*, more esthetically than affectively charged. A substratum of emotion still perceptibly endows the eclogue with a vigor of expression, a dynamic surge of feeling, that reflect Garcilaso's own temper and, reinforcing it, a legacy of the vigorous expressive tradition of fifteenth-century Castilian court and *cancionero* poetry. We are far from the statuesque characters and the processional movements of Sannazaro's *Arcadia*. The fluid onrunning Petrarchan strophe leads Garcilaso, at times with Sannazaro as intermediary, into an unraveling of the Latin lines that is never simply decorative or otiose. Lines multiply, their texture loosens, and Garcilaso's phrasing adjusts itself with ease to the Petrarchan schemes, longer and shorter breaths coming without forcing.

Sometimes variations made by Sannazaro upon Vergil offer Garcilaso channels toward further variations of his own. Such is the case with the invocation of the patron which in both the Spanish and the Latin poets follows upon the opening lines. Here it is the invocation of the Italian to his admired Cassandra Marchese in the fifth of the *Piscatorial Eclogues* composed by him in Latin that suggests itself to Garcilaso. In invoking a military leader (presumably Pollio), Vergil had briefly placed him in two imagined situations:

> Tu mihi, seu magni superas iam saxa Timavi,
> sive oram Illyrici legis aequoris, . . .
>   accipe iussis
> carmina coepta tuis . . .
>
> (8.6–7, 11–12)

Whether you are now passing the rocks of mighty Timavus or skirting the shore of the Illyrian sea, . . . receive the songs begun by your orders . . .

Sannazaro, with much incremental virtuosity, expands the alternatives to three:

> Tu mihi, seu doctas percurris Palladis artes
> . . . .

seu . . .
venatu Prochyten maternaque regna fatigas,
sive . . .
ludentes spectas Nereidas, en age nostros
(si quis honos pelagi) Cassandra, en aspice lusus.

(7–14)

Whether you are pursuing the learned art of Pallas . . ., whether
. . . wearing down Prochyte and your native realm with your
hunting, or whether . . . you are watching the Nereids at their
play, do come, Cassandra (if any honor attaches to the sea) and
observe my playing.

Garcilaso picks up Sannazaro's triadic pattern:

tú . . .
. . .
agora estés atento sólo y dado
al ínclito govierno del estado
albano; agora buelto a la otra parte,
resplandeciente, armado,
representando en tierra el fiero Marte;
agora . . .
. . . por ventura
andes a caza, el monte fatigando
. . .
espera . . .

(7–21)

You . . .
whether you now are tending
to lofty tasks of governance in
your Alban state; or busy elsewhere,
in glittering armor represent
fierce Mars on earth;
or whether . . .
. . . you perchance,
leading the hunt, wear down the hills
. . .
await the day . . .

The increased expansiveness of Garcilaso's lines arises easily and unostenta-
tiously from his skilled handling of the fluid strophic pattern. Sannazaro's
hunting alternative, applicable to either sex, suits his needs and is retained;
the land-based military possibility must be suggested by Vergil; while the

third one—civil governance—is appropriate purely to Garcilaso's own patron, the Duke of Alba.

Expansiveness becomes almost palpable in the lines which mark an exfoliation of the succinct Vergilian image of the pastoral ivy becoming interwoven on Pollio's brow with martial laurel (8.12-13):

> el árbol de victoria
> que ciñe estrechamente
> tu glorïosa frente
> dé lugar a la yedra que se planta
> debaxo de tu sombra y se levanta
> poco a poco, arrimada a tus loores.
>
> (35–40)

> let the victorious branch
> which tightly wreathes
> your glorious brow
> make room for the ivy growing
> in your shadow, cleaving
> as it mounts, to your acclaim.

The ivy creeping laterally around Pollio's brow symbolizes not only the offering of this product of Vergil's pastoral muse to Pollio, but Pollio's own share of literary achievement. Garcilaso's dependence as courtier on the Duke leads him to adopt a more deferential tone and to dwell on the upward progress of the plant from obscurity into a prominence guaranteed by the laurels which support it.

How, finally, might one describe the function of Sannazaro in relation to Vergil in the gestation of Garcilaso's *First Eclogue*? Garcilaso surely had known the Latin poet's eclogues since youth, before ever encountering Sannazaro. It seems likely that the latter's prime rôle was by his own example to lead Garcilaso back to Vergil. Such an assumption has the weight of textual evidence behind it: the evidently non-Vergilian phrase "Mantuan Tityrus" embedded in the fabric of a stanza otherwise woven entirely of topoi reworked from Vergil's second Eclogue:

> despectus tibi sum, nec qui sim quaeris, Alexi,
> quam dives pecoris, nivei quam lactis abundans.
> mille meae Siculis errant in montibus agnae;
> lac mihi non aestate novum, non frigore defit.
> canto quae solitus, si quando armenta vocabat,
> Amphion Dircaeus in Actaeo Aracyntho.
> nec sum adeo informis . . .
>
> (19–25)

I am scorned by you, Alexis. You do not even inquire who I am,
how rich in herds, how wealthy in snow-white milk. A thousand
lambs of mine wander on the mountains of Sicily. I lack fresh
milk neither in summer nor in winter. I sing songs such as
Amphion of Dirce was wont on Attic Aracynthus, whenever he
called his herds. And I am not so ugly . . .

Siempre de nueva leche en el verano
y en el invierno abundo; en mi majada
la manteca y el queso está sobrado.
De mi cantar, pues, yo te via agradada
tanto que no pudiera el mantuano
Týtero ser de ti más alabado.
      No soy, pues, bien mirado,
      tan difforme ni feo . . .

                                                    (169–76)

Ever fresh in my sheepcotes
the new milk flows; in summertime
and winter, cheese and butter abound.
And I've known you so pleased with my song,
you'd not have praised
Mantuan Tityrus more.
      All in all, no one can call me
      so ugly or ungainly . . .[9]

It was in the tenth *prosa* of Sannazaro's *Arcadia* that the periphrasis
"Mantuan Tityrus" had caught Garcilaso's eye. The context in which it
occurs there is revealing. The sage Opico has brought the lovelorn Clonico
to the sacred pine grove of Pan on an Arcadian mountain top to be cured by
the venerable priest of Pan, Enareto. In front of the cave containing the
statue of the god hangs "a beautiful large pipe . . . the like of which had
never been seen by shepherd in any wood." Enareto explains that this is the
pipe Pan found in his hands at the end of his fruitless pursuit of Syrinx.
"From him it succeeded, how I do not know, into the hands of a shepherd
of Syracuse . . . who, overtaken by envious death, made a final gift of it to
Mantuan Tityrus . . . who, when he went on to sing higher things, left it
hanging there." No successor has ever proved capable of playing on it
competently, though many have tried.[10]

Here was all the invitation Garcilaso needed to claim his place as a
successor to Vergil in a centuries-long song contest, a literary line still felt as
open-ended. In Garcilaso's lines the exemplum of Mantuan Tityrus simply
replaces the reference of Vergil's Corydon to Amphion of Dirce, similarly
inserted at the juncture of two exactly corresponding topoi—the shepherd's

never-failing milk and his championing of his appearance—both singers being invoked as major links in an age-old chain of pastoral song. In the passage of Sannazaro's tenth *prosa*, on the other hand, the context in which we find "Mantuan Tityrus" invoked is wholly distinct, as already seen. And when topoi expressive of pastoral merits or assets do occur in Sannazaro, the use of the third person instead of the first sets them further apart from their Vergilian source.[11] In a word, though Sannazaro does not always so clearly act as catalyst for a creative response to Vergil on Garcilaso's part, the present instance probably best characterizes his dominant function for the Spanish poet, who, once shown the way, could dispense with his guidance if he chose.

III

With Luis de León, the object of scrutiny becomes once again, as with Encina, a translation of the *Eclogues*, but my purpose will now be to discern in the performance of the translator the beginning stage of a major poet's art. From re-creation of Vergil to original creation is perhaps a considerable step; yet it will be possible, I think, to suggest how the poet's experience of the *Eclogues* helped him to take it. As regards Luis de León's handling of Vergil's text in comparison with Encina's procedures (no one else is known to have attempted the *Eclogues* in the interim), dissimilarities are more striking than affinities. The central difference is that in this exercise of Luis de León's early years—one cannot be more precise in dating—he is already the conscious literary artist visibly pursuing particular stylistic goals. The hand that translates the *Eclogues*, though lacking deftness, shows unmistakable signs of mastery to come, the mastery which will make his small number of compositions, largely written in a strophe perfected by Garcilaso, a landmark of Hispanic poetic expression. After glancing at the place the pastoral occupies in Fray Luis's poetic and spiritual world, I shall draw on portions of his version of the lament for Daphnis in the fifth Eclogue as a means of following him as he feels his way from the original language to the vernacular. Without entirely overlooking instances of unsuccessful groping, I shall concentrate on felicities in his techniques of adjustment and expansion, especially as regards his handling of rhetorical figures, of prosody, rhythm and meter, and of the phonic possibilities of Castilian.

The entrance of Luis de León into the Augustinian order in 1544, at the age of sixteen, enabled him to begin reaping the benefits of the rigorous classical training which its educational reforms had fostered. He could not have been too long in discovering that the temper of the Vergilian pastorals answered a deep need of his vigorous, active temperament for intervals of reflective calm, for inner and outer harmony, and for transcendence, the same need that the mystical tendency of much of his verse would seek to supply. It is affinities of sensibility that make the dominant Latin resonances of his verse Vergilian, despite a frequent sententious and lapidary cast reminiscent of Horace.[12] Notwithstanding his inclination toward Vergil, however, the vision Fray Luis holds of the pastoral exceeds the confines of any literary mode. For him, a Christian humanist and accomplished Hebraist and Hellenist, it embraces the Old Testament and the New, patriarchs and Good Shepherd; he finds a pervasive presence of the pastoral in the world he himself inhabits as well. The pastoral is all one, whether he encounters it in the *Song of Songs* ("all of it is a pastoral eclogue," he writes)[13] or among the Greeks and Latins, or indeed imposes its ideal upon a natural world contemplated through eyes steeped in the tradition of Augustine's neo-platonism and the Augustinians' emphasis on the continuing epiphany of Christ in the created world. He brings to his perception of the pastoral a Renaissance sensibility that re-experiences and recreates the substance of literary and sacred texts in terms of a human, natural, material world familiar to it, a world which arouses not misgivings but delight. For all its trials and imperfections, the world for him is far from being hollow, deceptive, and dangerous, as it already is becoming for some of his early baroque contemporaries.

"Pastoral life," says Marcello, one of the interlocutors in a conversation about the name "Pastor" in Luis de León's prose masterpiece, *The Names of Christ*, "has its delights, all the greater because they arise from the simplest, purest, most natural things: the sight of the open sky, the purity of the air, the configuration of the land, the green of the grasses, the beauty of roses and flowers ...." After mentioning the pastoral activity of the early patriarchs of the Old Testament, Marcello goes on to observe that "there is no poet who does not sing of the pastoral life and laud it." To which a fellow-monk adds: "If no one lauded it, sufficient for its praise would be what was said of it by the Latin poet who, in all he said, surpassed all others and in that poetry seems to surpass himself: so choice and elegant are the verses in which he speaks of it." Marcello replies in a clearly Augustinian-Platonic vein, referring to the shepherd's unimpeded vision of the air, the earth, and the other elements as a "kind of school of pure and true love." This is in explanation of the omnipresence of love in pastoral writing. He proceeds to evoke a vision of the elements in mutual embrace, placed in concert with the greatest harmony.[14]

Luis de León's translations of the *Eclogues*, as might be expected, are in the Italian hendecasyllables first practiced by Garcilaso and Boscán. The lines are disposed in one of two stanzaic patterns: *octavas reales* (*ottava rima*) or *tercetos* (*terza rima*), the latter being the case with the version of the fifth Eclogue, from which my samples are chosen. Aside from possessing greater innate esthetic sensitivity and having Garcilaso's practice to illumine him, Luis de León is by nature a finer and more exacting Latinist than Encina. His suppleness may be exemplified by the varied renditions of *decori* and *decus* scattered through lines 53-60 of his version in nouns and verbs:

> vitis ut arboribus decori est, ut vitibus uvae,
> ut gregibus tauri, segetes ut pinguibus arvis,
> tu decus omne tuis.
>
> (32-4)

as the vine is a source of beauty for trees, as grapes for vines, as bulls for herds, as corn for the rich fields, so you are a glory to mankind.

> tú de tu campo todo y compañía
> la hermosura fuiste y bien entero,
>   ansí como del olmo es alegría
> la vid, y de la vid son las colgadas
> uvas, y de la grey el toro es guía;
>   cual hermosea el toro las vacadas,
> como las mieses altas y abundosas
> adornan y enriquecen las aradas.
>
> (53-60)

You of all your countryside and company were the embellishment and entire good, as of the elm the joy is the vine, and of the vine the hanging grapes, and of the herd the bull is guide; as the bull embellishes herds of cows, as the tall and plentiful corn adorns and enriches the grainfields.[15]

Vergil's compactness allows a single term to function as tenor for four similes, but Fray Luis discovers that he can make the roominess and fluidity of his tercets effectively subserve the unpacking imposed by the semantics and syntax of the vernacular. In the course of expanding hardly more than two lines of Vergil, he produces eight hendecasyllables, not without amplification to be sure, yet without violating the semantic range of the single Latin word: *hermosura* (beauty, embellishment), line 54; *bien* (well-being, good), line 54; *alegría* (joy), line 55; *guía* (guide), line 57; *hermosea* (embellishes), line 58; *adornan y enriquecen* (adorn and enrich), line 60. Each of Vergil's condensed comparisons is extended into a clause; a given clause may embrace two line-units, be co-extensive with one, or cover less than one, with pauses correspondingly more or less marked at line-ends. (I shall return to the question of enjambment.) Monotony is avoided at no cost in smoothness, continuity, or cadence. One recognizes here skills that will distinguish the metrics of the original verse.

Like any translator, Luis de León must face the problem created by the resistance of the receiving language to stylistic possibilities admitted by the original. A typical instance involves the hyperbaton, especially as seen in the interwoven texture of Latin lines that break up syntagmatic flectional groups: *et foliis lentas intexere mollibus hastas* (31 "and to intertwine hard spears with soft leaves"). The line is particularly strong because syntax acts as a signifier in its own right. Here Fray Luis simply suppresses the adjectives: *Tú el enramar las lanzas has mostrado* (51 "You taught [us] how to decorate lances with boughs"). He partly makes up for the sacrifice of the expressive adjectives, however, by incorporating one in the verb: for the "intertwine" of the Latin, he gives us in *enramar* a verb that directly suggests intertwining with green branches (*ramas*). The Castilian line is certainly less expressive than the original, yet its effect is still vivid. With the loss of *mollibus* (soft), the translator loses the echo created by the *molli* of Vergil's line 38: *pro molli viola* ("instead of the soft violet"). As if sensing this, Fray Luis is also willing to relinquish the "soft" in his translation of that phrase, which becomes simply *en vez de la violeta* (67 "instead of the violet"). The Spanish poet's prudence in eschewing the reproduction of so complex a Latin syntactical design looks ahead to his practice in his original work. There, while hyperbata are frequent enough, the instances are extremely rare in which they exceed in complexity the simpler types acclimatized by the practice of earlier Italian and Spanish poets.[16]

Where a simpler hyperbaton is involved, Fray Luis already shows himself capable of strikingly beautiful effects, as in his rendering of Vergil's line 40—*spargite humum foliis, inducite fontibus umbras* ("Strew the ground with leaves, cover the founts with shade")—in his lines 70–71: *Pues esparcid ya rosas, poned velo / a las fuentes de sombra* . . . ("So strew roses now, place a veil / over the fountains of shadow . . ."). The interposition of *a las fuentes* between the usually inseparable noun and adjective of a single syntagmatic unit— perhaps simply the result of following what in the original is quite normal word order—adds a new and fertile layer of meaning to the line by making springs of shadow a metaphor for sources of sorrow. Of course, there are occasions when the creation of a Latinate hyperbaton comes off far less felicitously, as in the phrase *con traidora / y muerte crudelísima* (37–8, literally, "by a treacherous and death most cruel"), which renders the straight-forward adverbial *crudeli funere* ("by a cruel death") of Vergil's line 20. A technical inadequacy leads to padding and a forcing of rhyme in this case. Indeed, padding, to which the expansiveness of vernacular syntax and meter may all too easily lead, is a problem throughout. The yoking of lion, for example, as well as tiger, to Bacchus's chariot strikes one as bizarre.[17]

Fray Luis is sensitive to Vergil's artistry in foregrounding given effects by prominent placement of particular words: the note of coolness, for example, through the prepositive *frigida* of the *frigida flumina* (cool rivers) at the beginning of line 25. Unable to retain either the initial positioning or the connection of coolness with rivers, Fray Luis links coolness to the *frías / cuevas* (cool caves) which the lions of his version acquire. He underscores the coolness by placing the adjective last in the line and initiating with it a strongly felt enjambment. One detects here the touch of a translator, and artist, concerned with something more than immediate denotation, aware that on occasion the function a word fulfills within a broad context is as important as its particular placement in this context. The note of coolness serves here to create by contrast a sensation of heat in the whole pastoral scene.

The enjambment handled so expressively in this instance has many counterparts in Fray Luis's mature verse. Indeed, still within the present example one may point to an equally forceful and actually more concentrated use of this device: the supplying of *colgadas* (hanging), line 56, as prepositive epithet for *uvas* (grapes), line 57, precisely in a final "hung-over" position. (Vergil's *uvae*, line 32, is unmodified.) Luis de León's sensory imagination recreates the image by extrapolating visual, even tactile, properties left implicit in the original. Similarly, a keen ear tells him how to capitalize on the combined effect of resumption or new beginning and continuation implicit in the structure of the tercet, through repetitions absent from the Latin, e.g. the repetition of line 57 in his line 58 (cited above). A hint from Vergil has probably been the stimulus here: Fray Luis is in effect repeating the anadiplosis figure found only in Vergil's line 32 but half-expected in line 33 (cited above). In the process he achieves a pleasing lexical variation—*grey* versus *vacadas*—for which English is inadequate ("herd" as against "herd of cows") and an inversion of structure. These features, not present in the Latin, are very much at home in the Spanish, since they bind two tercets together in a chiastic relationship.

Moving on to more particularly phonic effects, one must take note, finally, of Fray Luis's ability, even at this stage of apprenticeship, to come up with hendecasyllables of superb cadence and sonic texture, which at times, like certain lines of his original verse, seem to foreshadow Góngora in their mastery of verbal music. Forgoing a detailed phonic analysis, one may simply point out examples, indicating dominant patterns of stress with grave accents:

Line 39: *tòda la deidàd que el àgua mòra* (o-a-a-o) ("all the gods that inhabit the waters"). The expressive pattern of the Spanish sonorities, which are reinforced by unstressed *a*'s, partially compensates for the specificity lost with the absence of Vergil's hazels, wood nymphs, and water nymphs of line 21: *vos coryli testes et flumina Nymphis* ("you hazels and streams bear witness to the nymphs").

Line 73: *Y con dolòr, pastòres, y̌ gemìd* (o-o-[i]-i) ("and with grief, shepherds, and moaning"). The shift from the persistent low *o*'s to the high *i*'s provides

unmediated support for the sense. The line makes phonically explicit a threnodic effect deducible from the original but not brought out there at this point.
Lines 76–8:

> Yò Dàfni descansàndo aquì repòso (o-a-a-i-o)
> nombràdo entre las sèlvas hàsta el cièlo, (a-e-a-ie)
> de hermòsa grèy pastòr muy màs hermòso. (o-ey-o-a-o)

> I, Daphnis, resting here repose, famous in the woods even to the skies, of lovely flock shepherd far more lovely.

Highly effective is this three-line rendering of Vergil's two-line epitaph:

> Daphnis ego in silvis, hinc usque ad sidera notus,
> formosi pecoris custos, formosior ipse.
>
>   (43–4)

> I was Daphnis in the woods, known hence even to the stars. Fair was the flock I guarded, fairer I.

Luis de León expands on the original only by making explicit in the first line the notion of repose left unstated by Vergil. Passing over the varied sonic patterns, one may observe how the verbal equivalent of smooth stone carving achieved in the chiseled Latin phrasing reappears in the Spanish in the well-joined syntax. The *aquí* of line 74 fits equally well with the preceding participle and the ensuing present indicative. The beautifully graduated effect of line 44 in the Latin, dependent mainly on the two degrees of the adjective, is effortlessly reproduced through the two degrees of the exact Spanish equivalent. The unavoidable unpacking caused by the compound nature of the Romance comparative is redeemed by the discreet stress on the monosyllabic *más*. This word is in turn eased into the line through a new alliteration carried by the adverb *muy*. The resultant polish is perhaps higher than that of the Latin, yet it does not strike one as excessive, probably because the whole line is so smoothly joined through a perfectly natural omission of articles. (This Latinate feature, unobtrusive here, will be a favorite with Góngora, though the effect sought by him will be pointedly classicizing.) One notes the same unobtrusiveness in the moderate end-stopping of the three lines: they comprise a triple unit, not a single one nor yet three separate units. Again the effect is of smooth joining, not unlike that of the original. In this same third line of the epitaph, finally, the chiasmus not present in the original keeps the comparative in which, unlike the Latin, the Spanish line ends from unbalancing it and assures by different means the same effect of subsidence the Latin gives.

With such textual observations as these in mind, one is not surprised to find that Luis de León is the first Spanish writer to champion the vernacular as an expressly artistic instrument, the first to draw attention to its phonic qualities, and to the lexical riches it has acquired.[18] In retrospective remarks on his translations one finds evidence of the sort of experience of the vernacular the discipline of translation brought him as well as an anticipation of more modern views on the subject of translation itself. Let a would-be judge, he says,

> first try out for himself what it is to translate elegant poetry from a foreign tongue to his own, without adding or removing any meaning, retaining as far as possible the figures of the original and its grace, and causing the verse to speak in Castilian not as something foreign and intrusive but as if born in it and native to it . . . It will be revealed that our language is most receptive to everything entrusted to it and is not harsh or poor, as some say, but abundant and like wax in the hands of those who know how to employ it.[19]

Even from my limited sampling, it is possible, I think, to conclude that Luis de León's versions are indeed operative in their own right and on their own terms, not without lapses but consistently enough to keep one aware that it is a promising poetic voice one is hearing. Throughout the versions of the *Eclogues* one detects a young artist finding himself as he probes the art of Vergil, creating on his own as he recreates his cherished model. So much does he sense in Vergil a kindred spirit that he is able to accept the Latin poet on his own terms, with almost no Christianizing, much less any "applying" of the text, and no alarm at his "pagan" sensuality.

Of the three poets examined, it is of course Garcilaso who has made the most significant creative use of Vergil. Unlike the others, Garcilaso was touched by the Vergil of the *Bucolics* at the peak of his powers. But it is Luis de León who displays the most discriminating and disinterested sensitivity to what moderns see as the special tonality, the consummate artistry of the *Eclogues*. After Luis de León, whose versions had to wait some three quarters of a century for publication (circulating in manuscript in the meantime), Vergil continues throughout the rest of the sixteenth century to be the most frequently published of classical authors in Spain, though soon the *Georgics* and the *Aeneid* overtake the *Eclogues* in favor.[20] But by then the *Eclogues* have played their part in the genesis of the modern Spanish lyric and one might even say, remembering Juan del Encina, in the rise of the Spanish drama.[21]

Notes

1. The texts and translations cited in this paper have the following sources. Translations of Vergil are from Michael C.J. Putnam, *Virgil's Pastoral Art: Studies in the "Eclogues"* (Princeton: Princeton University Press, 1970). For Juan del Encina, *Obras completas*, I, ed. Ana M. Rambaldo (Madrid: Espasa-Calpe, 1978) for the Spanish texts; English translations are my own. For Garcilaso de la Vega, *Obras completas con comentario*, ed. Elias L. Rivers (Columbus: Ohio State University Press, 1974); English translations my own. (I have attempted English metrical versions in order to give some notion of the quality of the original.) For Sannazaro, *Jacopo Sannazaro, Opere volgari*, a cura di Alfredo Mauro (Bari: Laterza, 1961) and, for the Latin pastorals, *Arcadia and Piscatorial Eclogues* (the latter bilingual), ed. and trans. Ralph Nash (Detroit: Wayne State University Press, 1966). Translations given are my own. For Luis de León, *Obras completas castellanas*, ed. Padre Félix García, 3rd ed. (Madrid: Biblioteca de Autores Cristianos, 1959). Translations my own.
2. See Henry W. Sullivan, *Juan del Encina* (Boston: Twayne, 1976), p. 41. Nebrija was surely aware of an Italian precedent, the translation into *terze rime* by Bernardo Pulci (Florence, 1481); the second edition of 1494 precedes the publication of Encina's *Cancionero* by just two years.
3. Original text reproduced in Antonio de Nebrija, *Gramática castellana*, ed. P. Galindo Romeo and L. Ortiz Muñoz, vol. 1 (Madrid: Junta del Centenario, 1946), p. 9.
4. In a papal bull of 1502 appointing Encina cantor of the Salamanca cathedral, the Borgia pope, Alexander VI, refers to him as his "intimate and constant table-companion" (Sullivan, p. 29). Citations from the *Bucólicas*, taken from the Rambaldo edition, will be incorporated into the text with the abbreviation *OC*.
4a. In the translation of the fourth Eclogue, however, Encina uses the twelve-syllable (four amphibrach) line in stanzas of eight lines.
5. Critics have sometimes read the insecurity of the New Christian into such touchiness. See, for example, Richard J. Andrews, *Juan del Encina. Prometheus in Search of Prestige* (Berkeley: University of California Press, 1959).
6. *Virgil's Pastoral Art*, p. 281.
7. In connection with a textual parallel between Juan del Encina and Garcilaso in the formulation of impossibility topoi occasioned by the "unnatural" defection of the beloved, Cesare Segre suggests that Garcilaso was familiar with Encina's translation of Eclogue 8. See "A Conceptual Analysis of the First Eclogue of Garcilaso," *PTL. A Journal for Descriptive Poetics and Theory of Literature* 2 (1977): 331n12.
8. This interpretation has been challenged of late. See Adrien Roig, "Quiénes fueron Salicio y Nemoroso?," *Criticón* 4 (France-Ibérie Recherche, Université de Toulouse-Le Mirail, 1978): 1–36. Roig's study sketches the interpretive history of the eclogue.
9. The one echo of Vergil missing here—the thousand lambs wandering on the mountains of Sicily—can be caught in the very next stanza, beautifully adjusted to actual Spanish practices undoubtedly recalled by Garcilaso from his youth:

> *No sabes que sin cuento*
> *buscan en el estío*
> *mis ovejas el frío*
> *de la sierra de Cuenca, y el govierno*
> *del abrigado Estremo en el invierno?*
>
> (189–93)

> You know there is no end
> to my flocks when in summer
> they seek the cool heights
> of the Cuenca peaks, and, winters,
> find sheltered pasture in Extremadura.

10. Ed. Mauro, p. 81.

11. *Et acciò che chi egli è occolto non ti sia, mille pecore di bianca lana pasce per queste montagne, nè di state nè di verno mai le manca novo latte, Del suo cantare non dico altro però che quando de amore liberato lo avrai, il potrai a tua posta udire; e fiati, son certo, giulissimo* (ed. Mauro, p. 73: "And in order that you may not remain unaware who he is, he grazes a thousand white-wooled sheep in these mountains, nor ever lacks fresh milk in summer or in winter. Of his singing I shall say only that when you have cured him of love, you will be able to listen to him at will and I am sure this will be most enjoyable for you").

12. So Padre García observes in *Obras completas castellanas*, pp. 14–15 and 1405–7.

13. In the Prologue to his translation from the Hebrew, *Obras completas castellanas*, p. 63.

14. *De los nombres de Cristo*, ed. Cristóbal Cuevas, 2nd ed. (Madrid: Cátedra, 1980), pp. 221–2.

15. For purposes of analysis I have kept the translation extremely literal.

16. See Rafael Lapesa, "El hipérbaton en la poesía de Fray Luis de León," in *Studies in Spanish Literature of the Golden Age Presented to Edward M. Wilson*, ed. R.O. Jones (London: Tamesis Books, 1973), especially pp. 146–7. One may note that in the next generation Góngora will not display Fray Luis's restraint. His incorporation of highly complex Latinate syntactical patterns will contribute to the difficulty but also to the brilliant artifice of his verse.

17. *Armenias curru subiungere tigris* (31 "to yoke Armenian tigers to the chariot") becomes: *Que por tu mano, Dafni, el yugo atado / al cuello va el león y tigre fiero* (49–50 "The lion and fierce tiger go with yoke bound to neck by your hand").

18. "I combine my words, I choose them and give them their places . . . For speaking well is no ordinary thing; it is a matter for special consideration, both in what is said and in the way it is said[,] . . . a matter of choosing suitable words from the common stock, being attentive to their sounds and even counting their letters at times, weighing and measuring them and bringing them together in such a way that one says what one intends to say, not only clearly but also harmoniously and sweetly." From the Dedication to the Third Book of the *The Names of Christ* (1585), ed. Cuevas, 2nd ed., p. 497.

19. *Obras completas castellanas*, p. 1427.

20. See Theodore S. Beardsley, Jr., *Hispano-Classical Translations Printed between 1482 and 1699* (Pittsburgh: Duquesne University Press, 1970).

21. The reader who wishes to look further into the subject of this essay may find one or another of the following studies helpful. The most important is Darío Fernández-Morera, *The Lyre and the Oaten Flute: Garcilaso and the Pastoral* (London: Tamesis Books, 1982). The second chapter, on Garcilaso's first eclogue, contains some emphases paralleling my own and adds others. Among the latter: the blending of the Petrarchan *in vita* and *in morte* autobiographical tradition with that of the pastoral; the Spanish concern with personal honor, which makes Salicio ashamed to be exposing his sufferings to the eyes of others; the connection of Salicio's tears with the "running water motif" prominent in all of Garcilaso's poetry. The chapters on Encina and on Garcilaso's first eclogue in Marcial J. Bayo, *Virgilio y la pastoral española del Renacimiento (1480–1550)* (Madrid: Gredos, 1970), are largely undocumented and lacking in concreteness. In Juan C. Temprano, *Móviles y metas en la poesía pastoril de Juan del Encina* (Oviedo: Universidad de Oviedo, 1975), an opening chapter on Encina's translation of Vergil's eclogues is concerned mainly with their millenarian context and their secular emphasis. Finally, James A. Anderson, *Encina and Virgil* (University, Mississippi: Romance Monographs, 1974), concentrates on the versions of the first, second, and fourth eclogues with a view to observing Encina's "artistic procedures" and "technical accomplishments," something Anderson attempts in a series of running and sometimes random comments.

VERGIL IN THE LIGHT OF THE SIXTEENTH CENTURY: SELECTED ILLUSTRATIONS

Ruth Mortimer

The two most accomplished illustrated editions of Vergil in the sixteenth century, one printed at the beginning of the century in Strasbourg and one at mid-century in Lyons, demonstrate techniques and philosophies of woodcut illustration enhanced by application to an author as rich in imagery as Vergil. The Strasbourg edition was the better known and the more influential, but it should be noted that it appeared at a time when close copying and borrowing of woodblocks were common among printers. It is fortunate that the illustrations most copied were faithful to the text. The Lyons woodcuts, small works of art, clearly appealed to a different reader of Vergil, less in need of instruction. The selection of illustration for the following plates was made from these two interpretations, with the addition of four portraits of Vergil that raise the question of the author figure in the sixteenth century. I have not transcribed lines of Vergil directly from the text pages reproduced, but have chosen to shape the captions to suggest special features of the text that are at work within the illustrations and were thus of interest to the sixteenth-century reader.

Plate 1

Vergil. *Opera*. Strasbourg, Johann Grüninger, 1502.
Eclogues IV, leaf C4^V (woodcut: 117x147 mm.)

Sicelides Musae, paulo maiora canamus!
non omnis arbusta iuvant humilesque myricae;
si canimus silvas, silvae sint consule dignae.

(*Eclogues* 4.1–3)

Muses of Sicily, let us attempt a rather more exalted theme.
Hedgerow and humble tamarisk do not appeal to all. If we must
sing of woodlands, let them be such as may do a Consul honour.*

The edition of Vergil's *Opera* printed in Strasbourg by Johann Grüninger in
1502 was a scholarly folio, edited by Sebastian Brant. The text was
surrounded by the notes of five different commentators and enlivened by
woodcut illustrations that form almost a sixth commentary. The commentators were Servius, Donatus, Cristoforo Landino, Antonio Mancinelli,
and Domicio Calderino, identified in the text by initials or abbreviations of
their forenames. Shown is the cut at the beginning of the fourth Eclogue.
Vergil and Caius Asinius Pollio stand over the cradle of Pollio's son. The
child celebrated in this eclogue is not named by Vergil, and the eclogue was
read by some Christian commentators as a prefiguration of the birth of
Christ. By labelling the child, the artist here emphasizes the critical
apparatus for this edition, which begins with notes on Pollio's role in the
capture of the city of Salona as the derivation of the name Saloninus for his
son. Vergil is crowned with laurel and richly dressed according to the tastes
of his sixteenth-century audience. On a volume as lavishly illustrated as this
one, the printer normally would employ several block cutters and probably
several artists to draw the scenes to be cut. The 1502 designers were
unusually attentive to the text. The cradle rests among the flowers of lines
18–23: *fundent cunabula flores*. The details of lines 31–3 that signify continued
exploitation of sea and land—the ships, the city walls, the plough—are all
there at the left side of the illustration. The Strasbourg blocks were copied
in Italy and France and dominated Vergil illustration for the first half of the
sixteenth century.

---

*On the source of translations and illustrations in this paper, see Note, p. 184, below.

poeta solus in laudem pollicnis & Salonini filii.   Aeglcga quarta,
Pollio quarta tuas laudes & fortia facta: Altius hic canitur:celebratur pollio:Cesar
Atcp Salonini sata immatura recenset,   Alter:&hic secli venturi scribitur ordo,

Icelides muse. S.
Asini Pollio du
ctor germanici
exercitus : captis
Salonis vrbe in
Dalmacia:meruit laurea
deinde consolatu : & eo-
dem anno suscepit filiu:
que a Salonis captis Sa
loninu vocauit. huic Vir
gili Genethliacon dicit :
qui statim natus risit.qd
parentibus omen fuit infelicitatis. Ipse enim inter primor
dia extinctus est. Sicelides grecum:nam latine Sicilienses
facit:id est Theocriti. Nam Theocritu (qui Syracusanus
fuit) imitat. AN. Sicelides. In antiquis etiam pluribus te
xtibus:& in illo qui in summi pontificis bibliotheca ma
ionibus characteribus scriptus est Sicelides per e no per i.
legi:quod gryce dixit,illis enim Sicelia:nobis aute Sicilia
dicitur.Celebratur hic Asinius Pollio qui orator & cosu
laris:vt docet Eusb.   de quo latius in Alexi. Fuit hi
storiarum &Tragediarum scriptor qui & de Dalmatie
triumphauit.Vnde Hora. Ode prima secundi voluminis
ad eu scribes. Cui laurus eternos honores Dalmatico pe
perit triumpho:Laudat hic eude a prudetia:a dignitate:
honore:ab eloquetie viribus.Dicunt alii a Salona Dal

Sicelides muse pau,
lo maiora canamus,
Non omes arbusta iuuant:humiles cp myrice,

matie vrbe capta : susce
ptum filium Saloninum
vocasse:qui & si parum
vixit:hic tame a Marone
cum patre celebratur.sed
laus ipsa talis est: q sepe
ad Augustum quocp re
ferenda e:vt suo loco do
cebimus.preterea in Stra
bone legisse memini:Sa
lone Salonarum. In Pli
nio Salona salone . Iracp
non recte Solone p o.in prima syllaba dicit.   Sicelides
muse:q scp Theocrito syracusano faustis:seu o Theocriti
cantus & carmina.   Sicelides. CRI. Deprecat errore:
si paulo sublimius quam pastoria res requirit canat.Di
xit autem Sicelides & non Sicilides . Nam cum vsus sit
patronymico nomie:quod potius grecum q latinu est.
deduxit ab eo quod est Sicelia: vt dicunt greci:& non si
cilia:vt dicunt latini.
b   Paulo maiora. S. Non multo. Nam licet hec egloga
discedat a carmine Bucolico:tamen aliqua operi apta in
serunt.   c   Arbusta.AN.id est minima et huilia.C.G
pprie arbustu sit locus costitus nouellis arborib q ex lo
minerie auulsa sunt:lemia q. appellat. voluit notare hu
miliores arbores,   d   Myrice. S. Virgulta huilia sunt Ar

Plate 2

Vergil. *Opera*. Strasbourg, Johann Grüninger, 1502.
Georgics, Book I, leaf H1^V (woodcut: 184x147 mm.)

Idcirco certis dimensum partibus orbem
per duodena regit mundi sol aureus astra.

(*Georgics* 1.231–2)

Wherefore the golden sun commands an orbit measured
In fixed divisions through the twelvefold signs of the universe.

In the Strasbourg woodcuts for book 1 of the *Georgics*, men working at farming occupations frequently are menaced by storms. The illustrations are not simple reference figures showing the performance of tasks; the anonymous artists were alert to the perils inherent in the relationship between man and nature defined by Vergil. For the passage where Vergil describes the ordering of the universe and the necessity for reading the night sky, the illustrator has used the convention of the diagram found in printed astronomical texts of the fifteenth century. Encircling the earth are the elements and the paths of the planets, crossed by signs of the zodiac. Dominating the diagram is Vergil's serpent constellation: "Here the great Snake glides out with weaving, elastic body" (1.244). One explanation for the four corner figures of the sower, the reaper, the woodsmen, and the mariner is in the few lines on weather watchers at the end of this passage. The mariner, however, is not "launching an armed fleet" (1.255) and is better suited to illustrate a Vergilian simile in the preceding passage, where the farmer is admonished to observe the stars "as carefully / As sailors . . . on windy waters . . ." (1.205–6).

c Iccirco . A. Vt tempa
discernam°: sol eni dator
est teporū & horarū. Nā
siderū cursus:recursusq̃.
(vt etiā Macro.libro.i.de
som.scribit) .moderatur
certa diffinitōie, Nā spa-
cū certa diffinitio est. d
nis intelligit. e · Dimensum partib°orbē. S Annū diui
sum in q̄tuor tpa: & .xii. signa ét. xii. menses accipim°.
f Duodena mūdi astra. A. Astra mūdi dixit:q̃ zodia-
cus circulus:& vn°:et insummo cēlo afig vtē mūd'vo
catunquē signis diuiduū vel distinctūvidem°:q̃ infixa cē

Certis partib°. A. De qnq̃ zo
Dimensum partib°orbē.

¶ Iccirco certis dimensum partibus orbem
Per duodena regit mūdi sol aureus astra,

lo ferūt. Diuidit aūt mū
dus p.xii. ptes equales q̃
dicūt signa vl'duodena
astra:De his ibi superius
patuit.ibi.Qua loc° Eri-
gone iter. g Regit ot
bē. A .Per duodēa astra:
Sol em (vt Pli.lib.ii.c.vi.docet) planetarū medi° fert:am
plissima magnitudine ac ptāte:nec tēporū mō terrarūq̃:
sed siderū euā: ipsorumq̃ rector: hic lucē rub° minustrat
auferutq̃ remeātus.lū & reliqua sidera occultat : hic vices
tempoꝝ annūcq̃ semp euanescētē ex via nature tēperat:
hic cēli tristiciā discutit:atq̃ etiā nubila hūani animi ser

Plate 3

Vergil. *Opera*. Strasbourg, Johann Grüninger, 1502.
Aeneid, Book I, leaf V5ʳ (woodcut: 177x153 mm.)

at domus interior regali splendida luxu
instruitur, mediisque parant convivia tectis:
arte laboratae vestes ostroque superbo,
ingens argentum mensis . . .

                                                    (Aeneid 1.637–40)

Within the palace gleam
the furnishings of royal luxury;
the feast is readied in the atrium.
And there are draperies of noble purple
woven with art; and plate of massive silver
upon the tables . . .

Book 1 of the Strasbourg *Aeneid* is illustrated with nine woodcuts. In the last
of these, Aeneas is in the palace of Dido. Achates meets Ascanius at the left
edge of the illustration, but Venus, in the upper left corner, carries off
Ascanius in order to enable Cupid, disguised as Ascanius (left foreground),
to practice his deception on Dido. The illustration takes the reader from the
entrance into Dido's palace to the close of book 1, where Aeneas is asked to
relate the story of Troy. Achates has moved into the main scene to a seat
beside Aeneas. Two minor figures—Bitias, who takes the cup of wine from
Dido after her libation to the gods, and the musician Iopas—are labelled.
The illustrator costumed his court figures for the year 1502 and offered a
picture of "royal luxury" immediately recognizable to his readers. The
cumulative effect of these illustrations, from block to block and from figure
to figure within the scenes, is that of a living Vergil reworked in the
Strasbourg image.

At domus interior regali splendida luxu

Instruitur: medi isꝗ parant cōuiuia tectis,

Arte laboratę vestes: ostrocꝗ superbo.

Ingens argentum mensis: cęlatacꝗ in auro

y At domus. D. Oñdit
ꝗ cū hospites recipimus:
domᵒ ꝓ coꝝ mentis est cō
poneda. Ergo cū accipien
dus esset Aeneas tantᵒ vir
domū regali luxu ꝑ se splē
dida:tn additis multis re
ꝑ trimᵒornauit. Ergo legē
dū domᵒ splēdida regali
luxu: et iteriecta mora di
camus instruit. ꝑ Inte
rior.D.Quia interim in exteriore parte troianos iduxerat:
interior melius solito ornabat. a luxu, S.abūdātia hic.
Alibi luxuria. Dat aūt semper poeta abūdātia extens gē
tibᵒ.Rōnis vero frugalirate:qui duobᵒbtūabisvtebant
ꝗ in atris edebant se dentes.luue.Quis fercula septe secre
to cenauit auus.lat virgi.Perpetuis soliti dapibᵒ cōsidut

mensis:C.Regali luxu.L.tā
to quāto regīna decebat.
Luxus aūt nō vituperaꝯ
i diuilimis:qm iꝺ opes fu
erūt suę. Vituperaꝯ i tenuī
cēsu.Qua ꝓpter recte Iu
ue. Atticᵒeximie si cōenat
laut habeꝯ. Si rutilus de
mēs:qd ei maiore cachin
no. Excipiꝯvulgi ꝗ miser
b Mediisꝗ parāt tectis.
D.Nā cū mīta turba esset accipiēda:alibi tot triclinio ste
ru nō poterat ıt.Omnia cōuiuia vehementer spendebant:
sed sunt in apparatu diuersitas:ꝓpter diīlāꝺ ꝑsonarū.Nā
hospites cū regina recepti sunt in ostro supbo . Tyrii vero
tanꝗ minoris dignitatis in vestibus pictis:vt in textu vl
debis, c Laborarę S laborę ꝑsuadę:vt laboratascꝗ ꝑ
V ♥

Plate 4

Vergil. *Opera*. Strasbourg, Johann Grüninger, 1502.
Aeneid, Book VI, leaf OO2^r (woodcut: 179x156 mm.)

Sic pater Anchises, atque haec mirantibus addit:
'aspice, ut insignis spoliis Marcellus opimis
ingreditur victorque viros supereminet omnis.'

(Aeneid 6.854–6)

So, while Aeneas and the Sibyl marveled,
father Anchises spoke to them, then added:
"And see Marcellus there, as he advances
in glory, with his splendid spoils, a victor
who towers over all!"

Anchises closes his prophetic recital in *Aeneid*, book 6, with the triumphant figure of the Roman general Marcellus (riding to victory in the foreground of the illustration), but Aeneas sees the doomed figure of the boy Marcellus, nephew of Augustus. The artist of this illustration moves outside of the text to introduce Vergil himself, with harp, reciting book 6 to Octavia, sister of Augustus and mother of the dead Marcellus. At the left, Augustus stands at the tomb of Marcellus and on the tomb are the scattered lilies to which Anchises refers in his lament for Marcellus. In the Strasbourg blocks, the time sequence of the narrative is followed in the grouping of labelled figures, so that each illustration, rather than arrest one moment in the text, works with the text through several events. The future shown to Aeneas is the past known to the poet. While Aeneas looks ahead to Vergil's own time and gazes at the boy—"And yet, around his head / black night is hovering with its sad shade!" (6.866)—the artist allows the reader to see even Vergil, although Aeneas does not.

C.q.d.tā admirabiles artes,& reliq̄rū omniū p̄clarissimē
qū salutē & dignitatē publicam continent. Nam bonum
quāto magis vniuersale est̄tāto preclarius: administratio
vero rei publicē oia cōplectit̄. Ergo cēteris oibus virtutib⁹
est pponēda. v Tibi.C.q.d.& nō aliis. x Pacis amo.
S.leges pacis: y Parcere subie.C.designat quid propriū
it eorū qui reipu. p̄sunt.Cū em̄ quies & pax̄ ciuitatis pri-

mū bonū sit:ea maxime rōne bella gerenda eē videantur:
vt nihil nisi pax quēsitū essev̄ deāt̄. Itaq̄ erit off̄ciū eorū:
qetos: & leg b⁹ obtēperātes tutos esse iubere:eosq̄ ab om
ni iniuria p̄hibere:superbos vero:& contumaces:et qui ad
uersus leges alienum otium sua immanitate conturbant:
bello insectari:& vt legib⁹ obtemperent, cogere & illorū
ceruices frangere.

¶ Spoliis mar.op. S.Hic
Gallos et pœnos equesto
certamine superauit.Virti
domarū erā Gallorū du
et manu ppria interemit:
& opima retulit spolia:q̄ dux detraxerat duci::sic Cossus
iam Tolūnio, C. Spoliis mar.op. Postulat loc⁹:vt de Ioue

¶ Sic pater anchises:atq̄ hęc mirātibus addit.
Aspice vt insignis spoliis Marcellus opimis

Feretrio quedā alt⁹ repus
tamus.Romulus ergo:ve
Dyonisius ha. Ceniensiū
exercitu i finee Romanos
irruēte cęso:vrbē ipsā igre
diens cenin̄ Acronē illius rege cū valida manu sibi obuiā
intra vrbē factā sua manu interfecit. superauit erā Antē

OO ii

Plate 5

Vergil. *Omnia opera*. Venice, Bartolomeo de' Zanni, 1510.
Title-page (woodcuts: each 92x136 mm.)

hic vir, hic est, tibi quem promitti saepius audis,
Augustus Caesar, divi genus, aurea condet
saecula qui rursus Latio regnata per arva
Saturno quondam . . .

(Aeneid 6.791–94)

This, this is the man you heard so often promised—
Augustus Caesar, son of a god, who will
renew a golden age in Latium,
in fields where Saturn once was king . . .

Two blocks printed together on a Venetian title-page of 1510 exemplify
aspects of author portraiture prevalent in the early sixteenth century.
Neither block was cut for this edition. The upper block is a composite
presentation portrait, in which Vergil kneels to present the *Aeneid* to
Octavianus (Augustus) while Maecenas and Caius Asinius Pollio stand
beside the volumes associated with them. Figures and books are carefully
labelled. The presentation scene occurs frequently in sixteenth-century
books; the combination of figures to cover the three Vergil works is a
significant variation. The block of six commentators below was adjustable.
The names were set in type outside the block, and the figures at the desks
are not true portraits of individuals but represent the writing of commentary as a scholar's occupation. This edition adds one more commentary, that attributed to Marcus Valerius Probus, to the five in the 1502
Strasbourg edition. The two center figures are slightly smaller, not through
any attempt at perspective rendering but because they were cut by another
artist to be inserted into the block to meet the required number of six
commentators; the same block is found in editions of Horace and Ovid
with an author figure in the central position. The repetition of such blocks,
from edition to edition, emphasized certain virtues of the classical text. In
both illustrations, the classical work is related to Renaissance concerns, the
practical matter of literary patronage and the collation and explication of
texts.

P.V.M.Omnia opera:diligenti castigatione exculta:aptissimilq ornata figuris:
comentantibus Seruio:Donato:Probo:Domitio:Landino:Antonioq Man
cinello uiris clarissimis.Additis insuper in Seruium multis:quæ dee
rant:græcisq dictioibus:& uersibus qplurimis:qui passim cor
rupte legebantur: in pristinum decorem restituis.

Plate 6

Vergil. *Bucolica, Georgica, Aeneis*. Venice, Gregorio de' Gregori, for Luc'
    Antonio Giunta, 1522.
Title-page (woodcut border: 268x184 mm.)

primus ego in patriam mecum, modo vita supersit,
Aonio rediens deducam vertice Musas;
primus Idumaeas referam tibi, Mantua, palmas . . .

                                                                (Georgics 3.10–12)

If life enough is left me,
I'll be the first to bring the Muse of song to my birthplace
From Greece, and wear the poet's palm for Mantua . . .

The architectural title-border, seen as a doorway or window to the text
within, was a principal element of Renaissance book decoration. The text
crowded onto this title-page for a 1522 Venetian edition of Vergil describes
the contents of the volume with laudatory adjectives. A catch-title, the
names of commentators and editors, and statements of new features such as
the index are printed in red. The border has Apollo in the upper piece and
the nine Muses in concert in the lower. The device of the publisher, Luc'
Antonio Giunta, is printed in red in the center of the lower piece. The
detachable side strips contain portraits of ten Latin authors, beginning with
Vergil at the top of the left column. The authors lean forward from shell
niches, partially tomb sculpture but brought to life by variety of dress,
gesture, and pose with their books, in a manner consistent with the
resurrection of their texts. A strip of modern Italian authors was cut later to
replace the right-hand column so that the border could be used on a 1529
edition of Dante; there Dante faced Vergil across his title-page.

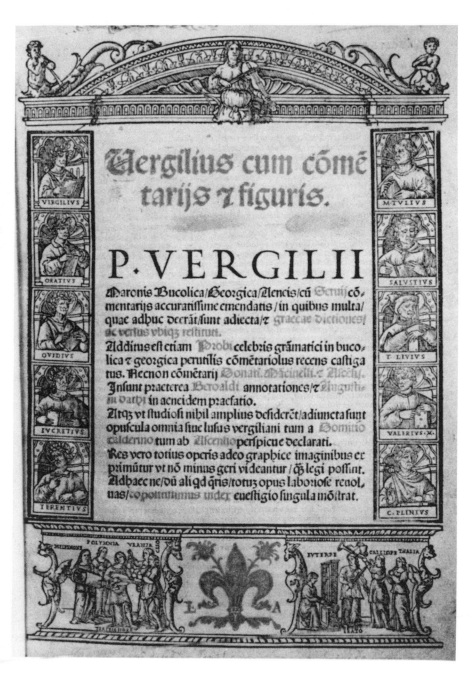

Vergilius cum cōmē tarijs ⁊ figuris.

P·VERGILII

Maronis Bucolica/Georgica/Aeneis/cū Serui cō
mentarijs accuratissime emendatis/in quibus multa/
quae adhuc decrāt/sunt adiecta/⁊ graecae dictiones/
ac versus vbiqʒ restitut.

Additus est etiam Probi celebris grāmatici in buco
lica ⁊ georgica perutilis cōmētariolus recens castiga
tus. Necnon cōmētarij Donati. Mācinelli. ⁊ Nicchy.
Insunt praeterea Beroaldi annotationes/⁊ Augusti
u vatij in acnei dem praefatio.

Atqʒ vt studiosi nihil amplius desiderēt/adiuncta sunt
opuscula omnia siue lusus vergiliani tum a Domitio
calderino tum ab Ascentio perspicue declarati.

Res vero totius operis adeo graphice imaginibus er
primūtur vt nō minus geri videantur/ōh legi possint.
Adhaec ne/dū aliqd ōris/totuz opus laboriose renol
uas/copoituiuimus uder euestigio singula mōstrat.

VIRGILIVS
HORATIVS
OVIDIVS
LVCRETIVS
TERENTIVS

M·TVLIVS
SALVSTIVS
T·LIVIVS
VALERIVS·M·
C·PLINIVS

MELPOMENE POLYMNIA VRANIA CLIO EVTERPE CALLIOPE THALIA

L A

Plate 7

Dante Alighieri. *La comedia*. Venice, Francesco Marcolini, for Alessandro
   Vellutello, 1544.
   Purgatorio, canto xxii, leaf AH1^V (woodcut: 127x104 mm.)

   Elli givan dinanzi, e io soletto
di retro, e ascoltava i lor sermoni,
ch'a poetar mi davano intelletto.

                                                         (Purgatorio 22.127–9)

   Those two were in the lead; I walked alone,
behind them, listening to their colloquy,
which taught me much concerning poetry.

Vergil as author figure was present not only in sixteenth-century editions of
his own works but throughout the first two canticles of Dante's *Divine
Comedy*. Illustration of the *Comedy* was carried from the manuscripts into
early printed editions. In a full sequence of illustrations, Dante and Vergil
appeared more than once within each illustration, to give a sense of their
progress. A pattern of illustration set in the fifteenth century was continued
into the sixteenth until 1544, when Francesco Marcolini had a new set of
blocks designed to take advantage of a new proficiency in block cutting and
to reflect a new concern for the geography of the poem developed by his
commentator, Alessandro Vellutello. The small figures have vitality, and the
enormity of their undertaking is conveyed by the overview of their situation
depicted for the reader. In the woodcut reproduced, Dante and Vergil have
been joined by Statius, and the figures labelled D, V, and S move upward
with Vergil always in the lead. Marcolini's artist obscured the fifteenth-
century distinction in costume between Dante and Vergil and dressed them
alike as classical poets. By 1544, this was not a naive interpretation but a
statement of the nature of the relationship between the two poets.

alcuna fonte, riuo, o fiume, oue poteſſero cō ſuoi caualli bere, Hauendo Bacco, per farli partir da
laſſedio, fatto ſeccar tutte lacque cherano intorno a Thebe, Pregaron adunque coſtei, che uoleſſe
inſegnar loro, oue poteſſero trouar de lacqua, laqual poſato il fanciullo in terra, per eſſer piu ſpe₃
dita, li conduſſe ne la ſelua Menea ad un fonte detto Langia, che per eſſer conſacrato a Nettuno,
Bacco non lhauea potuto far ſeccare, e tornata poi al fanciullo, lo trouò eſſere ſtato morto da un
ſerpente, Adunque nel limbo, con laltre famoſe donne di ſopra nomate, ſi uede Iſifile, che mo₃
ſtrò a gli Argiui il fonte Langia. Di Manto figliuola di Tireſia dicemmo nel xx. canto de l'In₃
ferno, Ma perche il poeta la ponga hora ne Limbo, hauendola poſta quiui ne la terza bolgia de
lottauo cerchio tra glindouini ſi è, per dimoſtrare, che quantunque foſſe ſtata peccatrice, ella ha₃
uea però laſſato al mondo fama di ſe. Di Thetis madre d'Achille, e di Deidamia con le ſorelle fi₃
gliuole di Licomede, dicemmo nel viiij. canto.

Plate 8

Vergil. *Les qvatre premiers livres de l'Eneïde*. Lyons, Jean de Tournes, 1552.
Aeneid, Book III, leaf H7ʳ (woodcut: 69x108 mm.)

Postquam res Asiae Priamique evertere gentem
immeritam visum superis, ceciditque superbum
Ilium et omnis humo fumat Neptunia Troia,
diversa exsilia et desertas quaerere terras
auguriis agimur divum . . .

(Aeneid 3.1–5)

The power of Asia and Priam's guiltless race
are overturned, proud Ilium is fallen,
and all of Neptune's Troy smokes from the ground;
this the Highest Ones were pleased to do.
Then we are driven by divine commands
and signs to sail in search of fields of exile
in distant and deserted lands . . .

The original 1502 Grüninger blocks for Vergil's *Opera* were transferred from Strasbourg to Lyons after 1515 and were used by several Lyons printers in the following decades. At mid-century, a newly illustrated *Aeneid* was begun by the Lyons printer Jean de Tournes, printing the French translation of the poet Louis Des Masures. The blocks are attributed to the major artist who worked for de Tournes, Bernard Salomon. Four blocks were ready for an edition of the first four books in 1552, and the remaining eight were added when the complete translation was published in 1560. The illustration was concentrated into single blocks at the head of each book, an epitome of the text to follow. In the block for book 3, the Trojan women surround the altar in the left foreground; below on the right Aeneas holds the branch from which the blood of Polydorus flows. These scenes are indicative of the sacrifices and warnings that make up the contents of book 3. The two royal figures in the middle ground are Helenus and Andromache. In the upper left are the fires and smoke of the erupting volcano Etna, forcing the terrified Trojans again upon the sea of exile, which opens out for them in the background. The technical accomplishment of these small blocks is considerable. A refinement of detail replaces the exuberance of the Strasbourg illustrations. De Tournes designed the page so that the Latin text appears as marginal notes. Vergil's text is there, but the emphasis is on the achievement of the translator.

LE III. LIVRE
DE L'ENEÏDE DE
VIRGILE.

 QVAND *les haults Dieux selon
leur fantasie
Eurent ainsi les richesses d'Asie,
Le Roy Priam, & sa gent de tout
poinct*

*Postquã res A-
sia, Priamíque
euertere gentem*

*Mis à l'enuers, ne le meritant point:
Quand le superbe Ilion fut rasé:
Et que de terre & du fons embrasé
Troye fumoit, ouurage de Neptune:
Diuers exil souz l'augure & fortune
Des Dieux du ciel, par mainte estrange terre
Fusmes contraints aller chercher & querre.*

*Immeritam visum
superis, cecidítá su-
perbum
Ilium, & omnis hu
mo fumat Neptunia
Troía:
Diuersa exilia, &
desertas quærere ter
ras
Augurijs agimur
Diuum : classemú
sub ipsa*

Donq'

Plate 9

Vergil. *L'Eneïde*. Lyons, Jean de Tournes, 1560.
Aeneid, Book VI, leaf S2^r (woodcut: 69x108 mm.)

at pius Aeneas arces quibus altus Apollo
praesidet horrendaeque procul secreta Sibyllae,
antrum immane, petit . . .

(Aeneid 6.9–11)

But pious Aeneas seeks the peaks where high Apollo
is king and, in a deep, enormous grotto,
the awful Sibyl has her secret home . . .

The distinctive feature of the artist Bernard Salomon's conception of book 6 in the complete twelve-book *L'Eneïde* of 1560 is the Sibyl's cave, where the *ostia centum* are beautifully arranged. The images in this woodcut—Aeneas and the Sibyl before Apollo in the cave (left foreground), the body of Misenus on the beach (upper right background), the cutting of the wood for the funeral pyre (lower center), the funeral pyre for Misenus (right midpoint), and Aeneas finding the golden bough (upper left)—cover the first 235 lines of book 6, i.e. the preparations for Aeneas' experience in the Underworld, but none of the horror of the text that begins at line 236. The placement of the figures is such that the reader who would follow the storyline must move his eye erratically within the illustration.

LE VI. LIVRE
DE L'ENEÏDE DE
VIRGILE.

 INSI *parla jettant larmes Enee:*
Si va singlant à course abandonnee.
Au port en fin de Cumes il arrive,
Venant surgir à l'Euboïque rive.
Tournent la prouë envers les eaux
salees:
Aux crocs de l'ancre accrochent les galees:
Le havre entier bordent les courbes pouppes:
Desembarquer se vont toutes les troupes
Des jeunes gens, & d'ardeur prendre port,
En se jettant de l'Hesperie au bord.
D'un dur caillou quelcun d'eux tirer tasche

Sic fatur lacrymãs:
classique immittit
habenas,
Et tandem Euboïcis,
Cumarum allabitur
oris.
Obuertũt pelago pro-
ras: tum dente tenaci
Anchora fundabat
naueis , & littora
curuæ
Prætexũt puppes, iu-
uenum manus emi-
cat ardens
Littus in Hesperium:
quærit pars semina
flammæ

s   2   L'ame

Plate 10

Vergil. *L'Eneïde*. Lyons, Jean de Tournes, 1560.
Aeneid, Book IX, leaf E4^r (woodcut: 69x108 mm.)

tum demum praeceps saltu sese omnibus armis
in fluvium dedit.

(Aeneid 9.815–16)

Then
he leaps at last and gives himself headlong,
together with his weapons, to the river.

Book 9 of the *Aeneid* begins with Iris sent from heaven to speak to Turnus
and ends with Turnus escaping from the angry Trojans by swimming the
river Tiber. Both of these scenes are in the Lyons woodcut for this book.
The rainbow comes down from the upper right corner, and Iris is seated on
it with Turnus standing facing her. The left side of the illustration is filled
with the battle at the city walls, the siege led by Turnus against the Trojans in
this book. A close examination reveals figures on the central tower and men
scaling the wall and falling from it. The soldiers at the river's edge detach
themselves from the thick of the battle. The final scene of the book is the
dominant one here, in the foreground, the figures of Turnus and his
pursuers very clear in the reader's mind even as he starts to read the text.
The *Eneïde* examples here reproduced demonstrate that the principle of
selection of material for illustration differs from book to book in this 1552–
1560 sequence. There is an active intelligence behind these illustrations,
challenging a responsive reader in the sixteenth century and in the
twentieth.

LE IX. LIVRE
DE L'ENEÏDE DE
VIRGILE.

 R ce pendant qu'es lieux, par longue
traite
Divers entre eux, ces affaires on
traite,
Du hault du ciel Iuno fille à Sa-
turne
Envoye Iris, sans arrest diuturne,
Devers Turnus au courage hardi.
Turnus adonq, au fort bois raverdi
De son ayeul Pilumne, d'adventure
Estoit assis sur la fresche verdure,
En la sacree & profonde vallee.

Atque ea diuersa penitus dũ parte geruntur:

Irim de cœlo misit
Saturnia Iuno

Audacem ad Tur-
num. luco tum forte
parentis

Pilumni Turnus sa-
crata valle sedebat.

E 4   Auquel

Plate 11

Vergil. *L'Eneïde*. Lyons, Jean de Tournes, 1560.
Aeneid, Book XII, leaf Q2^r (woodcut: 69x108 mm.)

olli sublimes armis animisque refecti,
hic gladio fidens, hic acer et arduus hasta,
adsistunt contra certamina Martis anheli.

(Aeneid 12.788–90)

Both men are high in heart; they face each other,
their arms and courage fresh again—one trusts
his sword; the other, tall and fierce, his shaft—
Aeneas, Turnus, breathless for Mars' contest.

The contest between Aeneas and Turnus is twice pictured in the final
woodcut in the de Tournes *Aeneid*, at the head of book 12. In the
foreground, at the right, the two men are alone in their struggle. At the left,
at a distance, the two armies, with spears and standards, are drawn apart as
spectators. The text reference is not entirely clear here. The position of the
two figures is that of victor and vanquished, and the contest before the two
armies did not end in this way. A similar license is evident in the upper
right, where Venus from a cloud hands down the healing stalk of dittany; in
the text, the goddess herself mixes the liquid applied to Aeneas' wound.
The Lyons woodcuts are less easy to read than the Strasbourg. The figures
in the story are part of a larger view. This expansion to landscape within the
small compass of these blocks is more than a summary of the text to follow.
It keeps before the reader the real plight of Aeneas in his search for a new
homeland. In the upper part of this last woodcut, left and right, the city on
hills, the islands in the sea, and mountains of the far shore, are a reminder
of the prospect for Aeneas and his descendants.

LE XII. LIVRE
DE L'ENEÏDE DE
VIRGILE.

 VRNVS *voyant au martial af-*
faire
Que les Latins, malaisez à deffai-
re,
D'un sort contraire en route ont
esté mis:
Qu'on le semond de ce qu'il ha promis:
Et que chacun le marque & note à l'œil:
Ard de soymesme en implacable dueil,
Et fierement esliève le courage.
Comme un Lyon qui aux champs de Carthage
Sent bien avant, d'une playe inferee

Turnus Vt infra-
Etos aduerso Mar
te Latinos
Defecisse Videt, sua
nunc promissa repo-
sci,
Se signari oculis : Vl-
tro implacabilis ar-
det,

Attollitq́, animos:
Pœnorum qualis in
aruis

saucius ille graui Ve-
nantum Vulnere pe-
Ctus

Q 2   'Par

Plate 12

Antonio Francesco Oliviero. *La alamanna*. Venice, Vincenzo Valgrisi, 1567.
La alamanna, Book I, leaf A8^V (woodcut: 145x85 mm.)

Vos, o Calliope, precor, aspirate canenti
quas ibi tum ferro strages, quae funera Turnus
ediderit, quem quisque virum demiserit Orco,
et mecum ingentis oras evolvite belli.

(Aeneid 9.525–8)

O you, Calliope, and all the Muses,
do you, I pray, inspire me: I must
sing of the slaughter and the deaths that Turnus
spread with his sword across the field of battle,
of those each fighting man sent down to hell;
unroll with me the mighty scroll of war.

The final reproduction in this series of plates is from a lesser work of the sixteenth century, whose author would have taken courage from the invocation quoted here as caption. The inspiration for Antonio Francesco Oliviero's epic poem on Charles V and the Schmalkaldic War is defined on several levels in the illustration for book 1. The poet is seated writing at a desk facing a landscape in which Homer and Vergil can be seen in conversation. On the first cloud level are the Muses, with sun, moon, and stars. In the upper part of the block, Oliviero's ultimate responsibility, as a Christian poet, is to God, here seen twice receiving messengers. The figures of Vergil and Homer are the closest to Oliviero, and they seem almost rooted in the earth. Rays of light descend upon them from the Muses. They are only part of a complexity of associations. The author's ambitions for this volume were not fully realized in the illustrations. The program of illustration proved too elaborate and was abandoned, with the printer's apologies, partway through the book. Nor did the text do justice to its models, but Oliviero, as a poet of the sixteenth century, saw Vergil before him.

Note

Plates 1–4, 6–7 are reproduced by permission of the Smith College Library Rare Book Room; plates 5, 8–12, by permission of The Houghton Library, Harvard University (plates 5, 8, 12 from the Department of Printing and Graphic Arts). Photography for plates 1–8 is by Stephen Petegorsky. English translations of Vergil are from: *The Pastoral Poems*, trans. E.V. Rieu (Baltimore: Penguin Books, 1961); *The Georgics*, trans. C. Day Lewis (London: Jonathan Cape, 1940); and *The Aeneid*, trans. Allen Mandelbaum (Berkeley: University of California Press, 1981). The Dante text and translation for plate 7 are from *The Divine Comedy: Purgatorio*, trans. Allen Mandelbaum (Berkeley: University of California Press, 1982).

VERGIL IN THE AMERICAN EXPERIENCE FROM COLONIAL TIMES TO 1882

Meyer Reinhold

In 1881, in commemoration of the nineteenth centenary of Vergil's death, Tennyson composed his stately eulogy "To Virgil." Across the Atlantic there was no American accolade, not even a ceremonial compliment in remembrance of Rome's greatest poet. Yet for about 250 years Vergil was a household word to numerous Americans, for study of his works was by tradition prescribed for those who pursued the academic curriculum in the grammar schools, academies, high schools, and colleges.

From early colonial times (with Harvard College and the Boston Latin School setting the models and standards) knowledge of the *Aeneid* was required of all college-bound students, with some variations in expectations and scope. The traditional admission requirements of the colonial colleges were maintained by the numerous colleges that sprang up like mushrooms in the first century of the national period. In the South, the Midwest, the western territories and states, likewise, knowledge of Vergil's *Aeneid* was mandated in entrance requirements of colleges. And in the curriculum of the colleges in the seventeenth, eighteenth and nineteenth centuries in America Vergil continued to be studied: college students were likely to read the *Eclogues* and *Georgics*.[1]

However, from this academic exposure to Vergil as teenagers and youths most Americans harbored memories of the *Aeneid* that were unpleasant, dolorous, even repugnant. For the text of the *Aeneid* as studied in the grammar schools, academies, and later the high schools simply served as a *corpus vile* for drilling grammar, construing and parsing Latin, or scanning verses. The author of an American edition of Vergil for schools and colleges in 1842 commented candidly on the folly of this age-old method of instruction. "Virgil," he wrote, "is more generally read and less

185

appreciated than any other classic . . . These elegant and delightful poems call up, in the minds of most persons, no more pleasant images than those of the spelling-book, the recitation room, and, perhaps, the rod." In consequence, he concluded, Vergil was generally neglected, read not as a poet, but "as a crabbed and difficult exercise in Latin."[2] In a similar vein John Trumbull (Yale 1769), one of the Connecticut wits, in his comic satire *The Progress of Dulness* (1772–1773) mocked the neglect of belles lettres in America: ". . . our youth with grammar teazing / Untaught in meaning, sense or reason . . . / From thence to murd'ring *Virgil*'s verse / And construing *Tully* into farce . . . / Read antient authors o'er in vain / Nor taste one beauty they contain."[3] Benjamin Rush, vociferous opponent of classical learning in America, in 1791 ridiculed the study of the *Aeneid* (as well as the *Iliad*) by mere boys, who, he said, carried away from school "but a smattering of the classics."[4] And Francis Hopkinson, first graduate of the College of Philadelphia, complained that teaching languages by means of grammar alone was sheer folly, and dismissed school masters as mere "Haberdashers of Moods & Tenses," with no feeling or taste for the authors they taught. "What would Virgil think could he hear his beautiful poems frittered into its grammatical component parts in one of our schools."[5] In 1806 study of the *Georgics* even on the college level was questioned as unprofitable for and unintelligible to youths because reading "this celebrated poem" requires technical expertise in agriculture, at times even in astronomy.[6] In 1811 a graduate of Phillips Academy Andover lamented the aims and methods of this early formal education as "excessive memorizing . . . of entire Greek and Latin grammars." "The whole business," he continued, "and it was the same all over the land, was a melancholy misunderstanding of the function of education."[7]

There was, moreover, a complex of cultural attitudes contributing to a widespread disparagement of Vergil that went far beyond this distasteful familiarity from school days. Many Americans were wary of his works on religious, moral, and political grounds. In the late seventeenth century Robert Calef of Boston, fulminating against the dangers of exposing children to "Heathen writers," condemned "the pernicious works of pagan learning in Virgil, Ovid, and Homer," and defended his own views with "If I err, I may be showed it from Scripture or sound reasoning, and not by quotations out of Virgil."[8] In 1769 John Wilson, teacher in the Friends Latin School in Philadelphia, motivated by Quaker utilitarian educational views and by moral and religious objections, resigned from his position, and wrote in his letter of resignation to the Overseers of the school that instruction in classical authors "is the grossest absurdity that ever was practiced. It has contributed more to promote Ignorance, Lewdness & Profanity in our Youth than anything I know . . . Will the Lasciviousness of

Ovid teach them Chastity? the Epicurean Horace Sobriety? the impudent Juvenal Modesty? or the atheistick Lucretius Devotion? & tho Virgil commonly is excepted from this guilty list yet with the impious Notion of both the 2nd and 8th Eclogues & his representing the Ungrateful Lustful Perfidious Aeneas as the particular Friend & Favorite of Heaven are shocking to every System of Morality."[9] Similarly, the Quaker teacher and humanitarian Anthony Benezet of Philadelphia deplored the religious and moral influence of Vergil, "the prodigious hurt done by these romantic & mad notions of heroism &c. which are early implanted in the tender minds from the use of these Heathen Authors Ovid, Virgil, Homer &c. which they are generally taught in, which nourishes the spirit of war in the Youth & in other respects is so diametrically opposed to our Christian Testimony."[10] Native American pragmatism, too, and the persistent quest for "useful knowledge" motivated many in their rejection of the Classics and Vergil. In New York William Livingston (later Governor of New Jersey) wrote in 1768: "We want hands . . . more than heads. The most intimate acquaintance with the classics will not move our oaks, nor a taste of the *Georgics* cultivate our lands."[11]

It was in the early national period that the most sustained challenge to the reputation of Vergil in America burst forth, at a time when rising nationalism created an American version of the "Battle of the Books," or "La Querelle des Anciens et Modernes," a vigorous debate which had exercized the French and English in the late seventeenth and early eighteenth centuries, coming to an end in Europe about 1720. In the nascent United States clamor arose for an instant indigenous American literature, accompanied by manifestoes of freedom from cultural dependence, depreciation of the great literary models of antiquity, denunciation of slavish imitation of them as absolute standards and deterrents to creative originality in America.[12] "We are called to sing a New Song," wrote Nathaniel Appleton, "a song that neither We nor our Fathers were able to sing before."[13] In the very first issue of the new national periodical, the *Massachusetts Magazine*, a poem entitled "Anticipation of the Literary Fame of America" predicted the rise of an American Livy, Cicero, Euripides, Ovid, Aristotle, Plato, and prophesied that "Some future *Virgil* shall our wars rehearse / In all the dignity of epic verse."[14]

Foreshadowing American aspirations for native epics, as early as 1772 Timothy Dwight (later president of Yale) at the age of twenty delivered in New Haven a disquisition in which he argued that the Bible as literature was superior to all ancient literary genres. "Shall we," he wrote, "be blind . . . to Poetry more correct and more tender than *Virgil*?" Further, he repudiated the conventional view that "*Homer* and *Virgil* . . . were sent into the world to give Laws to all other authors."[15] In 1791 a pronouncement was made that America had already produced a Homer, a Vergil, and a Horace.[16] The anonymous writer was alluding to Timothy Dwight himself, whose huge biblical epic, *The Conquest of Canaan*, had appeared in 1785, to Joel Barlow as the American Vergil—his epic *The Vision of Columbus* was first published in 1787—and to Philip Freneau as the American Horace.

Just as Dwight's *Conquest of Canaan* aimed at displacing Homer's *Iliad*, which had a greater appeal among Americans than the *Aeneid*, Barlow's American epic was composed to supersede the *Aeneid*. In 1807, to foster a new national literature with native didactic-moral-political content, Barlow produced a revised version of his epic entitled *The Columbiad*. In his Preface to this version of his epic on Columbus Barlow unleashed a vigorous assault on Homer for inculcating glorification of war, supporting the divine right of kings, and promoting military plunder, violence and false notions of honor. "The moral tendency of the Aeneid of Virgil," he added, "is nearly as pernicious," though Vergil's artistry elicited his grudging praise. "But Virgil wrote and felt like a subject, not like a citizen. The real design of his poem was to increase the veneration of the people for a master, whoever he might be, and to encourage, like Homer, the great system of military depradation."[17] Despite this denunciation, Barlow begins the *Columbiad* with a Vergilian echo: "I sing the Mariner who first unfurl'd / An eastern banner o'er the western world." Dwight's epic is virtually unknown today, and Barlow's *Columbiad*, despite its national theme and promotion of the doctrine of progress, remains one of the most dismal failures in the history of American poetry.[18]

In the South, in 1793 Richard Beresford of South Carolina attacked the moral content of both the Homeric and Vergilian epics. In particular he faulted "the pious Aeneas [who] took occasion to involve a homeless race of men in all the horror of desolation and slaughter," and he condemned Vergil's *parcere subiectis et debellare superbos* (*Aen.* 6.853) for its boast of the use of raw power to subdue others by force and keep them in obedience. "No longer are the *Iliad* and *Aeneid* perused as exemplars in moral, but in poetic excellence."[19] In the face of such harsh depreciation of the great ancient poets, Fisher Ames of Massachusetts, a fervent advocate of classical learning, declared that modern poets cannot find such inspiring themes as those of the *Iliad* and *Aeneid*, "for no such subject worthy of poetry exists [in the United States]. Commerce . . . is the passion of the multitude."[20] In 1814 the *Port Folio*, a prestigious Philadelphia literary magazine, in a display of national pride after the War of 1812, published an accolade, not to American poets, but to Vergil, who, it proclaimed, "wrote for *immortal renown*," while British poets wrote to please the multitude. "After a lapse of two thousand years, the writings of Vergil are still in the prime—the zenith of their fame. Two thousand years hence, what will have become of the writings of Lord Byron?"[21]

In the 1830s, as the influence of classical thought, literature, and symbols (except for the triumph of Hellenic Revival architecture) began conspicuously to wane, the militant South Carolinian anti-classicist Thomas Smith Grimké, moved by religious and patriotic fervor, dismissed Vergil (and Homer, too) as not providing either useful knowledge or edification for Americans. "As for their morals, who would be willing to have a son, or brother, like . . . the mean and treacherous Aeneas, the hero of the Aeneid, if indeed it has a hero." Grimké condemned Aeneas for meanness, ingratitude and perfidy toward Dido, and also for killing Turnus. "The beauties of Shakespeare are worth all the beauties of Homer and Virgil." Instead of these, Americans should read *Paradise Lost* and *Paradise Regained*. "I do not doubt, that the Paradise Lost is worth the Iliad, Odyssey, and the Aeneid all together; there is more sublime, rich and beautiful descriptive poetry in Childe Harold than half a dozen Georgics."[22] Indeed, so hostile was he toward Vergil that in his Phi Beta Kappa address at Yale in 1830 (the year of the nineteenth centenary of Vergil's birth) he proclaimed "I would rather read that great impeccable and glorious poem 'Gertrude of Wyoming' than the Fourth Book of the Aeneid."[23] This poem, written by Thomas Campbell, a Scot who had never set foot in America, was a romanticized narrative of the Wyoming Valley Massacre in eastern Pennsylvania in 1778, based on events involving American patriots and the Continental forces battling Loyalists and Indians in the Susquehanna River country. The poem created a sensation in America—it was even edited by Washington Irving. Campbell's admiring biographer later judged "Gertrude of Wyoming" to be a "third-rate poem, containing a few first-rate lines."[24]

While these negative attitudes of many Americans to Vergil—testy, deprecatory, hostile—derive, as indicated above, from various trends in evolving American society, the continuation of the traditional academic curriculum, the age-old aims of education and methods of instruction were barriers to both aesthetic appreciation of Vergil's works and illuminating understanding of his thought. Moreover, the textbooks employed in teaching Vergil's works continued to be uninspiring and unsuitable for the youthful students. The *Port Folio* might applaud the announcement of an American edition of Vergil's work thus: "for the production of correct taste in literature, we hope that the works of Virgil, one of the most splendid specimens of ancient wit, will be perused at every Grammar School and College in America."[25] But decade after decade school texts of Vergil were either far beyond the competence of boys and young men, or were so simplified and provided with so many crutches that initiative and challenge were destroyed. For many decades the Delphin text, by Carolus Ruaeus (Charles de la Rue, S.J.) held the field: the first American edition was published in Philadelphia in 1804, and it was frequently reprinted for decades thereafter. The commentary was in Latin, even the Preface. At the other extreme was the popular English Vergil by Davidson, first published in Britain in the middle of the eighteenth century: it provided the Latin text, the Latin in order of sense on the same page, and also an English translation and brief notes.[26] Vergil texts authored by Americans for use in schools and colleges began to appear early in the nineteenth century. The best known were those edited by Malcolm Campbell, by J.G. Cooper (to bridge the extremes of the editions of Ruaeus and Davidson), by Edward Moore, by G.A. Gould, and by Charles Anthon, whose editions were often reprinted and often criticized for hasty, careless workmanship, errors, and plagiarisms from German editions.[27]

Outside the walls of the schools and colleges, however, interest in Vergil's works, from colonial times through the nineteenth century, is evidenced by the frequency with which texts and translations of Vergil are found in private libraries.[28] Most Americans read Vergil in Dryden's translation, which was often reprinted in America well into the nineteenth century. In 1796 Caleb Alexander published a new prose translation of Vergil's works for school use. He hailed it proudly, but cautiously, in his Preface as "the first AMERICAN translation." "Elegant it cannot be," he wrote, but "Why should Americans be dependent on European translations and printers for the Latin or Grecian Classics?"[29] It is, however, noteworthy that while in the first decades of the nineteenth century a new verse translation of the *Iliad* was composed, by William Munford, a Virginian (a work that was the most distinguished translation of a classical work by an American in the early national period),[30] no American translation of the entire *Aeneid* (or extensive parts thereof) was undertaken in verse.

It is true that translations of limited parts of Vergil's works began to appear. In 1806 the *Port Folio* enthusiastically reprinted from the *Kentucky Gazette* "A New Translation of Virgil's First Pastoral."[31] This was an inelegant effort, in the form of a dialogue between Tityrus and Meliboeus; yet the editor of the *Port Folio* with patriotic zeal hailed it as a "very great curiosity," and commented that "A classical imitation, by a woodsman of the west is . . . stupendous . . . This forester's translation, though occasionally meritorious, does not always emulate the sense of the original. But we think the very attempt is wonderful in a savage region." In 1807 Lucius Manlius Sargent, Boston lawyer and litterateur, published a verse translation of the *Culex*. The influential *Monthly Anthology and Boston Review*, while doubting the authenticity of the *Culex*, and deploring the trivial nature of the theme, complimented Sargent on the accuracy of the translation, and saluted the publication of it as "this small accession to the specimens of American literature."[32] In 1814 the *Port Folio* printed a verse translation of *Aeneid* 2.268–80 by a youth of fourteen, which the editor praised as a creditable effort.[33] As a result, the editors solicited more verse translations of the *Aeneid*, proposing as texts two "beautiful and celebrated passages," 4.173–88 (beginning *Extemplo Libyae magnas it Fama per urbes*), and 4.693–705 (beginning *Tum Iuno omnipotens longum miserata dolorem*) The editor was sanguine that he could expect such an effort from "some of the literary youth of our country, to whom we cannot too often repeat the advice we have already given, *never to neglect their classical learning*."[34] Shortly after, they published translations of these passages (pp. 224–5, by "Vivian"); they were routine, uninspired versions. Not long after, there appeared a verse translation of the fourth Eclogue.[35] In 1820 William Ellery (Harvard 1747), signer of the Declaration of Independence, in his old age was engaged in translating part of the *Aeneid*.[36]

Despite these tentative efforts to create an "American Vergil," no creditable translations of Vergil appeared in the United States until the twentieth century. For Americans in the eighteenth and nineteenth centuries, in reading the *Iliad* and the *Aeneid* "it is not so much Homer and Virgil that we admire as Pope and Dryden."[37] Our marked "cultural lag" in regard to Vergil is highlighted by the many distinguished translations of Vergil's poetry in England, and by the high order of the scholarship on and appreciation of his works from the sixteenth to the nineteenth centuries. Similarly, in Latin America the influence of Vergil was substantial in these centuries. Translations, centos, imitations, echoes of the *Aeneid*, *Eclogues*, and *Georgics* abound in many Latin-American countries.[38]

It is also striking that the *Aeneid* did not share the popularity of the *Iliad* in America in these three centuries. This fact is noteworthy because a number of potentially transportable themes of the *Aeneid* did not, in general, leave their mark on American thought and literature: the birth of a new nation in a new land, the wandering of a divinely guided people, the struggle between the settlers and the native people, the transplantation of culture.

Far more in tune with American life and thought than the epic themes and grandeur of the *Aeneid* were the pastoral-agrarian models of the *Eclogues* and *Georgics*. From the seventeenth century well into the middle of the nineteenth, many aspects of American life combined to attract Americans to the idyllic landscape and fantasy of the *Eclogues* and the rural values and moral exaltation of agriculture in the *Georgics*: traditional American primitivism, the politico-ethical content of American agrarianism, the "Sabine Farm" ideal, and the paradigms of Cincinnatus and the virtuous Roman yeoman-citizen-soldier.[39] Particularly seductive and apposite were the moral didacticism of the *Georgics*, its message of the work ethic and the rewards of labor, and the anxieties in the *Eclogues* about the intrusion of history and the real world that threaten to shatter the sheltered pastoral retreat with its idealized *otium* and stability. The ideal of a rural retreat with intellectual pursuits as refuge from the city and the political world was widespread among Americans, both in the North and the plantations of the South.[40] "Vergil's *Eclogues* are the true fountainhead of the pastoral stream in our literature."[41]

Thus, while the *Aeneid* remained virtually untried by American translators, versions and imitations of the *Eclogues* and *Georgics* were not infrequently composed—none of them, it must be said, memorable. For example, a Pennsylvanian, calling himself Agricola, produced a mediocre imitation of a Virgilian pastoral, "The Squabble. A Pastoral Eclogue," in the form of a dialogue between Thyrsis and Corin.[42] In 1772 the poet Nathaniel Evans published "Daphnis and Menalcas. A Pastoral Eclogue"; and at the end of the eighteenth century John Miller Russell composed a verse translation of Eclogues 1–6.[43] Moreover, the *Georgics* (in translation) was a favorite of many Americans, for instance, Eliza Lucas Pinckney of South Carolina, one of America's distinguished women of the eighteenth century. In 1742 she wrote: "I have got no farther than the first volume of Virgil but was most agreeable disapointed [sic] by finding myself instructed in agriculture as well as entertained by his charming poem; for I am pursuaded that tho he wrote in and for Italy it will in many instances suit Carolina."[44]

Royall Tyler's autobiographical novel of 1797, entitled *The Algerine Captive* (the first novel about life in New England) contains numerous references to Vergil's works. The hero, Updike Underhill, son of a struggling framer, was sent to school, where for years he studied only Greek and Latin. Because of family financial difficulties Updike was called back to the farm, where he proceeded to give Greek names to all the farming tools, and to recite hexameter verses to the cattle. The only book he took with him into the fields was a copy of Vergil (the Delphin edition). One day he decided to try to apply some practical knowledge culled from the last book of the *Georgics*. He killed one of the family cows, and tried to raise a swarm of bees "after the manner of Virgil; which process, notwithstanding I followed the directions in the georgics, some how or other failed." Accordingly, he was sent away from the farm—back to school.[45] In the nineteenth century the *Eclogues*, in particular, transmitted "a delicate blend of myth and reality that was to be particularly relevant to American experience." Especially Eclogue 1, with its theme of the "Dispossessed," the invasion of history, intruding upon and unhinging the rural myth, had significant influences, especially upon Hawthorne, Thoreau, and Emerson.[46]

Indeed, despite the limited critical appreciation and superficial understanding of Vergil, there is not inconsiderable evidence of a variety of influences of Vergil on Americans from the seventeenth century on. The first native-born American poet, Benjamin Tompson (1642–1714, Harvard 1662), was a grammar school teacher of extensive experience in the Boston area. Although he wrote bad verse in English, he knew his Vergil. In his poem "New England's Crisis" (1676), about incidents in King Philip's War, he recalls Aeneas at the fall of Troy in describing a massacre by Indian warriors; and in praising the efforts of the women of Boston to help fortify the city, he quotes *Dux Foemina Facti*.[47] In "The Grammarian's Fame," in commemoration of Robert Woodmancy, he identifies in the imagined funeral procession a group of classical authors including Vergil (*Poems*, p. 117). It was Benjamin Tompson, too, who in 1702 wrote the Latin hexameters that serve as Preface to Cotton Mather's *Magnalia Christi Americana*. These lines of Tompson echo Virgilian phrases, notably from Eclogue 4.7: *Haec nova Progenies, veterum sub Imagine, coelo / Arte Tua terram visitans, demissa salutat* ("This new progeny, following the pattern of the ancients, visiting the earth by your skill, sent down from heaven greets you"); and from *Aeneid* 1.600: *Grates persolvimus omnes. / Semper Honos, Nomenque Tuum, Mathere, manebunt* ("All of us thank you. Your honor, your name, O Mather, will always abide").

Cotton Mather himself in his *Magnalia* sought to signal in the very opening words the epic grandeur of the exploits of the Puritan founding fathers in New England by analogy to the *Aeneid*: "I write the wonders of the Christian religion, flying from the Depravations of *Europe*, to the *American Strand*." While the analogy is not carried out systematically by Mather, among his numerous direct quotations and adaptations from Latin authors in the *Magnalia* there are thirty from Vergil, mostly from the *Aeneid*.[48] In his tribute to his famous teacher at the Boston Latin School, Ezekiel Cheever, Mather wrote in 1708: "Our stately *Virgil* made us but contrive / As our *Anchises* to keep him Alive . . . / Young *Austin* [i.e., St. Augustine] wept, when he saw Dido dead, / Tho' not a Tear for a *Lost Soul* he had: / Our Master would not let us be so vain, / But us from *Virgil* did to *David* train. . . ." And despite Puritan wariness about the corrupting influences of pagan literature, and traditional Puritan injunctions against aesthetic pleasure and belles lettres, Mather could write his son: "I cannot wish you a Soul that shall be wholly *unpoetical* . . . I wish you may so understand an *Epic* poem, that the Beauties of an *Homer* and a *Virgil* may be discerned with you."[49]

However trite and circumscribed the influence of Vergil's poem on American thought and literature, we can discern widespread familiarity in the facility with which Vergilian tags flowed from the pens and tongues of Americans—phrases, lines, passages. For example, at Harvard the Latin orations, e.g. of John Leverett (in 1672, 1678), were dotted with direct quotations and adaptations from Vergil.[50] Moreover, conventional general tributes to Vergil as poet and moral writer are scattered liberally through early American essays, poems, letters. A poem by the Bostonian Benjamin Church (Harvard 1754; physician, classmate of John Hancock), entitled *The Choice*, contains the lines: "*Homer*, great Parent of Heroick Strains, / *Virgil*, whose Genius was improv'd with Pains."[51] Francis Hopkinson wrote in 1762 in a commencement poem at his graduation from the College of Philadelphia:

> But now glad *Science* to this riper Age
> Unlocks the Treasures of the Classic Page . . .
> *Virgil* for him awakes the tuneful Lyre . . .
> Pious Aeneas! who attends thy woe
> But deeply feels the sympathetic Glow.
> Thro' ev'ry Page engaging Virtues shine
> And frequent Precepts grace each moral Line.[52]

In the rousing poem "The Rising Glory of America," authored by Philip Freneau and Hugh Henry Brackenridge, and recited at the commencement at Princeton in 1771, the influence of Vergil (and Milton) is apparent in the epic tone and phrases.[53]

But from all these comments and references to Vergil, whether laudatory or deprecatory, incisive analysis and understanding of him as poet and thinker rarely emerge. For example, in his elaborate description of the intellectual experience at Harvard at the end of the eighteenth century, the Rev. John Clarke, lauding the "Sacred Classicks" in general, expatiated on the virtues of Vergil. The limits of his appreciation are found in his praise of "his truly correct poems," "the beauties of his composition," "the smoothness of his numbers."[54]

In the first decade of the nineteenth century, in the midst of the great debate of the time on the suitability of the classical curriculum for America, there appeared a flurry of essays in praise of Vergil. *The Literary Magazine and American Register*, published in Philadelphia, printed a review of a new British translation of the *Georgics* (by Sotheby). The reviewer mused: "I have taken down from its shelf my old academic Virgil, over which I have kindled into rapture, and passed many a happy hour."[55] Later, the same magazine, in an ongoing debate on whether classical literature inculcated immoral and anti-Christian sentiments, extolled Vergil as prëminent in elegance and tenderness, despite his descriptions of war and battles, and the fact that his vision of the afterlife conflicted with Christian views.[56] The *Port Folio*, too, carried very superficial biographies and comments on the works of Vergil, bestowing high praise on "the prince of Latin poets."[57] In New England, the *Monthly Anthology and Boston Review*, assessing the extent of Vergil's imitation of his predecessors, concluded that in the *Bucolics*, except for Eclogues 1, 4, 5, and 6, Vergil's pastorals were but "elegant translations" of

Theocritus. "This is not said, however, to detract from his merit as a poet."[58]

Among the Founding Fathers the most fervent admirers of Vergil were Jefferson and John Adams. Jefferson's love of Vergil's poems was epitomized by him in the oft-quoted "But as we advance in life . . . things fall off one by one, and I suspect that we are left with Homer and Virgil, perhaps with Homer alone."[59] His second library (eventually sold by him to Congress) contained one of the largest assortments of Vergilian books in early America: a variety of texts, even Maffeo Vegio's *Thirteenth Book* (with English translation), the Dryden translation, an Italian verse version (by Annibale Caro), and a French translation (by Didot).[60] In his youthful commonplace book (composed mostly from 1764–1772), Jefferson copied a great range of quotations from classical authors. Yet there are only six passages from Vergil, four from the *Aeneid* and two from the *Eclogues*.[61] Jefferson was also interested in theories about Vergil's tomb, and cited lines from the poems in his comments on metrics.[62] But in his voluminous letters, essays, and speeches there is hardly any detailed evidence of his great love of Vergil. Indeed, as he grew older, under pressure of public affairs he confessed that his relish for poetry had deserted him, so that "at present I cannot read even Vergil with pleasure" (*Writings*, 8:65).

John Adams' devotion to Vergil was more varied—and vocal. In 1756, the year after his graduation from Harvard, he set himself the task of reading with care thirty to forty lines of Vergil every day.[63] At this time, too, he set down his thoughts on poetic genius and ranked, among the writers of antiquity, Homer, Vergil, and Ovid as "most perfect in their several kinds." In imagination even Milton's *Paradise Lost*, Adams judged, "falls short of the Aeneid of Iliad. . . ." The "Aeneid is like a well ordered Garden, where it is impossible to find any Part unadorned, or to cast our Eyes upon a single Spot that does not produce some beautiful Plant or Flower." In these musings when he expatiated on the beauties of country life, he quoted (with slight variation) *Georgics* 4.467–70, and commented that "in his Georgicks he has given us a Collection of the most delightful Landskips that can be made out of Fields and Woods, Herds of Cattle, and Swarms of Bees."[64] In an entry in his diary in 1758 he quoted *Aeneid* 4.2: *vulnus alit venis, et caeco carpitur igni* (which he translated thus: "He nurses a Wound in his Veins, and is consumed by a blind hidden fire") and then named five young men among his acquaintances consumed by secret fires of love. In the same year he was interested in poetic genius, and wrote to a correspondent on "sublime Passages in [various authors], including Virgill " Poetic genius, he wrote, has been exhibited "in a surprising degree by Milton, and Shakespeare, Homer, Virgil, &c."[65] On his voyage to France in 1778, when he experienced a fierce storm at sea, he noted in his diary that "every

School Boy can turn to more than one description of a storm in Virgil."[66] Adams' great library contained, like Jefferson's, various texts and translations of Vergil.[67] In retirement he was pleased to learn in 1823 that his grandson Thomas Boylston Adams had "made such progress in Virgil."[68] Yet during the Revolutionary War it was not poetry that Adams deemed essential for the times. In 1781 he exhorted his son John Quincy, then a student abroad: "In Company with Sallust, Cicero, Tacitus and Livy you will learn Wisdom and Virtue . . . You will ever remember that all the end of Study is to make you a good Man and a useful Citizen."[69]

For the revolutionary generation political science was at a premium, and the cult of antiquity was at its height in America, as the Founding Fathers ransacked the Roman and Greek classics for republican models and classical virtues. It was at this time that the Great Seal of the United States was created, its mottoes adopted from Vergil's poems. In 1782 (the year of the eighteenth centenary of Vergil's death) Congress approved the design of the official seal. One of the consultants to the committee that drew up the seal was Charles Thomson, Secretary of Congress, who had been a teacher of Latin in Philadelphia. The seal (now depicted on the obverse of the dollar bill), contains three Vergilian tags: ANNUIT COEPTIS, adapted from *Aeneid* 9.625 and *Georgics* 1.40, *Audacibus adnue coeptis*; NOVUS ORDO SEC-LORUM, adapted from *Eclogues* 4.5, *magnus ab integro saeclorum nascitur ordo*; and E PLURIBUS UNUM, adapted from *Moretum* 103, *color est e pluribus unus*. Of these three, the motto *e pluribus unum* appears to have been taken over, not from the *Moretum* directly, but from the legend on the title page of the British *Gentleman's Magazine*, popular on this side of the Atlantic.[70] These mottoes embodied a statement of the classical heritage and humanistic origins of the first modern republic, even if the heraldic emblems and the devices would have been understood only by educated Americans, most of whom had studied Vergil.

One such American was Peter van Schaack of Kinderhook, New York, whose love affair with Vergil continued throughout his life. A graduate of King's College 1766, lawyer and accomplished Latin scholar, he opted for the Loyalist cause, and so lived for seven years in exile until his citizenship was restored in 1784. His letters from abroad, to John Jay, and to his son and brother, display throughout Vergilian tags as well as appreciation and encouragement to continued study of his favorite author. In his exile Vergil was his solace, "my favorite," "the modest and amiable Virgil," "that sweet poet, about whom one may say *decies repetita placebit*."[71]

Among the early American national poets, too, Vergil exerted a substantial influence. One of the principal literary influences on the poems of Philip Freneau (1752–1832), America's first important poet, was Vergil. Freneau's poems are full of classical allusions, including echoes, epigraphs, and references from the *Aeneid*, *Eclogues*, *Georgics*.[72] John Trumbull's aesthetic appreciation of Vergil was more perceptive. In 1770 he composed, as a "collegiate exercise," a verse translation of the Orpheus and Eurydice story in the *Georgics*, entitled "The Speech of Proteus to Aristaeus." Trumbull set down first the Latin text of the seventy-five lines *Georgics* 4.453-527 (from *non te nullius exercent numinis irae* to *Eurydicen toto referebant flumine ripae*), then his translation in 104 lines of rhymed couplets.[73] Later, his influential poem *McFingal* (1782) contained imitations and adaptations from the *Aeneid*, e.g. the speech of Hector's ghost to Aeneas, and an adaptation of Aeneas' experience in Hades.[74] In the 1820s, in his old age, he judged that Vergil lacked Homer's descriptive skill, but noted Vergil had a penchant for the letter *m* (which Trumbull approved), and possessed "meritorious judgment," "force of expression," and "elegant correctness."[75]

Despite continuing assaults on classical learning in general and on Vergil in particular during the first century of the United States, pockets of appreciation and influence of Vergil in America continued. In the Adams family John Adams' admiration for Vergil was, as it were, a legacy. When John Quincy Adams was a young student abroad, his father urged him (the time is 1780/1) to "Study in Latin, above all, Virgil and Cicero."[76] At this time, when John Quincy translated the *Eclogues* in his notebooks he commented "What a difference between this study and that of a dry, barren Greek Grammar." In July 1783 he copied down the Latin text of all ten Eclogues, and for each wrote a translation in rhymed couplets; and in a collection of early translations made by him we find a copy of Dryden's version of "Virgil's Fourth Pastoral, or Pollio," followed by John Quincy's own prose translation of the first five Eclogues. Next he copied the text of *Georgics* 1.12-73, and (from November 1783 to February 1784) wrote a prose translation of all four books.[77] Later, when he wrote for the *Port Folio*, he reviewed a new English translation of the *Georgics* by William Sotheby (published in an American edition in 1808), giving it high praise and comparing it favorably to Dryden's translation. Adams here called the *Georgics* "the most perfect composition, that ever issued from the mind of man," lauding its "transcendent excellence." Some passages in the *Georgics*, he added, "have been the special delight of twenty centuries," and "will enrich the ear of harmony and transport the soul of fancy as long as taste and sentiment shall last among mankind." With characteristic American concern for practicality, he added that the didactic parts "will not be of much . . . use to our practical farmers."[78] John Quincy Adams kept six bronze busts in his study at Quincy which he called his "Household Gods." One of these was Vergil.[79]

The most extensive appreciation of Vergil that we have in America during the nineteenth century is to be found in the diary of John Adams' grandson, Charles Francis Adams. As a student in 1820 he was committed to daily study of Vergil (*Diary*, 1:4–7). In 1831 he decided to assess the genius of Vergil, who, he judged, would have risen to higher rank as poet if he had exhibited greater originality (4:114). Then in 1832 he began to read systematically through all of Vergil's works in Latin. About the *Eclogues* he commented that "they are fine specimens of the highest polish of which verse is susceptible. Vigorous but smooth (4:247). Then he read through the *Georgics* in less than a week, dismissing the details of "rural Economy" and lauding the *Georgics* as a whole as "models for that specimen of composition, a sign of which is that all subsequent times have only imitated them" (255). In the next five weeks he read through the entire *Aeneid*. "It is a very great mistake committed," he wrote, "to make boys or men read Virgil first and Homer afterwards" (255). The morality of book 4 he considered dubious—"The pious Aeneas is little better than a rascal for the desertion of Dido after seducing her," though he felt inclined to mitigate this criticism of Aeneas on the ground that it was "poetic" and, in any case, "agreeable to nature" (256). Book 6 he thought the masterpiece. "The imagination, the description, the versification combine wonderfully" (267). Taken as a whole the *Aeneid* is "an honour to the human intellect for imagination, for pathos, for perfect harmony, for beauty, and there is moral in it, so far as the Ancients allowed themselves to have moral" (279). The greatness of the *Aeneid*, he concluded, is unfortunately not appreciated by boys, who are too young for the experience and are poorly taught. "It is a great mistake I think to submit such things to be hammered over in such a way until return to them at a future moment is disgusting from the Associations it brings up" (276). Then from August 1833 to January 1834 he reread Vergil entire once more. On the *Georgics* he wrote: "I find the Poetry of the *Georgics* more exquisite than ever. The high polish, the ease and familiarity with which the versification is conducted, and the beauty of it throughout are now and must remain unequalled monuments of ancient mental exertion" (5.194).[80] Again he recorded his condemnation of Aeneas for his behavior toward Dido. "I do not greatly admire his hero in this business. His cold heartedness is a vice past defence" (213). But, taking the *Aeneid* as a whole, "I have read it with pleasure . . . I find repetition of a Classic only shows me how much I let escape before" (250). The absorption of Charles Francis Adams with Vergil was idiosyncratic, as it was with Henry Thoreau in the next two decades. Vergil was a leading inspiration for him, for descriptions of nature, for man's closeness to the soil, the idyllic pastoral life, and even the concept of a golden age. From 1837 to 1857 quotations from Vergil recur in Thoreau's writings—from the *Aeneid* as well as the *Eclogues* and *Georgics*. For example, in 1859 he recorded in his *Journal* that Vergil's account of a winter in *Georgics* 1.291 "applies well-nigh to New

England." In 1837 he found in the *Eclogues* confirmation of the eternal sameness of human beings: "I would read Virgil if only that I might be reminded of the identity of human nature in all ages . . . It was the same world, and the same men inhabited it."[81]

But by the middle of the nineteenth century the pastoral image had begun to fade in America. As industrialization burgeoned, assaults on the Vergilian pastoral mode mounted. In 1847, for example, on the day the Northern Railroad was inaugurated in New Hampshire, Daniel Webster, speaking at the ceremony, lauded railroads, progress, profits, and dismissed Vergilian pastoralism out of hand: "New Hampshire is no classic ground. She has no Virgil and no Eclogues." In 1850 Thomas Eubank, Commissioner of Patents, declared: "A steamer is a mightier epic than the Illiad [sic], and Whitney, Jacquard, and Blanchard might laugh even Virgil, Milton and Tasso into scorn."[82] In 1866, in an address before the prestigious Academy of Arts and Sciences in Boston, Jacob Bigelow, M.D., dismissed the works of Homer and Vergil because of the "absence of all moral or poetical justice" in them.[83] The transvaluation and transformation of society and education in America in the first hundred years of the nation is patent in the views of John Adams' great-grandson, Charles Francis Adams, Jr. In a Phi Beta Kappa address at Harvard in June 1883 he delivered a major assault on the traditional classical curriculum in the universities and colleges, declaring it irrelevant and useless.[84]

Thus by the last decades of the nineteenth century classical learning had ceased to provide "useful knowledge" to educated Americans in the received form of moral, political, and aesthetic models. It became a professional field, the province of classical scholars and teachers of the Classics. It is, however, mere coincidence that the first scholarly studies on Vergil's poetry in America were published at this time—just about the nineteenth centenary of Vergil's death. In July 1880, at the annual meeting of the American Philological Association in Philadelphia, Ernest G. Sihler presented a paper on "Virgil and Plato," which was that year published by the Association in its *Transactions*.[85] In the following years several articles on Vergil appeared in the *American Journal of Philology*.[86] But in the *Proceedings* of the Association for 1881, 1882, 1883 one looks in vain for even a mention of Vergil. No American classical scholar at the time, no teacher of the Classics, no American poet was moved to salute, with Tennyson, "Roman Virgil," "Wielder of the stateliest measure even moulded by the lips of man."[87]

Notes

1. See, e.g., Meyer Reinhold, *The Classick Pages. Classical Reading of Eighteenth-Century Americans* (University Park: Pennsylvania University State Press, 1975), pp. 3–6; Edwin C. Broome, *A*

Historical and Critical Discussion of College Admission Requirements, Columbia Univ. Contrib. to Philosoph., Psych., and Educ. 11.3–4 (New York, 1903), pp. 17–69; Frederick Rudolph, *Curriculum. A History of the American Undergraduate Course of Study Since 1636* (San Francisco: Jossey-Bass, 1977), pp. 29–39; Pauline Holmes, *A Tercentenary History of the Boston Latin School 1635-1935* (Cambridge: Harvard University Press, 1935), pp. 256–60, 264, 287, 330–31.

2. *P. Virgilii Maronis Bucolica, Georgica, et Aeneis*, ed. Francis Bowen (Boston: D.H. Williams, 1842), Preface.

3. *The Satiric Poems of John Trumbull*, ed. Edwin T. Bowden (Austin: University of Texas Press, 1962) Part I, lines 43–44, 49–50, 13–132.

4. Reinhold, 14–15; idem, "Opponents of Classical Learning in America During the Revolutionary Period," *PAPS* 112 (1968): 228–31.

5. *Miscellaneous Essays, and Occasional Writings* (Philadelphia: T. Dobson, 1792) 2:7, 57.

6. "Classical Obscurities," *The Literary Magazine and American Register* 6 (1806): 394–6.

7. Claude M. Fuess, *An Old New England School. History of Phillips Academy Andover* (Boston: Houghton Mifflin, 1917), pp. 170–71.

8. Richard M. Gummere, *Seven Wise Men of Colonial America* (Cambridge: Harvard University Press, 1967), p. 23.

9. James Mulhern, *A History of Secondary Education in Pennsylvania* (Philadelphia: University of Pennsylvania Press, 1933), pp. 43–4, 122; Edwin L. Wolf, "The Classical Languages in Colonial Philadelphia," in *Classical Traditions in Early America*, ed. John W. Eadie (Ann Arbor: University of Michigan Press, 1976), p. 71.

10. George S. Brookes, *Friend Anthony Benezet* (Philadelphia: University of Pennsylvania Press, 1937), p. 389, letter to John Pemberton, May 29, 1783; cf. letter to Robert Pleasants, Oct. 2, 1780, pp. 351–2, on the deleterious effect on religion from reading of Ovid, Vergil, and Horace.

11. *A Letter to the Right Reverend Father in God, John, Bishop of Landaff* (New York, 1768), pp. 23–4.

12. See, e.g., A. Owen Aldridge, "The Concept of the Ancients and Moderns in American Poetry of the Federal Period," in Eadie, *Classical Traditions*, pp. 99–108; Meyer Reinhold, "The Silver Age of Classical Studies in America, 1790–1830," in *Ancient and Modern. Essays in Honor of Gerald F. Else*, eds. John W. Eadie and John D'Arms (Ann Arbor: University of Michigan Press, 1979), pp. 181–9.

13. Cited by Russell B. Nye, *The Cultural Life of the New Nation, 1776-1830* (New York: Harper, 1960), p. 238.

14. By Cantabrigiensis, in *Massachusetts Magazine* (1789): 117–18.

15. *A Dissertation on the History, Eloquence and Poetry of the Bible* (New Haven: T. & S. Green, 1772).

16. By The Meddler, *New Haven Gazette* 1.4 (June 26, 1791).

17. Joel Barlow, *The Columbiad*, 2 vols. (Philadelphia: Conrad, Lucas, 1809), 1:v–vii; 2:184–95. On Vergil as subservient to Augustus, currying favor with a monarch, flattering him and his countrymen, cf. "Literature of the Ancients," by "R" in *Monthly Anthology and Boston Review* 4 (1807): 57, 59. George Bancroft, "Value of Classical Learning," *North American Review* 19 (1824): 130, also criticized Vergil for "servile adulation" and failure to sustain in his later work the "republicanism of his earlier days."

18. Similarly in France from 1653 to 1670 some dozen biblical and national epic poems were composed. Though all these turned aside from the contents of the great classical models, repudiating the themes and intellectual standards and values associated with antiquity, they all clung to classical form and style, as did Dwight's and Barlow's epics. And, like the American works, none of the French epics has enjoyed a lasting reputation. See Hans

Kortum, *Charles Perrault und Nicolas Boileau: Der Antike-Streit im Zeitalter der klassischen französischen Literatur* (Berlin: Rütten & Loening, 1966), pp. 136–45.

19. Richard Beresford, *A Plea for Literature, More Especially of the Literature of Free States* (Charleston, S.C.: Harrison & Bowen, 1793), pp. 29–30, 35.

20. *The Works of Fisher Ames*, ed. Seth Ames (Boston: Little Brown, 1854; rpt. ed., New York: B. Branklin, 1971). p. 468.

21. *Port Folio* 3rd ser. 4 (1814): 105–6 ("Ancient and Modern Poets").

22. Thomas Smith Grimké, *Oration on American Education* (Cincinnati: J. Drake, 1835), pp. 16–17, 39.

23. *Oration . . . before the Connecticut Alpha of the Phi Beta Kappa Society, . . . Sept. 7, 1830* (New Haven: Hezekiah Howe, 1831).

24. J. Cuthbert Hadden, *Thomas Campbell* (Edinburgh: Oliphant, Anderson & Ferrier, 1899), p. 97; cf. Charles Duffy, "Thomas Campbell and America," *AL* 13 (1941–1942): 346–55.

25. *Port Folio* 4 (1803): 286.

26. There were numerous editions of Davidson's Vergil published in America, e.g., *The Works of Virgil. Translated into English Prose*, 2 vols. (New York, 1811).

27. *The Works of Virgil*, ed. Malcolm Campbell (New York, 1803): this was in substance a revised version of Davidson's Vergil.; *P. Virgilii Maronis Opera*, ed. J.G. Cooper (New York: White, Gallaher & White, 1829); *The Bucolics, Georgics, and Aeneid of Virgil*, ed. Edward Moore (Boston: Bazin & Ellsworth, 1849); *Publius Virgilius Maro. Bucolica, Georgica, et Aeneis*, ed. B.A. Gould (Boston: Cummings, Hilliard, 1826): the text was based on editions of Heyne, Hensius, Burmann, and Wakefield; the *North American Review* 23 (1826): 220–24 published a very favorable review of Gould's Vergil by Sidney Willard, who praised it for accuracy of text, good typography, and avoidance of too much aid for the student; *The Aeneid of Vergil*, ed. Charles Anthon (New York: American Book Co., 1843); and *The Eclogues and Georgics of Virgil*, ed. Charles Anthon (New York: Harper & Brothers, 1847): Anthon's editions were attacked by the *North American Review* in 1849 and 1850 as impeding real progress in classical education in America because of their basic faults. Cf. Stephen Newmyer, "Charles Anthon, Knickerbocker Scholar," *Class. Outlook* 59 (1981–1982): 40–41.

28. See, e.g., *Matthew Carey's Catalogue of Books* (Philadelphia: D. Humphreys, 1794); *The Writings of Colonel William Byrd*, ed. John S. Bassett (New York: Doubleday, 1901), pp. 431–5; *Journal and Letters of Phillip Vickers Fithian, 1773–1774*, ed. Hunter D. Farish, new ed. (Williamsburg: Colonial Williamsburg, 1957), pp. 285–94 (catalogue of the library of Robert Carter); Edwin Wolf 2d, *The Library of James Logan of Philadelphia 1674–1751* (Philadelphia: Library Co. of Philadelphia, 1974), pp. 500–502; Reinhold, *Classick Pages*, pp. 133–6; Richard Beale Davis, *Intellectual Life in the Colonial South 1585–1763* (Knoxville: University of Tennessee Press, 1978), 2:506, 539–40.

29. Caleb Alexander, *The Works of Virgil. Translated into Literal English Prose* (Worcester: Leonard Worcester, 1796). The volume contained also the Latin text and brief notes. John F. Latimer, "American Scholarship and Caleb Alexander," *TAPA* 80 (1949): 403–12, is unduly charitable to Alexander's efforts at "scholarship."

30. William Munford, *Homer's Iliad*, 2 vols. (Boston: Little, Brown, 1846); cf. Meyer Reinhold, "Philhellenism in America in the Early National Period," *Class. Outlook* 55 (1978): 87.

31. *Port Folio* n.s. 1 (1806): 207–8.

32. 4 (1807): 211–13. On Sargent (1786–1867) see *Dictionary of American Biography*, 16:367–8.

33. *Port Folio* 3rd ser. 3 (1814): 593–4. The editor exhorted the young man "to perseverance in his classical studies, assuring him that nothing else is necessary to rank him, at no very distant period, among the elegant scholars in his country."

34. *Port Folio* 3rd ser. 4 (1814): 103–5.

35. By "C," *Port Folio* 3rd ser. 5 (1815): 294–8.

36. William M. Fowler, Jr., *William Ellery: Rhode Island Politico and Lord of Admiralty* (Metuchen, N.J.: Scarecrow Press, 1973), pp. 180-81.

37. John G. Gray, "Study of the Classics," *North American Review* 11 (1820): 415.

38. See, e.g., Martin L. Clarke, *Classical Education in Britain, 1500-1900* (Cambridge: Cambridge University Press, 1959), pp. 76, 169, 171; Tom B. Jones, "Classics in Colonial Hispanic America," *TAPA* 70 (1939): 37-45; Marcelino Menéndez y Pelayo, *Historia de la Poesía Hispano-Americana*, 2 vols (Santander: Aldus, 1948), 1:81-2, 92-3, 178-80, 222-3, 226; 2:226, 333, 363, 345-7; Irving A. Leonard, *Books of the Brave* (Cambridge: Harvard University Press, 1949), pp. 164, 208-9, 219. It is curious to find North Americans expending creative energies not on efforts to interpret and appreciate Vergil's works but on travesties. In Maryland the Rev. Thomas Cradock (1718-1770) wrote travesties (still unpublished) of all ten *Bucolics*. See Richard Beale Davis, *Intellectual Life*, 3:1393-5. In 1774 Rowland Rugeley published a travesty of book 4 of the *Aeneid*, inspired by Charles Cotton's well-known British burlesque of the *Aeneid*, titled *Scarronides*. See *The Story of Aeneas and Dido Burlesqued* (Charleston, S.C.: Robert Wells, 1774).

39. See, e.g., Douglass G. Adair, "The Intellectual Origins of Jeffersonian Democracy: Republicanism, the Class Struggle, and the Virtuous Farmer" (Diss., Yale, 1943), pp. i-ii, 27-30, 69-95, 272-95; Alfred W. Griswold, *Farming and Democracy* (New York: Harcourt, Brace, 1948), pp. 18-46; Leo Marx, *The Machine in the Garden. Technology and the Pastoral Ideal in America* (New York: Oxford University Press, 1964), p. 3; Meyer Reinhold, "Eighteenth-Century American Political Thought," in *Classical Influences on Western Thought A.D. 1650-1870*, ed. R.R. Bolgar (Cambridge: Cambridge University Press, 1979), p. 230.

40. Lewis P. Simpson, *The Dispossessed Garden. Pastoral and History in Southern Literature* (Athens: University of Georgia Press, 1975), pp. 1-3. An anonymous poem, "Old Virginia Georgics" (by a member of the patrician landed gentry of the South, who knew both the Roman authorities on agriculture and the *Eclogues* and *Georgics*) appeared in *Farmers Register* 1 (1834): 551-2. A satire on the lackadaisical farming of the time, it contained tags from the *Aeneid*, *Eclogues* and *Georgics*, and began with the lines: "I sing the tillage old Virginia knows, / Which cheats with hope the husbandman who sows; / Not such as Maro sung in deathless strains, / To piping shepherds and Italian swains." See Clarence Gohden, "Old Virginia Georgics," *SLJ* 11 (1978): 44-53.

41. Marx, p. 19.

42. 2nd ed. (Philadelphia: Anthony Armbruster, 1764). The anonymous author claimed in his Preface that "The following Piece was really written by a Country Farmer . . . from my Farm on the Banks of the River _____."

43. In *Poems on Several Occasions* (Philadelphia, 1772; rpt. New York, 1970), pp. 1-6. *The Pastoral Songs of P. Virgil [sic] Maro* (Boston: Manning & Loring, 1799).

44. *Letterbook of Eliza Lucas Pinckney 1739-1762*, ed. Elise Pinckney (Chapel Hill: University of North Carolina Press, 1972), pp. 35-6. She was the mother of two eminent South Carolinian political figures, Charles Cotesworth Pinckney and Thomas Pinckney. The *Georgics* and *Eclogues* were read and appreciated not only in the South but also on the landed estates of New York in the 1780s; see Henry C. van Schaack, *The Life of Peter van Schaack* (New York: D. Appleton, 1842), pp. 221, 230. In a letter to his son, written from London, where he lived in exile, van Schaack advised him to inform his farmers how husbandry was carried on in Vergil's time, "but do not quote the Georgics to them." "By the way," he wrote to him, "do you not often read the first Eclogue with peculiar sensibility when you think of public troubles. Who will be the happy man of whom it shall be said *Deus nobis haec otia fecit!*" Eclogue 1, he wrote, is "so suitable to the time."

45. *The Algerine Captive*, ed. Jack B. Moore (Rpt. Gainesville, Fla.: Scholars Facsimiles & Reprints, 1967), 1:41-2. Updike's father concluded (1:39) that "If Updike went to college, I should think he would learn, not *hard words*, but *useful things*."

46. Marx, pp. 19, 20-21, 243-4.
47. *Benjamin Tompson, 1642-1714. First Native Born Poet of America. His Poems*, ed. Howard J. Hull (Boston: Houghton Mifflin, 1924), pp. 29-30, 64, 70, 79. Cf. Richard M. Gummere, *The American Colonial Mind and the Classical Tradition. Essays in Comparative Culture* (Cambridge: Harvard University Press, 1963), pp. 145-6.
48. Cotton Mather, *Magnalia Christi Americana Books I & II*, ed. Kenneth B. Murdock (Cambridge: Harvard University Press, 1977), pp. 45, 89-90, 107, 200; Leo M. Kaiser, "On the Latin Verse Passages in Cotton Mather's *Magnalia Christi Americana*," *EAL* 10 (1976-1977): 301-6; idem, "Six Notes," *EAL* 13 (1978-1979): 298. The Vergilian quotations and adaptations are from all books of the *Aeneid* except 5, 8, 9, and 10.
49. Cotton Mather, *Corderius Americanus* (Boston: Nicholas Boone, 1708), p. 31; idem, *Manductio ad Ministerium. Dissertation for a Candidate of the Ministry* (Boston: Thomas Hancock, 1726), p. 38.
50. See, e.g., Leo M. Kaiser's skillful identification of Vergilian tags in "The Oratio Quinta of Urian Oakes, Harvard 1678," *Human Love* 19 (1970): 485-508; "Tercentenary of an Oration: The 1672 Commencement Address of Urian Oakes," *HLB* 21 (1973): 75-87; "John Leverett and the Quebec Expedition of 1711. An Unpublished Latin Oration," *HLB* 22 (1974): 309-16; "Seventeenth Century Latin Prose: John Leverett's Welcome to Governor Sir Edmund Andros," *Manuscripta* 12 (1974): 30-37; and "Prae Gaudio, Prae Luctu. The First Commencement Address of President John Leverett," *HLB* 24 (1976): 381-94.
51. Benjamin Church, *The Choice* (Boston: Edes & Gill, 1757), lines 75-6
52. Francis Hopkinson, *Science. A Poem* (Philadelphia: William Dunlap, 1762), lines 59-60, 63, 65 6.
53. *A Hugh Henry Brackenridge Reader, 1770-1815*, ed. Daniel Marder (Pittsburgh: University of Pittsburgh Press, 1970), p. 56.
54. John Clarke, *Letters to a Student in the University of Cambridge, Massachusetts* (Boston: Samuel Hall, 1796), pp. 45, 50-51. Cf. the superficial bantering mutual criticism in "A Dialogue between Homer and Virgil," in *Christian's, Scholar's & Farmer's Magazine* (Oct.-Nov. 1789): 465-6.
55. *Literary Magazine and American Register* 2 (1804): 112-17.
56. "Classical Literature," *Literary Magazine and American Register* 7 (1807): 392.
57. *Port Folio* n.s. 3 (1807): 164-9, 227-8; 5 (1808): 103- 6 ("Classical Learning"); 3rd ser. 4 (1814): 105-6.
58. Ibid. 6 (1809): 376-9 ("Theocritus and Virgil").
59. *Writings of Thomas Jefferson*, Memorial Edition (Washington, D.C., 1905), 18:448. The time is after 1789, probably during the years he served as Secretary of State.
60. *Catalogue of the Library of Thomas Jefferson*, ed. Millicent Sowerby, 5 vols. (Washington, D.C.: Library of Congress, 1952-1959), 3:419-23.
61. *The Literary Bible of Thomas Jefferson. His Commonplace Book of Philosophers and Poets*, ed. Gilbert Chinard (Baltimore: Johns Hopkins Press, 1928), p. 12. There are far more excerpts from Euripides (70), Homer (21), Cicero (20), and Horace (14).
62. In a letter to William Short, Sept. 20, 1788, *Writings of Thomas Jefferson*, ed. Paul L. Ford, (New York: Putnams, 1892-99), 5:51.
63. *Diary and Autobiography of John Adams*, ed. L.H. Butterfield (Cambridge: Harvard University Press, 1962) 1:37-8, 41.
64. Manuscript at Massachusetts Historical Society, *Adams Family Papers*, Microfilm Reel 187 ("Miscellany, Literary Commonplace Book"), pp. 31-8.
65. *The Earliest Diary of John Adams*, ed. L.H. Butterfield (Cambridge: Harvard University Press, 1966), pp. 68, 72-3, 76.
66. *Diary and Autobiography*, 4:13.

67. *Catalogue of the John Adams Library in the Public Library of the City of Boston* (Boston, 1917), pp. 256-7.

68. *Adams Family Papers*, Microfilm Reel 124 (the date is March 29, 1823).

69. *Adams Family Correspondence*, ed. L.H. Butterfield et al., 4 vols. (Cambridge: Harvard University Press, 1963-1973), 4:117.

70. See Gaillard Hunt, *History of the Great Seal of the United States* (Washington, D.C.: Department of State, 1909); Monroe E. Deutsch, "E Pluribus Unum," *CJ* 18 (1922-1923): 387-407; and Frank H. Sommer, "Emblem and Device: The Origins of the Great Seal of the United States," *Art Quart.* 24 (1961): 57-76. Benjamin Franklin's nephew Benjamin Mecom published for a few months in 1758 *The New England Magazine of Knowledge and Pleasure*, which carried on its title page the motto *E Pluribus Unum*.

71. *Dictionary of American Biography*, 19:213-14; see van Schaack, (n. 44, above) especially the letters from London 1778- 83, pp. 129, 206, 212, 220, 284, 338.

72. Harry Hayden Clark, "The Literary Influences of Philip Freneau," *SP* 22 (1925): 7, 20; Ruth W. Brown, "Classical Echoes in the Poetry of Philip Freneau," *CJ* 45 (1949): 32-3.

73. *The Poetical Works of John Trumbull* (Hartford: Samuel G. Goodrich, 1820), 2:131-8. The translation, however, appeared first in *The American Museum* 2 (1787): 95-7.

74. Canto 4, lines 81-9, 104-10, 610-12.

75. Victor E. Gimmestad, *John Trumbull* (New York: Twayne, 1974), pp. 131, 138; Katherine A. Conley, "A Letter of John Trumbull," *NEQ* 11 (1938): 372-4.

76. *Adams Family Correspondence*, 3:308-9; 4:144.

77. *Adams Family Papers*, Microfilm reel 13, Oct. 4, 1782; reel 238.

78. *Port Folio* 3 (1803): 43-4, 50-51, 58-9, 66-8. See Linda K. Kerber and Walter J. Morris, "Politics and Literature: The Adams Family and the *Port Folio*," *WMQ* 23 (1966): 455-6. The library of John Quincy Adams contained two texts of Vergil, including an edition published in London in 1824 which he annotated thoroughly, as well as a French translation.

79. *Diary of Charles Francis Adams*, ed. Aida di Pace Donald and David Donald (Cambridge: Harvard University Press, 1964-68), 3:vii. The others were of Homer, Socrates, Plato, Demosthenes, Cicero.

80. The text of the *Georgics* he used and annotated (see n. 78 above) had the following notation at the end in his hand: "These books have never been equalled."

81. *The Writings of Henry David Thoreau, Journal*, vol. 13, ed. Bradford Torrey (Boston: Houghton Mifflin, 1906; rpt. New York: AMS Press, 1968), entries under Nov. 20, 1837 and Dec. 13, 1859; Ethel Seybold, *Thoreau: The Quest and the Classics* (New Haven: Yale University Press, 1951), pp. 16, 29, 37, 55, 121-3; Henry D. Thoreau, *Journal vol.I, 1837-1844*, ed. John C. Broderick, et al. (Princeton: Princeton University Press, 1981), pp. 13-14, 93, 212, 217. Cf. Kenneth W. Cameron, *Companion to Thoreau's Correspondence* (Hartford: Transcendental Books, 1964), pp. 17, 35.

82. The last two quotations are cited in Marx, p. 203.

83. *Remarks on Classical and Utilitarian Studies* (Boston: Little Brown, 1867).

84. "College Fetich," in Charles Francis Adams, *Three Phi Beta Kappa Addresses* (Boston: Houghton Mifflin, 1907), pp. 3-47.

85. *TAPA* 11 (1880): 72-82.

86. Clement L. Smith, "Virgil's Instructions for Ploughing, Fallowing, and the Rotation of Crops. Georgics II, 43-83," *AJP* 2 (1881): 425-45; R. Ellis, "On the Culex and Other Poems of the Appendix Vergiliana," *AJP* 3 (1882): 271-84; and Thomas R. Price, "The Color System of Vergil," *AJP* 4 (1883): 1-20.

87. This article is a contracted version of a chapter from the author's *Classical Americana: The Greek and Roman Heritage in the United States* (1984), reprinted courtesy of Wayne State University Press.

STATIUS AND VERGIL: DEFENSIVE IMITATION

Gordon Williams

Statius was about thirty when Domitian became emperor and all of his poetry that has survived was written under the constraints of the Domitianic terror. But Statius was a court-poet, favored by Domitian, and he kept writing within the safe limits of panegyric and Greek mythology, though even that did not suffice to win him the coveted prize at the Capitoline poetic contest. In fact Statius' most severe anxiety did not arise from political oppression; it arose from poetic oppression, from a sense of the overpowering greatness of a predecessor. It is the purpose of this paper to explore Statius' response to Vergil and to define the difference in his relationship with other predecessors. More fully than any other poet of the period Statius reveals the essential problems of poetic imitation.

I. Some Examples of Imitation

The theme of cutting down trees to make a funeral pyre became a fixed feature of epic after Homer's treatment of Patroclus' funeral in *Iliad* 23 (117–20). It was imitated by Ennius and then by Vergil. This is Vergil's version:

> itur in antiquam silvam, stabula alta ferarum;
> procumbunt piceae; sonat icta securibus ilex
> fraxineaeque trabes cuneis et fissile robur
> scinditur, advolvunt ingentis montibus ornos.

(Aen 6.179 82)

Their path takes them into an ancient wood, the tall dwelling-place of wild beasts. Firs fall to the ground; the holm-oak rings to the blows of axes; oak and ash are split with wedges and cleft into great logs; they roll huge rowans down the mountains.[1]

207

Here, as Macrobius demonstrated is often the case, Vergil had in mind not only the passage of Homer, but also Ennius' imitation of that passage.[2] What he owes to Ennius is essentially the multiplicity of types of tree, five in each poet as against Homer's one (though they are different in the two Roman poets). There the similarity ends.[3] Ennius is deliberately ponderous and the decibel-level of his language is increased by every device of alliteration, assonance and onomatopoeia. The Vergilian description is swift (beginning with the impersonal verb *itur*), and the speed is maintained by the device of using verbs of each type of tree that express the progressive processing and transport of the wood. Also both Homer and Ennius describe the sound of the trees' fall, but Vergil leaves that implicit in the onomatopoeia of the final slow clause. Two ideas are added by Vergil that extend the range of a reader's perception: the wood is *antiqua* (an emotive word in Latin that expresses age and sanctity), and it is the home of wild animals. A pathos that resonates with the occasion of Misenus' funeral is resident in both ideas. What can be said about the relationship between the last passage and its two models is that there is *imitatio* but no *aemulatio*; the late poet is not challenging his predecessors, but rather using them as sources of inspiration. A reader is not being required to compare the text with its two sub-texts, though his aesthetic pleasure is probably increased by recognition.

Statius imitated the Vergilian passage in his description of the funeral of Opheltes in the *Thebaid*:

> sternitur extemplo veteres incaedua ferro
> silva comas, largae qua non opulentior umbrae
> Argolicos inter saltusque educta Lycaeos
> extulerat super astra caput: stat sacra senectae
> numine, nec solos hominum transgressa veterno
> fertur avos, Nymphas etiam mutasse superstes
> Faunorumque greges. aderat miserabile luco
> excidium: fugere ferae, nidosque tepentes
> absiliunt—metus urget—aves; cadit ardua fagus,
> Chaoniumque nemus brumaeque inlaesa cupressus,
> procumbunt piceae, flammis alimenta supremis,
> ornique iliceaeque trabes metuendaque suco
> taxus et infandos belli potura cruores
> fraxinus atque situ non expugnabile robur.
> hinc audax abies et odoro vulnere pinus
> scinditur, adclinant intonsa cacumina terrae
> alnus amica fretis nec inhospita vitibus ulmus.
> dat gemitum tellus.

(6.90–107)

Forthwith a wood, its ancient foliage never cut with steel, is laid low; no wood was richer than it in generous shade that had carried its head higher than the stars, grown to maturity between the glades of the Argolid and of Lycaeus: it stands divine in the sanctity of its great age, and it is said in its long life not only to have outpassed generations of men, but even to have survived to see changes among the Nymphs (95) and the flocks of Fauns. Pitiful death was imminent for that grove: the wild beasts fled, and birds leapt— terror drove them—from their warm beds; there falls the lofty beech, and the Chaonian grove and the cypress uninjured by winter, firs crash down that feed funeral fires (100), and rowans and holm-oak wood and yew feared for its poisonous sap, and the ash that will drink the unspeakable blood-letting of war and oak that is not to be assailed by decay. After that the audacious pine is cut and the fir whose wound is scented; the alder, companion of the waves, and the elm that is no poor host to vines bend their unshaven heads to the ground (106). The earth gives forth a groan.

With the exception of one detail, Statius' eye is fixed on the Vergilian description alone, and each idea is subjected to an expansion designed to exhaust its possibilities. So *antiquam* is echoed by *veteres* (90) and then expanded into fantasy by three lines (93–6) that make the wood outlast not just generations of men but even of (otherwise) immortal Nymphs and Fauns. Then *alta* is exaggerated so that the trees become higher than the stars. The pathos of the wood as home to the wild beasts is fully enacted by the poet in *miserabile* (96), in the warmth of the abandoned nests, and in the fear that motivates the abandonment. Each type of tree is then decorated with an elaborate ornamental phrase that in no way works for its place in the context. The one detail in which Statius goes beyond Vergil is the sound of the trees' fall, but this is transformed into a groan emitted by the stricken earth; pathos is closely allied to personification in poets of the period.

What can be said about Statius' treatment of the theme is that a reader's interest (and pleasure) is proportional to his capacity to recognise the ingenuity with which all potentialities in the Vergilian material have been exhausted. Consequently, knowledge of the sub-text is essential to appreciation of the text. The nature of that relationship will be discussed below.

Another theme in which Statius imitated Vergil is that of a single warrior fighting against a whole army.[4] Vergil used the theme in the scene at the end of *Aeneid* 9 where Turnus deliberately locks himself alone into the Trojan fort and challenges their whole army:

> ergo nec clipeo iuvenis subsistere tantum
> nec dextra valet, iniectis sic undique telis

obruitur. strepit adsiduo cava tempora circum
tinnitu galea et saxis solida aera fatiscunt
discussaeque iubae capiti, nec sufficit umbo
ictibus; ingeminant hastis et Troes et ipse
fulmineus Mnestheus. tum toto corpore sudor
liquitur et piceum (nec respirare potestas)
flumen agit, fessos quatit aeger anhelitus artus.

                                                              (806–14)

So the young man cannot sufficiently withstand them either with
his shield or with his right hand, so overwhelmed is he by spears
hurled from all around him. His helmet resounds with continuous
ringing round his hollow temples, and the solid bronze is torn by
stones and the crest is broken upon his head, nor can his shield
stand up (810) to the blows. Both the Trojans and lightning-swift
Mnestheus redouble their spear-throwing. Then sweat pours over
his whole body and makes a dark viscous stream; it is impossible
for him to breathe, and his gasping shakes his tired limbs.

Here again Vergil had in mind both Homer's description of Ajax against the
Trojan army in *Iliad* 16.102–11 and also Ennius' account of the tribune
Caelius' fight against the Histrian army (*Annales* 401–8 V.)[5] The movement
of Vergil's account follows Homer's closely, but its vocabulary echoes
Ennius, so that both sub-texts not only enhance a reader's appreciation but
are active in the text in a particular way: Turnus' bravery (as distinct from his
foolhardiness, which is condemned by the poet) is not only Homerically
heroic; it is also Italian and Roman—such men will guarantee Rome's
greatness. Here too, therefore, there is *imitatio* but no *aemulatio*, and there is
the additional feature that the sub-texts are active in the text (as they are not
in the Vergilian passage on tree-felling). There is one striking detail that goes
beyond both Homer and Ennius in "sweat flows in a pitchy river" (813–
14).[6] Conington says of this in his commentary: "*piceum* is a strange and
scarcely pleasing epithet, expressing, doubtless, the sweat as mingled with
dust and gore." The precise observation of unpleasant detail and the
distaste are typical of Vergil.

    Lucan challenged this treatment by Vergil with a characteristic ex-
pansion in this description of the Caesarian Scaeva's lone stand against the
whole of Pompey's army (6.192–225). The physical weaknesses of weariness, sweat, and breathlessness are omitted in the interest of hyperbolic
heroism and strength. Enjoyment of horror for its own sake takes the place
of Vergilian distaste.

    Statius twice made use of this theme, both times of Tydeus. The first
time is when Tydeus, returning alone from Thebes to Argos, is caught in
night-ambush by a whole army:

haec intonat; ast tamen illi
membra negant, lassusque ferit praecordia sanguis.
iam sublata manus cassos defertur in ictus
tardatique gradus, clipeum nec sustinet umbo
mutatum spoliis; gelidus cadit imber anhelo
pectore, tum crines ardentiaque ora cruentis
roribus et taetra morientum aspargine manant.

(2.668–74)

So he thunders; yet nevertheless his legs are letting him down, and
the blood strikes wearily at his heart. Now his uplifted hand is
expended on useless blows (670) and his steps are slowed; and the
boss cannot hold together the shield with its hides ruined; a chill
rain streams down his panting breast; finally his hair and burning
face are flooded with a bloody dew and the filthy spatterings of the
dying.

The second time is in the long scene that leads up to Tydeus' act of
cannibalism and his death:

et iam corporibus sese spoliisque cadentum
clauserat, unum acies circum consumitur, unum
omnia tela vovent; summis haec ossibus haerent.
pars frustrata cadunt, partem Tritonia vellit,
multa rigent clipeo. densis iam consitus hastis
ferratum quatit umbo nemus, tergoque fatiscit
atque umeris gentilis aper; nusquam ardua coni
gloria, quique apicem torvae Gradivus habebat
cassidis, haud laetum domino ruit omen, inusta
temporibus nuda aera sedent, circumque sonori
vertice percusso volvuntur in arma molares.
iam cruor in galea, iam saucia proluit ater
pectora permixtus sudore et sanguine torrens.

(8.700–712)

And now he had enclosed himself with bodies of the dead and their
weapons. The enemy is being used up on him alone, for him alone
all weapons pray. Some stick in the surface of his bones, some miss
and fall to the ground, some Athene plucks out, many bristle on his
shield. The boss, sown with a dense crop of spears, shakes an iron-
bound grove, and on his back (705) and shoulder his family boar-
hide gapes in rents; gone is the tall glory of his crest, and the Mars
that occupied the peak of his fierce helmet falls off, no happy omen
for its owner. The bare bronze is branded onto his temples, stones
strike his helmet and fall ringing about his armor (710). Now there
is blood inside his helmet, now a black torrent of mixed sweat and
blood drenches his wounded chest.

These are widely different variants that deliberately draw attention both to one another and to their model in Vergil's account of Turnus. The earlier passage closely follows Vergil; only the detail of breathlessness is omitted for the moment (to allow Tydeus to deliver a thunderous speech—*intonat*, 668). The tiredness arises from the effort of continuous killing (Tydeus slays all of his enemies, sparing only one to carry the news to Thebes). In each phrase Statius has found a strikingly original way of expressing an idea of Vergil's; this is particularly clear in the detail of his shield being ruined: *clipeum nec sustinet umbo / mutatum spoliis* (671-2 "the boss cannot hold up the shield which is altered for the worse in its spoils"). Here *spolia* has an unexpected sense: a *spolium* is something stolen or stripped from an enemy; here it must have the sense of "hide," that is, the skin stripped from an animal.[7]

In the later passage, Statius certainly challenges Vergil and (in a sense) himself; but he also challenges Lucan. Not only does he produce, for instance, his own original version of Vergil's *piceum flumen* in lines 711-12, but he adapts phrases of Lucan also. It is especially notable that he devises a surprising locution for the idea of many spears sticking in Tydeus' shield: *densis iam consitus hastis / ferratum quatit umbo nemus* (704-5 "the boss, thickly sown with spears, makes a grove of iron quake"). Lucan said *densamque ferens in pectore silvam* (205 "displaying a dense wood on his breast"). Both poets use the metaphor of a cluster of spears as a grove of trees; Lucan hyperbolically placed the grove in Scaeva's own chest. Statius not only expanded the metaphor by using *consitus* (the planting of the grove), but in transferring the grove from a man's chest to his shield he was returning to the passage of Vergil from which Lucan derived his hyperbole. In *Aeneid* 10.883-7 Mezentius, riding in a circle, fixes spear after spear in the shield of Aeneas, who pivots, holding it out to protect himself, and *immanem aerato circumfert tegmine silvam* (887 "swings round a huge wood on its brazen covering").[8] Such a "correction" of a predecessor by return to the revered master-poet, Vergil, is characteristc of Statius. It can be seen also in the detail of Tydeus' helmet (706-10). Lucan said of Scaeva: *et galeae fragmenta cavae compressa perurunt / tempora* (193-4 "and his hollow helmet in fragments galls and crushes his temples"). Lucan had to envisage a Roman legionary helmet. Statius could go back to Vergil's Homeric helmet, with an expansion of Vergilian details, though at the same time he took over and intensified Lucan's idea of "galls" (*perurunt*) into "is branded onto his temples" (*iniusta*).

II. The Nature of Statius' Imitation

Two apparently opposed ideals are clear in Statius' poetic composition: an instinct for brevity and a delight in expansion.[9] Both derive from a desire for originality. On the one hand originality could be attained by linguistic ingenuity that focused on the single phrase. This technique is most clearly illustrated by the love of the *sententia* or epigram that characterizes the writing, both prose and verse, of the whole of this period. The *sententia* had a very wide range of tone from the highly cerebral wit of Lucan's *victrix causa deis placuit sed victa Catoni* (1.128 "the winning cause found favour with the gods, the losing with Cato") to the pathos of Statius' authorial comment that foreshadows the disaster and death of Dymas and Hopleus—*invida fata piis et fors ingentibus ausis / rara comes (Theb.* 10.384-5 "Fate is grudging to the loyal and luck rarely accompanies great exploits"). Such authorial in-trusions into the text are very infrequent in Vergil, but become char-acteristic of epic in the Silver Age.[10] Another way in which this instinct displays itself is more common in Statius; this is the linguistic ingenuity that produces an unexpected and often puzzling locution. In such locutions the ingenuity of the poet demands a like ingenuity on the part of the reader. What Statius is particularly adept at doing is taking a bold locution from a predecessor and pushing it to a further extreme of unexpectedness. A good example of this has already been noted in the movement from Lucan's use of *perurere* to Statius' *inurere*. But Statius practises this art on all of his predecessors and especially on Vergil. For instance, Vergil wrote of a soldier deeply asleep, *toto proflabat pectore somnum (Aen.* 9.326 "he was snoring out sleep from his whole chest"). Statius converted this to *anhelum / proflabant sub luce deum (Theb.* 2.76-7 "they were snoring out the panting god in the light of day"). He is describing men so drunk that they are still deeply and noisily asleep even in the daylight after a night of orgies. The god is Bacchus, the orgy was in celebration of his birthday, but he is also a metonymy for wine and by enallage receives the adjective that expresses the breathlessness which he causes. The link with Vergil's expression was created for Statius by the fact that the Rutulians, attacked by Nisus and Euryalus in *Aeneid* 9, were in a drunken sleep (164-5 and 189-90). Such imitation of predecessors is constant in Statius, and such is the degree of ingenuity he brings to it that recollection of the predecessor's phrase is often required for full under-standing.[11]

It is of the nature of such locutions that their intent and ingenuity are a direct function of their brevity. The apparently opposed ideal of expansion, clear in all the writers of this period, was not really opposed. Brevity and expansion have this in common: they narrow the area of concentration to the least possible. In the case of brevity it is the single phrase; in the case of expansion it is the single idea. So in the example of the theme of trees being cut down, the single idea contained in Vergil's adjective *antiquam* is given three expansive treatments by Statius which are designed to exhaust not only all the thematic potentialities inherent in it but the emotional as well. Similarly the poet exhausts as he enacts all the emotional potentialities of

Vergil's *stabula . . . ferarum*. The trees mentioned by Vergil are expanded by linear extension at the same time as each tree is decorated with ingeniously devised ornamental phrases. The recognition of such expansion as a legitimate aesthetic device goes back to Hellenistic poets, but in Latin it is virtually the creation of Ovid. In *Metamorphoses* 10.86-105, for instance, he plays with Orpheus' virtuosity in causing trees to uproot themselves and follow his music in a portrait of a bare hillside suddenly covered with no less than twenty-seven different trees (accommodated in seventeen hexameters). After Ovid, lists become a permanent feature of poetic composition. Here, too, the focus of concentration is narrowed to a single idea. The poetry of Vergil was especially valuable to successors simply because he was content to suggest both emotions and ideas that the reader was left to perceive for himself, and he was therefore a prime source for various modes of imitation not only by Statius but by all poets of the period.

However it is important to recognise that it was characteristic not only of Statius but of the process of imitation generally in this period to use a multiplicity of models. It has already been seen how Statius used Lucan, and the importance of Ovid to all of these poets is easily seen; Ovid was the poet who transformed poetic composition to adapt it to the new conditions of the late Augustan and post-Augustan era. Statius made use of all his predecessors from Vergil onwards, and to some extent he used the others as a filter to mediate the oppressively blinding genius of Vergil to his own gaze. One example will illustrate this process. Lucan met the challenge of Aeneas' descent into the Underworld in *Aeneid* 6 by dividing his response. In the sixth book of the *Bellum Civile* he converted the descent into the horrific portrait of Sextus Pompeius summoning up from the Underworld and consulting the witch Erichtho. But he also challenged Vergil's account of the Sibyl's prophetic ecstasy by a long-drawn-out account of Appius Claudius' consultation of the Delphic oracle in his own fifth book (71-236). Statius imitated Lucan's technique and divided his own response to *Aeneid* 6. He ended *Thebaid* 7 with a rococo description of the descent of the prophet Amphiaraus beneath the earth (771-823); this device then enabled him to open *Thebaid* 8 with a long description of the Underworld and of Pluto's reaction to this invasion of his territory (1-126).

III. The Anxiety of Imitating Vergil

Imitation of predecessors (*imitatio exemplorum*), as distinct from the Aristotelian concept of the imitation of life (*imitatio vitae*), became a problem of great importance both practically and theoretically in the post-Augustan period. Of course it had long existed before that, especially for Greeks.

Dionysius of Halicarnassus, writing under Augustus, diagnosed the excellence of Demosthenes' style as being the product of eclectic imitation of a whole range of models (*Demosthenes* 33) In his *De imitatione* (of which only a few fragments exist) he even worked out a theory of poetic inspiration in which the poet's soul is excited by reading a great predecessor; here he anticipated the much fuller expression of this theory by Longinus (*On the Sublime* 12.2–14).[12]

But the whole concept of such imitation was open to a paralysing objection: an imitation is by definition inferior to an original.[13] Quintilian expressed the objection thus: *adde quod, quicquid alteri simile est necesse est minus sit eo quod imitatur, ut umbra corpore et imago facie et actus histrionum veris adfectibus* (*Inst.* 10.2.11 "add this consideration: whatever imitates something else must be inferior to what it imitates, just as a shadow is inferior to the substance, a portrait to the [actual] features, or the simulations of actors to real feelings"). When the same objection had been made with characteristic bluntness by the elder Seneca, he supplied the traditional answer at the same time: *non est unus, quamvis praecipuus sit, imitandus quia numquam par fit imitator auctori; haec rei natura est: semper citra veritatem est similitudo* (*Controv.* 1 *praef.* 6 "no one model, however excellent, should be imitated since an imitator is never the equal of his original; this is the truth of the matter: a copy always falls short of the reality"). By the ordering of his formulation, the elder Seneca was able to evade the problem whether imitation of many models does in fact correct the essential flaw in imitation. Quintilian does not pretend to have an answer to the problem, but he still insists on the necessity for a plurality of models. He has a strange reason for this: he admits that one model is quite sufficient (as long as it is Cicero), but since one cannot imitate anyone perfectly, many models are preferable (10.223–6).

How then to escape the disabling sense of inevitable decline that seems the lot of the imitator? This is not faced explicitly by Quintilian; it was too troubling a question for a determined optimist. Instead an influential point of view is just allowed to appear, though its strength is never tested against the enemy. Quintilian is committed, as a teacher must be, to the possibility of development: that is, to asserting that the movement downhill can be reversed. He does this by an argument that, if pursued to its conclusion, would deny the importance of imitation. He asserts that no development is possible for those who only imitate (*nihil autem crescit sola imitatione*, 10.2.9). One must aim at the highest, not follow the traces of others: *nam qui hoc agit ut prior sit, forsitan, etiamsi non transierit, aequabit* (10 "for a man who concentrates on surpassing may well, even if he does not succeed, come level"). The idea seems to be that one must go beyond imitation to actual rivalry of models. This is then converted into the proposition that if imitation is carefully eclectic and well judged (27), and if to this the imitator adds his own individual talents, then such a man could be the consummate orator (*perfectus orator*) that we are seeking; in fact this should be more possible now than ever because so many excellent models already exist, and men will be able to praise those great men not only for having surpassed their predecessors but also for having taught their own successors (28). This extraordinary example of wishful thinking depends on faith in a concept that had a long previous history—the inspiring power of *aemulatio*. Later, Quintilian actually states his preference for the practice of paraphrase instead of translation on the ground that it provides the possibility of struggling against and rivalling the original in expression of the same ideas (10.5.5).

The basic idea here was expressed by Dionysius of Halicarnassus when he said that emulation (in a literary sense associated with imitation) "is an activity of the soul stimulated to admiration of what it perceives to be beautiful."[14] It is not at all clear that Dionysius regarded this as more than a way of explaining how the latecomer, perforce an imitator, could still experience the sense of inspiration. There is no evidence that he used the concept, as Roman writers did, as a means of escaping from the burden of the tradition and the oppressive sense of inevitable decline. Yet he may have done so, because he regarded a return to the pure Attic style of the fifth century by means of imitation as the only path to salvation from present-day decadence.

Roman writers, however, certainly seized on the idea as offering the hope of doing more than dispiritedly following in the tracks of their great predecessors. In fact, it became an essential element in their imitation to draw explicit attention to their models and so to invite the audience to judge the success of their rivalry. The attitude is perfectly expressed in a perceptive comment by the orator Junius Gallio on his friend Ovid's procedure; it is reported by the elder Seneca that: *hoc autem dicebat Gallio Nasoni suo valde placuisse; itaque fecisse illum quod in multis aliis versibus Vergilii fecerat, non subripiendi causa, sed palam mutuandi, hoc animo ut vellet agnosci* (*Suas.* 3.7* "Gallio used to say that this phrase [of Vergil's] greatly pleased his friend Ovid, who consequently did what he did in the case of many other verses of Vergil—[he made use of it], not with any intention of plagiarising but of openly borrowing, with that very idea in mind of having [its origin] recognised"). The procedure is easily detected, and it is writ both large and small especially in the *Metamorphoses*, but Ovid did the same thing with other predecessors such as Propertius and Tibullus in other works.

This is to be distinguished to some extent from the idea that originality can be achieved by using not one but many models. Both ideas offer comfort to the imitator in this period. The idea of emulation opens up the possibility of surpassing; the use of many models allowed the hope of creating something that could not, *ex hypothesi*, have existed before. The younger Seneca exploits the psychology of that hope in letter 84 to Lucilius. He uses the honey-gathering of bees as an analogy to the procedure of the imitator and draws this conclusion:

> hos quoque apes debemus imitari, et quaecumque ex diversa lectione congessimus, separare (melius enim distincta servantur); deinde adhibita ingenii nostri cura et facultate in unum saporem varia illa libamenta confundere, ut, etiamsi apparuerit unde sumptum sit, aliud tamen esse quam unde sumptum est appareat.
>
> (5)

> we too should imitate those bees and separate out everything we have collected from our varied reading (for they are better preserved if kept separate); then, by applying our own inborn diligence and skill, we should blend all those flavors into one single savor such that, even though its origin may be clear, it may also be clear that it is different from its origin.

So multiple models could give hope of creating an impression of originality. But, paradoxically, challenge of a recognisable model opened up the possibility of surpassing it; however the audience was the only judge of success and had to be able to recognise the model. So in the latter case the writer had to take the risk of inviting comparison. From this another curious feature of the period took its origin: this was the constant and deliberate re-use of material that had already been exploited by predecessors. The more familiar the material, the greater was the challenge.[15] Contemporary rhetoric was encouraging to this point of view, and, in fact, it is most strikingly represented in the *controversiae* and *suasoriae* recollected and recorded verbatim by the elder Seneca. The basis of this idea lay in the concept of *inventio*. The word suggests imaginative creation, but it came to have a much more restricted sense in an age in which the pressure of ideas was low. The discovery involved in *inventio* was the full exploitation of all the potentialities latent in a given body of material. The opportunity lay open to a later writer to show that a predecessor had neglected certain aspects of the material that were now available to the ingenuity of the latecomer. It was Vergil's "negative capability" that made him so resourceful a model to his successors. The body of material and consequently the relationship between the earlier and later treatments could vary greatly. It could be restricted in scope, and the variation could reside in a chain of details; this is the case with the passages examined above in Section I. But the material could be extensive and the relationship could be structural rather than a question of corresponding details. This is the case with Statius' episode involving the two young heroes Hopleus and Dymas, which has a clear relationship to Vergil's account of the exploit of Nisus and Euryalus.[16]

Vergil modelled his episode on the night foray of Odysseus and Diomedes in *Iliad* 10. However he introduced a dramatic complication in making Nisus and Euryalus lovers, and he underlined this in the portrait he gave of the pair and their conduct during the foot race, one of the funeral games for Anchises in *Aeneid* 5. The actual exploit is similar to that in *Iliad* 10. Statius' episode (*Theb*. 10.347–448) is totally different, except that it takes place at night. Hopleus and Dymas set out to recover the bodies of their princes (*reges*) in order to give them burial. They are discovered; Hopleus is killed and Dymas commits suicide. There is no relationship of any kind whatever between the pair; both are instead devoted to, and apparently lovers of, their princes, Tydeus and Parthenopaeus: *dilecti regibus ambo, / regum ambo comites* (348–9 "both of them loved by their princes, both of them companions of their princes"). The relation to the episode of Vergil is thus purely structural. But Statius calls specific attention to it by closing the episode with an apostrophe to the pair that imitates Vergil's similar apostrophic closure:

> tales optatis regum in complexibus ambo,
> par insigne animis, Aetolus et inclitus Arcas,
> egregias efflant animas letoque fruuntur.
> vos quoque sacrati, quamvis mea carmina surgant
> inferiore lyra, memores superabitis annos.
> forsitan et comites non aspernabitur umbras
> Euryalus Phrygiique admittet gloria Nisi.
>
> (*Theb*. 10.442–8)

> In such a way both of them, the Aetolian and the famous Arcadian, a pair distinguished for their courage, breathe out, in longed-for embraces of their princes, their matchless souls, and they delight in death. You too have been made immortal, although my poetry soars from an inferior lyre, and will outlive the remembering years. Perhaps furthermore Euryalus will not disdain your shades as companions nor the glory of Phrygian Nisus.

There are features here that are echoed in the extraordinary personal *sphragis* which ends the epic and which is imitated from Ovid's closure to the *Metamorphoses*; both endings hope for future life for their epics. This is Statius':

> Durabisne procul dominoque legere superstes,
> o mihi bissenos multum vigilata per annos

Thebai? iam certe praesens tibi Fama benignum
stravit iter coepitque novam monstrare futuris.
iam te magnanimus dignatur noscere Caesar,
Itala iam studio discit memoratque iuventus.
vive, precor; nec tu divinam Aeneida tempta,
sed longe sequere et vestigia semper adora.
mox, tibi si quis adhuc praetendit nubila livor,
occidet et meriti post me referentur honores.

(Theb. 12.810–19)

Will you endure in time to come and will you survive your master
and be read, o my *Thebaid* over whom I labored twelve wakeful
years? Even now here in my lifetime Fame has laid down a
welcoming road for you and makes a start on displaying your
originality to future generations. Even now noble and heroic
Caesar deigns to recognise you, and the youth of Italy is eager to
learn and memorize you. Live on, that is my prayer; but do not
compete with the divine *Aeneid*; just follow a long way behind and
never cease to adore her footsteps from afar. If any trace of Envy
clouds your brightness still, it will soon perish and well-deserved
honors shall be paid to you after I am dead.

There is here a curious combination of diffidence and pride, of confidence
and uncertainty. It is quite unlike the situation in the first poem of Catullus
where the initial self-depreciation in the address to Cornelius Nepos is
ironically contrasted with the prayer to his Muse for long life in the final
couplet. What Statius expresses in both apostrophes is a sense of inferiority
to the *Aeneid* along with a pathetic hope that it may be unjustified. Nisus and
Euryalus may perhaps accept Hopleus and Dymas as friends; his *Thebaid* is
original (*novam*, 12.813); he is already famous; Domitian recognises him,
and young men of Italy learn his poetry by heart (12.814–15); if anything
clouds his present glory it is due to Envy (12.818–19).

Other references to his *Thebaid* display a similar anxiety. For instance, in
the course of a long poem addressed to Vitorius Marcellus, he says:

nos otia vitae

solamur cantu ventosaque gaudia famae
quaerimus. en egomet somnum et geniale secutus
litus ubi Ausonio se condidit hospita portu
Parthenope, tenuis ignavo pollice chordas
pulso Maroneique sedens in margine templi
sumo animum et magni tumulis accanto magistri.

(Silv. 4.4.49–55)

I console a life of leisure with song and pursue the joy of ever-shifting Fame. Here am I seeking sleep and my family shore, where foreign Parthenope drowned herself in an Ausonian harbor. I pluck frail strings with feeble fingers and, sitting on the edge of Maro's shrine, I take heart as I sing at my greater master's grave!

But later he says:

> Nunc si forte meis quae sint exordia musis
> scire petes, iam Sidonios emensa labores
> Thebais optato collegit carbasa portu,
> Parnasique iugis silvaque Heliconide festis
> tura dedit flammis et virginis exta iuvencae
> votiferaque meas suspendit ab arbore vittas.
>
> (87-92)

If you want to know what my Muse is beginning: my *Thebaid*, her Sidonian labors completed, has furled her sails in the long-hoped-for haven, and on the ridges of Parnassus and the glades of Helicon has offered incense and the entrails of a virgin heifer on the festival flames, and has hung my garlands on a votive tree.

He goes on to say that he is now writing his *Achilleid*. In another poem, addressed to Vibius Maximus, he says this:

> quippe te fido monitore nostra
> Thebais multa cruciata lima
> temptat audaci fide Mantuanae
>   gaudia famae.
>
> (*Silv*. 4.7.25–8)

My *Thebaid*, tortured much with the file under your trusted guidance, strains with audacious tones for the joy of Mantuan Fame.

In his preface to the first book of the *Silvae*, he explains that he has long hesitated whether to publish these impromptu pieces; "For why should I burden myself with the responsibility of this further publication when I am still fearful for my *Thebaid*, although it has left my hands?"

Part of his anxiety relates to his failure at the Capitoline poetic contests, which he mentions with shame and guilt in poems addressed to his wife (*Silv*. 3.5.28–33) and to his dead father (5.3.225–33). References to Envy are designed to alleviate that pain.[17] But the real source of his anxiety lies in his constant and overt imitation of the *Aeneid*. He shows no such anxiety in imitating Lucan, or in his most explicit imitation of Valerius Flaccus, whose account of the women of Lemnos (briefly narrated in *Argonautica* 1.82–427) he imitated in *Thebaid* 5.27–498.[18] This imitation was deliberately made into a challenge to his predecessor since the story had no relevance in the *Thebaid*, and it took a digression of nearly three books to accommodate it. Anxiety only came with imitation of the *Aeneid*, and that was because, as was explained above, contemporary theory justified imitation by regarding it as emulation and so as providing the possibility of surpassing the predecessor. Statius could not face the clear implication of that in the case of Vergil, and so he sought defence in representing imitation of the *Aeneid* as conforming to the theory by which an imitation is inevitably inferior to the original; but this applied only to the *Aeneid*, and his confusion and discomfort appear clearly in the uneasy combination of hope and uncertainty.

The unique nature of these expressions of obsessive anxiety—that is, their status as something quite other than rhetorical exploitation of a convenient theme—can be assessed by comparing them with Statius' treatment of Lucan's relationship to Vergil. In *Silvae* 2.7 Statius wrote a poem addressed to Lucan's wife on the anniversary of the dead poet's birthday. A major theme is Lucan's literary fame, based especially on his *Bellum Civile*. The greater part of the poem is occupied by the poet's report of a long address (41–104) by Calliope to the new-born Lucan. She asserts that the *Iliad*, the *Odyssey*, and the *Argonautica* are hackneyed (48–51), and that Lucan's *carmen togatum* (epic on Roman citizens) marks him as a bolder poet (*fortior*, 53). She predicts that he will write the *Bellum Civile ante annos Culicis Maroniani* (74 "before the age at which Vergil wrote the *Culex*"), and that he will surpass Ennius, Lucretius, Varro of Atax (who wrote an *Argonautica*), and Ovid (75–8).[19] She concludes with a climax:

> quid maius loquar? ipsa te Latinis
> Aeneis venerabitur canentem.
>
> (79–80)

> What greater praise can I utter? The *Aeneid* itself shall actually pay homage to you as you sing to the people of Latium.

The clear implication of this is that the *Aeneid* will recognise the *Bellum Civile* as at least equal to itself and probably superior. In accordance with this Statius, in the introductory section of the poem, apostrophises Vergil's birthplace and warns *Baetim, Mantua, provocare noli* (35 "Be careful not to challenge Baetis, Mantua!"). So Lucan's birthplace can claim a poet who cannot be challenged by Vergil's. Again Lucan's superiority to Vergil is implied. That is typical rhetorical treatment of a theme without regard to its truth, and Statius did not hesitate to challenge Lucan. It was only the oppressive pre-eminence of Vergil that aroused anxiety in him, compelling him to express the doubts that he yet hoped might be misplaced.

IV. The Changed Nature of Intertextuality

The texts of the *Iliad* and of the *Odyssey* are active in the text of the *Aeneid*: that is, the poet wrote his *Aeneid* in such a way that knowledge of the texts of Homer is essential for full understanding of it.[20] This linkage of texts and sub-texts takes various forms and can be used for various purposes. The sub-text may provide a framework for judgment; an example that is not Homeric is the exploitation of a reader's knowledge of the Medea of Apollonius Rhodius to define and evaluate the situation of Dido. Or it may be used for irony, as when Turnus' view of himself as an even greater Achilles is undercut by the clear appropriateness of Hector's situation to his own. Or it may be used to measure the distance from a conventional heroic world and so particularly to define the novelty of Aeneas as a new kind of human being in the Homeric world. These are all large-scale relationships between text and sub-text. But there are also constant small-scale relationships as, for instance, when the poet uses of Turnus a striking simile of a stallion that Homer had applied to Paris; the conjuction invites, in fact demands, an assessment of the similarities between Paris and Turnus.[21]

What is characteristic of this intertextuality is this. Vergil's appeal to Homer is not to Homer as a given body of text, or even to Homer as a poet; it is to Homer as a witness, recording historian and imaginative inhabitant of the world which he himself created. That is the world in which Vergil locates himself and his reader. It is the referentiality of the text of Homer that concerns him.

It is quite different with Statius, and the difference can be measured in the apostrophe to Hopleus and Dymas quoted above. That passage carries on its face an appeal to the text of the *Aeneid* in its form, its placement, and its extent. He too, like Vergil, is speaking of himself as a poet; and he too, like Vergil, is mistrustful of his success.[22] But here the similarity ends. Statius is thinking of himself as a poet, but not in relation to his two heroes, and he is not hoping that he has done justice to something that in some way lies objectively outside the text. He is thinking of himself in relation to Vergil, and he is hoping that his treatment of a similar theme will measure up to Vergil's—in some degree. Nisus and Euryalus are for Statius in Vergil's text, not in Vergil's world; and Hopleus and Dymas are thought of as in Statius' text. So the hoped-for acceptance of the latter pair by the former is enacted in a purely textual world.

In fact the contribution that the sub-text is qualified to make to the reading of the text has nothing whatever to do with its interpretation, only with its evaluation. A clear distinction is being made between form and content, and it is only the former that is relevant. Statius appeals to the

Aeneid as a particular network of signs, not so much a sub-text as a parallel text to which the reader must make reference every now and then. In a curious way the poet's communication with the reader is not mediated at the level of the text; instead the poet is somehow in direct contact with the reader, above the head, as it were, of the text. Poet and reader are in a mutually agreed-on conspiracy concerning the text which exists, for this purpose, at the same level as a series of similar texts. The process of *aemulatio* demands this constant extraction of the reader from the imaginative world created in the text so that he can notice the manner of its creation and evaluate that manner against a series of predecessor texts.

Statius did not create this new type of intertextuality, but he was the most powerful exponent of it for later antiquity and for the Renaissance. The cause of his influence lay not only in the power of his poetry, but also in the explicit anxiety of his imitation of the *Aeneid*. Sympathy could easily be felt for a poet oppressed by the sense of a great predecessor's presence, and no one could fail to admire the honest expression of that anxiety.

Notes

1. All translations are mine; they are literal and intended merely as guides to the Latin texts.
2. *Saturnalia* 6.
3. For more detail, see Gordon Williams, *Tradition and Originality in Roman Poetry* (Oxford: Clarendon Press, 1968), pp. 263-5.
4. See Williams, *Change and Decline* (Berkeley: University of California Press, 1978), pp. 199-205.
5. For details, see Williams, *Tradition*, pp. 687-9.
6. Williams, *Change*, pp. 200-201.
7. For this interpretation see H.M. Mulder, *Publii Papinii Statii Thebaidos Liber Secundus* (Groningen: De Waal, 1954), ad loc.
8. Used directly by Statius at *Thebaid* 5.533.
9. For these as general features of writing in this period see Williams, *Change*, pp. 213-32.
10. Ibid., pp. 232-46.
11. It is clear for instance, in *Thebaid* 2.671-2 when compared with the corresponding words from *Aeneid* 9.810-11 (see above).
12. See the edition of D.A. Russell (Oxford: Clarendon Press, 1964), ad loc.
13. On this and what follows see especially Elaine Fantham, "Imitation and Decline," *CP* 73 (1978): 102-16.
14. Russell, p. 113; cf. G. Kennedy, *The Art of Roman Rhetoric* (Princeton: Princeton University Press, 1972), pp. 347-8.
15. See Williams, *Change*, pp. 193-213.
16. On this see especially B. Kytzler, "Imitatio und aemulatio in der Thebais des Statius," *Hermes* 97 (1969): 209-19, and D. Vessey, *Statius and the Thebaid* (Cambridge: Cambridge University Press, 1973), pp. 110-17.
17. This is not affected by the fact that Envy was a traditional topic.

18. See Erich Burck, *Vom Römischen Manierismus* (Darmstadt: Wissenschaftliche Buchgesell-schaft, 1971), pp. 75ff., and Vessey, pp. 165ff.
19. It does not matter that the *Culex* was a later forgery; Statius (like everyone else) believed it a genuine work of Vergil's youth.
20. On this feature see Williams, *Technique and Ideas in the Aeneid* (New Haven: Yale University Press, 1983), chapter 5.
21. Ibid., pp. 82-3.
22. On this aspect of the apostrophe in *Aeneid* 9.446-9 see Williams, *Technique*, pp. 205-7, 226-31.

"TAKEN FROM BRINDISI": VERGIL IN AN OTHER'S OTHERWORLD

Allen Mandelbaum

I. Old, New, and Old Renewed

Neither citing, mining, nor emulating Vergil is the same as abducting him. And the Dante of the *Comedy*, poet of persons, is not only appropriator and innovator, but abductor of others—the living (Branca Doria, *Inf.* 33, and Dante himself) and the dead—into his otherworld.

The prince of the abducted through *Purgatorio* 26 is Vergil. The frame of his abduction is Dante's obsessive chiming on "old" and "new," *antico* and *nuovo* in the *Comedy*. The topos of *nuovo* is not new. It is a common-place that serves three generations of Italian poetry of the Duecento and has Provençal antecedents.[1] But the *antico* is a Dantesque innovation, for which the central passage has as its summative line: "I recognize the signs of the *old* flame" (*Purg.* 30.48). Above all, the joint presence in the *Comedy* of both *antico* and *nuovo* is a radical innovation. The fable corresponding to this innovation is Dante's double rivering: with Lethe, a traditional given, and with Eunoë, his own addition. And the river that restores the memory of the good that we have done may also be the river of poetic confluence; and drinking from Eunoë, for which thirst may indeed be limitless, is a precondition for being "remade" (*Purg.* 33.127–45).

Without unduly fanatic concern with triple repetends, we need to see in juxtaposition *Purgatorio* 30.34–54, with its three *antico*'s and three *Virgilio*'s, and 33.142–5 with its *novelle*, *rinovellate*, and *novella*:

> E lo spirito mio, che già cotanto
> tempo era stato ch'a la sua presenza
> non era di stupor, tremando, affranto,
>   sanza de li occhi aver più conoscenza,

225

per occulta virtù che da lei mosse,
d'antico amor sentì la gran potenza.
    Tosto che ne la vista mi percosse
l'alta virtù che già m'avea trafitto
prima ch'io fuor di puërizia fosse,
    volsimi a la sinistra col respitto
col quale il fantolin corre a la mamma
quando ha paura o quando elli è afflitto,
    per dicere a Virgilio: "Men che dramma
di sangue m'è rimaso che non tremi:
conosco i segni de l'antica fiamma."
    Ma Virgilio n'avea lasciati scemi
di sé, Virgilio dolcissimo patre,
Virgilio a cui per mia salute die'mi;
    né quantunque perdeo l'antica matre,
valse a le guance nette di rugiada
che, lagrimando, non tornasser atre.

                                             (Purg. 30.34–54)

    Within her presence, I had once been used
to feeling—trembling—wonder, dissolution;
but that was long ago. Still, though my soul,
    now she was veiled, could not see her directly,
by way of hidden force that she could move,
I felt the mighty power of old love.
    As soon as that deep force had struck my vision
(the power that, when I had not yet left
my boyhood, had already transfixed me),
    I turned around and to my left—just as
a little child, afraid or in distress
will hurry to his mother—anxiously,
    to say to Virgil: "I am left with less
than one drop of my blood that does not tremble:
I recognize the signs of the old flame."
    But Virgil had deprived us of himself,
Virgil, the gentlest father, Virgil, he
to whom I gave my self for my salvation;
    and even all our ancient mother lost
was not enough to keep my cheeks, though washed
with dew, from darkening again with tears.

and

    Io ritornai da la santissima onda
rifatto sì come piante novelle
rinovellate di novella fronda,
    puro e disposto a salire a le stelle.

                                               (Purg. 33.142–5)

From that most holy wave I now returned
to Beatrice; remade, as new trees are
renewed when they bring forth new boughs, I was
    pure and prepared to climb unto the stars.

Abductions and appropriations include, of course, Dante's Romance
antecedents. The *Purgatorio* is surely a Romance collegium where, from
Casella's singing of *Amor che ne la mente mi ragiona*, to Sordello, to Oderisi's
comments on fame in canto 11, through to Bonagiunta da Lucca, Guido
Guinizzelli, Forese (not only friend but poet), and Arnaut Daniel, Dante
establishes the nature and limits of his and others' achievements in the
Romance mother tongue. To these, many now would add the travail of the
Fiore and the *Detto*; and all would acknowledge as the most clamorous, most
exacerbated point of Dante's Romance encounters Arnaut Daniel. If the
Fiore and the *Detto* are way stations to lexical abundance, Arnaut Daniel is
the patron of lexical limitation and compression, and prosodic arabesque.
He presides over Dante's entry into what I think of as the prosodic
hallucinarium, that halfway-house in which technique becomes an end in
itself. To that hallucinarium, to *trobar ric* and *trobar clus*, Dante is surely
indebted for his taste for periphrasis. If Arnaut, in his *Lo ferm voler*, can
speak of a mother as *lu seror de mon oncle*, Dante need not turn to antiquity for
serpentine adornment.

    And yet there is in Dante an obsessive movement past the Roman
collegium into the uniqueness of being granted a vision "most unusual for
moderns" (*Purg.* 16.42–3), with the implication that the craft of the *Comedy* is
also exceptional among moderns. However warm Dante's relation to his
Romance predecessors, it is antiquity he hopes to join or asserts he has
joined. In that sense, Dante's Eclogues, his first work in Latin verse and his
last poetic work except for the *Paradiso*, is—even if by way of a Vergilian text
prior to the *Aeneid*—the final emblem of his appropriation of antiquity.
Poetic antiquity means Vergil, Ovid, Lucan, Statius.

    But it is essentially through Vergil that Dante takes heart, through
Vergil's work that he can confront his own journeying and his making. In
Dante's establishing the right of poetry—of fiction—to share the depth and
scope of the discourse of philosophy and theology, Vergil's is the only poem
in the available past that can serve Dante as exemplar for the cultural
supremacy of *fictio*. (Perhaps we should be grateful that Latinity has no
equivalent of an Aristotle: however warm Dante's feelings for Cicero are, he
seems to know that Cicero is no Aristotle.) From the abducted, embodied
shade of Vergil, he draws more life than any living body can provide.

    Much modern speculation on the pairing of the poets emphasizes the
political sections of the *Convivio* and the shrill, dazzling ideological
pamphleteering of the *Monarchy*. In relation to craft and making, that view

can conclude with Whitfield: "Few pairs of poets are in effect in most things so dissimilar as these who have been cast so long, so intimately together."[2] Whitfield's Vergil, taken alone, is very different from the less imperial Vergil that—I trust I can say without chauvinism—Americans have "discovered" or chosen to see over these last decades. Then again, a less imperial Vergil would, at first glance, only widen the divide between Vergil and the very pro-Imperial Dante.[3] Whitfield was gunning for Auerbach's view, in "Figura," of Dante's Vergil as "Vergil himself."[4] But Auerbach's emphasis on the Camilla passage as an index of the Vergilian sublime is somewhat different from the direction in which I shall go. Nor am I intent on figural constructions.

But exegesis need not involve total contestation. Any of us would have to allow that the historical Vergil, over the time he has spent in Dante's Limbo, has had rather more theological indoctrination than we might expect from a cultured Augustan. And to the question "When Dante imports into his other world the shade of Vergil, the man who wrote the *Aeneid*—whose body, 'taken from Brindisi . . . now belongs to Naples'— does he transform the poet?", the answer is, "Of course he does."

Yet there are a number of ways in which Dante's Vergil and the author of the *Aeneid* may indeed be interior paramours, ways in which their linkage moves beyond the brief discussion of personification in the *Vita Nuova* and even beyond the more intimate urgency of Vergil's presence in some sections of the *Convivio*. In sum, however much the *Comedy* is a summa of Dante's long experimentation, of his restless wandering as poet and prose writer, his apprenticeship in—and mastering of—many styles, the eruption of both the *Comedy* and of Vergil in the *Comedy* is volcanic. It is as if a writer who

> would resurrect,
> as soon as he assumes that just
> one life is seldom quite enough,
> had, with a loud, Pelean cloud,
> removed a sanitary shroud
> and freed another Lazarus.

But, I suggest, the ardor that moved Dante to free that Lazarus was not unenlightened *ardore*.

II. A Divan of Likenesses

A divan is an inventory, an account-book, a ledger, but it is also linked to custom-house, with the implication in custom-house of carrying across a boundary—here the boundary between Latin and the mother tongue.

1. Trying to establish continuity between the *Comedy* and Dante's earlier works, we have, collectively, attempted to squeeze Vergilian sense out of and into the ethically elevated or sublime of the canzoni of the *Convivio* or the canzoni that would have been candidates for inclusion in the *Convivio*, had it been completed. (We should almost certainly be grateful that that banquet of wisdom, that parade of the poet's learning, a distillation of Dante's encounter with philosophy, an arena for allegorical analysis and— Dante's outpouring of autobiographical need—the justification of his life by the learned exile, was never completed.) I am a little disheartened now by the attempt to ride those canzoni that hard. It is the spaciousness of Vergil that they cannot foreshadow, a temporal spaciousness, a comprehension of past and present and future that seems central to Dante's need for Vergil in the *Comedy*. For Büchner, this was Vergil's innovation, even with reference to antiquity.[5] (Though book 6 certainly sees some— discrepant—possibility of eternal, cyclical return.) In other words, the Dante of eros and ethics is not yet the Dante of the *Comedy*, the man who enters, with violence, into the realm of the polis in time, the Dante who has read his Hegel carefully and, more significantly, read his Vergil more carefully than Hegel did.

The programmatic thrust of Dante's entry into history conforms to Whitfield's view of the *Aeneid* as a "celebration of the plenitude of Rome." But more important is Dante's entry into history as such. This is the pre-program in Dante, his leaving of the limited language and prosodic hallucinarium of eros, the space of his Romance origins, for the wider temporality of Vergilian fiction: not the plenitude of Rome, but the plenitude of recorded and still-to-be-recorded time.

2. Despite our emphasis after Auerbach on *sermo humilis*, we know how deceptive Dante's plain style can be. It might be better to read *lo bello stilo che m'ha fatto onore* (*Inf.* 1.87 "the noble style for which I have been honored") as Boccaccio did, as a solecism in which Dante substitutes the past tense for what is indeed a future tense, applying it to the work he is *about* to write;[6] to see in his *poema sacro*, an analogue for Macrobius's sense of Vergil's *Aeneid* as a "sacred poem"; and thus to assign to Dante a full Macrobian awareness of the range of Vergil's styles, his plurality, and the many variables that can, in Vergil, fill the same formal container. (It is this emphasis on Vergilian variety that Dryden recovers, at least programmatically, in his Introduction to the *Sylvae*, with its deep awareness of Vergil's variety as against Ovid's sameness.)

I should most tellingly center that learning by Dante of the Vergilian lesson on his learning—as he writes the role of the verse paragraph, the longer, more sustained breath that only Vergil can teach. If Auerbach emphasized the *allora* of canto 10, I should see the contre-rejet of *quando* at canto 26.90 as one crucial index of the sustained breath. This breath for me is the most apparent presence of the historical Vergil the poet within the poem. Less obviously, however, there is always in Vergil a mode of deriving length out of briefer, paratactic units. Think of this for a moment not in relation to Dante's closet Ovidianism, but to the way in which, out of a paratactic string in the Dares and Entellus passage of book 5 of the *Aeneid*, Vergil arrives at a sustained thread on which he strings multiple likenings:

> ille, velut celsam oppugnat qui molibus urbem
> aut montana sedet circum castella sub armis,
> nunc hos, nunc illos aditus, omnemque pererrat
> arte locum et variis adsultibus inritus urget.
>
> (439–42)

> The other—just as one who drives against
> a towering city with siegeworks, or camps
> with arms beneath a mountain fortress—scans
> now this approach, now that, explores the ground
> with skill, and tries, in vain, shifting attacks.

> Entellus viris in ventum effudit et ultro
> ipse gravis graviterque ad terram pondere vasto
> concidit, ut quondam cava concidit aut Erymantho
> aut Ida in magna radicibus eruta pinus.
>
> (446–9)

> Entellus spent his strength upon the wind;
> his own weight, his own force, had carried him
> heavy, and heavily, with his huge hulk
> down to the ground; just as at times a hollow
> pine, torn up from its roots on Erymanthus
> or on the slopes of giant Ida, falls.

> nunc dextra ingeminans ictus, nunc ille sinistra.
> nec mora nec requies: quam multa grandine nimbi
> cuminibus crepitant, sic densis ictibus heros
> creber utraque manu pulsat versatque Dareta.
>
> (457–60)

> and now his right hand doubles blows and now
> his left; he knows no stay nor rest; just as
> storm clouds that rattle thick hail on the roofs,
> so do the hero's two hands pummel, pound
> at Dares, blow on blow, from every side.

This is a lesson Dante *comes* to most brilliantly in canto 25 of the *Inferno*, the metamorphosis passage:

Ellera abbarbicata mai non fue
ad alber sì, come l'orribil fiera
per l'altrui membra avviticchio le sue.
   Poi s'appiccar, come di calda cera
fossero stati, e mischiar lor colore,
né l'un né l'altro già parea quel ch'era:
   come procede innanzi da l'ardore,
per lo papiro suso, un color bruno
che non è nero ancora e 'l bianco more.

(58–66)

No ivy ever gripped a tree so fast
as when that horrifying monster clasped
and intertwined the other's limbs with its.
   Then just as if their substance were warm wax,
they stuck together and they mixed their colors,
so neither seemed what he had been before;
   just as, when paper's kindled, where it still
has not caught flame in full, its color's dark
though not yet black, while white is dying off.

But it is the end of book 5 of the *Aeneid* that carries perhaps a deeper lesson, with almost no string of likenings adorning the paratactic thread of fable. It is telling itself, fabulation, that engenders the poetry. The *Vita Nuova* is not devoid of narrative, but it needs the schizophrenia of prosimetrum to sustain that narrative. In the *Commedia*, Dante learns the urgency of narrative and narrative time as the principal agents of poetic invention and conviction. The Vergilian sublime does not lie, as Auerbach would have it, in the buoyant bravura and prestidigitation of the Camilla passage at the end of book 7; it lies in passages like the Palinurus passage at the end of book 5. That lesson works against the Kant-Poe-Croce line of the modern apotheosis of the short poem, implicitly supported by the Jakobsonian model of the poem as a synchronic condensation of redundancies and repetitions. That model, denying linear time, emphasizing information but not the *order* of information, is foreseen by Dante and rejected by him in his need to write a *Comedy* and not a *canzoniere*.

3. The prose of the *Convivio*, however arduous, is only journeymanlike when compared with the didactic force of *Aeneid* 7.724–51; and it is only that Vergilian exposition that can bring Dante close to the didactic cadenzas of *Purgatorio* 16, 17, and especially 25.37–108.

4. I have already referred to the contre-rejet of *quando* in *Inferno* 26.90, where one asymmetrically placed "when" closes a tercet and opens a speech that will only conclude fifty-two lines later. That is the fourth *quando* in the *Comedy* in line-terminus position—and it is the most pregnant. It is as if Dante, in working, had learned the potential of "when," just as a later

poet in Rutherford would learn the potential of "upon." This emblematic
"when" stands against the onset of mechanical, symmetrical, anaphoric
che's in initial position in the third line of tercets in the first canto of the
Inferno. But Dante's learning is not linear; there are relapses. The most
blatant-yet-bravura relapse into anaphora lies in wait in *Purgatorio* 12 (25–
63). There, in a thirteen-tercet sequence, we find three sets of four tercets
each, with the key-word in each set repeated at the beginning of four tercets,
and the thirteenth, concluding tercet repeating the respective onset-words
of each of the three tercet-sets at the beginning of each of its three lines.
This bravura is compounded by the acrostic play of the initials of the three
tutelary words—*vedea, O, mostrava*—forming "V O M," "man." And this
bravura we all have noted. But in our attention to this most un-Vergilian
passage, a passage still mortgaged to the Romance and late-Latin hallucinarium, we may have neglected a possible insidiousness concerning
techné in the comment of Dante's Vergil after this massive finger exercise, a
comment that might well have come from the historical Vergil: *non è più di
gir sì sospeso* (*Purg.* 12.78). This could amount to, "It's time to set these
images aside": these images—and perhaps this mode.

5. Dante's rhyme emphasis is, of course, a Romance inheritance and—
perforce—un-Vergilian. And for Dante's rejection of proximate rhyme
there is the Romance *rimas dissolutas* antecedent. But I may not be driving
too far in seeing some muted Vergilian caution, some Vergilian un-
percussiveness, in a form generated by rhyme *distance*. (Though Dante,
since he is a drummer, will often forget that caution and bind different
rhyme sets together through consonance and assonance, through the many
demi-links the hallucinarium affords.)

6. Dante is a most adroit user, especially in the *Purgatorio*, of the styleme
of "I am" followed by the proper name. Its chief incarnation is the
Provençal *ieu sui Arnaut*, citation-steal from Arnaut Daniel (*Purg.* 26.142),
and its first incarnations are the negative of *Inf.* 11.32, *io non Enea, io non Paolo
sono*, and then the affirmative, *I' son Beatrice* (*Inf.* 27.70). The proper name is
one part of natural language that mimes—and engenders—poetic language.
It is the emblem of poetry as nominalization (only a part of Dante's poetic,
but there nevertheless), for the proper name collapses class and mem-
bership in the class into one. Even the reading aloud of a catalogue list, with
that most elementary of structures, the alphabet, to be found in a telephone
book, or an unalphabetic random sampling of registered voters, gives us
some poetic lift. (And the pairing of the un-pairable proper name and the
common noun in a rhyme pair yields even more poetic surplus.) But in *io
son*, it is the coupling of that already-poetic proper name with the
pronominal, indefinite, hovering shifter of "I am" that condenses the

chiaroscuro of shadowed presence emerging into the light of particularity. If my fable has been centered on antiquity, one might see Arnaut's *ieu sui Arnaut* as condensing not only Romance origins but Vergil's *Polydorus ego* (*Aen.* 3.15 "I am Polydorus"), moving from mystery into light. The tale of Polydorus oversees the wood of the suicides; the styleme of the "I" and proper name waits—for its full array—for the *Purgatorio*.

Some Vergilian quotient of mystery is present, too, in Dante's tactic not of naming but of namelessness in the long wait between Dante's *io sol uno* and Beatrice's utterance of his name, "Dante," and, more hauntingly, in Matilda's nameless appearance in the Earthly Paradise, where the *donna soletta*, the "solitary woman" (*Purg.* 28.40) waits for some six cantos to be named.

7. Aeneas is not Vergil, but the seeing Aeneas as exile is certainly a fundamental envisioning of the historical Vergil. And the gateway to the *Comedy* as a *Danteid* is indebted to the beginning of book 3 of the *Aeneid*, with its *feror exul in altum* (3.11), its exile going out across the waters.

8. Dante's coupling of the insubstantiality of shades with his intense somatic interests, the thematic of the body (as if—certainly in much of the *Inferno*—he were ready to forget the insubstantiality of shades), has some premonition in the Deiphobus of book 6 of the *Aeneid*. The shades bring us to the *Comedy* as a diary of the dead, but with an autonomization of the act of dying, an emphasis not on the "ethical" place in the other world of the one who has died, but on the circumstances of his death. Here the line does run from Palinurus and Deiphobus to Manfred and Buonconto, and I, though many would disagree, would add Dante's Ulysses to this list, seeing him as one who speaks not of his sin but of the manner of his death. (Extending this, it should be observed here that only in the act of suicide is the moment of death absolutely coincident with the moment of sin.) That world of the dead is, too, the place not only of encountering but of re-encountering: Aeneas re-encountering Dido, Dante re-encountering Beatrice—and re-speaking the words of Vergil's Dido at the crucial point of his re-encountering.

9. The divan can also array the span of consciousness in the *Purgatorio*, not so much in the presence of its three dreams as in its obsessive concern with labile states of consciousness: waking vision, sharp thought, random thought, reverie, dream, and fantasy—and, even more hauntingly, the paralimnions of each state (even as Dante has examined his shoreline of Purgatory itself).[7] No poet before him does this so fully. But Vergil is aware of the alternations of sleep and waking and of the shifting dream-waking of Turnus at the end of book 12, and could well have invited Dante toward that range.

10. The first nine entries in the divan prepare the way for our return now to Dante's chiming on *nuovo*—for our seeing, at this point, his very first use of re-newing:

> Ahi quanto a dir qual era è cosa dura
> esta selva selvaggia e aspra e forte
> che nel pensier rinova la paura!
> Tant' è amara che poco è più morte;
>
> (*Inf.* 1.4–7)

> Ah, it is hard to speak of what it was,
> that savage forest, dense and difficult,
> which even in recall renews my fear:
> so bitter—death is hardly more severe!

In relation to line 6, Tommaseo had long since called attention to *Aeneid* 2.3, *Infandum, regina, iubes renovare dolorem*; and Mazzoni, more recently, has called Tommaseo's conjunction of the two lines "not very relevant." At this point, we might look more kindly at Tommaseo's suggestion. Dante, through his use of himself as witness, would move from the epic world of the preterite into the now of direct vision. Dante feels the power of witnessed recounting in Aeneas's tale in books 2, 3, and 4, but he displaces the I-tale to his own enlarged book 6. On that *cammin*, he collapses our by-now-conventional distinction between the voyager and the scribe into the renewal that memory effects. He brings himself into the now of the act of writing or transcribing, and us into the recurring now of our renewing. That *now* joins the *now* of many of the vehicles of Dante's similes—the mode of likening for which the historical Vergil was also the guide and maker.

11. Dante the maker knew when to dismiss Vergil, but Vergil of all poets is the poet who knows when to disappear, and that knowledge is shared by Dante's Vergil and the author of the *Aeneid*. Yet as moving as Vergil's final disappearance in the *Purgatorio* is (see above for *Purg.* 30.49–54), the most Vergilian moment of his absence is to be found in the opening of canto 2 of the *Inferno*. There, with three Vergilian night scenes behind him, Dante forgets the presence of Vergil and concentrates on Dante's own shadowed aloneness—in that aloneness remembering Vergil most:

> Lo giorno se n'andava, e l'aere bruno
> toglieva li animai che sono in terra
> da le fatiche loro; e io sol uno
> m'apparecchiava a sostener la guerra
> sì del cammino e sì de la pietate,
> che ritrarrá la mente che non erra.
>
> (*Inf.* 2.1–6)

The day was now departing; the dark air
released the living beings of the earth
from work and weariness; and I myself
    alone prepared to undergo the battle
both of the journeying and of the pity,
which memory, mistaking not, shall show.

Vergil as vanisher, however, is anticipated in the self-delimiting sadness of
Purgatorio 3:

"State contenti, umana gente, al *quia*;
chè, se potuto aveste veder tutto,
mestier non era parturir Maria;
    e disïar vedeste sanza frutto,
tai che sarebbe lor disio quetato,
ch'ctternalmente è dato lor per lutto:
    io dico d'Aristotile e di Plato
e di molt' altri"; e qui chinò la fronte,
e più non disse, e rimase turbato.

                                          (37–45)

"Confine yourselves, O humans, to the *quia*;
had you been able to see all, there would
have been no need for Mary to give birth;
    You saw the fruitless longing of those men
who would—if reason could—have been content,
those whose desire eternally laments:
    I speak of Aristotle and Plato—
and many others." Here he bent his head,
and said no more, remaining with his sorrow.

This Vergil emerges from a Limbo of antiquity somewhat different from
Mandelstam's image of the four poets in a huddle of *Inferno* 4 as "a pleasant
Orphic chorus, where the four together while away a tearless eternity in
literary discussion."

If that self-delimiting Vergil is not *the* historical Vergil, he certainly is a
possible historical Vergil, the Vergil of the sorrow of reason. And this brings
us to . . .

III. . . . The Other Side of the Ledger-Divan

Vergil may have conjured sitting at The Total Table, becoming the poet
both of the polis—of historical time—and of the cosmos. Certainly, Georgic
2.475-94 adumbrates that possibility. We may, with Putnam, see his

rejection of that possibility already implicit in the passage itself.[8] Or we may see the shadow of Lucretius as too massive to allow emulation. All that lingers of that possibility in the *Aeneid* is Iopas at the end of book 1.[9] Vergil does range, but he delimits his range—he knows that he is (and we are?) not "able to see all" (see *Purg.* 3.38 above).

Dante knows no limits. He drums against the walls, the All of the universe. But he tries to *realize* the All; with the God-term at hand and in heart, he does not harp on the *word* "all." And it is a harping (Aeolian and otherwise) on the word "all" that substitutes for the realization of all in much poetry since Wordsworth. "All" and other words of The Total Table, including "whole" and "world," became the automatic triggers for our modern sublime. Wallace Stevens murmured, "The death of one God is the death of all." Not at all. Remove "all" from "and all that mighty heart is lying still," and Westminster Bridge collapses. Consider, too: the anaphoric litany in "Tintern Abbey" of "all thinking things . . . all objects of all thought . . . all things . . . all that we behold . . . all the mighty world . . . all my moral being"; Tennyson's "Love and Duty," with its "all things good . . . all things ill . . . all good things . . . all the heart" (though Tennyson's work as a whole is less "all"-infected—his not un-hilarious "All Thoughts, All Creeds" is indeed an early, unheeded antidote against the All); Swinburne's "all things made . . . all men woven . . . all lives in-wrought . . . all the choir of lives . . . all men's feet or chains or wings . . . the whole world's waters . . . the whole world's fiery forces . . . the whole world's wrath and strength . . . the whole world's pity and sorrow" in the Prelude to *Tristram of Lyonesse*; and Rossetti's "all hearts . . . all things" and "all mankind . . . all in each" of two of his tautest lyrics, "Heart's Hope" and "The Sea Limits."

Our century does not lessen the litany. The Eliot of "Prufrock," with "all" as its most frequent line-end word, may have ironized on "all," but not the Eliot of "Little Gidding," where Juliana of Norwich is hardly mocked with "all shall be well . . . all manner of thing shall be well . . . and all shall be well and all manner of thing shall be well." Even the briefest glance at a Yeats mosaic would find as tesserae the poet who would "call to my own opposite, summon all" and "call to the . . . one who yet shall . . . disclose all that I seek" ("Ego Dominus Tuus"), the Yeats who has "all dishevelled wandering stars" at the end of "Who Goes with Fergus?", and the poet who cannot inscribe the five stanzas of "Byzantium" without "all that man is . . . all mere complexities of fury." Stevens himself may not call on "all," but he does call on a long, at-times-fanatic set of Total-Table words, from the superlatives of "On the Road Home"—"largest . . . longest . . . roundest . . . warmest . . . closest . . . strongest"—to other instances of this and other modes of totalizing that populate his work: "the centre of reality," "the absolute foyer," "the central man," "the central evil, the central good," "the final chants," "the acutest end," "the total building," "total dream," "extremest book," "wisest man," "first canto," "first idea," "final canticle." In Stevens there is more often more control of these counters than there is in Yeats, but even in Stevens, the title of one of his richest late lyrics may be, with its total-word, "world," more Polonius-like, more trombone-like than oboe-like, in "The World as Meditation."

The poet who would "call to . . . summon all," through the long history of rhyme-pairs, can call to our minds the terminal "all"-"fall" couplet in sonnet 16 of Spenser's *Ruines of Rome* and the "all"-"fall" couplet in sonnet 12 of that sequence. Indeed, of the 33 sonnets in the *Ruines*, "all" appears twelve times in the last two lines and three times in the first two lines. We can also recall the carnival of "all" in Shakespeare's sonnet 31 and the "all"-"call" rhyme-pairs of sonnets 40, 109, and 117—and other Scrutinists would add the "all"s in the final lines of 129, 132, 133, 135. The annalist of rhymes would surely add much from Donne and his richer rhyme-family (all - fall - shall - ball - festival - gall - liberall - essential - celestial - sphericall - cardinall-minerall) and, from Herbert's scoriae, cite the prose of his "Outlandish Proverbs" 413, with the implicit octosyllabics of, "My house, my house, though thou art small, thou art to me the Escuriall," where the "all" in "Escuriall" is hardly buried. This is only a small part of the tale, small part of the concordance-*cum*-discloser. But I would not construct a lexical annex to the prosodic hallucinarium.

It is the Ur-Patron of "All" that we must seek, the ultimate source for the promotion of that and kindred terms. Here, Eliot can be helpful. For in "Little Gidding" he was drawing on that century, the fourteenth, which produced the most powerful propagator All has ever had, a near-contemporary of Dante, who died some six years after the Tuscan: Meister Eckhart. In Eckhart "all" stands side by side with the God-term, but no one before him—or, I should say, since—has released the potential of "all" as he did:

Who thus possesses God in his essence, seizes God in the manner of God, and for him God shines in all things, for all things have for him the taste of God and he sees His image in all things . . . Or more: he who loves a thing ardently and with all his powers, so that he has neither taste nor heart for anything else; and indeed, it matters not where he is nor with whom, or what he has undertaken or does—his love is never spent within him; in all things, he finds the mirror of what he loves and what he loves is all the more present for him as his love grows stronger. This man does not seek repose, because no inquietude perturbs him . . .[10]

There are many "all"s between Eckhart and ourselves; and many of our "all"s do not stand with the God-term, but as surrogates for it. For much of our use, in Wordsworth and after, of "all," we can say this: unlike Victor Hugo (and unlike our writers of prose—Melville, Dickens, Joyce), our poets have not "swallowed all of the language" but simply "swallowed 'all'." In us, the latter-day progeny of Eckhart, we may find something akin to Arnold Ehrhardt's description of the Alexandrian situation, and some approximation of what our "all" has become in his reference to "meaningless magic words":

> As a whole such a magic papyrus presents an unwholesome mixture of human, all too human, desires; meaningless so-called magic words; fanciful, sometimes disgusting magic actions and recipes; and finally invocations and prayers, which stand out by their higher stylistic level. All magic invocations, and ours are no exception from the rule, follow a line of combined blackmail and flattery.[11]

Vergil refuses to sit at The Total Table—at either the substantial table of Dante or at the more modern table, where "all" is ephemeral murmur. This may make him an unassimilable teacher, the poet of "unlikeness" in any divan that tallies affiliations between antiquity and modernity. And it may qualify Dante's profoundest dream, the dream of resurrection of the father, as unrealizable or as another of what Dante calls his "not false errors" (*Purg.* 15.117).

As for Vergil's and Dante's dreaming on or foreseeing us, they might—in their divans—register our invasive "all"s as false errors.

Notes

1. For *nuovo* as a common-place, see Mario Marti, *Storia dello stil nuovo* (Lecce: Milella, 1966), 1:207–12; and Eberwein-Dabcovich, "Das Wort 'novus' in der alprovenzalischen Dichtung und in Dantes Vita nova," *Romanistisches Jahrbuch* 2 (1949): 171–95.
2. The sentence concludes J.H. Whitfield's "Virgil into Dante" in *Virgil*, ed. Donald R. Dudley (New York: Basic Books, 1969), pp. 94–118. Another version of this sentence concludes his "Dante's Virgil" in the *Books Abroad* special issue, *A Homage to Dante*, May 1965, pp. 136–40. Also see his "Dante e Virgilio," in *Le parole e le idee*, 7:1–2 (1965), and his earlier volume, *Dante and Virgil* (Oxford: Blackwell, 1949).
3. The only Italian critic to see Vergil as less imperial—closer to the later American image—was not a Latinist but the poet Giuseppe Ungaretti. For my own indebtedness to Ungaretti's vision of Vergil, see the Introduction to *The Aeneid of Virgil* (Berkeley: University of California Press, 1972, 1981).
4. Erich Auerbach, "Figura," in *Scenes from the Drama of European Literature* (New York: Meridian Books, 1959), pp. 11–76; his Vergil *sich selbst*, Vergil "himself," is on p. 70.
5. Karl Büchner, *Virgilio*, ed. Mario Bonaria (Brescia: Paideia, 1963), pp. 530–31.

6. Boccaccio's gloss of *Inf.* 1.87 is *ad loc.* in his *Esposizioni sopra la Comedia di Dante*, ed. Giorgio Padoan (Milan: Mondadori, 1965).

7. I have dealt with Dante's gamut of states of consciousness in "'Rumenando e mirando'; la capia di Dante," in *I linguaggi del Sogno*, ed. Vittore Branca, Carlo Ossola, Salomon Resnick (Florence: Sansoni, 1984), pp. 407–416.

8. Michael C.J. Putnam, *Virgil's Poem of the Earth* (Princeton: Princeton University Press, 1979), pp. 145–51.

9. A very useful run-through of ways of reading Vergil's Iopas is in Ettore Paratore's edition of the *Eneid* (Milan: Fondazione Valle and Mondadori, 1978) 1:236–7.

10. "Reden der Unterweisung," in Josef Quint's modern German translation, vol. 5 of Quint's edition, p. 510.

11. Arnold Ehrhardt, *The Beginning: A Study in the Greek Philosophical Approach to the Concept of Creation from Anaximander to St. John* (Manchester: Manchester University Press, 1968), p. 177.

VERGIL IN SHAKESPEARE: FROM ALLUSION TO IMITATION

Robert S. Miola

Surprisingly slight and desultory is the extant criticism on Vergil's presence in Shakespeare's art. Although Plutarch, Ovid, and Seneca have attracted much scholarly attention, no systematic study illuminates the complex and pervasive influence of Vergil on Shakespeare.[1] Few have seriously considered the subject; fewer have navigated safely past the Scylla of broad, interpretive generalization and the Charybdis of narrow-minded *quellenforschung*. The general neglect derives partly from the obvious differences in genres and subjects of the two artists. It derives as well from the long-standing conception of Vergil as learned and meticulous craftsman and that of Shakespeare as Fancy's child, warbling native woodnotes wild. John Dryden recognized the contrast between the two orders of genius in his celebrated comparison of Shakespeare to Homer and Jonson to Vergil.[2] And Joseph Addison sharpened and canonized the distinction by placing Shakespeare among those writers who possess nobly wild, extravagant, and natural talent, and Vergil among those who form "themselves by rules" and work within the "restraints of art."[3]

The biographical fallacy dividing Vergil from Shakespeare, of course, does justice neither to the Roman's genius nor the Englishman's art. Nor can it diminish or obscure Vergil's ubiquitous influence on the art and culture of the Renaissance. Central to such diverse figures as Dante, Ariosto, Tasso, Montaigne, Spenser, and Milton, Vergil clearly transcended the boundaries of artistic temperament and taste. To those in the age of imitation he was the preeminent poetical authority, the noblest and highest fountain of Latin eloquence. Annotated by Servius, Donatus, Ascensius and others, allegorized by men like Fulgentius, Silvestris, and Landino, appropriated by almost all writers of pastoral and epic, the works of Vergil were a centerpiece for European literary and popular traditions.[4] In Shakespeare's day one met Vergil everywhere: in anthologies of *sententiae* and in *florilegia*; in rhetorical handbooks and classical dictionaries; in the works of classical and contemporary writers and artists; in editions and translations of the *Eclogues*, *Georgics*, and *Aeneid*. As T.W. Baldwin has demonstrated, the works of Vergil, parsed and pored over by countless schoolchildren, were practically unavoidable steps on Shakespeare's road to Parnassus.[5]

Throughout his career Shakespeare shows a working familiarity with Vergil's text and a strong attraction to his art. In early works like *Titus Andronicus* and *Lucrece* Shakespeare's allusions to Vergil smell of the lamp: they are labored, ostentatious, and self-congratulatory. Later, by about the turn of the century, the allusions become subtle and sharply controlled. In *Julius Caesar* and *Hamlet* smoothly-integrated allusions to Vergil provide point and irony. In Shakespeare's last phase extensive treatment of Vergilian idea and image broadens allusion to eristic imitation. The final mode is radically transformative: in works like *Antony and Cleopatra* and *The Tempest* the Vergilian sub-text assumes new life and meaning as Shakespeare adapts it to articulate his own visions of love and civilization.

I

Like Ovid, Vergil appears at first in Shakespeare's mannered and self-conscious allusions. Shakespeare's earliest Roman play, *Titus Andronicus* (1593–94), is a chrestomathy of Latin scraps and fragments boldly pasted together. With partial success, the play attempts to incorporate Vergilian motifs into a dramatic structure. Vergilian and Ovidian allusions to the iron age combine to depict a world wherein *pietas*, the quintessential Vergilian virtue, lies vanquished.[6] During the course of the action two sets of brothers take arms against each other; one helpless bystander endures his brother's misfortune and madness, his niece's mutilation, his nephews' death or banishment. One mother sells her child for gold while another encourages her sons to acts of rape and murder. A Roman father slays his son and then his daughter. After the Roman royal family dine on a gory Thyestean banquet, the play ends in a spasm of murder and revenge.

Such impious Romans, of course, are not fit inhabitants for the promised city of the *Aeneid*, that vision of peace and order ruled by Augustus, *divi genus, aurea condet / saecula qui rursus Latio regnata per arva / Saturno quondam* (6.792–4 "son of a god, who will renew a Golden Age in Latium, in fields where Saturn once was king"). Shakespeare's portrayal of the decaying Roman Empire in *Titus Andronicus* provides a rude ending to Vergil's dream. His Lavinia, regrettably coarse in conversation (2.3.66ff.),[7] bathetic in injury, and desperate in revenge, pointedly opposes Vergil's, that silent and shadowy figure who waits for the great forces of history to decide her fate. Although both Lavinias are contested brides who cause strife between rival leaders, the rape and mutilation of the helpless woman in the play grimly parody the marriage of the destined wife in the epic.[8] Whereas the wedding of Aeneas and Lavinia begins Roman civilization and Empire, the rape of Shakespeare's Lavinia brutally expresses the savagery that ends Roman civilization and starts a new and barbaric dispensation.

Shakespeare also portrays Titus Andronicus in Vergilian terms, as a type of Aeneas. Like Aeneas, Titus is "Pius" (1.1.23). At the funeral of his sons, it has long been noted, he echoes the conversation of Aeneas and Sibyl in hell (6.318ff.). Later, reminded of his daughter's mutilation, Titus sees himself as Aeneas in Carthage, forced to retell the story of Troy and to relive his anguish:

> Ah, wherefore dost thou urge the name of hands,
> To bid Aeneas tell the tale twice o'er
> How Troy was burnt and he made miserable?
>
> (3.2.26–8)

Of course, the Vergilian allusions here, blended with references to Seneca and Ovid, are merely indecorous shreds from the original robes. Costumed in them, Titus appears ludicrous and artificial rather than tragic and human. Unlike Aeneas, who weeps at suffering, growing wiser and richer in sorrow, Titus tears passion to tatters and goes mad.

Shakespeare invokes Vergil to help shape character and theme in *Titus Andronicus*. Yet the effort is comparatively clumsy and juvenile: the allusions to Aeneas and Lavinia are crudely and baldly inappropriate rather than ironic. They are stitched on to the play rather than woven into its fabric. Shakespeare is clearly excited by the *Aeneid* as subtext but he is overwhelmed by it as well, unable to control fully the powerful resources at his disposal. After invoking Hecuba to illustrate Tamora's grief (1.1.135ff.), for example, he indiscriminately invokes her again to illustrate Lavinia's (4.1. 20ff.). Dido, for another example, appears incongruously in Tamora's seduction of Aaron the Moor:

> And after conflict such as was suppos'd
> The wand'ring prince and Dido once enjoyed,
> When with a happy storm they were surpris'd,
> And curtain'd with a counsel-keeping cave,
> We may, each wreathed in the other's arms
> (Our pastimes done), possess a golden slumber.
>
> (2.3.21–6)

The absurdity of the parallel here between the illicit lovers (especially that between Aaron and Aeneas) is matched only by the absurdity of Dido's reappearance at the end of the play. A Roman urges Lucius:

> Speak, Rome's dear friend, as erst our ancestor,
> When with his solemn tongue he did discourse
> To love-sick Dido's sad attending ear
> The story of that baleful burning night,
> When subtile Greeks surpris'd King Priam's Troy.
> Tell us what Sinon hath bewitch'd our ears,
> Or who hath brought the fatal engine in
> That gives our Troy, our Rome, the civil wound.
>
> (5.3.80–87)

The general analogy between shattered Troy and Rome can hardly justify the pointless evocations of Dido and Sinon.

Although drawn largely from Ovid and Livy, *The Rape of Lucrece* (1593–94) provides another illustration of Shakespeare's early engagement with Vergil, an engagement which has all the intensity and rashness of young love. For some two hundred lines in the poem Lucrece muses over an imaginary depiction of Troy. The dramatic situation of this *ekphrasis*, as well as its substance and effect, owes much to Vergil's model in *Aeneid* 1.[9] Aeneas weeps at a depiction of Troy in Carthage, but takes comfort in the sympathetic portrayal of his suffering. Similarly alone and estranged from familiar surroundings, Lucrece weeps to look on her present sorrow pictured forth in "Troy's painted woes" (1492). Like Aeneas, she focuses on the human tragedies of the war, the struggles between Greeks and Trojans "from the strond of Dardan, where they fought, / To Simois' reedy banks" (1436–7), and the destruction of the city, bright with fire. Although Shakespeare draws upon the thirteenth *Metamorphoses* as well as the *Aeneid*, his *ekphrasis* expresses a Vergilian sense of Greek perfidy, Trojan help-lessness, and pervasive doom.[10] The vicarious experience of Trojan woe brings Lucrece, as it does Aeneas, "from the feeling of her own grief" (1578) to comfort and relief. She marvels at the sympathetic imagination of the "well-skill'd workman" (1520) who understands the tears of things and whose heart, like those of the Carthaginians and the Trojans, is touched by mortal sorrows.

Shakespeare's remembrance of Troy in *Lucrece* draws also upon Vergil's second *Aeneid*. In the climactic incident of the *Iliupersis*, Pyrrhus, animated by his father's fury, breaks through various gates and doors to reach the innermost chambers of Priam's house. Priam, horrified, sees Pyrrhus and prepares to defend his home:

urbis uti captae casum convolsaque vidit
limina tectorum et medium in penetralibus hostem
arma diu senior desueta trementibus aevo
circumdat nequiquam umeris et inutile ferrum
cingitur, ac densos fertur moriturus in hostis.

(507–11)

When he saw the fall of the captured city, saw
the doors of the house wrenched off, and the foe
in the heart of his home, old as he is, he vainly
throws his long-disused armour about his aged
trembling shoulders, girds on his useless sword,
and rushes to his death among his thronging foes.

Arrogantly, Pyrrhus scorns Priam, slaughters one of his sons, Prince Polites, and then kills the aged King on one of his own altars.[11] The invading Pyrrhus, who slays a son and then a father, violates person, household, and family. Profaning the residence of the household gods, his attack on the *penetralia* is an attack on all the spiritual and physical principles necessary for human life, *quae ad vitam sunt necessaria*, as Servius put it. No wonder Aeneas comments, *ferit aurea sidera clamor* (488 "The din strikes the golden stars").

The importance of this incident to Shakespeare's dramatic imagination is clearly evident in *Lucrece* (and, as we shall see, in *Hamlet*). The pictorial representation of Priam's death arrests Lucrece's gaze and closely mirrors her own predicament:

Many she sees where cares have carved some,
But none where all distress and dolor dwell'd,
Till she despairing Hecuba beheld,
Staring on Priam's wounds with her old eyes,
Which bleeding under Pyrrhus' proud foot lies.

(1445–9)

Seeing in Hecuba an image of her own grief, Lucrece assumes the identity of an onlooker and achieves some distance from her situation. However momentary and illusory, the identification with Hecuba enables Lucrece to give tongue to unspeakable sorrows. As the imaginary *ekphrasis* works its magic, she envisions herself as Priam:

To me came Tarquin armed so beguild
With outward honesty, but yet defil'd
With inward vice: as Priam him did cherish,
So did I Tarquin, so my Troy did perish.

(1544–7)

Here Lucrece becomes the central figure in the Trojan tragedy, "slain" by the barbaric invader in the *penetralia* of her home. Tarquin, like Pyrrhus, is a cruel and bloody usurper armed with a gleaming weapon. Like the Greek, he breaks through locks and doors until he reaches the inmost recesses of his victim's home. Both invaders aim at the very center of civil stability, the mid-point of the concentric circles of social order, and both attack with the fury of their fathers. Their deeds crack the foundations of civilized life and turn the city into wilderness.

Extended allusion to Vergil allows Shakespeare to portray various vignettes from the epic tradition and to present a mythological perspective that expresses the various levels of Lucrece's violation. But the artificial and stylized *ekphrasis* intrudes upon the narrative of the poem. It is a heavy rhetorical device bolted on rather than fitted in. Moreover, as in *Titus Andronicus*, the handling of classical allusions in *Lucrece* shows a lack of firm control. The opening ten stanzas of the *ekphrasis* labor to provide totally extraneous commentary on the figures of Ajax, Ulysses, Nestor, Achilles, and Hector. This throat-clearing completed, the climactic invasion sequence quickly loses power and focus. Lucrece sees herself as mourning Hecuba and murdered Priam, momentarily as Helen, "the strumpet that began this stir" (1471), and then as Priam again. This last identification is made not with the murdered king but, surprisingly, with the gullible ruler who listened to Sinon's lies. In an equally unchronological and anti-climactic progression, the conceit proceeds to cast Tarquin as terrible Pyrrhus, fond Paris, and finally deceitful Sinon. One cannot help thinking that the *ekphrasis* is too long and too ingenious, especially as Priam appears one other time in it with no reference to anyone in the poem, as the doting father who should have restrained Paris's lust (1490). The extraneous characters and ever-shifting identifications vitiate the allusions even as they display the poet's youthful ardor and eagerness. Enamored with Vergil and the possibilities of allusion, Shakespeare is unable to subordinate the sub-text to the demands of the text. The poet has yet to discipline his imagination and to master the subtle art of classical allusion.

II

By the turn of the century, with almost a decade's writing experience behind him, Shakespeare becomes more fluent and self-assured in his continuing dialogue with Vergil. The initial infatuation is succeeded by mature understanding. The ingenious conceits and awkward gesturing of the early works now give way to sharply controlled allusion. In *Julius Caesar*

(1599), for example, Cassius evokes a well-known Vergilian scene in order to denigrate Caesar:

> I, as Aeneas, our great ancestor,
> Did from the flames of Troy upon his shoulder
> The old Anchises bear, so from the waves of Tiber
> Did I the tired Caesar.

(1.2.112–15)

Shakespeare here alludes to the archetypal scene of *pietas*,[12] memorialized on Roman coins and celebrated often by ancient writers. In addition to Vergil's account, Ovid's brief sketch of the Trojan war in *Metamorphoses* 13 includes reference to the episode (624–6) and Propertius alludes to the scene in an elegy (4.1.43–4), as does Seneca in *De Beneficiis* (3.37.1).

Later generations followed Vergil and the ancients in regarding the carrying of Anchises as a supreme example of *pietas*, the virtuous respect for gods, country, and family. Commentators on Vergil provided appropriate glosses, ranging from the brief but touching paraphrase of Donatus to the elaborate and learned moral essay of Pontanus, replete with classical, medieval, and Renaissance allusions, as well as various analogues.[13] The lessons of the grammar school on Vergilian *pietas* were reinforced by various sources: by collectors of proverbs like Erasmus, for example;[14] by compilers of classical lore like Aelianus;[15] by cataloguers of moralized antiquity like Ravisius Textor;[16] and by emblematists like Alciati and Whitney.[17] Interestingly enough, the Vergilian emblem was also recalled on stage by one of the characters in *The Tragedie of Caesar and Pompey* (pub. 1607), a play often cited as a possible source for *Julius Caesar*.[18] By the time of Cassius' allusion, the original Vergilian passage and its moral significance were commonplaces of Renaissance humanism.

Seen in the Renaissance context, the irony of Cassius' allusion clearly emerges. His appropriation of the famous scene urges not humble filial piety but arrogant self-assertion and murderous betrayal. Cassius' awkward repetition of the first-person singular subject ("I ... Did I ...") suggests the fumbling impatience of his self-assertion in the conceit and in the play. Cassius casts himself as a new Aeneas here, one unwilling to shoulder the burden of the past but destined to found a new Rome. He sees Caesar as a new Anchises—weak, old and troublesome—one who should not be carried on the shoulders of true Romans but thrown off. In so doing, Cassius replaces the articulated emblem of *pietas* with the unarticulated emblem of *impietas*, the image of the son slaying the father. To be true sons of Rome, Cassius argues, he and Brutus must murder Caesar, the *pater patriae*. Cassius' allusion to the *Aeneid* repudiates its most important virtue—*pietas*, one of the fundamental principles of Roman civilization.

Shortly after, Cassius, recalling his conduct during the storm, again appears in the role of Aeneas:

> For my part, I have walk'd about the streets,
> Submitting me unto the perilous night;
> And thus unbraced, Casca, as you see,
> Have bar'd my bosom to the thunder-stone;
> And when the cross blue lightning seem'd to open
> The breast of heaven, I did present myself
> Even in the aim and very flash of it.
>
> (1.3.46-52)

This bravado has no basis in Plutarch but most probably originates in Shakespeare's remembrance of *Aeneid* 5.685-95, where Aeneas bares his chest to the gods, invites the thunderbolt to strike, and witnesses as an answer to his prayers a divine tempest. Once again, Cassius envisions himself as Aeneas, just before chiding Casca for not having "those sparks of life / That should be in a Roman" (1.3.57-8). Yet, as before, there is certain irony in Cassius' imitation of Aeneas. Aeneas bares himself as a gesture of piety, as an expression of his humility and his dependence on the gods.[19] The storm is a reward for piety and a sign of divine favor. Cassius' baring of his chest after the storm has begun is an arrogant assertion of self, a gesture which brashly proclaims his own manhood and courage, and assumes rather than petitions the favor of the gods. Unlike the clumsy stitching and patching earlier, Shakespeare here weaves Vergilian images into powerful dramatic symbols.

No less striking and skillful is Shakespeare's use of Vergil in *Hamlet* (1600-1). Welcoming the players to Elsinore, Hamlet remembers from a recent play Aeneas' tale to Dido concerning Priam's slaughter and Pyrrhus' revenge:

> "The rugged Pyrrhus, like th' Hyrcanian beast—"
> 'Tis not so, it begins with Pyrrhus:
> "The rugged Pyrrhus, he whose sable arms,
> Black as his purpose, did the night resemble
> When he lay couched in th' ominous horse,
> Hath now this dread and black complexion smear'd
> With heraldy more dismal: head to foot
> Now is he total gules, horridly trick'd
> With blood of fathers, mothers, daughters, sons,
> Bak'd and impasted with the parching streets,
> That lend a tyrannous and damned light
> To their lord's murther. Roasted in wrath and fire,
> And thus o'er-sized with coagulate gore,

With eyes like carbuncles, the hellish Pyrrhus
Old grandsire Priam seeks."
So proceed you.

(2.2.450–65)

First Hamlet assumes the role of storyteller Aeneas, the exemplar of filial piety. This assumption suggests Hamlet's struggle to act the role of pious son, to render service to his father by killing Claudius. Hamlet then surrenders the speech to the First Player, who proceeds with the narration of Pyrrhus's "roused vengeance." Now a spectator, Hamlet sits rapt with attention as the tale of bloody murder unfolds. He curtly admonishes Polonius for complaining about the length of the speech and urges the actor, "Say on, come to Hecuba" (501). Clearly, Hamlet sees Pyrrhus, the fierce son of Achilles who slays a king to avenge his father, as an idealized image of himself. And just as clearly, Hamlet sees Hecuba, stock example of grief and loyal mourning, as an idealized image of his mother, Gertrude. The art of the speech here dramatically and pointedly rebukes life: the heroic images of Troy ironically expose Elsinore's degeneration, Gertrude's inconstancy, and Hamlet's vacillation. After the players leave, Hamlet lacerates himself with self-reproach:

But I am pigeon-liver'd, and lack gall
To make oppression bitter, or ere this
I should 'a' fatted all the region kites
With this slave's offal.

(577–80)

Like the *ekphrasis* in *Lucrece*, the allusion to Pyrrhus in *Hamlet* is stylized and set apart from the surrounding action. It is a rhetorical set piece recited on cue by two actors. Unlike the earlier references to *Aeneid* 2, however, this one is subtle and complex. The self-conscious artificiality in manner and style reveals Hamlet's preoccupation with art and with the power of playing. In fact, Hamlet is shamed by the Player's shedding of real tears for the fictional characters. So forcing the "soul to his own conceit," the Player weeps, thereby entering the imaginary scene and becoming a participant. The power of art and the artistic imagination transforms reality, creates it anew in the present. Recitation of Pyrrhus's revenge can thus help Hamlet to perform his own. Through the magic of art, the allusion may transform the rapt gazer, Hamlet, into the pitiless avenger, Pyrrhus.

Although the inspiration for the Pyrrhus speech derives ultimately from *Aeneid* 2, its lurid and melodramatic style are reminiscent as well of Ovid and Lucan.[20] Shakespeare overlays the incident with Marlovian sensationalism, not to parody quaint theatrical styles as has been suggested, but to portray the internal drama of his main character.[21] To Hamlet, fascinated and horrified, the prospective murder of Claudius must seem as bloody, bombastic, and oversized as the narrated murder of Priam. To complicate matters further, there is even a fleeting parallel between Priam and the elder Hamlet, two cruelly murdered kings and fathers.[22] In art's many-faceted mirror the archetypal assassin, Pyrrhus, the royal assassin, Claudius, and the would-be assassin, Hamlet, all appear as images of each other. No wonder Hamlet stares in stupefaction. In order to avenge his father he fears that he must become his enemy Claudius and also another Pyrrhus, roasted in wrath and fire, horridly tricked with blood and gore.

Examination of Shakespeare's Vergilian allusion here leads us through the twisted corridors of the royal palace and through the labyrinth of hope and fear in Hamlet's mind. What is more, the speech and Hamlet's reaction to it resonate throughout the play. When Hamlet stands with drawn sword over the praying Claudius, for example, we recall Pyrrhus over Priam:[23]

> lo his sword,
> Which was declining on the milky head
> Of reverent Priam, seem'd i' th' air to stick.
> So as a painted tyrant Pyrrhus stood
> [And,] like a neutral to his will and matter,
> Did nothing.
>
> (477–82)

Of course it is the differences between Hamlet and Pyrrhus that obtain here: Pyrrhus's sword comes down like the "Cyclops' hammers" (489), whereas Hamlet walks away and waits for a better time. So too in the rest of the play. Hamlet never becomes the savage Pyrrhus, inhuman avatar of revenge. Instead, he becomes more noble and humane. Unlike the impious violator of all civilized value, Hamlet expresses faith in the Providence that brings all to completion:

> There is special
> providence in the fall of a sparrow. If it be now,
> 'tis not to come; if it be not to come, it will be
> now; if it be not now, yet it will come—the readiness
> is all.
>
> (5.2.219–22)

Calm, faithful, ready to meet his end, he finally kills Claudius and dies in peace. His final revenge presents to us an unresolved paradox, one central to Shakespearean tragedy: the man of *pietas* and humanity acts in impious *furor*. This is, of course, the paradox central to the *Aeneid*, especially evident in the final books as *pius* Aeneas ruthlessly slays Magus and Turnus.

In Shakespeare's middle phase, then, allusion to Vergil is complex and controlled. The allusions in *Julius Caesar* and *Hamlet* create a standard by which the speakers judge themselves and are judged. In *Julius Caesar* Shakespeare draws on the literary and emblematic traditions descending from a famous Vergilian scene in order to expose Cassius' pretensions. In *Hamlet* another Vergilian scene provides richly satisfying ironies and develops themes. The reworking of *Aeneid* 2 in *Hamlet* contrasts neatly with Shakespeare's reworking in *Lucrece* and clearly illustrates artistic development. In the mature work, overwrought style and attention to detail are not merely clumsy contrivances but purposeful in the relevation of character. Shakespeare here creates a revenger antithetical to Pyrrhus, who represents all that Hamlet can never be. In this play as in the final ones, Shakespeare shows his increasing mastery and maturity. By this time he has learned to subordinate the sub-text to his own text, and to harness the inexhaustible energy of allusion. Such knowledge brings new freedom and power.

III

In Shakespeare's final phase, as in *Hamlet*, Vergil is a pervasive presence, a deep source that, directly or indirectly, shapes character and action. Yet, at the last, the dramatist shows increasing skill and boldness in allusion. In *Antony and Cleopatra* (1607–8), Antony's famous comparison of himself and Cleopatra to Aeneas and Dido clearly illustrates the point:

> Eros!—I come, my queen!—Eros!—Stay for me!
> Where souls do couch on flowers, we'll hand in hand,
> And with our sprightly port make the ghosts gaze.
> Dido and her Aeneas shall want troops,
> And all the haunt be ours. Come, Eros, Eros!
>
> (4.14.50–54)

Antony's vision of Aeneas and Dido reunited in Hades is his own creation. In the sixth *Aeneid*, of course, Dido's shade coldly and silently turns from Aeneas to rejoin her former husband, Sychaeus. By misconstruing the famous scene, Shakespeare transforms the epical love story into a reflection of Antony's own desires and aspirations. After Antony, unlike Aeneas, decides the archetypal conflict between love and duty in favor of love, he hopes to live forever with Cleopatra in the next life.

Throughout *Antony and Cleopatra*, Shakespeare turns to *Aeneid* 4 and boldly reshapes Vergilian scenes.[24] Antony's first leave-taking of Cleopatra (1.3), for example, follows the scenic rhythms established by Vergil's Aeneas and Dido. Dido, we recall, knows (*praesensit*, 4.297) that Aeneas is preparing

to leave before he breaks the news to her. So Cleopatra divines Antony's
intentions before he can reveal them:

> *Ant.*	Now my dearest queen—
> *Cleo.*	Pray you stand farther from me.
> *Ant.*	What's the matter?
> *Cleo.*	I know by that same eye there's some good news.
> What, says the married woman you may go?
> Would she had never given you leave to come!
>
> (1.3.17–21)

Before Aeneas has a chance to speak, Dido berates him for betraying her
love and breaking his promises:

> dissimulare etiam sperasti, perfide, tantum
> posse nefas tacitusque mea decedere terra?
> nec te noster amor nec te data dextera quondam
> nec moritura tenet crudeli funere Dido?
>
> (305–8)

> Deceiver, did you even hope to hide
> so harsh a crime, to leave this land of mine
> without a word? Can nothing hold you back—
> neither your love, the hand you pledged, nor even
> the cruel death that lies in wait for Dido?

Similarly, Cleopatra denies Antony the chance to speak and berates him for
his perfidy:

> *Ant.*	Cleopatra—
> *Cleo.*	Why should I think you can be mine, and true
> (Though you in swearing shake the throned gods),
> Who have been false to Fulvia? Riotous madness,
> To be entangled with those mouth-made vows,
> Which break themselves in swearing!
>
> (26–31)

Later, Dido reminds Aeneas that she granted mercy and hospitality to him,
a wretched castaway and beggar (*eiectum litore, egentem*, 373). Angrily, she tells
him to leave: *i, sequere Italiam ventis, pete regna per undas* (381 "Go then, before
the winds to Italy. Seek out your kingdom over seas"). Likewise, Cleopatra
reminds Antony of his former suppliance and tells him to leave:

> Nay, pray you seek no color for your going,
> But bid farewell, and go. When you sued staying,
> Then was the time for words; no going then.
>
> (32–4)

Aeneas' response is *pauca* (333), "brief" as well as "small," compared with Dido's large passion. He blames *fata* (340) for shaping his life and tells Dido to cease complaint as he does not search for Rome voluntarily:

> desine meque tuis incendere teque querelis.
> Italiam non sponte sequor.
>
> (360–61)

> No longer set yourself and me
> afire. Stop your quarrel. It is not
> my own free will that leads to Italy.

Antony also lays the blame for his departure on an unapproachable abstraction, the "strong necessity of time" (42), and bids the angry queen, "Quarrel no more" (66). Shakespeare follows Vergil very closely here, even going so far as to transfer Dido's speechlessness—*incipit effari mediaque in voce resistit* (76 "she starts to speak, then falters / and stops in mid-speech")—to Cleopatra:

> Something it is I would—
> O, my oblivion is a very Antony,
> And I am all forgotten.
>
> (89–91)

The Vergilian undertones that Shakespeare sounds throughout the play enrich Cleopatra's final moments. Cleopatra's death scene incorporates and transforms Dido's. Both women decide to commit suicide because they suffer from broken hearts and because they fear imminent conquest. Dido's companions help prepare a purgation ritual; Cleopatra's handmaids help prepare a sacrificial rite. Dido retreats into the locked *penetrale* that contains Aeneas's sword, clothing, and the familiar bed, *notumque cubile* (648); Cleopatra withdraws into the monument, also an epithalamial tomb, a place of marriage and self-immolation. Before dying, both queens recall the first meeting with their lovers, both receive kisses and loving ministrations from their companions, and both give the lie to Mercury's cruel jeer, *varium et mutabile semper / femina* (569–70 "an ever / uncertain inconstant thing is woman").

And yet, the differences between the fourth *Aeneid* and *Antony and Cleopatra* remain fundamental. Vergil's Dido is a tragic figure whose leave-taking expresses broken-hearted pathos and chthonic rage. Shakespeare's Cleopatra is in the parallel scene essentially comic, a consummate actress whose quicksilver shifts of mood bewilder and captivate her Roman lover. So too are their deaths dissimilar. Whereas Dido dies bitterly and tragically,

Cleopatra dies triumphantly and joyfully. Her glazed rapture (5.2.76ff.) replaces Dido's grim curse (607ff.); and Antony's transformation from guest to husband ("Husband, I come! / Now to that name my courage prove my title!" 5.2.287–88) neatly reverses Aeneas' degeneration from husband to guest: *hospes, / (hoc solum nomen quoniam de coniuge restat)* (323–4 "I must say 'guest': this name is all / I have of one whom once I called my husband").

In this play allusion broadens to eristic imitation as Shakespeare recalls an entire episode—its characters and thematic implications. Lying below the surface of Shakespeare's text, the Aeneas and Dido story deepens and enriches the play. It must be observed, however, that Shakespeare here appropriates Vergilian ideas for most un-Vergilian ends: namely, for the glorification of Antony and Cleopatra. The play rewrites the fourth *Aeneid* and reverses its values. In this work the playwright molds a Vergilian episode into radically new shape and form. The sub-text provides the material for its own counter-statement, for the articulation of a fundamentally different vision.

Such transformative imitation is also evident in Shakespeare's final masterpiece, *The Tempest*.[25] The Vergilian presence makes itself felt conspicuously in 3.3, wherein Ariel dressed as a harpy descends to confront Alonso, Sebastian, Antonio, and the rest. Obviously, Shakespeare here imitates the harpy episode of *Aeneid* 3. In both scenes winged harpies shatter an island banquet and astonish shipwrecked voyagers. A struggle ensues but ends quickly as the humans discover that they cannot harm the supernatural creatures. Vergil's *sed neque vim plumis ullam nec vulnera tergo / accipiunt* (242–3 "No blow can wound their wings or scar their backs") echoes in Ariel's proud notice of his untouched "plume" (65). After both battles one harpy speaks with divine authority. Celaeno, eldest of the Furies (*maxima Furiarum*, 252), repeats the message of Jupiter and Phoebus Apollo; Ariel, also a minister of "Fate" (61), speaks for omniscient "pow'rs" (73). Both accuse the dazed listeners of wrongdoing and promise grim punishment: Celaeno prophesies that the voyagers will eat their tables from hunger, and Ariel threatens "Ling'ring perdition (worse than any death / Can be at once)" (77–8).

The manifest differences between the two scenes, however, reveal the purpose of Shakespeare's elaborate imitation. Ariel, we observe, differs sharply from Celaeno, that hideous creature of filth and ordure. He merely enacts a charade for Prospero, who greets him warmly after the performance:

> Bravely the figure of this harpy hast thou
> Perform'd, my Ariel; a grace it had, devouring.

Of my instruction hast thou nothing bated
In what thou hadst to say.

(83-6)

As in *Lucrece* and *Hamlet*, Shakespeare frames the Vergilian allusion in art
and artifice. Much like the Player at Elsinore, Ariel acts out a Vergilian role
to instruct his audiences on stage and in the theatre. His dire threat, unlike
Celaeno's, points the way to forgiveness and reconciliation. "Heart's
sorrows / And a clear life ensuing" (81-2), Ariel promises, will guard the
amazed auditors from the wrath of the powers above. Here the curse of the
screaming harpy yields to the reassuring admonition of a benevolent spirit;
the epic ordeal becomes an internal drama of penitence and salvation.

In his own way, Shakespeare thus follows the well-trodden paths of
allegorical humanism. Commentaries on classical texts in the Middle Ages
and Renaissance frequently transformed classical characters and incidents
in this fashion, to accord with Christian values. Cristoforo Landino's
enormously influential *Camaldolese Disputations*, for example, provides an
instructive parallel to Shakespeare's revision of *Aeneid* 3 in *The Tempest*.
According to Landino, the harpies represent Avarice: their faces are pale
and haggard from desire; they have hooked claws for grasping, which drag
men down into bestiality; the broken banquet suggests that Avarice is born
of stupidity and baseness of spirit and prefers death to the diminishment of
treasure. The Trojans strike at the harpies ineffectually but, Landino tells us,
the creatures may be easily repelled, *si fortē generosumque sumamus animū* ("if
we assume a brave and generous spirit").[26] Landino's confrontation
between Avarice and the brave and generous spirit glosses interestingly
Shakespeare's confrontation between those grasping villains—Alonso,
Sebastian, and Antonio—and the forgiving Prospero.

The Tempest represents the culmination and conclusion of Shakespeare's
relationship with Vergil. In it the playwright ponders an essentially Vergilian
concern—the cost of civilization in human terms. Unlike the Roman poet,
however, Shakespeare does not end his vision in epic action, but in
recognition of the human capacity for spiritual growth. "The rarer action
is / In virtue than in vengeance" (5.1.27-8); and Prospero, wiser and
sadder, learns finally to put *furor* aside for forgiveness. This option, of
course, is not open to Aeneas, who must, to his own sorrow, end in furious
and bitter triumph over Turnus.[27] Yet, despite these differences, the two
conclusions are similar in spirit: they are in their own ways sad victories,
shadowed over by the same exhausted awareness of evil, suffering, and loss.
The weary Aeneas finally understands what is needed to build the high
walls of Rome, and the weary Prospero returns to Milan, where "Every
third thought" is his grave (5.1.312). In such transformative imitation, as in

the early and middle allusions, there is meaningful tribute. Shakespeare, even as he adapts Vergil, acknowledges for all time the importance of his work, the keenness of his understanding, and the lasting power of his art.[28]

Notes

1. For evidence of the general neglect see Geoffrey Bullough's *Narrative and Dramatic Sources of Shakespeare*, 8 vols. (London: Routledge and Kegan Paul, and New York: Columbia University Press, 1957–75), a thorough compilation that does not reprint a single passage from Vergil as source, possible source, or analogue. John W. Velz, "The Ancient World in Shakespeare: Authenticity or Anachronism? A Retrospect," *ShS* 31 (1978): 1–12, notes this lacuna in Shakespeare scholarship and calls for remedy (12). The most complete study of Vergilian influence to date is T.W. Baldwin, *Shakspere's Small Latine & Lesse Greeke*, 2 vols. (Urbana: University of Illinois Press, 1944), 2:456–96, although the emphasis is almost exclusively on verbal echoes and allusions.
2. *Of Dramatic Poesy: An essay* (1668) (ed. George Watson), 1:70.
3. [Joseph Addison], *The Spectator* (ed. Donald F. Bond), No. 160 (Monday, September 3, 1711), 2:129.
4. See Domenico Comparetti, *Vergil in the Middle Ages*, trans. E.F.M. Benecke (London: Sonnenschein, 1895).
5. *Small Latine*, passim.
6. See my *"Titus Andronicus* and the Mythos of Shakespeare's Rome," *ShakS* 14 (1981): 85–98. For a different view of the Vergilian elements in the play see Andrew V. Ettin, "Shakespeare's First Roman Tragedy," *ELH* 37 (1970): 325–41.
7. I have used G. Blakemore Evans, ed. *The Riverside Shakespeare* (Boston: Houghton Mifflin, 1974) for all references to Shakespeare's works.
8. First to notice the contrast between the two Lavinias was Robert Adger Law, "The Roman Background of *Titus Andronicus," SP* 40 (1943): 146.
9. See the analysis of T.W. Baldwin, *On the Literary Genetics of Shakspere's Poems & Sonnets* (Urbana: University of Illinois Press, 1950), pp. 143–6.
10. These are the qualities discussed by R.D. Williams, "The Pictures on Dido's Temple (*Aeneid* I.450–93)," *CQ* n.s. 10 (1960): 145–51.
11. Servius, whose commentary Shakespeare may have read, provides an interesting gloss to Vergil's *medium in penetralibus hostem* (508):

> sane penetralia proprie deorum dicuntur, non numquam etiam imae et interiores partes privatarum domorum vocantur, unde et penum dicimus locum ubi conduntur quae ad vitam sunt necessaria.

> Certainly the word *penetralia* refers properly to the chambers of the gods, but sometimes to the deepest and most interior parts of a private house, whence we name the place for storing food *penetralia*, that is, the place where we keep all things which are necessary for life.

Servianorum in Vergilii Carmina Commentariorum, Editio Harvardiana, Special Publication of the American Philological Association, No. 1, 2 (Lancaster, Pa., 1946), p. 450.

12. The locus classicus, of course, is *Aeneid* 2, wherein the son takes the father on back and carries him from burning Troy:

> ergo age, care pater, cervici imponere nostrae; ipse
> subibo umeris nec me labor iste gravabit; quo res
> cumque cadent, unum et commune periclum, una salus
> ambobus erit. mihi parvus Iulus sit comes, et longe
> servet vestigia coniunx.
>
> (707–11)

> Come then, dear father, mount upon my neck;
> I'll bear you on my shoulders. That is not
> too much for me. Whatever waits for us,
> we both shall share one danger, one salvation.
> Let young Iülus come with me, and let
> my wife Creüsa follow at a distance.

13. Donatus writes: *pater, inquam, non tibi desunt meae ceruicis obsequia, iam imponere humeris meis, pondus tuum deliciae meae sunt, facit pietas leue, quod putas esse grauissimum, sarcinam tuam libenter tolerabit affectus* ("father, I say, my neck is willing to do its duty and lays the charge on my shoulders. Your burden is my joy. My love and respect makes light what you consider so heavy and will gladly bear your pack as well"). Vergil, *Opera* (Venice: Iuntus, 1544), reprinted in *The Renaissance and the Gods*, No. 7, 2 vols. (New York and London: Garland, 1976), 1:230ᵛ). For the Pontanus essay see Jacobus Pontanus (Spanmüller), *Symbolarum Libri XVII Virgilii* (Augsburg, 1599), reprinted in *The Renaissance and the Gods*, No. 18, 3 vols. (New York and London: Garland, 1976) vol. 2, cols. 961–4.

14. See *Adagiorvm Chiliades, Omnia Opera* (Basel, 1536), 2:326–7.

15. See *A Registre of Hystories*, trans. Abraham Fleming (London: T. Woodcocke, 1576), fol. 39ᵛ–40.

16. See "De Amore Liberorvm in parentes," in *Theatrvm Poeticum atque Historicum* (London, 1609), p. 557.

17. See emblem 195, "Pietas filiorum in parentes," in Andrea Alciati, *Emblemata cvm Commentariis* (Padua: P.P. Tozzi, 1621), pp. 828–31; Geffrey Whitney, *A Choice of Emblemes* (Leyden: Christopher Plantyn, 1586), p. 163.

18. In *The Tragedie of Caesar and Pompey, or Caesars Revenge* (London: N. Fosbrooke and I. Wright, 1607), Cato Junior says to his father (note the Senecan formulation):

> Father I go with a more willing minde,
> Then did *Aeneas* when from *Troyan* fire,
> He bare his Father, and did so restore:
> The greatest gift hee had receiued before.
>
> *(sig. E)*

19. Donatus explains (*Opera* 1:315):

> Cum videret Aeneas auxilio suorum, hoc est humanis
> nixibus contra tantam perniciem nauium opem competentem
> ferri non posse. tum discissa ab humeris veste, quod
> signum fuit doloris maximi, quoniam pius fuit, hoc est
> deorum purissimus cultor, superum numen restinguendo
> incendio supplice voce posecebat in auxilium.

> When Aeneas saw that with the aid of his own men, that
> is, with human efforts, no help that would avail could
> be brought against the great damage to his ships, then
> he tore off the garment from his shoulders, which was a
> sign of great grief. Since he was pious, that is, a
> most devout worshiper of the gods, he humbly begged the
> divine powers for help in extinguishing the flames.

20. The Vergilian inspiration is evident in the general conception of Troy, Pyrrhus, and Priam and in specific details like Priam's "antique sword," which is adapted from *inutile ferrum* (*Aen.* 2.510). For interpretations of the Pyrrhus speech similar to mine but differing in emphasis, see Arthur Johnston, "The Player's Speech in *Hamlet*," *SQ* 13 (1962): 21–30; Joseph Westlund, "Ambivalence in The Player's Speech in *Hamlet*," *SEL* 18 (1978): 245–56; the notes of Harold Jenkins, ed. *Hamlet* (Arden edition) (London: Methuen, 1982), esp. pp. 478–81. On the Ovidian style of the speech see Harry Levin, *The Question of Hamlet* (New York: Oxford University Press, 1978), p. 144; on the Lucanic see J.A.K. Thomson, *Shakespeare and the Classics* (New York: Barnes & Noble, 1952), pp. 230–31; Emrys Jones, *The Origins of Shakespeare* (Oxford: Clarendon, 1977), pp. 275–7.

21. See the debate in Furness' Variorum edition, 1:180–86.

22. See Maurice Charney, *Style in Hamlet* (Princeton: Princeton University Press, 1969), pp. 96–7, for an analysis of imagistic connections between the two figures.

23. Ibid., p. 14.

24. In modeling his Cleopatra on the epic Dido, he is following Vergil, who used a similar phrase to describe both queens' deaths: Dido is *pallida morte futura* (4.644), Cleopatra, *pallentem morte futura* (8.709). Others who have noted some parallels between Shakespeare's Cleopatra and Vergil's Dido include Ernest Schanzer, *The Problem Plays of Shakespeare* (New York: Schocken Books, 1963), pp. 159ff.; and Janet Adelman, *The Common Liar: An Essay on "Antony and Cleopatra"* (New Haven and London: Yale University Press, 1973), pp. 71ff.

25. The play is usually not considered Vergilian despite J.M. Nosworthy's notice of Vergilian elements in it, "The Narrative Sources of *The Tempest*," *RES* 24 (1948): 281–94.

26. I quote from Thomas Herbert Stahel, S.J., "Cristoforo Landino's Allegorization of the *Aeneid*: Books III and IV of the *Camaldolese Disputations*," dissertation, Johns Hopkins University, 1968, sig. Giiii.

27. I am here indebted to Robert Wiltenburg's "The *Aeneid* in *The Tempest*," a paper delivered at the Seventh Annual Mid-Hudson MLA Conference, Marist College, 1 December 1981, forthcoming in *Shakespeare Survey*.

28. This essay, condensed and adapted from a manuscript, was submitted early in 1982 at the invitation of the editor. While the essay was unfortunately delayed in press, the manuscript saw the light of publication as *Shakespeare's Rome* (Cambridge: Cambridge University Press, 1983). This set of circumstances accounts for the replication here of passages in the book. Since the submission of the essay, scholarship relevant to it has appeared, most notably, Thomas M. Greene, *The Light in Troy* (New Haven: Yale University Press, 1982) and Barbara J. Bono, *Literary Transvaluation* (Berkeley: University of California Press, 1984). Greene discusses the varieties and uses of imitation in Renaissance poetry, and Bono traces the adaptations of the Aeneas and Dido story from Vergil up to Shakespeare's *Antony and Cleopatra*.

VERGIL'S *GEORGICS* AND *PARADISE LOST*: NATURE AND HUMAN NATURE IN A LANDSCAPE

Stella P. Revard

When Milton in book 3 of *Paradise Lost* describes his dilemma as an epic poet undertaking his great work, he deliberately and clearly echoes those lines from the *Georgics* where Vergil before him had expressed his doubts about his calling to greater poetry. That it is these modest verses (2.475ff.) and not the more adventurous ones from the seventh book of the *Aeneid* (37–45) that Milton chooses to allude to is significant, for it tells us not only how closely Milton read the *Georgics*, how important it was to him as a poem, but also how he saw the Vergil of this middle work already as an epic poet, creating in it a design worthy of emulation. Critics of Milton's poetry have long recognized the importance of the *Georgics* to him, but they have focused upon its influence either in early works such as *L'Allegro* and *Il Penseroso*, where it is seen as influencing the "pastoral" genre, or in late works such as *Paradise Regained*, where, they argue, it determines the four-book structure, the middle style, and the didactic tone.[1] When critics and editors have looked at the *Georgics*' impact on *Paradise Lost*, they have given their attention for the most part to the many verbal echoes that occur, from Milton's famous evocation of Vergil's bees in book 1 (768–75) to his simile of the careful Plowman in book 4 (983–5).[2] Although now and then they have noted a resemblance between Vergil's landscapes in the *Georgics* and the scenes in Eden or have remarked that Adam and Eve are, like the protagonists of Vergil's poem, farmers, they have not gone beyond these echoes and resemblances to inquire whether they indicate a more basic relationship in the intellectual, moral, and symbolic designs of the two works.[3]

The *Georgics* has much in common with *Paradise Lost*, as much in its way as has the *Aeneid*, which has universally been recognized as an important

259

model for Milton. Because of its twelve-book epic structure, its scenes of council and war, and its famous description of the underworld, the *Aeneid* has seemed closer to *Paradise Lost* and has overshadowed the *Georgics*.[4] Its claims to priority appear less pressing, however, once we remember that Milton loudly proclaimed that he was not merely imitating classical epic, that his subject transcended the plight of Cytherea's son or "the rage / Of Turnus for Lavinia disespoused" (9.16–17), that few sections of his poem deal with arms and the man and many with God's dispensation to man, and finally that the central sections of *Paradise Lost* describing Adam and Eve in the garden are georgic in manner and style. Though sometimes dismissed as a handbook for farmers, a work that tells when to turn the soil and how to care for vines, breed cattle, and keep bees, the *Georgics* is a serious symbolic poem, was so regarded by the Renaissance, and thanks to the work of Klingner, Wilkinson, and Otis is so recognized in the twentieth century.[5] In dealing with nature, Vergil's purpose is to inquire into man's relationship with the permanent and enduring aspects of the world, to seek, moreover, how a divine plan lies behind a natural world that is sometimes harsh and indifferent, at other times nurturing and providential. In focusing upon the farmer, Vergil is looking at man in his most primitive but ordered state, a kind of universal man or everyman produced by a nurturing god, who has in turn placed nature in his care. Implicitly, Vergil contrasts the farmer and his way of life with urban man, enhanced with the luxuries of his more advanced culture but continually threatened by political dissension and war. By so doing, Vergil can question whether urban man truly has advanced, and how the perils that he faces resulting from his inability to control ambition, greed, and human passion compare with the perils of inhospitable nature, disease, and natural disaster that the farmer faces. Finally, looking backward at the Golden Age, Vergil considers if it was well lost and whether a new Golden Age is possible in which not only individual happiness is assured, but also the collective security of an equal republic on earth.

In its scope and aims the *Georgics* is a short philosophical epic whose real subject is the human condition and whose true purpose is precisely that of *Paradise Lost*: to justify God's ways to man. Its importance for *Paradise Lost* is clear when we consider that Milton, like Vergil, was trying to write a philosophical and didactic work, not merely an epic of man's fall, and was intent on exploring the relationships of man to nature and to God. Vergil's farmer could be a positive model for Milton as he created Adam, his own primitive man and everyman, for like the farmer Adam knows that the world has been placed in his care, that he is responsible for his own happiness, and that he must work to maintain it. It is often remarked that Milton has not made paradise a place of pastoral *otium*; unlike the hexaemeral poets who preceded him, he has given Adam and Eve responsibilities: to cultivate the garden and in so doing to cultivate their own humanity. Like Vergil's farmer, they must learn how to deal with their environment, in an easy and positive way before the fall, with difficulty but with hope afterwards. Although Milton dramatizes only the events up to the exclusion from the garden, by reference and extended narrative, he keeps all of history before us, and thus like Vergil he considers the whole range of history from the creation until the prophesied renewal of the Golden Age.

As we evaluate Vergil's influence upon Milton, we must acknowledge that while their views of history are complementary and Milton can easily adapt the views of Vergil on such matters as the Golden Age, as he drew from and adapted material from other classical poets, as a Christian he could not exactly follow Vergil's now stoical, now epicurean point of view. For Milton the loss of Eden was tragic. Vergil sometimes praises, sometimes regrets the passing of the Golden Age. He seems to share Hesiod's opinion that the Golden Age was a primitive state that Jupiter ended wisely in that human beings needed the challenge of adversity and discipline of work in order for society to progress and the arts and sciences to evolve. Yet, he undoubtedly associates the end of the Golden Age with the beginning of strife on earth and frequently harkens back to the time when war, strife, and crime were unknown and man lived in peace with man and in harmony with nature. He would not have used the term "fallen" to describe modern man, as Milton does, but he has little trouble painting a picture of the vice and degeneracy of modern life to which Milton would readily assent, nor does he hesitate to make the farmers the only ones among men in whom the goddess Astraea, departing from the earth, left a vestige of her rule (2.473-4).[6] Hence he provides for Milton in the just farmer a model for his prelapsarian Adam and in his view of man degenerate since the Golden Age an approximate version of the Christian fall.

I

There are two ways in which the *Georgics* exerts an effect on *Paradise Lost*: first as, in many sections but especially in book 2, it presents man in an idealized relationship to nature and the gods of nature, and second as it shows how man has "fallen" from that ideal state and must struggle with himself and nature in a hostile world. Brooks Otis has demonstrated how books 1 and 3 by and large portray the more pessimistic view, whereas 2 and 4 show mostly the happy association between man and nature.[7] In book 2 Vergil discusses the planting of trees and the tending of vines and points out how, if man plants proper crops for each soil and climate, nature will produce abundantly. Nature almost seems to call out to man to cultivate the land: *et dubitant homines serere atque impendere curam?* (2.433 "And do men hesitate to sow and tend their care?"). A life spent close to nature has special rewards for man, because it is the kind of life the gods ordained for him from the beginning. Throughout the *Georgics* Vergil shows how man prospers when he governs his life by the diurnal and seasonal rhythms that govern nature. In an idyllic passage in book 3 he describes the satisfactions of the rural day, telling how in the warm season, when the west wind blows, the shepherd leads out his flocks to enjoy the tender grass, both he and his animals spending the day in the lovely fields until they return at sundown with the cool star of evening (3.322–38). Once more in book 4, in a digression on gardens, he shows how man can live happily on earth, if he will stay close to nature and tend it conscientiously (4.116–48). Vergil calls to mind an old Corycian, who from a few acres of unproductive land created a small paradise where, happy as a king, he kept his bees and cultivated a garden that he himself had laid out and bordered in lilies, verbena, and poppies. His were the first rose of spring and the earliest apples of autumn; when winter gripped the land elsewhere, he was cutting hyacinth. The husbandman in book 2 also enjoys, like the shepherd and the old Corycian, a Golden-Age happiness in temperate Italy, where he industriously tends and prunes his vines and grafts his fruit trees. There is more than an incidental likeness between these portraits of happy farmers in idealized country settings and the portraits of Adam and Eve in Eden. Their work in paradise is very like that of the husbandman of *Georgics* 2, for like him they prune plants, lop overgrown vegetation, tend young plants, prop and bind others. Adam in book 4 describes in detail the work they do (4.437–38); and Eve in book 9, whom Milton frequently compares to the agricultural deities Pales, Pomona, and Ceres, carries rude gardening tools and plans her day of pruning and cultivation (9.205–12). Like the old gardener of book 4, she has laid out for herself her own garden and has bordered it with flowers, a spot Milton calls "more delicious than those gardens feigned / Or of revived Adonis, or renowned / Alcinous" (9.439–41). The daily routine that Adam and Eve follow in their gardening is like that of Vergil's farmers and herdsmen; for, as John Knott has observed, they rise at dawn, go forth to work, take refuge from the heat of the sun at noon, and retire at evening.[8] Milton has taken care in books 4, 5, and 9 to illustrate the pattern of their day, and has in fact made Adam comment upon the sense of order it gives to their lives and the closeness to God that following the rhythms of nature makes them feel. Adam regards the work and order of the day as ordained by God: "God hath set / Labour and rest, as day and night to men / Successive," appointing for man his "daily work of body or mind," and so declaring the dignity of man and of work (4.612-14, 618-20). Both Adam and Eve feel a sense of vocation to their work and regard this alternation of work and recreation as part of the sweetness of the garden.

Nature for Vergil's farmers and for Adam and Eve is the gift of the gods; reverence towards it and its creator is a prime responsibility. Vergil has filled his nature, as L.P. Wilkinson has observed, with numinous presences, rural deities who preside over the land, the gods of harvest, agriculture, and of the flock: Ceres and Bacchus, Pales, Pan and Apollo Amphrysus.[9] He celebrates the closeness to the gods that the farmer feels through his association with nature and remarks on the good fortune of that association: *fortunatus et ille, deos qui novit agrestes* (2.493 "Fortunate also is he who loves the country gods"). The farmer remembers these gods at planting and harvest time with his prayers and his worship. Milton's Adam and Eve begin and end each day with hymns to God, wherein they thank him for his bounty and pray for its continuance. Their great thanksgiving hymn of book 5, though drawing its language from the psalms and canticles, recalls the reverent attitude of the Vergilian farmer and the praise of the nature deities that Vergil included in his invocations to books 1 and 2. In these invocations, Vergil addresses Bacchus and Ceres as the divine forces and principles behind the order of nature: *o clarissima mundi / lumina, labentem caelo quae ducitis annum* (1.5-6 "O most illustrious lights of the world, who lead the moving year from heaven"). He then thanks them for the rich gifts of nature that they have bestowed on man and pleads that they yet be present and propitious to man. Adam and Eve, in celebrating the "glorious works" of the Almighty (5.153), also extol the divine presence in "these [his] lowest works," and pray that God "be bounteous still / To give us only good" (205-6). Both Vergil and Milton in the hymn and invocation are thanking the god of nature for what he has given man through nature, recognizing implicitly that a friendly nature is the greatest of divine gifts, without which man cannot survive.

Although both poets acknowledge that nature after the Golden Age can be harsh and indifferent, they portray life as paradise on earth when nature and God smile on man. In book 2 of the *Georgics* it is almost as though Vergil were describing Italy during the Golden Age. Beginning with the opening passage on trees (9-135), Vergil stresses the abundance, variety, and beauty of nature. Trees come in all kinds—poplar, willow, elm, cherry, bay, myrtle, olive—adapt themselves to different climates and soils, grow spontaneously and fruitfully. Vergil dwells on the familiar popular associations of some trees—the olive with peace, the myrtle with love, the elm and its vine with fruitful marriage—associations which, not surprisingly, also recur in *Paradise Lost*. Calling Italy the Saturnian land, Vergil describes how its rivers run gold, and its fields are free of poisonous snakes and predatory lions and tigers. Its landscapes have pleasant and grateful changes, for there are vineyard and farmland, lakes and caves, cool valleys and meadows where cattle low and one may rest under the shade of trees. Vergil deliberately dwells in book 2 (in contrast to 1 and 3) on scenes of spring and ripening summer, suggesting that the present rural Italy is indeed Golden-Age Italy, for it seems to reproduce with its temperate climate the conditions of the Golden Age:

> hic ver adsiduum atque alienis mensibus aestas:
> bis gravidae pecudes, bis pomis utilis arbos.
>
> $(2.149-50)^{10}$

> Here is continual spring and summer beyond its usual months;
> Twice a year the cattle bear, and twice serviceable are the trees with apples.

Milton has carried over into *Paradise Lost* more than a few notions of Golden-Age nature from Vergil. Milton's Eden, like Vergil's Italy of *Georgics* 2, is a place of beauty, variety, and abundance. The rivers of Eden, like those of Italy, run gold: "crisped brooks, / Rolling on orient pearl and sands of gold" (4.237-38). The animals roam freely, untroubled by predators or poisonous snakes; the serpent in Eden is still innocuous. Trees in great variety mark the landscape of Eden; Milton names their kinds— "Cedar, and pine, and fir, and branching palm" (4.139)—and dwells upon the "mantling vine" and the myrtle-crowned bank with their associations of fertility and love. There is variety and change also in the expanse of landscape: "lawns, or level downs, and flocks / Grazing the tender herb, . . . palmy hillock, or the flowery lap / Of some irriguous valley" (4.252-5). To sum up these effects Milton tells us that Eden compares with no other land; it surpasses them all:

>   Not that fair field
> Of Enna . . . . nor that sweet grove
> Of Daphne by Orontes, and the inspired
> Castalian spring, might with this Paradise
> Of Eden strive; nor that Nyseian isle
> Girt with the river Triton . . .
> Nor where Abassin kings their issue guard,
> Mount Amara . . .
>
> (4.268-9, 272-6, 280-81)

In a like strategic moment, when he wishes to sum up the beauties of Italy,

Vergil has summoned forth a roll-call of names, not the same names, but ones rich in evocative meaning and sonorous beauty:

> Sed neque Medorum silvae, ditissima terra,
> nec pulcher Ganges atque auro turbidus Hermus
> laudibus Italiae certent, non Bactra neque Indi
> totaque turiferis Panchaia pinguis harenis.

(2.136–9)

> But neither the Median forests, that rich land, nor
>   fair Ganges,
> Nor Hermus rolling in gold
> Compares with Italy—no, not Bactra nor the Indies
> Nor all Arabia's acres of spice-enrichened soil.[11]

It seems more than likely that this roll of exotic places, used with the device of negative comparison to heighten the suggested superiority of Italy to all other lands, was the model for Milton's roll-call in *Paradise Lost*. Milton's repetition of the negatives, "not, nor, nor, nor," echoes Vergil's "neque, nec, non, neque." Both poets, moreover, are working to create the same effect: namely, to connect the richness and beauty of far-off and exotic lands with that of Eden or Italy, and yet with the repeated negatives to place their own paradises high above the others.

It is more, however, than an occasional borrowing or a series of scattered effects, a list of which might also be collected from other classical or Renaissance poets, that links Milton's concept of nature in *Paradise Lost* with Vergil's in the *Georgics*. It is rather the moral tone that each poet adopts in insisting that the order and beauty of nature comes from the divine and the fervor that each manifests in showing how nature inculcates reverence and virtue in man. For both poets an intimate relationship exists between God, nature, and man, one fostered by the fact that nature and man are God's creation. Milton begins his description of Eden by telling us that God created the garden and caused it to grow out of the fertile ground. Vergil, describing the coming of spring, makes the father god Jupiter responsible for the fertility of the land. Jupiter as husband descends into the embraces of his wife and in divine sexual union causes life on earth to begin:

> tum pater omnipotens fecundis imbribus Aether
> coniugis in gremium laetae descendit, et omnis
> magnus alit magno commixtus corpore fetus.

(2.325–7)

> Then the upper air, the Father Omnipotent, in fertile showers descends into the lap of his joyful spouse and in union with her great body greatly nurtures all fruit.

As the father god rouses nature, spring comes to the earth: birds begin to sing, animals to seek one another in love; the fields grow moist and warm under the breath of the west wind, and the grass starts to grow. This description of the return of spring to the earth reminds Vergil of the first great spring of creation: *ver illud erat, ver magnus agebat / orbis* (2.338–9 "Spring it was, great spring was working upon the earth"). He imagines that the east winds then spared their wintry gusts and there was a truce between cold and warm, for had there not been such, neither man nor animals nor the tender plants of the earth could have survived. The indulgence of heaven and the generative force of the great father god are necessary both at the initial creation of the earth and at each spring when life once more is renewed. Vergil implicitly links divine favor and the primordial fertility of the land.

The metaphor of the "omnipotent father" descending to his spouse was much commented on by Renaissance mythographers and interpreters of Vergil. Conti, for example, connected it with Homer's description in *Iliad* 14 of Zeus and Hera making love and causing the flowers to spring up about them. He identified Jupiter as Aether, the upper air, and Juno as Aer, the lower air, and said that the commingling of the two caused rain. Other commentators saw Jupiter as the life-giving rain coming down to impregnate the earth with his showers.[12] Milton's use of the metaphor indicates his knowledge of both Vergil's original passage and the commentaries, for he specifically indicates that Jupiter's love for Juno causes the showers of spring. Vergil uses his metaphor to introduce his section on spring; Milton adapts it to conclude his description of Eden's eternal spring. Milton at the outset tells us that God causes Eden to grow out of the fertile ground; he continues by describing how nature comes alive in this eternal spring. Flowers appear, the vine "gently creeps / Luxuriant," the birds "their choir apply," and "airs, vernal airs" breathe "the smell of field and grove," attuning "the trembling leaves" (4.256–66). The procession of spring is guided by divine forces, and Milton makes these the classical deities of the Golden Age: "Universal Pan / Knit with the Graces and the Hours in dance / Led on the eternal spring" (266–8). The same gods that inhabit Vergil's georgic world inhabit Milton's paradise. At the end of his description of the garden, Milton introduces Adam and Eve as lords of the growing paradise. By describing Adam's hyacinthine hair and Eve's golden ringlets that wave "as the vine curls her tendrils," Milton makes his human couple part of the nature they govern and even implies that their nature, like that of the garden, wants the gentle training and governance of which Vergil speaks so fully in the *Georgics*. Finally, he shows Adam and Eve in conversation with one another and has Eve recount her first meeting with Adam and her yielding to him in love. Now Milton links Adam and Eve not only with nature, but with the gods, employing the simile of Jupiter smiling on Juno to describe their union:

> he [Adam] in delight
> Both of her beauty and submissive charms
> Smiled with superior love, as Jupiter
> On Juno smiles, when he impregns the clouds
> That shed May flowers . . .
>
> (497–501)

But, as he has compared his human couple to the very gods that Vergil makes the initiators of the spring, he has come full circle in his description of Eden. For it was the Christian omnipotent father, Jupiter's counterpart, who, Milton says at the outset, first caused all things to grow. As they embrace, Adam and Eve, acting the parts of the Vergilian nature gods, Jupiter and his spouse, conclude the great cycle of fertility that God had set in motion and show us how the human love that will guarantee the continuance of the cycle is related to the divine love that initiates it.

The final sections of *Georgics* 2 examine the benefits of a life spent close to nature and contrast the joys that the countryman knows with the sophistications of the city. These passages have provided Milton with a model for the domestic life that Adam and Eve lead in Eden. Vergil begins with an outburst of praise for the good fortune of the farmer:

> O fortunatos nimium, sua si bona norint,
> agricolas! quibus ipsa procul discordibus armis
> fundit humo facilem victum iustissima tellus.
>
> (2.458–60)

> O all too happy farmers, if they might know their own good, for whom, far from clashing arms, the most just earth pours forth, of herself, an easy living from the soil.

Though the gods have ordained for the farmer a life of toil, they have provided compensatory rewards: the beauty of nature that surrounds him, a proper reverence for man and god, a life free from fraud. He does not possess a stately mansion or know pomp and luxury, but he is free from strife and civil discord. He plucks the fruit from the bough and reaps the crops that the earth has borne for his gathering; he has no poor to pity or rich to envy. Concluding with a harvest scene, Vergil describes the farmer, keeping holiday surrounded by his family and friends. Before him are the fruits of the earth that his labor has produced and that he is willing to share with others:

et varios ponit fetus autumnus, et alte
mitis in apricis coquitur vindemia saxis.

(2.521–2)

Autumn places its varied fruits before them, and above the ripe
vintage is warmed on sunny rocks.

The farmer crowns the brimming bowl with wine and remembers to pour a
libation to the god of harvest who has given him this abundance. Such a life
as this, Vergil tells us, man lived in the Golden Age, before the sound of the
trumpet was heard or the din of the sword on the anvil. For the farmer it is
almost as though Golden-Age life were yet possible—if he remain far from
the corrupting luxury of the city and the harvest of strife and war that
civilization has wrought.

Praise of the happiness and virtues of country living is common enough
in the Latin literature that preceded and followed Vergil, as critics have
amply demonstrated.[13] What makes the encomium in *Georgics* 2 and not
some of these others an appropriate model for Milton is that Vergil has
depicted the husbandman in terms of Golden-Age man, has pointedly
contrasted him with the city man, and has used this comparison and
contrast in the harvest scene to sum up his belief that the gods through
nature have taught man proper virtue and reverence. In book 5 of *Paradise
Lost*, when Milton wishes to demonstrate Adam's proper regard for God,
man, and nature, he echoes Vergil's harvest scene in language and concept.
Milton's scene shows Adam and Eve receiving the angel Raphael as their
guest and offering him the fruit Eve has gathered and prepared—"bounties
which our nourisher . . . hath caus'd / The earth to yield" (5.398–401). The
table on which Eve places the dinner fruits recalls the "table" heaped with
autumn harvest in the *Georgics*: "All autumn piled, through spring and
autumn here / Danced hand in hand" (4.394–5). The simple abundance
that they share and the unaffected welcome that they offer the heavenly
stranger seem to Milton to excel the pomp of luxurious state, and he offers
a contrast between Adam's single greeting and the "tedious pomp that waits
/ On princes, when thir rich retinue long / Of horses led, and grooms
besmeared with gold / Dazzles the crowd" (5.354–7). We remember
Vergil's dismissal of the proud ceremony of stately houses and his
preference for the farmer's "wealth" of natural setting. Eve, like a harvest
goddess serving the bounty of the garden, and Adam, holding holiday like
the husbandman of Vergil's poem, are Golden-Age characters such as Vergil
called to mind at the end of *Georgics* 2.

II

The conclusion of *Georgics* 2, where rural contentment reigns, is a marked contrast to the final passages of book 1, where the war god rages and the world rushing onward to ruin is likened to a speeding chariot that the driver tries vainly to control. Vergil conceives of war not merely as an institution that threatens the quiet of country life, but also as the greatest evil that civilized life has inflicted on man. Milton shares his view and adopts his device of contrasting war to the peace of georgic life. After his description of Golden-Age Eden where strife is unknown, Milton presents the beginning of strife in the universe with Satan's unholy war, the repercussions of which will eventually mar the quiet of Eden. Neither Vergil nor Milton has created the picture of the happy husbandman or of prelapsarian Adam and Eve simply to indulge in idealized fancy. They have a moral point to make in showing us what the world could be like if man had curbed or could learn to curb his pride, ambition, and greed. Hence Vergil's apostrophe to the fortunate farmers to know their own good must be taken as a serious injunction, for it tells man to cherish a life far from clashing arms, a life which only man's knowledge and sober moral choice may guarantee.

That Milton has chosen to echo this injunction at the end of book 7 of *Paradise Lost* is extremely significant. It occurs in the chorus of angels who have witnessed Messiah's ending of the war in Heaven, his setting forth and his return from creating the earth. They praise jointly Messiah's quelling of the "proud attempt / Of spirits apostate" and his creation of a new order of men, and speaking directly to men in an apostrophe, they advise them to know their happiness aright:

> Thrice happy men,
> And sons of men, whom God hath thus advanced,
> Created in his image, there to dwell
> And worship him, and in reward to rule
> Over his works . . . thrice happy if they know
> Their happiness, and persevere upright.
>
> (7.625-9, 631-2)

The final sentence, of course, is almost a direct translation of Vergil's words to the farmers quoted earlier: *O fortunatos nimium, sua si bona norint / agricolas!* (2.458-9). In telling his farmers to understand wherein their happiness consists Vergil is suggesting that man's condition on earth lies in his own power, in the proper appreciation of what he has. The husbandman can

choose to continue this state by his own industry and by a proper reverence
for the gods and nature. Obedience to the dispensation of Jove will mean
that he will not stray into the ruin caused by idleness, dissension, and wars.
Vergil makes a direct moral link between the choice of the lowly wise life
close to nature and the bounteous rewards from Jove in vouchsafing that
the husbandman will enjoy in peace the easy living that the just earth pours
forth. Milton's adaptation of the lines carries with it the moral weight of the
original as well as a specific application to the situation of Adam and Eve.
Like the farmers, Adam and Eve are told to value a humble life, close to
nature and to God; they are advised that the continuation of their happiness
consists in understanding, in knowing it truly. Obedience to the sole
injunction of the Christian God and obedience to the dispensation of Jove
are corollary conditions for the continuance of happiness. And the ruin of
war, which Milton has just illustrated in the war in Heaven, and which
Vergil constantly alludes to throughout the *Georgics*, is the symbolic penalty
for the "fall." Both Milton and Vergil see the happiness of man deriving
from correct understanding and correct choice; and they both imply that
man's wisest choice is a life close to nature and to God.

The passages on rural happiness in book 2 provide the greatest number
of direct links between the *Georgics* and *Paradise Lost*, but as the discussion of
their views on war has demonstrated, Vergil was more than a guide to
Milton on Golden-Age life. There are, it is true, fewer direct echoes of the
Georgics in those sections of *Paradise Lost* that deal with life after the fall.
There continues to be, however, a remarkable consonance in point-of-view.
Although Vergil can rejoice in the Saturnian delights of agricultural Italy, he
was aware that life for the farmer and for man in general was often a tragic
struggle against overwhelming adversity. In nature and in civilized life
things tend to the worse: *sic omnia fatis / in peius ruere ac retro sublapsa referri*
(1.199–200 "So by fate all things rush to the worse, and sliding away, fall
back"). It is almost as though man, as Vergil tells us in the simile that
follows, were an oarsman rowing against the flow of a river, never able to
relax for a moment, lest he be borne away by the current (201–3). Milton
takes a similarly pessimistic view of life after the fall, with order constantly
giving way to disorder, as the world rolls on to judgment day, "to good
malignant, to bad men benign, / Under her own weight groaning" (12.538–
40).

What is interesting here is that both Vergil and Milton depict the effects
of man's fall in nature and in the altered relationship of man to nature and
to God. The Vergilian storms and plagues of books 1 and 3 are graphic
examples of a nature alienated from man; the assaults of sexual passion, of
ungovernable ambition and pride, that Vergil shows afflicting beast and
man are evidence of alienation from God. Vergil believes, as does Milton, in

a benevolent divine providence, but he shows that the gods have, for the most part, left man to fend for himself. If the condition of Vergil's happy husbandman in book 2 resembles that of Adam before the fall, the struggle of the less idealized farmer and herdsman of *Georgics* 1 and 3 resembles his state after the fall. Vergil's farmer and Adam must learn to deal with a hostile environment that is no longer kind but portends harm to man and beast. Vergil advises the farmer to watch the signs in nature and the heavens and to pray to the gods for relief when worse comes to worst. Milton shows that Adam too must learn to provide for himself: to clothe himself against the weather and to borrow warmth from fire. In this he has the support, if not the assistance, of heaven: Adam tells Eve, "How much more, if we pray him, will his ear / Be open, and his heart to pity incline, / And teach us further by what means to shun / The inclement seasons" (10.1060-63). Heaven can instruct man to read nature, but man must rely on his intelligence and ingenuity to survive. Milton seems deliberately to heighten the resemblance between Adam and classical man expelled from the Golden Age. He alludes to the classical fables of Deucalion and Pyrrha and to the account Lucretius gives of primitive man's discovery of fire.[14] The hardships that the universal farmer faces in Vergil's *Georgics* are now exactly applicable to Adam, who must with labor earn his bread, and it seems difficult to believe that when Milton came to describe the Adam of book 10, he did not think of Vergil's farmer.

Among such hardships are those brought on by ungovernable elements without and within man, the first symbolized by the violence of weather, the second by the afflictions of disease and the unruliness of sexual passion. Vergil and Milton share the belief that until the passing of the Golden Age man did not know "pinching cold and scorching heat" (10.691). Both poets show us how the army of winds assaults the earth, ravaging sea and land and leaving man helpless before its savage force (*G.* 1.311-34; *PL* 10:687-706). Adam, observing the "outrage from lifeless things," cries out in despair over the ruin of his temperate paradise; Vergil's farmer, just as he is bringing the reaper to his fields, sees wind and rain tear up his heavy crop, leaving him nothing but stubble.[15]

Disease similarly afflicts "fallen" man, and both poets use descriptions of pestilence to show how man is helpless before another ungovernable aspect of nature. Vergil focuses upon one specific plague; he analyzes its symptoms, describes its course in sheep and cattle, and shows how it spreads even to man.[16] Milton catalogues a number of different physical ills found in the lazar house, beginning with "convulsions, epilepsies, fierce catarrhs" and ending with "wide-wasting pestilence" (11.483-7). Both poets allude to the suffering of the victims: Milton to the tossing, groans, and despair of the sick, Vergil to the dumb anguish of the dying animal

(3.515–26). Although each poet in turn notes that disease in man often comes from his own excesses, neither is unsympathetic to the misery of nature burdened and consumed by pestilence, and both implicitly glance backward at the happiness of Golden-Age man. In *Paradise Lost* Milton has Adam lament that man, once so blessed, should now be so wretched and degraded. Vergil has so placed his account of the plague at the end of *Georgics* 3 that it necessarily calls to mind the idyll of the Golden Age that ends book 2. Man's present misery for both recalls his former happiness.

In book 3, almost as a prelude to the passage on disease, and in book 4 in the account of Orpheus' journey to the underworld, Vergil looks at length at what he obviously regards as yet another legacy of the fallen world: ungoverned sexual appetite. In the golden world, when the father god awakens love in all creatures, sex is a beneficent force. Now, however, though necessary for generating most species, it is, unless strictly controlled, more often a bane than a blessing. In man or in animal—for love is the same for all (*amor omnibus idem* 3.244)—sex is almost a disease that consumes and weakens, sapping virtue and undermining reason. Among animals Vergil recommends that the sexes be kept apart except at mating; left to their own devices they court disaster. The female wantonly seduces the male and causes rivalry among her suitors, and to illustrate such behavior Vergil alludes both to the courtship of the cow and bull and to the competition among Helen's suitors that caused the Trojan War. Females under the influence of sexual passion run mad: lionesses desert their cubs; and mares, the most wanton of all animals, wildly bolt to the north and are impregnated by the wind (3.245–83). Males too, and among these he includes the unnamed Leander, cannot be restrained when stirred by passion and rush often unwittingly to their own death. Orpheus, whose story is recounted in book 4, is the most celebrated victim of *furor amoris* and also the most tragic human figure in the *Georgics*. His fatal yielding to love becomes for Vergil a symbol of tragic human fate.

Milton's defense of sexuality in the great marriage hymn of book 4 and his characterization of human love in book 8 as the means of ascent to heaven and the sum of earthly bliss might at first lead us to believe that he could little agree with Vergil's strictures in the *Georgics*. But we must remember that these idealized views of love apply to Adam and Eve in their wedded joy before the fall and that for Adam at least the surrender to *furor amoris* leads to consequences hardly less dire than those suffered by Leander and Orpheus, Vergil's two human lovers. Ungoverned sexual passion for Milton is not only a result of the fall but also its means. It causes the original tragedy on earth and is symptomatic of much in the human condition that continues to bring woe. To look at Adam's fall then in light of Vergil's analysis of the Orpheus myth in *Georgics* 4 is to see how the two poets have dealt with man's fatal disposition to fall.

It is clear that in placing the account of Orpheus' descent to the underworld and death near the conclusion of the *Georgics* and within the symbolic story of Aristaeus' regeneration of his lost hive Vergil meant for it to sum up, in many ways, his consideration of man and his destiny in the world. Orpheus, the archetypal lover and poet, is representative of failing mankind and stands obviously in contrast to Aristaeus, the bee-keeper, who successively overcomes his tragedy. Both young men are goddesses' sons who undergo trial in order to recover devastating losses: Aristaeus the loss of his bees, Orpheus the loss of his wife Eurydice. Their fates are interlinked in that it was Aristaeus who through pursuing Eurydice in passion inadvertently caused her death, and Orpheus who in anger at Aristaeus' crime led the nymphs to punish him with the loss of his bees. Following their respective losses, each young man attempts by undergoing a descent into the underworld and a trial of his steadfastness to bring back to life that which was taken from him. Aristaeus succeeds; Orpheus fails. Success is possible for the first because he governs his passions, fulfills the requirements of the gods, and having undergone trial and purification, regains what was lost. Success eludes Orpheus because he fails to fulfill the one strict law or condition that Proserpine has given him: just at the moment of victory he is overcome by the madness of love, looks back, and loses Eurydice forever to death. He himself becomes the victim of the love-mad Thracian women. For Vergil, Orpheus is more than an unwary lover; he is tragic humankind, unable to govern his passion and pathetically responsible for his own lot.

Vergil's rendering of the climax of the account, told in "slow motion," heightens the pathos of Orpheus' predicament. The poet focuses with great intensity on the moment of choice. Orpheus and Eurydice have almost reached the upper air, she following close behind her husband as Proserpina's condition prescribed. Orpheus stops. Eurydice is at the point of daylight, his own again, when a sudden madness seizes him, a madness that might be forgivable if Hell knew how to forgive. Overcome, he looks back, and all is lost, his labor vain and his pact with Pluto null:

cum subita incautum dementia cepit amantem,
. . . victusque animi respexit.

(4.488-91)

when suddenly a madness seized the unwary lover, . . . and conquered in his heart, he looked back.

Thunder echoes throughout Hades, and death begins to take hold of Eurydice once more, as we hear her parting words: *Quis et me . . . miseram et te perdidit?*' (4.494 "Who has doomed me, miserable, and you with me?").

Eurydice knows that their fates are intertwined and that Orpheus will follow her in death. She stretches out her hands to him, his no longer, and as she disappears Vergil recounts Orpheus' thoughts at what seems a final and irrevocable doom:

> quid faceret? quo se rapta bis coniuge ferret?
> quo fletu Manis, quae numina voce moveret?
>
> (4.504–5)

> What could he do? Where turn with his wife twice snatched away?
> With what lament move the Shades, the gods with his voice?

In his final agony Orpheus knows that he can do no more than await his own death and release from life, which occurs when the Thracian women tear him apart and throw his head and harp, yet sounding the name of Eurydice, into the Hebrus.[17]

Throughout his work, Milton is fascinated with the figure of Orpheus, and the account of his loss of Eurydice and his death appear and reappear there.[18] It seems likely that when he sought a model for the tragic human being and the tragic lover, he would have turned to Vergil's Orpheus, who seals his fate by choosing to surrender to passion. Though Milton undoubtedly knew both Vergil's and Ovid's versions of the Orpheus story, it is Vergil's, I believe, that he is following in *Paradise Lost*, in that Vergil's rendering stresses the tragedy of choice that Orpheus seems resistlessly led to. Vergil tells Orpheus' story sympathetically, but he makes it clear that Orpheus is responsible for his own fate, however unavoidable and forgivable that fate appears to be. Adam, similarly, is for Milton what Orpheus was for Vergil: a tragic human being (representative of mankind), who breaks a god-given command for love. His situation, like Orpheus', is pathetic, since he feels compelled by his all-consuming feeling for his wife to risk disobedience. Though the poet recounts Adam's fall with great compassion, he leaves us with no doubt that the *furor amoris* that blinded such lovers as Orpheus led Adam to sin. He traces in "slow motion" Adam's reaction to first seeing Eve and his determining to die with her. Milton's technique is comparable to Vergil's, and there are even some interesting echoes of phrase. The situation is, of course, somewhat different: Adam looks upon Eve, "defaced, deflowered, and now to death devote" (9.901), and "horror chill / Ran through his veins" (9.890–91); he determines to die with her.[19] His choice is deadly, for it not only confirms Eve's loss of paradise, but results in his own and in all mankind's. He cries out first on Eve's loss, "How art thou lost, how on a sudden lost" (9.900), then upon his own necessary involvement in her fate, "mee with thee hath ruined" (9.906), recognizing, as did the dying Eurydice, that he is doomed with his spouse. As he wonders how he can live without Eve, his words echo those of Orpheus immediately after Eurydice's second death:

How can I live without thee, how forgo
Thy sweet converse and love so dearly joined,
To live again these wild woods forlorn?

(9.908–10)

His projected fate, life in "wild woods forlorn," describes exactly the life Orpheus will live without Eurydice. The bond of nature draws Adam to his wife and, determining not to lose her, he eats the forbidden fruit. In order to show the "cosmic" implications of the deed, Milton recounts how "Earth trembled from her entrails . . . and nature gave a second groan, / Sky loured, and muttering thunder, . . . / Wept" (9.1000–3). In the Vergilian Hades, Tartaros resounds with thunder just at the moment Orpheus turns to his wife and breaks the divine command.[20]

It is clear from the frame story in which Vergil sets the account of Orpheus that however sympathetic he is to Orpheus, he believes that mankind must learn to make wiser choices.[21] For he shows that what the tragically failing lover does not do, the god-man Aristaeus will: be steadfast, obey, conquer, and so bring life and not death to himself and others. As Orpheus represents tragic man, Aristaeus represents potentially triumphant man. The Vergilian gods have not doomed Orpheus (he has doomed himself), for there is good fortune, favor, and ultimately salvation, not only for Aristaeus, but for his fellow men. Through him, the archetypal beekeeper and genius for the Vergilian farmer, the means to regenerate lost hives becomes known to man. Aristaeus obviously is for Vergil the greater man, the heroic god-man who redeems his fellows from tragedy; he is the symbol of hope for the future and promise of regeneration. It is not hard to see why the frame of the Orpheus episode, as well as the episode itself, held meaning for Milton, who could adapt its non-Christian symbols to his Christian design. As Orpheus contrasts with Aristaeus as man to god-man, so Adam looks to the second Adam, Christ, the "greater man" who comes to "restore us, and regain the blissful Seat" (1.4–5). The Son will lay down his life for love of man, triumphantly effecting the release from death that Adam with his passion-motivated sacrifice could only parodically and ineffectively attempt. Like Aristaeus, Christ, as Milton recounts in the final book of *Paradise Lost*, will bring life out of death. Hence Aristaeus' victory over death was for Milton the non-Christian symbol for the ultimate regeneration that he as a Christian poet made the theme of his epic. Aristaeus' patience during trial also has meaning for the depiction of Christ in Milton's other epic, *Paradise Regained*; the successful resistance of evil is, after all, a prime georgic virtue.

III

Because he recognized the many ways in which the *Georgics* involved themes and characters that were meaningful to his own "georgic" epic, Milton no doubt felt a special affinity with Vergil, for he adopts as his own the confession the Latin poet makes in the course of the *Georgics* about his relationship with the Muses and his hopes and fears for himself as a poet. Milton too had hitherto been, like Vergil, a poet of nature; he too had had epic aspirations. Twice before, when he wrote in his poetry about poetic plans, he had employed Vergil's "georgic voice": to ask in *Ad Patrem* that the Muses raise his strain to a higher pitch, and to request in *Epitaphium Damonis* that life enough remain to him to write his poetry. His words in the latter, *O mihi tum si vita supersit* (168), are almost a direct citation of Vergil's *modo vita supersit* (G. 3.10). In *Paradise Lost* 3, when he reflects once more on his poetic vocation, it is the modest words of the *Georgics* that sound in his memory. At the end of book 2 Vergil expresses the hope that because of his great love of the Muses they will through their power open the secrets of nature to him:

Me vero primum dulces ante omnia Musae,
quarum sacra fero ingenti percussus amore,
accipiant caelique vias et sidera monstrent,
defectus solis varios lunaeque labores.

(2.475–8)

First, before all, may the sweet Muses, whose sacred emblems I bear, struck with great love, accept me in truth, and show me the pathways of heaven and the stars, the several eclipses of the sun and the labors of the moon.

Yet, despite these high hopes, he doubts his human resources and fears that the cold blood about his heart (*frigidus . . . circum praecordia sanguis*, 484) may bar his way and keep him lowly and inglorious. If so, he is content to remain the humble lover of stream and valley. Vergil's dedication, as well as his hopes and fears, apparently spoke deeply to Milton. He declares that he is a lover of the countryside and a servant of the Muses, one who ceases not "to wander where the Muses haunt / Clear spring, or shady grove, or sunny hill, / Smit with the love of sacred song" (3.27–9). Even while voicing a preference for the songs of Sion, it is Vergil's lines and words, *ingenti percussus amore*, nor at this point scripture that he quotes, making, as Douglas Bush observed, pagan utterance reinforce his Christian motives.[22] Vergil's hopes that the Muses will reveal to him the secrets of nature are also on Milton's lip as he prays that he may "see and tell / Of things invisible to mortal sight" (3.54–5). He also shares Vergil's fear that personal limitations may somehow prevent him from fulfilling his epic plans:

> higher argument
> Remains, sufficient of itself to raise
> That name, unless an age too late, or cold
> Climate, or years damp my intended wing.
>
> (9.42–5)

In more adventurous moods, the confident plans that Vergil and Milton voice for a future epic belie fears and dismissals. At the beginning of *Georgics* 3, Vergil tells that he will venture on a poetic theme that will exalt him:

> temptanda via est, qua me quoque possim
> tollere humo victorque virum volitare per ora.
> primus ego in patriam mecum, modo vita supersit,
> Aonio rediens decucam vertice Musas;
> primus Idumaeas referam tibi, Mantua, palmas,
> et viridi in campo templum de marmore ponam
> propter aquam, tardis ingens ubi flexibus errat
> Mincius et tenera praetexit harundine ripas.
>
> (3.8–15)

> I must attempt a path by which I also can exalt myself from the earth and, a victor, fly on the lips of men; first, if life enough remains, returning to my country, I shall be the first to bring back the Muses from the peaks of Aonia; first to restore to you, Mantua, Idumaean palms and build in the green fields a marble temple beside the water, where the broad Mincius wanders in slow windings and adorns its banks with slender reeds.

Vergil's ambition that his name fly on the lips of men and that he, an Italian, bring the Greek Muses to his country and erect there a marble temple on the bank of Mincius are appropiately epic aims that Milton in the various proems of *Paradise Lost* clearly espouses as his own. He invokes at the outset the aid of the Muse for his "adventurous song, / That with no middle flight intends to soar / Above the Aonian Mount" (1.13–15). He pursues "things unattempted yet in prose or rhyme" (16), convinced that his argument is "not less, but more heroic" than those of classical epic (9.14). Only his conviction that Christian poetry should celebrate themes more noble than Vergil's projected celebration of the victories of Caesar divides him from the Roman poet.

In recent years critics have suggested that Vergil had already moved with the *Georgics* into the realm of semi-epic, for its themes and design, though on a smaller scale, are already those of epic, and its philosophical passages presage those in the *Aeneid*. Milton, I believe, recognized the epic potential of the *Georgics* and valued it precisely because it spoke of the dignity of the rustic and humble in terms that could be adapted to heroic design. He may have recognized too that Vergil himself was more at home with the rural Muses and the celebration of simple good than with martial polemics. Milton in principle could appreciate georgic simplicity in *Paradise Lost*, for therein he most highly praises the virtue that "by small" accomplishes "great things, by things deemed weak / Subverting wordly strong" (12.566–8). In the *Georgics* Vergil first tries his epic tones and under the guise of speaking of agricultural lore discourses on elemental themes that touch all human beings. Hence, this rural masterpiece has become the marble temple which, beside the wandering Mincius, contains secrets for future epic poets to attend to.

Notes

1. For its influence on *L'Allegro* and *Il Penseroso*, see Sara Ruth Watson, "Milton's Ideal Day: Its Development as a Pastoral Theme," *PMLA* 57 (1942): 404–20; for the influence of the *Georgics* on *Paradise Regained*, see Louis L. Martz, *The Paradise Within* (New Haven: Yale University Press, 1964), p. 175, and *Poet of Exile* (New Haven: Yale University Press, 1980), pp. 293–304; see also Andrew V. Ettin, "Milton, T.S. Eliot, and the Virgilian Vision: Some Versions of Georgic," *Genre* 10 (1977): 233–58; Anthony Low, "Milton, *Paradise Regained*, and Georgic," *PMLA* 98 (March 1983): 152–69. Milton commends the *Georgics* in "Of Education," *Complete Prose Works* (New Haven: Yale University Press, 1959), 2:394–6.

2. A list of echoes from the *Georgics* is found in the index to the Columbia edition of Milton's *Works*, gen. ed. Frank Allen Patterson (New York, 1931–38); also see (listed under Vergil), Charles Grosvenor Osgood, *The Classical Mythology of Milton's English Poems* (New York: Henry Holt, 1900). See also notes to *Paradise Lost*, ed. Thomas Newton (London: C. Hitch & L. Hawes, 1757). Newton identifies and comments on classical echoes. He compares the "careful Plowman," who "doubting stands / Lest on the threshing floor his hopeful sheaves / Prove chaff (*PL* 4.983–5), with Vergil's careful farmer, who fears that instead of fruit he may find his hoped-for crop empty ears: *sed illos / exspectata seges vanis elusit avenis* (*G.* 1.225–6). Milton's description of the bees who "Pour forth their populous youth about the hive" (*PL* 1.770) Newton suggests comes from *Georgics* 4.21–22: *cum prima novi ducent examina reges / vere suo ludetque favis emissa iuventus* ("When the new kings lead out the first swarms; the spring being theirs, the youth play, sent forth from the hive"). Translations are mine, unless otherwise indicated. Quotations from Milton's poetry are cited by book and line number from *The Poems of John Milton*, ed. John Carey and Alastair Fowler (London: Longman, 1968).

3. John R. Knott, *Milton's Pastoral Vision* (Chicago: University of Chicago Press, 1971), groups georgic and pastoral influences on *Paradise Lost*; Dennis Burden, *The Logical Epic* (London: Routledge and Kegan Paul, 1967), argues the importance of work (a typical georgic activity) in the garden. Recently, however, Anthony Low has suggested that *Paradise Lost* reflects "a broad general movement from pastoral to georgic." He sees angels and men in heaven and on earth enjoying until they sin a pastoral ease, but afterwards with the war in heaven and the fall entering the hard georgic world (Low, pp. 156–8).

4. The vast majority of echoes from the *Aeneid* occur in books 1 and 2 (the description of Hell) and in 5 and 6 (the description of the war in Heaven). Robert M. Boltwood considers some of these parallels in "Turnus and Satan as Epic Villains," *CJ* 47 (1952): 183-6.

5. Friedrich Klingner, *Virgil Georgics* (Zurich: Artemis Verlag, 1963); L.P. Wilkinson, *The Georgics of Virgil* (Cambridge: Cambridge University Press, 1969); Brooks Otis, "The Georgics," *Virgil, A Study in Civilized Poetry* (Oxford: Clarendon Press, 1964). Also see two recent books on the *Georgics*: Michael C.J. Putnam, *Virgil's Poem of the Earth: Studies in the Georgics* (Princeton: Princeton University Press, 1979); Gary B. Miles, *Virgil's Georgics: A New Interpretation* (Berkeley: University of California Press, 1980).

6. Milton names Astraea in "On the Death of a Fair Infant" (52-4) and alludes to her in "On the Morning of Christ's Nativity" (141-2).

7. Otis, pp. 166-7.

8. Knott, pp. 47, 89.

9. Wilkinson, p. 13.

10. Comparable spring passages occur in Ovid, Horace, and the Homeric Hymn to Apollo. Newton comments that "all the poets favor the opinion of the world's creation in the spring." He lists Vergil's passages in the *Georgics* with *Metamorphoses* 1.107: *Ver erat aeternum, placidique tepentibus auri / Mulcebant Zephyri*.

11. The translation is from C. Day Lewis, *The Eclogues, Georgics, and Aeneid of Virgil* (London: Oxford University Press, 1966). The passage usually cited for comparison with *PL* 4.268-81 is Spenser's description of the Bower of Bliss (*Faerie Queene* 2.12.52). Although Spenser catalogues a number of earthly paradises (among them, Eden), he does not make use of negative comparison or employ a grammatical construction that either echoes Vergil or looks forward to Milton. Milton may have known Abraham Fleming's translation of the *Georgics* (London: Thomas Woodcock, 1589) and his rendering of this and other passages.

12. Conti, *Mythologiae* 10, see Juno. Also see Newton's note on this passage (p. 297) and Fowler's (p. 642). Fleming's rendering of this passage offers both interpretations:

> Bicause th' almightie father (Ioue, or comfortable aire)
> Dooth then come downe into the lap or bosome of his wife
> Glad (Iuno, or cheerefull earth) with frutefull showres of raine:
> And he[t] great (Ioue) being ioyned with his body great to th' earth
> Doth nourish all the yoong . . . (p. 29)

Also see Peter Ramus' commentary on the *Georgics* (Frankfurt: A. Wechelus, 1584); Servius' and Ascenius' commentaries in such editions as that of the *Bucolics* and *Georgics* (Paris: I. Parvus, 1529); also the commentary by Hermann Torrentinus (Venice, 1499).

13. See Miles, pp. 4-64.

14. See John Milton, *Complete Poems and Major Prose*, ed. Merritt Y. Hughes (New York: Odyssey Press, 1957), pp. 431n, 433n. See also *Georgics* 1.62 and the note in T.E. Page, ed., *Bucolica et Georgica* (London: MacMillan and Co., 1898).

15. Milton directly echoes Vergil's description of penetrating cold in 1.93, *Boreas penetrabile frigus adurat* ("the piercing cold of the North wind burns"), when he describes how the parching air of Hell "Burns frore, and cold performs the effect of fire" (2.595).

16. Wilkinson, p. 99; Putnam, pp. 231-2; Miles, p. 223.

17. Newton argues that *Paradise Lost* 2.787-9, the description of the name "Death" resounding through Hell, is an imitation of Vergil's repetition of the name "Eurydice" on the lips of the dead Orpheus.

18. See especially *L'Allegro*, 145-50; *Il Penseroso*, 105-8; *Lycidas*, 58-63; *Paradise Lost* 7.32-8.

19. The slackness, horror, and loss of feeling that Adam experiences are typical Vergilian effects, as Fowler notes, citing several instances in the *Aeneid* (p. 907).

20. Once more a typical Vergilian effect. As Dido yields to Aeneas, the earth resounds and thunder moans (*Aen.* 4.167-8).
21. See Brooks Otis' discussion of the Orpheus account, p. 200ff. Putnam comments that Aristaeus survives when Orpheus does not because "he can balance his humanness with his immortal pedigree" (p. 321).
22. Douglas Bush, "Virgil and Milton," *CJ* 47 (1952): 180.

READING VERGIL IN THE 1690s

Steven N. Zwicker

The subject of this essay is not quite so general as my title suggests; what I am immediately concerned with is not the ways in which Vergil was read in the 1690s but the way in which Dryden read Vergil, translated Vergil, and might have wanted his translation to be read. The 1697 *Virgil* is a meditation on the language, culture, and politics of Vergil's poetry; it is as well a set of reflections on English politics in the aftermath of the Glorious Revolution. In the materials that Dryden attached to his edition and in the translation, the poet directly and obliquely argued the connections of Trojan, Roman, and English histories. The ways in which Dryden thought about Vergil and about his own task as translator can be approached by reading together the prefaces and postscripts, the plates and subscriptions, and the translation itself. What emerges from such an exercise is a sense of the continuities in theme and anxiety among the "texts" of this book, an understanding of the task and achievement of the translator as Dryden might have conceived them and as his readers in 1697 might have experienced them.

I

The *Dedication of the Aeneis* is one of the longest and least esteemed of Dryden's critical essays. By the poet's own admission, the *Dedication* is a rambling discourse without the shape or method of the work that he claims as his model (655).[1] Nor is shape the only problem. There are as well questions of Dryden's originality as a theorist, his handling of critical commonplaces, and the lengthy digressions. The remarks on heroic verse are often literal translations and transcriptions from the authorities, and what Dryden does develop as his own suggests idiosyncrasy rather than originality.[2] What, for example, are we to make of Dryden's remarks on the rival claims of Aeneas, Helenus, and Priamus to the Trojan crown (541), his assertion that Aeneas's sovereignty is an example of elective kingship (588), or the peculiar reading of book 4, which Dryden construes as Vergil's currying favor with a Roman public that despised Carthage and with a Roman emperor who had recently arranged his own divorce (1090 – 1140)?

But the *Dedication* is not wholly a patchwork of commonplaces and crotchets. The force and originality of this piece are not to be found in a new theory of the epic or an appreciation of Vergil's poetry, but in a reading of Vergil's politics that enables us to see how the translator understood and used the *Aeneid*. For Dryden, the business of Vergil's poem is politics in Augustan Rome, not the mythology of empire but political revolution. The ostensible subject of Vergil's poem is the myth of Aeneas, but for Dryden the identity of Aeneas is Augustus Caesar. The function of Vergil's poem is to celebrate Augustus Caesar, and its moral is political obedience. Vergil's intention was to be useful to his government, to argue the necessity of union and to confirm the Romans in their obedience to Caesar (470). And into this scheme Dryden fits the whole of the *Aeneid*, its most famous and frequently translated episodes, its minor characters, its central action, its mythology, its remaking of Homer, and the poem's conclusion.

Dryden's preoccupation with Vergil's politics was not of course disinterested history; he turns to Rome in the century of the Caesars in order to explore the bearing of ancient on contemporary affairs of state. England and Rome are the central analogues in the *Dedication*, and that equation is first suggested some few hundred lines into the essay at a point where Dryden begins a defense of the Roman poet: "I must now come closer to my present business: and not think of making more invasive Wars abroad, when like *Hannibal*, I am call'd back to the defence of my own Country. *Virgil* is attack'd by many Enemies: He has a whole Confederacy against him, and I must endeavour to defend him as well as I am able" (318). Vergil was the most esteemed of ancient poets, this epic revered as the culmination of a form that expressed for Renaissance poets and theorists the highest attainment of the literary intellect. The defensive posture follows not from Dryden's understanding of Vergil's condition but from the translator's sense of his own embattled circumstance. The letters that Dryden wrote in the 1690s convey the self-portrait sharply and poignantly.[3] By defending Vergil, Dryden undertakes a reading of the Roman poet and a justification of his own circumstance. The coincidence of poet and translator emerges from the large analogy that Dryden pursues through his description of politics in Augustan Rome: ". . . we are to consider [Virgil] as writing his Poem in a time when the Old Form of Government was subverted, and a new one just Established by *Octavius Caesar*: In effect by force of Arms, but seemingly by the Consent of the *Roman People*" (366). Dryden is describing Roman politics in the century of the Caesars, but the language suggests as exactly the Jacobite reading of the Glorious Revolution.

Stuart loyalists maintained that the Revolution was effected by force of arms, that it was an invasion conducted under the pretense of a protection of property and liberty, a subversion of the government that had altered fundamental laws and constitutions. Through the summary of Roman political history, Dryden outlines the course of politics in late seventeenth-century England:

> The Commonwealth had receiv'd a deadly Wound in the former Civil Wars betwixt *Marius* and *Sylla*. The Commons, while the first prevail'd, had almost shaken off the Yoke of the Nobility; and *Marius* and *Cinna*, like the Captains of the Mobb, under the specious Pretense of the Publick Good, and of doing Justice on the Oppressours of their Liberty, reveng'd themselves, without Form of Law, on their private Enemies. *Sylla*, in his turn, proscrib'd the Heads of the adverse Party: He too had nothing but Liberty and Reformation in his Mouth; (for the Cause of Religion is but a Modern Motive to Rebellion, invented by the Christian Priesthood, refining on the Heathen:) . . . Such was the Reformation of the Government by both Parties. The Senate and the Commons were the two Bases on which it stood; and the two Champions of either Faction, each destroy'd the Foundations of the other side: . . . So the Fabrique of consequence must fall betwixt them: And Tyranny must be built upon their Ruines. This comes of altering Fundamental Laws and Constitutions . . . . Thus the *Roman* People were grosly gull'd; twice or thrice over: and as often enslav'd in one Century, and under the same pretence of Reformation. (370)

The application to English political history from the civil wars through the end of the century would have been difficult for Dryden's audience to resist. Not only do key words and phrases in this passage argue those connections, but the whole scheme of political history as disguise fits both the conduct and perception of politics in the later seventeenth century.[4] Some among Dryden's audience would have resented or scorned his implications in this narrative, but all would have recognized the contemporary meaning of its language, the special fit of Roman history to English politics.

Roman history afforded general analogies with English politics; it allowed as well more daring particulars, and occasionally in the *Dedication* Dryden risks such particulars: "The last *Tarquin* was Expell'd justly, for

Overt—Acts of Tyranny, and Male-Administration; for such are the Conditions of an Elective Kingdom" (444). The application of this passage is obvious: the conflation of tyranny and elective kingship is an insult to William III and to his supporters. The satiric literature of the 1690s had made current the identification of William and Mary with Tarquin and Tullia,[5] those models of despotism and filial impiety; but the slur on elective kingship aims at constitutional rather than personal issues. The parliamentary convention of 1689 had scrupled so minutely over the language with which to describe James's departure from England to avoid two implications, that William's descent was an invasion and that his title was founded on election or conquest.[6] And the parliamentary bill for the exclusion of James, Duke of York, had been defeated in 1681 on the strength of the argument that such exclusion would turn the kingship into elective monarchy; none who supported William would have had his title hinged on so precarious a term.

Nor is Tarquin the only analogue for the English king. There are comparisons with Aeneas and Augustus, and a rather pointed contrast with Latinus, that paradigm of kingly legitimacy. The ways in which Aeneas and Augustus are used to think about William is one of the most complex issues in the *Dedication* and translation. Dryden's strategy is not to make either Aeneas or Augustus directly analogous with William but to present the ancient figures in a language that would argue the circumstances of William's kingship. Hence the long and peculiar passage on succession and title as they bear on Aeneas's claims to the Trojan office:

> *Aeneas* cou'd not pretend to be *Priam*'s Heir in a Lineal Succession: For *Anchises* the Heroe's Father, was only of the second Branch of the Royal Family: And *Helenus*, a son of *Priam*, was yet surviving, and might lawfully claim before him. It may be *Virgil* mentions him on that Account. Neither has he forgotten *Priamus*, in the Fifth of his *Aeneis*, the Son of *Polites*, youngest Son to *Priam*; who was slain by *Pyrrhus*, in the Second Book. *Aeneas* had only Married *Creusa*, *Priam*'s Daughter, and by her could have no Title, while any of the Male Issue were remaining. In this case, the Poet gave him the next Title, which is, that of an Elective King. (541)

Dryden has Vergil raise the subject of elective kingship so that he can scorn the legitimacy of William's rule and warn those who claim for the Dutchman the sanctity and rights of lineal descent that they have in fact sanctioned revolution and usurpation. The debate over the nature of William's title had not been settled in 1689; it was raised throughout his kingship, and with special force the year before the *Virgil* publication. The assassination plot of 1696 had caused parliament to vote an Association proclaiming loyalty to William III as rightful and lawful king.[7] But in the debate over the Association, even so late as 1696 and even in the face of the plot, members of parliament still scrupled over the title.

Dryden's Vergil depicts Aeneas's Trojan office as elective kingship so that Augustus Caesar might be instructed in the character and dangers of such a title. The analogy is two-fold: first, between the Vergilian models of elective kingship—Aeneas, Mezentius, and Tarquin—and William III; second, between the Roman emperor and the English king. The Vergilian models, pious and restrained in the person of Aeneas, but brutal and corrupt in the persons of Mezentius and Tarquin, demonstrate the extremes. Augustus Caesar, conqueror and despot, needs the instruction of Vergil's poem so that he might become the best of the bad lot to which he belongs. By arguing that Vergil draws Aeneas to the measure of Augustus Caesar, Dryden is free to raise the problems of Caesar's kingship as they are illustrated in Vergil's epic. The distortion is curious, but with William in mind we can see its point: "Our Poet, who all this while had *Augustus* in his Eye, had no desire he should seem to succeed by any right of Inheritance, deriv'd from *Julius Caesar*; such a Title being but one degree remov'd from Conquest. For what was introduc'd by force, by force may be remov'd" (553). In this complex arrangement of poetic models and historical figures, William falls somewhere between Aeneas and the worst examples, Mezentius and Tarquin. One assumes that Dryden found a greater affinity between Tarquin and William than between Aeneas and William, but perhaps the closest analogue is Caesar. The language in which Dryden casts Vergil's deliberation over the character of Aeneas's sovereignty and the nature of Caesar's rule is strikingly appropriate to the debate over the revolutionary settlement: under what conditions had William entered the country and by what rights did he now wield power? The whole of this problem is reflected in the translation, especially book 7, Aeneas's entry into Latium, where the steady shading of the language, the consistent impulse to render entry as conquest, can only be the translator brooding over the injustice and perhaps the inevitability of such conquest, of Latium by Aeneas and of England by William III.

The contemporary application of the whole discussion of legitimacy and sovereignty is sharpened by the introduction of Latinus:

> Our Author shews us another sort of Kingship in the Person of *Latinus*. He was descended from *Saturn*, and as I remember, in the Third Degree. He is describ'd a just and a gracious Prince; solicitous for the Welfare of his People, always Consulting with his Senate to promote the common Good. We find him at the head of them, when he enters into the Council-Hall. Speaking first, but still demanding their Advice, and steering by it as far as the Iniquity of

the Times wou'd suffer him. And this is the proper Character of a
King of Inheritance, who is born a Father of his Country. *Aeneas*,
tho' he Married the Heiress of the Crown, yet claim'd no Title to it
during the Life of his Father-in-Law. (561)

Perhaps the idea of Latinus as James II—gracious father to his people and
sage parliamentarian—would have roused the scorn of much of Dryden's
audience, but who could have missed the analogy between Aeneas and
William, the thrust of the end of this passage?

Not all contemporary issues are argued so openly as this. Some topics
are raised only by allusion and not pursued through extended analogy. But
we can hear the contemporary overtones in Dryden's handling of such
themes as ingratitude and constancy. Gratitude was a linch-pin of Stuart
politics,[8] and the language of Dryden's *Dedication* in 1697 conjures a
powerful political argument that takes meaning not only from the disloyalty
of those who raised arms against James II but from the whole history of
disloyalty to Stuart kings, above all from that highest crime of regicide
which gave particular force to this theme: "want of Constancy, and
Ingratitude after the last Favour, is a Crime that never will be forgiven"
(953). There are also glancing references to "dispensing powers." Dryden
treats this subject in purely literary terms, but none who heard the phrase
could ignore its political meaning, the long history of a struggle between
two Stuart kings and the truculent parliaments that were unwilling to have
their laws abrogated at will by kings bent on what parliament thought was
the destruction of the Protestant religion and the imposition of Catholic
slavery:[9] "Any thing might be allow'd to his Son *Virgil* on the account of his
other Merits; That being a Monarch he had a dispensing Power, and
pardon'd him . . . . To Moralize this Story, *Virgil* is the *Apollo*, who has this
Dispensing Power. His great Judgment made the Laws of Poetry, but he
never made himself a Slave to them" (1046). Vergil, like Apollo, could
supersede mechanical rules for the same reason that a "Monarch may
dispense with, or suspend his own Laws, when he finds it necessary to do
so; especially if those Laws are not altogether fundamental" (1080). And
similar reference is made to the coinage crisis under the guise of poetics:
"Words are not so easily Coyn'd as Money: And yet we see that the Credit
not only of Banks, but of Exchequers cracks, when little comes in, and
much goes out" (2105). The enormous expenditures that supported
William's land wars are clearly alluded to here and in the passage on the
"coining" of words (2167).[10] Taken individually, such references—and there
are more in the *Dedication*[11]—do not account for the political argument of
this preface; but seen in the context of the general analogy that Dryden
explores between ancient and contemporary politics, they become part of a
larger argument whose structure must occasionally be inferred, but whose
meaning cannot be in doubt.

II

But Vergil's text was more than an occasion for glancing reference to contemporary political topics, more than a vehicle for criticizing William III, more even than a way of running a commentary on the character of the Glorious Revolution. Dryden saw in Vergil an image of himself as civic poet: a man of letters sustaining and criticizing the mythology of empire, analyzing political issues, and praising and blaming those patrons, statesmen, and ideologues who shaped and enacted the affairs of state. Indeed, for Dryden politics and empire were always seen in terms of personality, and in what Dryden construed to be Vergil's practice of rewarding friends and punishing enemies[12] the translator saw or imposed his own powerful instincts as panegyrist and satirist. Vergil used his poem as the text for such allusion, but Dryden, who intended no continuous allegory by his translation, found another way of binding his contemporaries to Vergil. The whole problem of contemporary reference emerges most clearly in Dryden's discussion of book 5 in the *Dedication*:

> Neither were the great *Roman* Families which flourish'd in his time, less oblig'd by him than the Emperour. Your Lordship knows with what Address he makes mention of them, as Captains of Ships, or Leaders in the War; and even some of *Italian* Extraction are not forgotten. These are the single Stars which are sprinkled through the *Aeneis*: But there are whole Constellations of them in the Fifth Book. And I could not but take notice, when I Translated it, of some Favourite Families to which he gives the Victory, and awards the Prizes, in the Person of his Heroe, at the Funeral Games which were Celebrated in Honour of *Anchises*. I, Insist not on their Names: But am pleas'd to find the *Memmii* amongst them, deriv'd from *Mnestheus*, because *Lucretius* Dedicates to one of that Family, a Branch of which destroy'd *Corinth*. I likewise either found or form'd an Image to my self of the contrary kind; that those who lost the Prizes, were such as had disoblig'd the Poet, or were in disgrace with *Augustus*, or Enemies to *Mecenas*: And this was the Poetical Revenge he took. For *genus irritabile Vatum*, as *Horace* says. When a Poet is throughly provok'd, he will do himself Justice, however dear it cost him, *Animamque, in Vulnere ponit.* I think these are not bare Imaginations of my own, though I find no trace of them in the Commentatours: But one Poet may judge of another by himself. The Vengeance we defer, is not forgotten. (496)

There can be no question of the personal significance of this issue for the translator. Praise and blame were central imaginative modes for Dryden; and whether or not he simply imagines them in Vergil, the very discovery or imposition of likeness argues their significance in the translation and their importance for understanding the role of the plates and subscriptions in Dryden's book. These plates allowed Dryden the play of contemporary reference which he insisted that Vergil had once enjoyed.

Little is known of this aspect of the 1697 *Virgil*.[13] What I offer is speculation, but sufficiently congruent with Dryden's reading of book 5 in the *Dedication* and with the character of the plates and subscriptions themselves to justify exploration. The publication of books by subscription was not new in 1697.[14] Since early in the century, scientific texts had been issued by subscription, and by midcentury some entrepreneurs were publishing books by subscription for profit. Chief among them was John Ogilby, who had himself translated Vergil in 1649 and issued this translation in 1654 in folio with engravings and subscriptions from a number of important royalists.[15] In the last two decades of the century, the number of subscription books grew considerably. The most important literary publication by subscription before the *Virgil* was a 1688 edition of *Paradise Lost* which Tonson published with great commercial success. In the Milton, subscribers are listed at the front; in the *Virgil*, a two-guinea pledge bought the subscriber a position in such an alphabetical list, and a five-guinea subscription entitled the patron to have his name and crest attached to one of the 101 plates in the book. The plates of the 1697 *Virgil* are those originally engraved for Ogilby, but with two modifications: the consistent hooking of Aeneas's nose so that the hero bore a likeness to William III— Tonson's idea of a compliment[16]—and the addition of line numbers to the lower portion of the plate.

From correspondence between Dryden and Tonson, we know that both poet and publisher sought subscribers for the project, but we do not know which of the two sought specific subscribers nor who matched plate with patron.[17] What we can see is that in a number of instances the fit of plate and text to subscriber clearly argues the function of the plate and text as commentary on the subscription. The overlapping ties of friendship, patronage, and politics allow us to speculate on where Dryden may have determined the assignment of the subscription.

There are, to begin with, some cases in which the plate obviously joins with the text to compliment a patron. In the "Postscript" to the *Aeneid*, Dryden praises the generosity of William Bowyer, at whose country estate he had translated parts of the *Georgics* and *Aeneid*. The second Georgic, Vergil's great praise of country life, is prefaced with a pastoral scene dedicated to Bowyer.[18] The third plate of this Georgic, attached to the lines, "I teach thee next the diff'ring Soils to know; / The light for Vines, the heavyer for the Plough," is dedicated to George London, who was "his Majesty's gardiner." Anthony Henley, wit and politician, known for his generous patronage, is given the lavish picnic in book 7 of the *Aeneid*;[19]

George Stepney, amateur poet, member of Lord Dorset's circle and diplomat and ambassador to the Germanies, is given the plate illustrating *Aeneid* 7.290, Ilioneus's embassy to Latinus; and the plate for *Pastoral 5*, illustrating the apotheosis of Daphnis, is dedicated to James Bertie, Earl of Abingdon, clearly a reminiscence of the themes of *Eleonora*, Dryden's poem commemorating the death and celebrating the apotheosis of Bertie's wife in 1692.

In addition to plates of individual compliment, there is a group of engravings with altars, sacrifices, and divining scenes which are dedicated to Roman Catholics:[20] the most interesting of such assignments is the plate dedicated to James Cecil, Earl of Salisbury. His plate depicts Laocoon struggling with serpents to save his children. In 1697 the current earl was the six-year-old James Cecil, son of James, fourth Earl of Salisbury, who had turned Catholic in 1688, plotted against William, and was jailed in the Tower of London until 1692, shortly before his death. Perhaps the plate is intended as a memorial to Salisbury, Catholic and Jacobite, wrestling with the fates on behalf of his child. Although the facts of Salisbury's life might be construed in other terms, the commemorative design of the plate seems plausible given Dryden's religion and politics.[21] More complex are those plates in which both political and personal compliment are paid. One of the most interesting of these is the dedication of the third plate in the *Pastorals* to Charles Sackville, Earl of Dorset, longtime patron and friend of Dryden. Dorset was the man to whom Dryden had dedicated the *Essay on Dramatic Poesy* (1668) and the *Discourse Concerning Satire* (1697). In both, Dorset is cast as arbiter of literary taste. In the Pastoral to which his subscription is fixed, Dorset can be understood as Palemon, the figure called to judge the singing contest of Damaetas and Menalcas. The assignment echoes Dorset's role as Eugenius in the *Essay*, and is neatly folded into the assignment of the next plate to Lord Buckhurst, Dorset's nine-year-old son. Vergil dedicated his fourth Pastoral to Pollio—consul, patron, and critic—and in the assignment to Buckhurst, Dryden suggests that the child is Salonius and the father Pollio, thus extending the compliment of the earlier plate. Dorset is the generous patron imagined now as arbiter of taste and civic personality. Moreover, Dorset and Buckhurst as Pollio and Salonius allow Dryden to become Vergil to this generous patron and man of great affairs. Finally, in book 7 of the *Aeneid*, the plate that illustrates the wounding of Sylvia's doe is dedicated to Mary Sackville, Dorset's daughter. In this dedication, Mary Sackville is the tender-hearted Latian maid and Dorset becomes "*Tyrrheus*, chief Ranger to the *Latian* King" (676), hence loyal retainer of Stuart monarchy, an allusion to a happier past that Dryden shared with Dorset. The use of plates to compliment patrons and reward friends is the most obvious allusive facet of the subscription list, a way for the translator to see

Vergil's themes of loyalty, virtue, and friendship expressed in his own social
and political world, and the number of such complimentary assignments is
large. I have not touched on the assignment of plates depicting a valiant
though doomed Turnus to Ailesbury (*Aeneid* 8.1) and Ormond (*Aeneid*
12.1360), perhaps Dryden's valediction to a noble though fated cause. But
compliment was not the only function of these plates. Dryden claims that
Vergil's poem not only rewarded friends but also punished enemies. Indeed
Dryden insists on this aspect of Vergil's poem though he confesses
singularity in that perception: "I think these are not bare Imaginations of
my own, though I find no trace of them in the Commentatours" (513). The
subscription assignments afforded Dryden the occasion to act on the same
impulse, to fit plates to subscribers so that the assignment might function
ironically or derisively. Such cases are more difficult to establish than the
complimentary assignments because the ironic mode had of necessity to
function more obliquely. Dryden understood that he would have had to
proceed with caution in this way, but he also insisted on the compulsion:
"When a Poet is throughly provok'd, he will do himself Justice, however
dear it cost him" (512).We do not know what, if anything, such assignments
might have cost Dryden, but it is inviting to speculate on Sir Robert
Howard's response to the plate which his five-guinea subscription had
bought. A recent biography of Howard argues that old enmities between
the poet and his brother-in-law had been resolved in the 1690s.[22] But one
wonders with Dryden if personal resentments were ever completely
abandoned, and what effect Howard's quite vocal role in the Convention
Parliament might have had on Dryden's feelings. Howard was a member of
the parliament meeting in 1689, and in its proceedings his voice is heard
stridently denouncing James II and arguing in the most extreme and
insulting language that James had abdicated the throne and that William
rightfully succeeded him as king.[23] It seems unlikely that Dryden would
have been wholly ignorant either of such opinions or of the vehemence with
which they were held or expressed.

　　Howard's subscription resulted in the most personally insulting of the
assignments. The plate which appears in book 10 and is referred to in line
450, depicts the battle of Aeneas with Cydon's seven brothers:

　　Then wretched *Cydon* had receiv'd his Doom,
　　Who courted *Clytius* in his beardless Bloom,
　　And sought with lust obscene polluted Joys:
　　The *Trojan* Sword had cur'd his love of Boys,
　　Had not his sev'n bold Brethren stop'd the Course
　　Of the fierce Champion, with united Force.

　　　　　　　　　　　　　　　　　　　　　(10.449–54)

Not only is the assignment damaging and insulting in the way it focuses the plate and hence the figure of Howard on Cydon, but Dryden's translation coarsens that figure, makes specific and harsh a condemnation which in Vergil is certainly oblique. Vergil's discreet *sequeris Clytium infelix, nova gaudia Cydon* (325 "the unhappy Cydon follows a new love")[24] becomes, in Dryden's translation, harsher and more direct; and Dryden's next line (452) makes quite explicit the proposed castration of the figure. We don't know that Dryden translated these lines with Howard in mind, nor have we evidence that Dryden made the assignment. But the relations between Dryden and Howard suggest that Dryden's "vengeance deferred" has not been forgotten in this plate.

Personal insult was not of course the only derisive use to which the plates were put; as in the case of complimentary assignment, those plates which could be treated in political terms offered Dryden a way of thinking about contemporary politics in relation to his great task as translator. An exemplary case is the assignment to Henry Viscount Sydney of the first plate of book 7 which depicts Janus, keeper of the gate.[25] The subject of this book is Aeneas's entry into Latium; that and such subsidiary themes as lineage, succession, and conquest which are developed through the book as a whole allowed Dryden to read Vergil very closely here as a commentary on the politics of the Glorious Revolution. On the translation of the book I shall comment shortly; but the assignment of the initial plate to Sydney we might consider in the light of these facts of Sydney's political career: that he was one of the seven men who signed the invitation to William, that the invitation was in his own hand, that he joined William in Holland before the invasion, that he was one of the few Englishmen whom William trusted over the whole of his administration, and that he was a politician famed as "the great wheel on whom the revolution turned."[26] The only other subscriber who signed the invitation to William, Charles Talbot, Duke of Shrewsbury, is given the first plate to book 11, which depicts the head and armor of the dead Mezentius, Vergil's atheist and tyrant ("curs'd *Mezentius*, in a fatal Hour, / Assum'd the Crown, with Arbitrary Pow'r," 8.630). In the plate that opens book 7, Sydney is linked with Janus, who in Vergil's language is simply *bifrontis*; for Dryden, he is "ancient *Janus*, with his double Face, / And Bunch of Keys, the Porter of the place" (245). The details of key and office Dryden seems to have invented; they appear in neither the Lauderdale nor the Ogilby translations.[27] But if Dryden conceived of Sydney in terms of his political career, then to characterize him as keeper of the gate certainly sharpens our perception of his role in the Revolution. Sydney's titles as Major General of the Ordinance and Warden of the Cinque Ports, both recorded in the legend to the subscription, allow a blameless meaning for Dryden's details, but they do not deny the suggestive and damaging association of Sydney and Janus as wardens who have betrayed the palace to foreign guests. Swift wrote of Sydney in the 1690s, "he was an old vitious illiterate Rake without any sense of Truth or Honor."[28]

III

Thus far I have attempted to delineate a poetics of translation in a specific political circumstance, to show the bearing that Vergil's Roman history might be seen to have on English political life in the later seventeenth century, and to suggest how Dryden's book as a whole can be understood as an interpretation of Vergil. Central to my thesis about translation as commentary is of course the translation itself. And the evidence here is striking. Not only is there a steady shading of the translation, a heightening of political themes and topics throughout the poem, but at crucial points where the subject matter of Vergil's poem could be brought directly to bear on contemporary political issues Dryden's attention to that contemporaneity is unfailing.

To make a translation is not of course to write an allegory, but for Dryden the contemporary point of reference must have pressed frequently near the text. Even in what is taken to be the most hurried of his jobs, the translation of book 1 of Tacitus's *Annals*, a comparison of Latin, French and English texts reveals some striking instances where Dryden is rethinking Tacitus so that the *Annals* reflect political issues of special concern to him in the 1690s.[29] In translating Vergil, a task which Dryden invests with enormous personal and professional significance, there can be no doubt of the steady pressure that his own political concerns exerted on the rendering of this political epic.

While there is hardly space in this essay to consider the whole of the *Virgil*, book 7 with its attention to foreign settlement, lineal descent, and the role of fate in politics, must have been of special interest to Dryden. The book opens with a memorial to Caieta, a name fixed to the shore of the bay where Aeneas anchors his ship before entering Latium:

> Tu quoque litoribus nostris, Aeneia nutrix,
> Aeternam moriens famam, Caieta, dedisti
> Et nunc servat honos sedem tuus; ossaque nomen
> Hesperia in magna, si qua est ea gloria, signat.
>
> (*Aen.* 7.1–4)[30]

In Dryden's translation there is a slight departure in the last line quoted, and this turn points a theme important to the translation as a whole and recurrent in Dryden's late poetry. Vergil invokes Caieta as a "name" giving deathless fame to the shore, if there is any glory at all after death. Dryden renders the passage:

> And thou, O Matron of Immortal Fame!
> Here Dying, to the Shore has left thy Name:
> *Cajeta* still the place is call'd from thee,
> The Nurse of great *Aeneas* Infancy.
> Here rest thy Bones in rich *Hesperia*'s Plains,
> Thy Name ('tis all a Ghost can have) remains.
>
> (7.1–6)

The initial line is invention and the first rhyme coupling declares Dryden's theme, but the turn in line 6 is particularly interesting since it reveals Dryden thinking directly on Vergil's language. Vergil's construction is conditional; Dryden's is declarative. The change is slight, but not so the glory that attaches to name, a glory underscored by Dryden's insertion of "still" in line 3, and a glory that had come to have considerable force for Dryden in the 1690s. In his work of these years there appears a constellation of remarks on name.[31] The variations on this theme often appear in obvious places, dedications to those great families still able or willing to oblige the poet, where the celebration of name is a standard panegyric topic. But now it seems to have a special urgency and is invariably linked to succession and lineal descent. Name embodies the virtues of family, virtues heritable, passed from one generation to the next as estates, as indeed crowns, ought to be passed. But name takes a new precedence over estate and over office. Of course place and name are not always antipodal, but when Dryden now contemplates these themes, name is the bulwark against the vagaries of fortune, it has a substance beyond anything with which it had previously been invested.[32] A more obvious turn from Vergil's language and a more explicitly political theme emerges at the close of the prophecy concerning Lavinia:

> Id vero horrendum ac visu mirabile ferri.
> Namque fore illustrem fama fatisque canebant
> Ipsam, sed populo magnum portendere bellum.
>
> (*Aen* 7.78–80)

What Dryden does with these lines is to turn war into political revolution:

> The Nymph who scatters flaming Fires around,
> Shall shine with Honour, shall herself be crown'd:
> But, caus'd by her irrevocable Fate,
> War shall the Country waste, and change the State.
>
> (117–20)

The crown of line 118 is a new and suggestive detail, but the significant change is the revolution of line 120. Vergil prophesies war, *magnum bellum*; Dryden prophesies waste and "change of State." The transformation picks up a slight change at line 103, where Vergil's *externum ... virum* (68-9), a stranger, becomes Dryden's "foreign Prince." In Vergil this stranger rules in a lofty citadel, *et summa dominarier arce*; in Dryden, "The Town he conquers, and the Tow'r commands" (Vergil 70, Dryden 106). The first half line draws our attention: Dryden was not running a parallel between historical events but rather turning Vergil toward the 1690s, and the congruence is not left at the level of implication. Aeneas and William are foreign princes, fated to rule, conquerors and revolutionaries, and the introduction of such detail could not have been adventitious.

At line 253, Vergil's Latinus dwells upon marriage rites, *thalamo*; Dryden has him ponder "Succession, Empire, and his Daughter's Fate" (346). The extension is deliberate, the preoccupation again political, and the issue succession. And Juno's dark prophecy of Trojan and Rutulian blood for Lavinia's dowry (Vergil, 318) is similarly extended:

> With Blood the dear Alliance shall be bought;
> And both the People near Destruction brought.
> So shall the Son-in-Law, and Father join,
> With Ruin, War, and Waste of either Line.
>
> (438-41)

What in Vergil is suggestion Dryden makes particular and disastrous. Amata's foreign heir in Vergil (*gener externa ... de gente*, 7.367) becomes Dryden's "usurper" (595). What is passive in Vergil becomes active in translation; what is fate in Vergil and hence inscrutable Dryden turns to conquest, to personal ambition, to political revolution. Similar themes are explored in other books, and Dryden's preoccupations as translator are those that he reveals in book 7. At the opening of book 10, Venus and Juno rehearse the causes and character of the war that now unfolds between Trojans and Rutulians. Again, Trojan entry is made to conjure the image of invasion and conquest. In part the translation is exact; but Dryden also invents and at points shades the political idiom to accommodate his own concerns with the injustice of the Revolution: "Hard and unjust indeed, for Men to draw / Their native Air, nor take a foreign Law." (10.114-15). The tone is resentful and xenophobic; the language has no counterpart in Vergil. Nor does the following: "Realms not your own, among your Clans divide" (120). Dryden is translating *avertere prada* (78), to carry off plunder, with the latter phrase; and the closing lines of this passage draw the *Aeneid* close to the charges laid against the expanding European war which Dryden and others claimed was draining the English treasure in an endless European adventure, resulting moreover in the awards of lavish grants and estates to foreigners. The topics derive from Vergil, but the particular thrust of the language is Dryden's own:

> You think it hard, the Latians shou'd destroy
> With Swords your *Trojans*, and with Fires your *Troy*:
> Hard and unjust indeed, for Men to draw
> Their Native Air, nor take a foreign Law:
> That *Turnus* is permitted still to live,
> To whom his Birth a God and Goddess give:
> But yet 'tis just and lawful for your Line,
> To drive their Fields, and Force with Fraud to join.
> Realms, not your own, among your Clans divide,
> And from the Bridegroom tear the promis'd Bride:
> Petition, while you publick Arms prepare;
> Pretend a Peace, and yet provoke a War.
>
> (112–23)

The same issues of legitimacy and conquest are explored at the opening of book 6, where Dryden makes significant changes as Aeneas ponders his fate and begs of the gods something like peaceful retirement:

> Tuque, ô sanctissima vates
> Praescia venturi: da (non indebita posco
> Regna meis fatis) Latio considere Teucros,
> Errantesque Deos, agitataque numina Trojae.
>
> (6.65–8)

Dryden translates these lines:

> And thou, O sacred Maid, inspir'd to see
> Th' Event of things in dark Futurity;
> Give me, what Heav'n has promis'd to my Fate,
> To conquer and command the *Latian* State:
> To fix my wand'ring Gods; and find a place
> For the long Exiles of the *Trojan* Race.
>
> (6.100–105)

Vergil's Aeneas begs shelter and settlement; he specifically rejects empire. Dryden's Aeneas would "conquer and command the *Latian* State." Vergil's qualifications are ignored, and the whole passage is rendered in a language charged with the political currents of the 1690s. These are not random turns in the translation, but a consistent way of seeing Aeneas's entry as conquest and violation.

At the close of book 6, Dryden takes another such occasion to sharpen the political and topical meaning of Vergil's poem. In the underworld, Aeneas sees the cheats and frauds who violate domestic and civic bonds, abuse clients, and profane sacred rites:

> Hic quibus invisi fratres, dum vita manebat,
> Pulsatusve parens, & fraus innexa clienti;
> Aut quis divitiis soli incubuêre repertis,
> Nec partem posuêre suis, quae maxima turba est;
> Quique ob adulterium caesi, quique arma secuti
> Impia, nec veriti dominorum fallere dextras:
> Inclusi poenam expectant.
>
> (608–14)

The passage offered Dryden an interesting temptation:

> Then they, who Brothers better Claim disown,
> Expel their Parents, and usurp the Throne;
> Defraud their Clients, and to Lucre sold,
> Sit brooding on unprofitable Gold:
> Who dare not give, and ev'n refuse to lend
> To their poor Kindred, or a wanting Friend:
> Vast is the Throng of these.
>
> (824–30)

Dryden must have been thinking directly on the royal family at the beginning of this passage. At each juncture Dryden turns the language so that the application is exact. Vergil's brothers suffered hatred, Dryden's brother is defrauded of a claim; Vergil's parent is beaten, Dryden's parents are expelled; and the half-line at 826, the usurpation of the throne which focuses the first two violations, is Dryden's invention. The reshaping of the lines is so obvious here that we seem to be dealing not with Dryden's political anxieties simply pushing forward in the act of translating, but with a specific and sharp rebuke being administered by clear changes in Vergil's language. Nor is this quite all. Vergil's misers brood over their wealth and neglect to lay aside part for their own. Dryden's misers neither give nor lend, denying both friend and family. Does the poet imagine his own neglect in these lines? The linking of royal and personal misfortune is not beyond the poet, and while the suggestion of his own misfortune is oblique it is also characteristic.[33]

Conquest, imposition, violation, and usurpation are steady themes in Dryden's translation; and it is a consistent act of the translator to use such language in rendering passages which in Vergil seem neutral or only obliquely political. Nor of course is Dryden's impulse to translate one set of terms with another limited to the transformation of entry into conquest. There are a number of related themes and to grasp their interconnections we would need to examine the whole translation at length, but a striking example that complements those we have looked at is Dryden's handling of the concept of fate.

The role of fate in the disposition of governments was much debated after the Glorious Revolution.[34] As in the Engagement Controversy, men were both privately and publicly concerned with discovering or disputing those sanctions that allowed the disavowal of sacred oaths and the swearing of loyalty to a new regime. Those who favored a providential view of the Glorious Revolution, a view which allowed them to abjure oaths of nonresistance and loyalty to the person and government of James II, argued that the revolution was providential, that indeed William of Orange had been swept across the channel by a Protestant wind. But Jacobites and nonjurors scorned such an argument; common theft could also be justified by this logic. And though Jacobites acknowledged the turn of fortune's wheel, they refused to understand the Revolution as the design of heaven. In Dryden's translation it is hardly surprising that we should experience Vergil's gods in somber terms. The neutral future, the promised day, the destined land, these and a number of other of Vergilian topoi are consistently darkened and undercut. We are made to feel the active malignance of gods who in Vergil are detached or indifferent. Such language as "dark futurity," "fate's irrevocable doom," and "fatal place of rest" shapes our perception of the fates in Dryden's translation. Throughout, we experience Dryden's response to the idea of gods as political agency, and on such a subject it is not surprising that the temperament is melancholy. The language suggests not so much the construct of historical analogy through which Dryden might intend to parallel the furies in English and Roman politics, but rather a general and philosophical point of view that I think could hardly be detained from expression. Here is Aeneas from book 2 contemplating the fall of Troy:

Apparent dirae facies, inimicaque Trojae
Numina magna Deum.
Tum vero omne mihi visum considere in ignes
Illium, & ex imo verti Neptunia Troja.
Ac veluti summis antiquam in montibus ornum
Cum ferro accisam crebrisque bipennibus instant
Eruere agricolae certatim; illa usque minatur,
Et tremefacta comam concusso vertice nutat:
Vulneribus donec paulatim evicta, supremum
Congemuit, traxitque jugis avulsa ruinam.   (622–31)

And here is Dryden's version of this scene:

I look'd, I listen'd; dreadful Sounds I hear;
And the dire Forms of hostile Gods appear.
Troy sunk in Flames I saw, nor could prevent;
and *Ilium* from its old Foundations rent.
Rent like a Mountain Ash, which dar'd the Winds;
And stood the sturdy Stroaks of lab'ring Hinds:
About the Roots the cruel Ax resounds,
The Stumps are pierc'd, with oft repeated Wounds.
The War is felt on high, the nodding Crown
Now threats a Fall, and throws the leafy Honours down.
To their united Force it yields, though late;
And mourns with mortal Groans th' approaching Fate:
The Roots no more their upper load sustain;
But down she falls, and spreads a ruin thro' the Plain.

(842–55)

There are a number of small, quite delicate changes here, and the shifts of emphasis and slight additional generalizations have the effect of enlarging Vergil's scene. Dryden acknowledges the way in which Vergil uses the fall of the ash as an emblem for the destruction of Troy,[35] but he also uses Vergil's simile to suggest the fate of Stuart monarchy, the fall of that "nodding Crown" whose demise "spreads a ruin thro' the Plain." The vocabulary in this scene is tinged with the fate of Stuart monarchy.

Such a tempering of language is characteristic of the translation as a whole, overt when Vergil's poem touches such subjects as conquest and lineage, subtler and less pressing when Dryden treats the gods or the bonds of oath and nature. Here political and ideological preoccupations are suggested by a slight movement of language toward the translator's own concerns. What is striking about the political axis along which this translation was made is the diversity of tone which it allowed. At this point in his career Dryden's intimacy with, indeed possession of, Vergil's text was so complete and so powerful that the movement of Vergil's poem into English came at a constantly changing pace and over a very broad spectrum of suggestion, implication, and argument.

Near the close of the *Dedication*, Dryden wrote of the language of his translation, "I carry not out the Treasure of the Nation, which is never to return: but what I bring from *Italy*, I spend in *England*: Here it remains, and here it circulates; for if the Coyn be good, it will pass from one hand to another." The remark suggests a contrast between the literally debased currency of the 1690s and Dryden's "coining," which, I suspect, he knew would be valued and endure; but the real contrast that Dryden is after is not wholly contained by the metaphor. What he wants to juxtapose is king and poet, warfare and translation. This poem reverses the history of luxury and decline: Dryden's trade with the ancients and moderns enriches England; King William's wars end in waste and destruction. The suggestion is bold but, under the screen of this translation, not unlikely for Dryden to have made.

There is something touching if incongruous about the circumstances and the daring of the whole project. When Dryden began to translate the works of Vergil, he had been ejected from the laureateship, had converted to Roman Catholicism, and had maintained what can only seem to us a preposterous loyalty to James II; for these principles he had lost favor and patronage. He was a man precarious in his safety, his health, and his finances, dependent on the leavings of a few minor gentry and loyal patrons who bore him no grudge in what he himself perceived as rather shabby circumstances. And yet he now chose to make an English *Virgil*, to translate a poem of empire and sublimity, not perhaps the most likely enterprise for this old age. Dryden took up the translation because he needed money; but he also knew that an English *Virgil* would honor the Roman poet and enshrine the translator who thought himself Vergil's likeness and heir. By maneuvering the *Aeneis* into an opposition stance, such a work gave this Jacobite a way of asserting his literary and political identity. The translation of Vergil allowed Dryden to see himself as patriot; it allowed him to celebrate as the Roman nobility those families that still obliged him, and to scorn the revolution that had displaced the legitimate king and poet laureate with tyranny and the mob. The analogy with Rome provided a language and a history for such assertions. How clearly the political assertions were perceived in 1697 is difficult to say; but Dryden's *Virgil* also suggested eternity, and in that invocation the poet was not wrong.[36]

Notes

1. Here and throughout, references to and quotations from the *Dedication* and the translation are from James Kinsley's edition, *The Poems of John Dryden*, 4 vols. (Oxford: Clarendon Press, 1958), vol. 3.
2. For Dryden's uses of Segrais, Vida, Le Bossu, Dacier, Scaliger, Henisius, and Bochart see W.P. Ker, *Essays of John Dryden*, 2 vols. (Oxford: Clarendon Press, 1900), 2:293–306; and Kinsley, 4:2038–48.
3. *The Letters of John Dryden*, ed. Charles E. Ward (Durham, N.C.: Duke University Press, 1942).
4. On this theme see Howard Nenner, *By Colour of Law* (Chicago: University of Chicago Press, 1977); James Rees Jones, *Country and Court: England, 1658–1714* (Cambridge: Harvard University Press, 1978), pp. 1–10; and Steven N. Zwicker, "Language as Disguise: Politics and Poetry in the Later Seventeenth Century," *Annals of Scholarship* 1.3 (1981): 47–67.

5. Mainwaring, "Tarquin and Tulia," *Poems on Affairs of State* (New Haven: Yale University Press, 1971), vol. 5, ed. William J. Cameron, pp. 46–54, 298.

6. See "Conference on 'abdicated' and 'vacant', 1689," in E. Neville Williams, *Eighteenth-Century Constitution* (Cambridge: Cambridge University Press, 1960), pp. 20–26; the proceedings can be followed at greater length in Cobbett, *The Parliamentary History of English* (London: T.C. Hansard, 1809), 5:31–110.

7. The language of the Association can be found and the response followed in *A Collection of the Parliamentary Debates* (London: J. Torbuck, 1739), 3:58–63; or Cobbett, *Parliamentary History*, 5:987–92. See, as well, Jane Garrett, *The Triumphs of Providence, the Assassination Plot of 1696* (Cambridge: Cambridge University Press, 1980), chap. 9.

8. See John Wallace on benefits and gratitude, "John Dryden's Plays and the Conception of a Heroic Society," *Culture and Politics from Puritanism to the Enlightenment*, ed. Perez Zagorin (Berkeley and Los Angeles: University of California Press, 1980), pp. 113–34.

9. A discussion of the suspending and dispensing powers and some of the documents in the conflict can be found in John Phillips Kenyon, ed., *The Stuart Constitution, 1603–1688* (Cambridge: Cambridge University Press, 1966), pp. 401–13.

10. On the coinage crisis see Henry Horwitz, *Parliament, Policy, and Politics in the Reign of William III* (Manchester: Manchester University Press, 1977), chaps. 7–8.

11. See, for example, the reference to bribery and foreign influence, 1880; the additional reference to the coinage crisis, 2185; the reference to succession, 588; or the passage on the Dutch, 1883.

12. Dryden was hardly alone in his perception of the *Aeneis* as a party poem; Spence quotes Pope on this point, "The *Aeneid* was evidently a party piece, as much as *Absalom and Achitophel*. Virgil [was] as slavish a writer as any of the gazetteers." Joseph Spence, *Observations, Anecdotes, and Characters of Books and Men*, ed. James M. Osborn (Oxford: Clarendon Press, 1966), 1:229–30; cf. Voltaire on Vergil, *Essai sur la poésie épique* in *Oeuvres complètes*, ed. Louis Moland (Paris: Garnier, 1877–85), 8:326. The most elaborate reading of contemporary reference in this period is a pamphlet entitled *Turnus and Drances: Being an attempt to shew, who the two real Persons were, that Virgil intended to represent under those two Characters* (Oxford: W. Owen, 1750).

13. Professor William Frost, editor of the Vergil for the California Dryden, is concurrently working on the plates and subscriptions; we have arrived independently at a similar notion of the function of the plates and at similar readings of the Howard and Salisbury subscriptions.

14. See S.L.C. Clapp, "The Beginnings of Subscription Publication in the Seventeenth Century," *MP* 29 (1931): 199–224, and 30 (1932): 365–79; and "Subscription Publication Prior to Jacob Tonson," *Library* 4th ser. 13 (1932): 158–83.

15. Professor Annabel Patterson is currently at work on the politics of the Ogilby plates and translation.

16. *The Letters of John Dryden*, p. 93.

17. Ibid., pp. 80 & n4, 85–6, and 88.

18. All plates are from *The Works of Virgil* (London: Jacob Tonson, 1697).

19. *DNB*, Henley.

20. *The Works of Virgil*, pp. 298, 318, 371.

21. *DNB*, Salisbury (James Cecil); *Poems on Affairs of State*, 5:355, 417n.

22. H.J. Oliver, *Sir Robert Howard* (Durham, N.C.: Duke University Press, 1963), pp. 297–9.

23. Lois Schwoerer, "A Journal of the Convention of Westminster begun the 22 of January 1688/9," *Bulletin of the Institute of Historical Research* 49 (1976): 242–63.

24. Something of the decorum of Vergil's passage is suggested by the Loeb translation at this point: "Thou, too, hapless Cydon, while thou followest thy new delight, Clytius, whose

cheeks are golden with early down—thou hadst fallen under the Bardan hand and lain, O piteous sight, forgetful of all thy youthful loves, had not thy brethren's serried band met the foe. . . ." *Virgil with an English translation by H. Rushton Fairclough* (Cambridge: Harvard University Press, 1950), 2:193.

25. See *DNB*, Sidney; Jones, *Country and Court*, pp. 246, 265; Horwitz, *Parliament, Policy and Politics*, pp. 66-7, 93, 219; *Poems on Affairs of State*, 5:62, 165-6, 460-62.

26. Jones, *Country and Court*, p. 246.

27. The Ogilby translation was of course the book from which the plates for Dryden's *Virgil* were drawn, and the borrowings from Ogilby have been treated by Proudfoot, *Dryden's Aeneid and Its Seventeenth Century Predecessors* (Manchester: Manchester University Press, 1960); the use that Dryden made of the Lauderdale translation, which he knew in manuscript form, has been studied by Margaret Boddy, "Contemporary Allusions in Lauderdale's 'Aeneid'," *N&Q* 9 (1962): 386-8; "Dryden-Lauderdale Relationships," *PQ* 42 (1963): 267-72.

28. Swift, *Prose Writings*, ed. Herbert Davis (Oxford: Blackwell, 1962), 5:194-5.

29. Dryden's translation of Book 1 of Tacitus's *Annals* was part of a composite translation of the *Annals* published in 1697 by Mathew Gilliflower. What little attention has been given to this translation seems all to derive, directly or indirectly, from Gordon's derisive remarks in his preface to his own translation of Tacitus, *The Works of Tacitus . . . translated by T. Gordon* (London: T. Woodward, 1728). The mistaken notion that Dryden worked directly from a French translation by Amelot de la Houssaye comes from Gordon's remark that "Dryden has translated the first Book; but done it almost literally from Mr. Amelot de la Houssaye, with haste and little exactness, that besides his many mistakes, he has introduced several Gallicisms: he follows the French author servilely, and writes French English . . . at best 'tis only the French Translator ill translated, or ill imitated" (sigs. Bl^r-Bl^v). Gordon was presumably trying to enhance his own claims as translator, but this judgment, apparently without benefit of inspection, is repeated in so recent a work as Howard Weinbrot, *Augustus Caesar in 'Augustan' England* (Princeton: Princeton University Press, 1978), p. 29: "Ignorance of Dryden's sources—Amelot rather than Tacitus—has led to some curious generalizations regarding the development of English prose style." In fact, Dryden seems to have had both the Latin and French in front of him and a careful comparison shows not that he translated from the French but that he translated from the Latin, at times using de la Houssaye, but often enough working out the English for Tacitus's difficult and enigmatic Latin on his own.

30. Vergil's Latin is quoted from the Delphin edition that Dryden used in preparing his translation, *P. Virgilii Maronis, Opera . . . Secunda Editio* (Amstelodami, 1690); cf. Arvid Losnes, "Dryden's *Aeneis* and the Delphin Virgil," in M. Sofie Røstvig et al., *The Hidden Sense* (Oslo: Universitetsforlaget, 1963).

31. See, e.g., *Eleonora*, 193-204; the Dedication of *Fables*, 10-16, 24-50, 60-63, 180-82; *To Her Grace the Dutchess of Ormond*, 141-50, 165-8; and, of course, *To my honour'd Kinsman, John Driden of Chesterton*.

32. The fullest exploration of name and lineage in Dryden's late poetry is the verse epistle that Dryden wrote to his namesake and cousin, John Driden of Chesterton, "To my Honour'd Kinsman"; the contemporary political themes of the poem have been most recently examined by Elizabeth Duthie, "'A Memorial of My Own Principles': Dryden's To My Honour'd Kinsman'," *ELH* 47 (1980): 682-704.

33. See, for example, the passage in *The Hind and the Panther*, 3.304-5, "That suff'ring from ill tongues he bears no more / Than what his Sovereign bears, and what his Saviour bore."

34. See, e.g., Thomas Wagstaffe, *An answer to a late pamphlet, entitled obedience and submission to the*

present government (London: J. Hindmarsh, 1690), p. 43; John Kettlewell, *Of Christian Prudence or Religious Wisdom; not Degenerating into Irreligious Craftiness, in Trying Times* (London: J. Hindmarsh, 1691), p. 84.

35. Hobbes read the passage in Vergil in the same manner, "To the Reader, Concerning the Virtues of an Heroic Poem," *The English Works*, ed. W. Molesworth (London: J. Bohn, 1844), 10:ix.

36. A version of this essay appeared originally as chapter 6 of *Politics and the Language of Poetry* (Princeton: Princeton University Press, 1984) and is printed here with permission of the Press.

AMERICAN SCHOLARSHIP ON VERGIL IN THE TWENTIETH CENTURY

William R. Nethercut

The history of any branch of scholarship is a history of the people drawn to that study: the most notorious riddle posed to man in antiquity had his own name as its answer.[1] Vergil holds up a mirror to us, from which, as we move from decade to decade, a changing image shines. In the following pages, it may be hoped that we shall come to understand more clearly the relationship between the vigorous disputes over the *Appendix Vergiliana* — a *cause célèbre* of criticism for twenty years (1920–1940) — and the reassessment of the *Aeneid* as a poem ambiguous about Roman destiny which has been the vogue in the United States since 1965. We shall have also to inquire why the *Bucolics* (the "Eclogues") commended themselves next to scrutiny, while it has been only since 1979 that the *Georgics* have come into their own. Apologies are owed, at the start, to many scholars born in this country who have written graceful and illuminating studies on Vergil, but whose names may not appear: I have limited myself to works which especially seemed to set or to represent a given trend of analysis. Apologies likewise must be offered to classicists in Canada, who are as "American" as every map of this continent declares us all to be, and to numerous English or European colleagues who reside here more or less permanently and who have contributed greatly to our major universities. It is a pleasure, by contrast, to acknowledge the assistance provided for the preparation of this review by the bibliographies published for Vergil by G.E. Duckworth (1940–56, 1957–63) and annually since 1963 by A.G. McKay for *Vergilius* and the Vergilian Society of America.[2]

I. The Minor Poems Attributed to Vergil

In the early years of this century, we find only occasional papers on Vergil in the major American journals. A quick scan of the four most significant publications yields, for *Classical Philology*, only two between 1906 and 1920; for *Harvard Studies in Classical Philology*, 1896–1920, two on Vergil's *Bucolics*; for the *American Journal of Philology*, 1899–1920, five (two on the *Georgics* and British poets, two more producing a critical commentary on the first book of the *Aeneid*, and one other, a series of notes on the *Ciris*); for the *Transactions and Proceedings of the American Philological Association*, 1896–1918, five abstracts in the "Proceedings" section on the *Aeneid*, one abstract on the *Georgics*, with one regular article on Catalepton 2. In all, over eighty annual volumes with but sixteen presentations given to Vergil; of these, no more than two address the *Appendix* of short poems collected under his name (I.M. LINFORTH, 1906; H.R. FAIRCLOUGH, 1916).

This changes rapidly. In 1919, in a lengthy survey in *Harvard Studies*, E.K. RAND reviewed the lesser works of Vergil's youth and argued that the several compositions fit easily into progressive stages leading to artistic maturation. Rand was encouraged to accept the works as genuine by a growing tendency among German scholars to consider it probable that a certain number of the poems in the *Appendix Vergiliana* were authentic. In 1920, T. FRANK published a tightly analyzed reconstruction of "Vergil's Apprenticeship." The *Culex*, he said, antedates Horace's second Epode, which in turn humorously undercuts Vergil's praise of country simplicity by exposing the yet greater appeal of the city with its "detested" financial opportunities. To Horace's irony the celebration of rustic virtues at the conclusion of *Georgics* 2 gave a morally earnest rebuttal. Frank went on to pursue the relationship which Vergil may have enjoyed with Valerius Messalla Corvinus: Messalla's pastoral poetry inspired the *Elegia in Messallam* which we find in Catalepton 9, a poem Vergil did not publish when Messalla returned on the losing side after Philippi (42 B.C.). The *Ciris*, dedicated to a Messalla, seems to look back at the *Culex*: the earlier poem is the product of a light and learned muse (*Cul.* 35–6); the second epyllion will move beyond this to work out an impressive tapestry, as it were, which will be Greek in design (*Cir.* 19–26). The "Attic garden" (of Epicurus) in which the poet of the *Ciris* finds inspiration for his work (*Cecropius . . . hortulus, Cir.* 3) need not compel us to assume that Vergil traveled to the East. The oriental fulsomeness of the proem to the *Georgics* and the suggestion that the new Caesar is a *praesens deus* (*B.* 1.41) derive from the opportunity for study Vergil enjoyed with the Epicurean Philodemus, who came to Italy from Gadara in Syria. In 1922 Frank put out a brief biography of Vergil, drawing upon the more detailed arguments to which I have alluded.

The assumptions of Rand and Frank flew in the face of European scholarship. The thesis of F. Skutsch[3] that the *Ciris* was not the work of a later poetaster but stood close to Catullus and might well he the work of Cornelius Gallus was considered radical and was attacked vigorously by the energetic Leo.[4] The groundswell which Rand felt would bolster his own acceptance of the *Appendix* as legitimate was not sustaining itself. German dissertations had already, many years before, established the Ovidian quality of the language of the *Appendix* in its entirety. In England, W.R. Hardie (1916) had drawn a clear line between the metrical art of the *Culex* and *Ciris*: the *Ciris* resembled Catullus 64, not only in the doubled spondaic closure of a number of its lines, but in its percentage of "Golden Lines" (*Ciris*: 15.5%; Catullus 64: 14.5%) and fondness for hyperbata; the *Culex* eschewed, comparatively, such architectural niceties, and in its use of nominative participial phrases dangling over several feet of the hexameter it seemed to Hardie unequivocally not Vergilian.[5] One could not expect, therefore, that the interpretations of Rand and Frank would remain unchallenged.

During the years 1920–1931 R.S. RADFORD directed a series of articles against the proposition that any of the Vergilian *Appendix* had in fact been Vergil's own work. In an initial paper (1920), he posited that, as earlier German scholarship had shown, the *Ciris* and *Culex* were more reasonably by the young Ovid. Ovid's impressive contribution to Latin metrics had been the re-forming of the mainly spondaic hexameter into one rapid with dactyls. In both *Ciris* and *Culex* the first foot is distinctly dactylic (*Ciris*: 66.8%; *Culex*: 67.1%). In 1921 Radford explored first a thesis to which he was to return in successive publications: that while the language of the short poems is Ovidian, Ovid in his known works quotes from the *Culex* and *Ciris* and *Moretum*, thus placing them before his erotic and epic verses; that the situation sketched at the beginning of the *Ciris*—a sojourn in Athens to concentrate on philosophy and writing—corresponds indeed to the year 18 B.C., when Ovid withdrew from competition for the quaestorship, gave up the political career which he had led his father to believe that he would dutifully pursue, and made a new start on his own terms. Radford also considered it possible that Ovid "impersonated" Vergil in such early efforts as the *Culex* and especially the *Catalepton* (in which the names of Vergil's friends and teacher appear) so that his poetic career would escape his father's detection: Ovid tells us that his early poetry was worked out secretly (*suum furtim Musa trahebat opus*, *Tr.* 4.10.20).

Welcome support for Ovid's hand in the *Appendix* was forthcoming the following year (1922) from the pen of H.R. FAIRCLOUGH, an important figure in Vergil studies—three of the six abstracts in the *Transactions* which I mentioned earlier, an article on Catalepton 2 in the same series, and the two papers on Vergil in *Classical Philology* between 1906 and 1920, were by him—and the translator for the Loeb Classical Library of the *Appendix Vergiliana* in 1918. Fairclough searched the vocabulary of the minor poems and found a greater percentage of non-Vergilian words than of non-Ovidian. R.F. THOMASON, a student of Radford's, followed with an examination of the *Ciris* and Ovid (1923): the terms for color in the *Ciris* are those preferred by Ovid rather than those frequent in Vergil. Vergil likes greens and blues, and is more sombre; Ovid is bright, taking *flavus* over *fulvus* for yellow, *nigrans* (glossy black) over *ater* (dull black), *candidus* (luminous white) before *albus* (dull, dead white). In 1923 R.G. KENT's investigation of different kinds of elision disclosed that the *Culex*, like Ovid and unlike Vergil, favors, beyond all other types of elision, that of the enclitic -*que*. The *Culex* simultaneously is very low on the elision of words ending in -*m*, which Vergil in his accepted works grew to prefer (in this, agreeing with his friend Horace). E.H. STURTEVANT (1923) placed the *Ciris*, *Culex* and *Aetna* either among Vergil's recognized poems or with those of Ovid: both poets achieve, 99% of the time, the coincidence of metrical ictus with natural stress in the last two feet of the hexameter; and this is the case as well in the three poems I have named. Other poets fall below this norm, sometimes with marked divergence (Ennius managed coincidence in only 92% of his verses; Horace and Lucilius create a smooth closure for their hexameters in 95% of their work). Imperial epic, however—Lucan, Statius, Silius—conformed predictably to the Vergilian and Ovidian standard.

A critique of methodology was in order. R.B. STEELE (1925) objected that the statistical report of Fairclough contained a fundamental distortion: he had compared the complete vocabulary of the *Appendix* with Vergil's, but only the non-Vergilian portion with Ovid's; had the procedure been reversed, the results would have turned around to make the poems distinctly Vergilian. There was a second and obvious problem: any poet uses a vocabulary which is particular to the subject he happens to be describing; change the topic, and the language alters. F.W. SHIPLEY (1926) added that there are more Ovidian words in the *Bucolics*, *Georgics*, and *Aeneid* than in the *Culex*: would this prove them to be by Ovid? Furthermore, a large number of these non-Vergilian, "Ovidian" words were in Catullus and Lucretius.

Two approaches had been tried: biographical reconstruction, stylistic analysis. The first continues to be open to the charge that its practitioners use the traditions about Vergil's life to justify whatever scenario they may wish to create for any of the shorter poems.[6] The second is frustrating because it sometimes produces contradictory results and because so many minutiae can be entailed, each point of which requires extended concentration with little clear gain in the end. Summarizing the status, in 1930, of the Vergilian *Appendix*, H.W. PRESCOTT wrote, with vivid and sympathetic frustration:

> All such minute consideration of internal evidence by modern scholars often seems to a detached onlooker as a veritable game of battledore and shuttlecock. The expert in metric dilates on trochaic caesuras or hephthemimeral caesuras, and immediately a brother-expert rises to observe that caesuras of no significance have been wrongly included in the evidence, and sooner or later somebody is sure to emerge with a contention that caesuras in general are without the significance attached to them by students of metric . . . Bewildered by the variety of opinion, the observer forgets his interest in the problem of authorship and decides to write an eassy on the criticism of criteria or on the intricacies of human behavior. (pp. 56-7)

A positive result of the internal analysis favored during the 1920s was to place at least the *Culex* and *Ciris*, the longest poems in the *Appendix*, close to Vergil and Ovid, which would account for their attribution to Vergil in the first instance.

Although statistical studies passed out of vogue during the 1930s, a contemporary exhaustive publication of the different patterns of dactyls and spondees in the first four feet of the hexameter, by G.E. DUCKWORTH (1966), claims authenticity for the *Culex* and *Moretum*. The completeness of these data might be taken for a firmer criterion than the matter raised by one of the editors of the recent Oxford text of the *Appendix* (1966): W.V. CLAUSEN (1964[2]) argues against the *Culex* as Vergilian on the basis that verbal repetitions in *successive* lines (as in *Cul.* 32-6) are not Vergil's way (he compares *magnus* as a unifying motif in Eclogue 4.5, 12, 22, 36, 48, 49). The style of the *Culex* in these lines is not that of Eclogue 4. At the same time, the observation that the *Ciris*-poet prefers *nec* to *neque* (29:4) does make us look toward provenance in the generation following Vergil (CLAUSEN, 1964[1]); the Augustans had begun to choose *nec*, but not in such overwhelming proportions.

A third basis upon which to seek authorship was developed by R.B. STEELE in two papers published in 1930 and in several monographs which date from this period. Later poets, even Ovid himself, borrowed from the *Culex*, *Ciris*, and *Moretum*. However, to prove that one poem is under contribution in a second may be tricky. To take one example we have already mentioned: T. Frank's view that the praise of the country in the *Culex* offered Horace the occasion, in Epode 2, for a whimsical reply, rests upon the pairing of such poems as Epode 16 and Eclogue 4, in which it is held that Vergil pointedly refuted Horace's pessimism. The actual language the second Epode and *Culex* share is similar because similar subjects are being treated. Recently, the study of the *Culex* passage has been taken farther than comparison of vocabulary by the Canadian scholar A.A. Barrett: the *Culex*'s praise of the countryside comes after Lucretius 2.14–33 because the rhetorical structure and connecting particles of Lucretius are identically arranged in both texts—to a point; but after this, the *Culex* adds something more, building upon Lucretius. Yet Barrett cannot be certain that the end of the second Georgic, which also adapts the structure of Lucretius' passage, may not have been worked out previously, or at least independently of the *Culex*.[7]

Another witness to our perplexity as we attempt to found the priority of one text upon its apparent use by a second author is present if we compare the work of R.B. STEELE (1930[1]) and of the newest editor of the *Ciris* R.O.A.M. Lyne.[8] In preparing his edition, Lyne was struck by usages common to the *Ciris* and to Statius; he remembered aptly the venomous first Satire of Persius, which spits forth loathing at the affectations of late first-century A.D. spondaizers who froth at the mouth with Alexandrian circumlocutions. The *Ciris*, Lyne interestingly suggests, is such a product from Statius' and Persius' own day.[9] Steele, on the other hand, viewed the shared language of the two as evidence that Statius, who copied Vergil in so much, did the same in this case.

Is any part of the *Appendix* rewarding as literature? After the debates over Vergil's biography, Ovidian vocabulary, borrowings from the *Ciris* or *Culex*, or borrowings within these texts from Vergil and Ovid and Catullus (A.R. BELLINGER, 1922, found a Catullan reminiscence at least once every eleven lines in the *Ciris*), after elision and stylistics, American scholarship, having brought to bear something of the technological assumptions of the 1920s and 1930s, grew weary at so inconclusive an endeavor. A refreshing and potentially pivotal new start was made by L. RICHARDSON, JR. (1944) in a Yale Prize-winning essay which analyzed with great care the structural and dramatic theory which the *Ciris*, *Culex*, and *Moretum* share with Catullus 64 (the Wedding of Peleus and Thetis) on the one hand, and with the *Bucolics* and *Georgics* of Vergil on the other. Unlike German scholarship, American classicists had studied the *Culex* so long with so intensively straight a face that the possibility of enjoyment of this Latin seemed to have vanished in the distance. Yet Richardson revealed it to be full of gaiety and clever humor. The chariot of the sun is introduced to demarcate the different stages of the passing day, from the rose-tinged dawn when the shepherd sets out into the morning to the onset of black night when the ghost of the gnat he swatted will arise to confront him from the underworld. Only two scholars have followed Richardson in awakening us to appreciation of this poetry: in Canada, A.A. Barrett[10] and in the United States, D.O. ROSS, JR. (1975) have given us pleasure in the *Culex*.

Barrett showed the artistic discrimination with which the *Culex*-author by varied and colorful repetitions structures the praise of country life (such repetitions were approved by Richardson but occurred too closely together for Clausen); he also defended the infamous lines which E. Fraenkel (1952) and others before him had used to show how the *Culex* misappropriates what is suitable in Vergil.[11] Ross would place the *Culex* and *Moretum* later as parodies—for example, it is humorous to see how the shepherd in the *Culex* remains standing through all the verses which digress on the joys of nature and then finally, a complex series of digressions ended, sits.

II. The *Aeneid*

I have described the work of Richardson as "potentially pivotal" for subsequent study of the *Appendix*. Its contribution—how one might demonstrate the attractiveness of a longer poem through exposition of its structure—was not pursued in greater detail for the *Appendix*, but can now be seen as a clear link between the scholarship of the first decades of this century, when researchers analyzed the *Ciris* and wrote more papers on it than on whole books of the *Aeneid* (so Thomason, p. 240) while glimpsing the great epic romantically through a haze of gold, and the period 1950–1970, when the *Appendix* had ceased to exist, so to speak, for Americans, who had now turned their attention to the proportioning and verbal patterning of the *Aeneid*. This investigation attempted more than the earlier search for authenticity; before all else, one wished to understand in what light, finally, Vergil had viewed the Roman Revolution. Why had he set the end of his story in anger and darkness, almost as if to subvert the golden revelation given to Aeneas in the underworld in book 6? The urgency the reviewer senses in reading again the many papers on the meaning of the *Aeneid* was nourished by the great tension within the United States between souls resisting the war policy of successive administrations and souls affronted by attacks on their ears, property, and patriotism, and again between those who opposed governmental coercion seeking to effect social change and many others who welcomed both.

If we sample at random discussions from before World War Two, we learn that Vergil was a sincere propagandist for Augustus and that Aeneas represents an idealization of what had made and would now make Rome great (M.G. MURPHY, 1926), that a Great Cause must have a Great Leader (F.J. MILLER, 1928), and that Aeneas, so far from being the automaton he seemed in discharging his destiny, suggests how a Great Leader can also be a man of deeply felt emotions (C. KNAPP, 1930–31). War led us to balance the sympathy of Vergil (and of Aeneas) for the underdog (E.A. HAHN,

1925) against morality itself, which demanded, for Americans, that the evil be punished (J.N. HRITZU, 1945–46); and the contest of inimical ways of life allowed us to approach the Roman's feeling for the rightness and necessity of Aeneas' triumph over Turnus:

> Men grow sensitive to the values of their national traditions and come to cherish them not only in periods of enlargement, like the Augustan or Elizabethan, but even more when the survival of these traditions is threatened, and most intensely when nationality itself is lost. (M. HADAS, 1948, p.409)

Yet American scholars did not characterize Turnus as *ein Staatsfeind* (an enemy of the State):[12] he was instead a tragic, even sympathetic, character (G.E. DUCKWORTH, 1940), not unlike Milton's Satan (P.M. BOLT-WOOD, 1951–52), who upon review could be found to have killed the young Pallas in self-defense. Such an adversary, in a story in which Free Will was commingled with personal error and human choice (DUCKWORTH, 1955–56), enhanced the significance for all men of Aeneas' actions. It was popular, from 1930–1960, to reflect on the double tragedy of Dido and Turnus (E.K. RAND, 1931; V. Pöschl, 1950); the *Aeneid* was being read as a work of world literature. The study of its architecture, its craft, its debt to Alexandrian and Republican poetical theory, and with this the questioning of Vergil's intentions, was now to begin.

Four publications by DUCKWORTH (1954, 1957, 1960, 1962) represented, in order, first, a parallel arrangement of books in the two halves of the *Aeneid* (in books 1 and 7 Juno stirs up trouble and the Trojans come to shore, books 2 and 8 contrast the end of Troy with Aeneas' new country and allies, books 4 and 10 are special in the tragic intensity of the loss of Dido and that of Pallas and Lausus); again, a tripartite division among books 1–4 (darker in tone with Troy and Dido lost), 5–8 (bright and full of promise), 9–12 (dark once again with conflict); and thirdly, an organization which, whether coincidentally or by design, appeared the result of mathematical proportioning. Such construction emerged especially from the examination of three passages in which two that corresponded (*A, A'*) were set to frame a third passage (*B*) as a centrepiece. There was little hesitation in accepting Vergil's fondness for tripartite sectioning: an example ready to hand is the way in which books 1 and 4 (on Aeneas' stay in Carthage) embrace 2–3 (the flashback on Troy's destruction and the wandering which followed). Most scholars preferred, however, not to look further at mathematics and to ask, instead, what Vergil achieved by separating *A* and *A'* by *B*.

In the case of books 1 and 4, it was recognized that repetition afforded Vergil the opportunity to undercut and reverse the direction of what he had set forth previously. Dido's *curses* on Aeneas in 4.382–4 throw back in his face his *prayer* for her rewards in 1.603-5 (P.R. MURPHY, 1956); Dido, described as *dux* (leader) in 1.364, appears before us momentarily in 4.165 as *dux*, until we find that it is Aeneas, not Dido, to whom *dux* attaches: her efficacy passes from her in book 4. After Pöschl, F.L. NEWTON (1957) elaborated the manner in which Dido, compared to Diana, goddess of the hunt, in book 1, is transformed, in the imagery of book 4, into a deer (Diana's special animal) wounded by a hunter's arrow. B. FENIK (1959) next showed that the Trojans, invaded and destroyed in *Aeneid* 2, are hinted in book 4 to have reversed roles with the pernicious Greeks back in 2: Dido and Carthage suffer much as the Trojans did before.

The importance of repetition and reversal in the *Aeneid*, particularly as (in Fenik's article) they illumined the developing character which Aeneas and his followers now maintain with those they come to meet, gave impetus to an increasingly doubtful reading of the poem. In 1961 K.J. RECKFORD set much of the language in the opening portion of book 7 and of the second, largely ignored, half of the *Aeneid*, in disturbing context with the Greeks' treacherous encroachment upon Troy in book 2. In fact, B.M.W. KNOX (1950), in an admired paper which proved seminal for American Vergilian critics, had noted how the fiery omen which does not harm Ascanius at the end of book 2 is recapitulated in the fire which does not injure Lavinia in book 7; however, Knox did not press the possibly negative implications of several other parallels: if Aeneas puts on Greek armor and tears part off a Trojan building, fitting in with the Greeks in appearance and action when Troy is burning, and if the fires which shine at the end of book 2 are described in language which recalls the serpents and the Greeks that attack Troy earlier, it may have been Vergil's design to show, for Aeneas, only a moment of wild passion—a starting point for his maturation—and, for the fiery omens, an affirmation answering Troy's collapse. It was more the mark of the 1960s to tolerate the keen ambiguity of Vergil's double-edged symbols. In 1963 A. PARRY wrote movingly about the "two voices" of the *Aeneid*: one of resonance for Rome's past and of perhaps muted hope for her future, and a second, "private" voice of sentiment for all she had lost. The most striking symbol of all for Vergil's ambivalence was the magical golden bough which will follow those whom fate has chosen, but which hangs back; which, for all its beauty, is itself dead (mistletoe) amidst a forest ever green (R.A. BROOKS, 1955; C.P. SEGAL, 1965-66). Others went farther: M.C.J. PUTNAM (1965) elicited book 12 of the *Aeneid* as a jarring re-enactment, but in reverse, of the taking of Troy in book 2: what happened to Troy at the hands of the Greeks in book 2 is now visited by Aeneas and his men upon the Latins.

This more forceful thesis divided response. R.A. HORNSBY (1970) felt, after studying Vergil's similes, that Putnam had laid too much weight on some. W.S. ANDERSON, who had defended Aeneas against the charge of acting like Paris (1957), now preferred (1966) to stress the richness of Vergil's ambiguity: man must act to destroy nature, in a sense, in order to build his human future; even so, Aeneas is compared to a farmer who "attacks" the bees' hive with smoke and fire, so that he can harvest their honey to sustain himself. The imperative of man's social dream makes inevitable the loss of what is natural. Others, moreover, found it less consistent with their own belief of how literature is created to suppose that Vergil wrote so selectively as to use words only two or three times in far removed passages of the *Aeneid* to make a point. This objection may fail to take into account what we have learned about poetical theory in Rome.

On the opposite side, W.R. NETHERCUT (1971–72), in support of Putnam, developed more completely the suggestion latent in Fenik and present in Putnam's essays that the reversal of Aeneas' men into Greeks (with book 2 as the initial definition of "Greek") is a major plan for the second half of the *Aeneid*: the obvious use of Achilles as a model for Aeneas here has a much wider and pervasive context—the Greeks and what resembles them being purveyors of *furor*, of unreasoned, destructive action. Nethercut charted the major images through the *Aeneid* and noted the transformation of the arrow and flame and meteor into Aeneas' shield which flashes like a blood-red comet bringing sickness to men in book 10, and the *Dira*, serpent and winged arrow at once, as it hurtles to earth to confound Turnus in book 12. The development connecting ambiguous images in the first part of the *Aeneid* with negative or destructive transformations as we approach its close will not allow us to think that the *Aeneid* aims, above all, at a positive statement about Rome and Augustus. B. OTIS (1964), whose compendious study of all Vergil preceded by just a year Putnam's own collection of essays, held that it is misleading to emphasize Aeneas' irrationality at the moment he kills Turnus: Turnus gives the lie to his own entreaty by Aeneas' parents, since he wears the buckler he stripped from Pallas, whom he sent back to his father, Evander, with the words "as he deserves you" (*qualem meruit*, 10.492). PUTNAM now has marshalled as evidence (1981) the opportunities Aeneas has had throughout the epic to respond differently at the last than he does: our primary concern must not be with Turnus' guilt or innocence but with what Aeneas chooses for himself, for his personal history is the point of the poem.

We may summarize by noting that, whereas the complaint used to be that the *Aeneid* is a story of too dedicated a hero who displays little personal passion and follows the gods' directions (Knapp labored to make the point that Aeneas is a "real" person capable of genuine and disruptive emotions), we have come to grant Aeneas all the lack of discipline, all the ungovernable frenzy, that any "real" man does have, only to feel uncomfortable about it.

We have seen a peculiar blend of personal licence, governmental abuse, controversial policies and social discord since 1960; and while World War Two probably brought us closer, in heightened awareness of nationhood, to what Romans might identify in Vergil's poetry, the special pain of internecine conflict may be an even more significant path by which we have approached the poet's personal sensibilities.

Although European scholars have registered little sympathy with the reading of the *Aeneid* we have evolved, in America at least— to judge by almost a decade of derivative articles—the impression continues to prevail that Vergil was indeed concerned with the precarious balance men try to preserve between energetic action and impulsive decisions which are carried through, clouded by passion, and bring doom (cf. M.A. DI CESARE, 1974, amplifying G.E. DUCKWORTH, 1955, on Nisus and Euryalus in book 9 and on Turnus in books 10 and 11); and that this concern is attached to the epic's protagonist, and by extension to Rome's leader. G.K. GALINSKY (1966), for example, has pointed out how the example of Hercules makes clear to Aeneas how one destined to quell the serpents of this world—the Hydra and the twin snakes sent by Hera to kill the baby Hercules—can himself be seized by blind fury and come to resemble a snake as he throttles Cacus. In all this it is helpful to read H.-P. STAHL (1981), who distinguishes between different kinds of *furor* in Vergil and in this way allows us to cultivate flexibility, too easily lost to a generation of critics advancing in age. Most European scholars would agree with Stahl's reservations about the usual contemporary American interpretation.

Since much has been made of the comparison of Aeneas to the Greeks of the *Iliad* for a negative reading of the second half of the *Aeneid*, it is most profitable to follow G.K. GALINSKY's review (1981) of the role of Homeric parallels in the last part of the poem. Galinsky counters the contention that Aeneas could possibly have spared Turnus. Roman religious practice would have wanted Turnus to consecrate the spoils of Pallas to Jupiter; it is in this sense, i.e. to expiate his sin, that Turnus is said to be "sacrificed" (*Pallas te immolat*, 12.948-9). Furthermore, Aeneas' defeat of Turnus was *the* tradition of all which allowed the Trojans to assume superiority in Italy; how could Vergil not have had Aeneas crush his enemy? The debate will surely continue. In the meantime, Galinsky will preclude any facile schematization of Aeneas as this or that Homeric or "Greek" hero, and will encourage us to concentrate on the national coloring of Vergil's employment of mythological figures. Also helpful is the careful and engaging introduction to the *Aeneid* of W.S. ANDERSON (1969), a model of fairness to all we should know and now imagine we have discovered about Vergil.

A very different general study of the *Aeneid*—one whose opening chapter concisely reviews reaction to the *Aeneid* in England and Germany during the 1800s—offers a deep look into those precise instants in passages of the *Aeneid* which unravel our security in the world's order and leave all dissolved. The darkness in Vergil of which W.R. JOHNSON (1976) writes has nothing to do with architectural schemes or verbal reminiscences; it lies beyond *furor* and politics, in the poet's heart.

The last architectural diagram for the *Aeneid* was printed in 1963 (Otis). Its scheme moved far away from Duckworth's tripartite organization and was almost wholly chiastic with no real "center" framed by the mirroring books—to a degree, a distortion. R.J. ROWLAND, JR., 1981–82, now defends cogently the centrality of book 7: it is here that we see gathered, albeit ironically in opposition to Aeneas, a true *tota Italia*. The purpose of such antiphonal panelling, Otis urged in a similar structural analysis of Propertius' *Monobiblos* (1965), was to awaken an ironic tension by playing off the later member of each pair against the first. It is such a chiastic premise that led Putnam and others to study carefully the verbal harmonies between books 2 and 12, the first chiasm in Otis' view (books 1 and 7 he placed outside of his diagram as introductory units for each half). As we have remarked, this mode of analysis calls forth the ambiguities which, before all else, have occupied American scholars. A second, earlier, view of the poem's development contributes a different perspective: the "trilogy" of which Pöschl and Duckworth wrote is less artificial and encourages us to read Vergil in a linear manner, passing from one stage (*A*, then *B*) to another (*A'*). Book 3 can be shown to prepare for the structure of Aeneas' journey through book 6 (R.B. LLOYD, 1957); and book 5—which begins the central section of the trilogy—not only takes up from books 3 and 4, but also looks ahead to book 8, thus creating a firm continuity for the *B*-section, both as it is unified internally and as it develops smoothly out of what precedes it (GALINSKY, 1968). The transitional and preparatory role of book 5 vis-à-vis book 6 has received handsome elaboration by PUTNAM (1962). The journey of the epic hero in truth combines both a linear and chiastic side (Otis, 1963); at its end, the wanderer must suppress the past which becomes his victim (NETHERCUT, 1973). This, then, has been another reading of the *Aeneid* in the United States: within the context of psychology and comparative literature, the journey of the hero of many masks. This approach helps us to understand the *Aeneid* also in a literary way, generically, rather than in a political manner alone.[13]

III. The *Bucolics*

We have studied two foci of Vergilian criticism in the United States during this century: the pursuit of the identity of the author or authors of the *Appendix Vergiliana* in the 1920s and 1930s; the analysis, in the 1960s and 1970s, of carefully staged subversions in Vergil's story of Rome. The first passion of commentators, largely statistical, drew strength from the confidence of the years before World War Two: confronted with inconsistencies (as in the *Appendix*) or economic depression, the American had faith that if he persisted, attentive to each detail, and if he marshalled his facts, he could establish identity. *Pathei mathos*; the world was knowable. The second style of scholarship grew out of the first; the discovery of structural norms in the verses of a poem (e.g. tolerance of hiatus, the clash or harmonization of spoken accent and metrical pulse, the ratio of spondees to dactyls) led naturally to the survey of internal relationships between different sections of a poem; this, in turn, disclosed apparent symmetries and the "framing" devices of which German scholars had written earlier. To a generation which struggled to integrate the stand-off in Korea and the deadlock or reversal in Viet Nam with the heady victories over Germany and Japan at the conclusion of World War Two, Vergil's recapitulations seemed more often to undermine, rather than to confirm, an initial impression.

The reading of Vergil's pastoral poems, the *Bucolics* (or "Eclogues" as they are popularly called), developed chapters in a similar sequence: at first fertile ground for sleuths tracking the identity of the shepherds with whom Vergil furnished his Arcadia, these poems came later to compose a balanced structure of response. The interpretation of this architecture, however, has moved in a different direction from the inferences drawn from the plan of the *Aeneid*. Its consciousness belongs to the 1970s (the first book on Vergil's pastoral poetry to appear in this century in America was published by M.C.J. PUTNAM in 1970), not, as with the central studies of the *Aeneid*, the 1960s. It seeks to answer a problem raised by the negative reading of the *Aeneid*, itself one of the counter-theses in which that decade abounded. Later readings of the *Bucolics* do not insist, as the new wave of *Aeneid* studies may have seemed to do, that we choose one side or the other: that we remain at the last more moved by the inevitable glory which destiny promised to Augustus and his people, i.e. by the brilliance of books 6 and 8; or, conversely, that we find ourselves persuaded by the precarious ultimate moment of book 12. The more recent criticism of the *Bucolics* emphasizes, by contrast, "suspension amid contraries, rest amid disturbance" (C.P. SEGAL, 1965, p. 244; amplified now by P. ALPERS, 1979, pp. 96–154). The violation of life which we cannot escape is at least partly compensated by the continuing beauty of each added day. This is the mind of a nation which has survived, partially torn but essentially entire, yet with perhaps less energy to commit to any single standard. Structure, from this vantage, appears more naturally linear and forward-moving (J.B. VAN SICKLE, 1978); rigorous enclosure and chiastic ribbing (as in Otis) are reinterpreted by Alpers: the enfolding panels of the *Bucolics* hang suspended across a *fulcrum*, Eclogue 5. The flexibility of this metaphor stands in sharpest distinction from the architectural imagery of the 1950s and 1960s (one remembers Grimal's comparison of the Actium-poem in Propertius' fourth book to the keystone which distributes evenly the weight of an imposing structure).[14]

The *Bucolics* date well before the *Aeneid*. G.W. BOWERSOCK, 1971, and W.V. CLAUSEN, 1972, have shown, respectively, that Octavian, not Pollio, is addressed at the beginning of Eclogue 8—the trip took place in 35 B.C.— and that the altar upon which monthly sacrifices will be renewed to a young god in Eclogue 1 is an oriental conceit suitable for the year 35 B.C. when Octavian could appear as a savior for Rome, having secured her grain supply by defeating Sextus Pompey, but not consonant with the period 41/40, when his land policy in northern Italy divided her people. Nevertheless, for the reasons given above, we can readily understand why American consideration of Vergil's pastoral poems was delayed.

Before 1940, almost nothing was seen on the *Bucolics* in the United States. There are incidental remarks in the "Proceedings" section of *Transactions and Proceedings of the American Philological Association* from 1930 on, but apart from two papers in *Harvard Studies* (W.W. Fowler, 1903,[15] and C.N. JACKSON, 1914), and a brief opinion in *Classical Philology* (E.T. SALMON, 1939) on the identity of the child in Vergil's "Messianic Eclogue," Eclogue 4, there is general silence. Pastoral poetry, with its mists and fantasies, its withdrawal from what is clear and concrete, was, one may surmise, fundamentally unappealing to American tastes. When this literature begins to attract attention, it is for the challenge it holds for the scholar who would make it more clear by tacking down firmly the personalities and identity of the different figures in Vergil's scenes. An exhaustive attempt to demonstrate who was who in Arcadia had been made by Herrmann in 1930;[16] Rose (1942)[17] had opposed English common sense to his French colleague's elaborate reading *à clef*. Whenever lines have been drawn in issues of scholarship, Americans have preferred traditionally to push for a solution, to expose an answer. We have seen this in reviewing the *Appendix*: the poems there must be by Ovid, or by Vergil himself; there is little satisfaction in confining oneself to stating the obvious uncertainties. Something of the same impulse toward closure, manifest also in the debate over Vergil's intentions in the *Aeneid* (and visible in our arguments that the babe in Eclogue 4 was a real child, as opposed to the symbolic figure of Fowler and Rose), attracted speculation.

E.A. HAHN (1944) accepted certain identities: Daphnis as Julius Caesar, Silenus in Eclogue 6 as Vergil's Epicurean teacher Siro, the wonder-child in 4 as the baby who was named Julia. She was more interested, however, in studying the development of the poetry book through the development of its characters: e.g. Corydon is unrequited in Eclogue 2, but he wins the singing match in 7. Hahn divided the *Bucolics* into three triads and demonstrated elegantly how the *dramatis personae* of each triad, the natural scenery salient in each set of three, and even the two major modes of discourse—dialogue and monologue—converge in the finale, Eclogue 10. Going beyond the literary *masques* of Herrmann, J.J.H. SAVAGE (1958, 1960) urged that the allegory in Eclogues 1–3 was political and could be dated to the years 40–38 B.C., when "courtship" and co-existence dominated the concerns of Rome. According to Savage, Galatea in Eclogue 1 and Alexis in 2 (Vergil's counterpart for Galatea in Theocritus, Idyll 11) would be Sextus Pompey, commander of the seas south and west of Italy, who robbed the state of grain from Africa.

One of the last papers to investigate the individuals in the *Bucolics* appeared in 1967 (W.R. NETHERCUT). In *Aeneid* 8 Vergil uses the poplar (its color and mythological associations) to associate Aeneas with Hercules. Similarly, in the *Bucolics* he uses the beech (*fagus*) which joins Tityrus, whose land has been restored to him in Eclogue 1, with Corydon in 2, who petitions a young boy in the city (Tityrus had done this in 1); with Corydon in 7, who joins the favoring presence of his boyfriend with the prosperity of his fields; and with Menalcas in 5, who, like Tityrus in 1 and Corydon in 7, sings a song of pleasure for the world's restoration and renewal. This would point us toward a study of the *Bucolics* by the role or posture of its *personae*, rather than by concentration upon their biographies. Following this approach, we can detect, in Eclogue 2, a restatement on the more whimsical and detached level of literary and amatory cliché, of the painful problem which Eclogue 1 sets out from contemporary Roman history: the necessity of petition to the city by those whose family lands were threatened.

Such restatement at a different level functions importantly to create a dynamic which informs the poetry book. E.W. LEACH (1966, 1974) represents pastoral poetry as a poetry of withdrawal but also of inevitable return, for which her paradigm is Corydon in Eclogue 2. But the structure of the *Bucolics* overall displays this rhythm as well. We withdraw progressively from the mingled happiness and anguish in Eclogue 1; through the more removed recasting in 2 of Tityrus' entreaty of the young city-dweller; to Eclogue 3, in which the dialectic of Vergil's first poem is lightly replaced by alternating distichs of purely sportive song (B.B. POWELL, 1976, provides an excellent elucidation of the literary humor of Eclogue 3), and in which the singers' words are said to "drench" the fields: *claudite iam rivos, pueri; sat prata biberunt* (3.111 "Shut the sluice-gates, boys; the meadows have drunk enough!"). These words allow us to put aside the fire linked with Corydon's passion in Eclogue 2. SEGAL has shown, further, (1967) how Eclogue 3 subtly prepares, amid its jests, for Vergil's higher mode in the serious poems, 4 and 5. Song, however, cannot change reality: so Corydon (G.K. GALINSKY, 1965), and so the development of the book, which returns us through song-contest (Ecl. 7) and love's torture (Ecl. 8) to the unsettled world (in Ecl. 9) we first saw in the opening poem.

But this return leaves us in greater darkness than ever (see Putnam's powerful projection of the sombre hues of Eclogue 9—1970, pp. 293-341). Otis, in his discussion of the structure of the *Bucolics* (pp. 128-43), contrasted the second half, with its poems dominated by destructive or irrational love, and the strongly Roman-patriotic orientation of the non-Theocritean pieces in the first half. He noted that just as Eclogue 9 is more negative than Eclogue 1, so 6 inverts the direction of 4, which it balances in the book's structure: 4 tells of an age of gold now to come; 6 chronicles the decline of human history from Pyrrha and Deucalion to the passion-ridden generations which have descended into our own time. And SEGAL (1969) emphasized that the introductory poem of the second half, Eclogue 6, is thoroughly ambivalent: every encouraging image is found, upon closer inspection, to gleam dubiously.

There have been two defences against final pessimism. The first is structural. The *Bucolics* do not end with Eclogue 9, but with a coda, Eclogue 10, which summarizes the preceding nine poems (as Hahn showed) and which breaks the reader free from the cycle of withdrawal and return. (Richardson compared Eclogue 10 to the song of the *Parcae* in Catullus 64, which opens a new dimension after the concentric composition of the poem to that juncture; he commended it as a Latin innovation to prolong interest beyond the completely framed architectures of Hellenistic Greek poetry.) Furthermore, the interest of the second half of the *Bucolics* is especially to create a new style in pastoral: J.P. ELDER (1961) called attention to the Callimachean program at the start of Eclogue 6 and drew together into a poetics the different genres which Z. STEWART (1959) had recognized in Vergil's catalogues. The most patient and valuable analysis of the developing poetics in the whole work is by J.B. VAN SICKLE (1967, 1978): Vergil deploys a traditional style of pastoral at first, so that there may emerge in three evenly-spaced poems—Eclogues 4, 7, and 10—a poetry which returned past Theocritus to Arcadia itself. Van Sickle is more careful than his predecessors to clarify the different registers (bucolic, georgic, civic-heroic) which Vergil may combine in a single poem. His demonstration that we should read the *Bucolics* in a linear and dynamic manner, rather than chiastically, should serve as a welcome example for subsequent interpretations of other Latin poetry books. Insofar, then, as Vergil can be seen to have planned change into his book, we may conclude less with an impression of human fortunes in disarray than with an increasing interest as we understand the poet to be building toward the completion of a new design.

A second defence against the apparently negative coloring in the latter part of the *Bucolics* may be found if we examine what we believe to be the significance of the landscape in Vergil's pastoral. Putnam assigns importance to a raven croaking in the empty trunk of a wasted tree, to a tomb marking the mid-point of a journey, to the comparison of Rome to a tall cypress, tree of death. Such details seem eloquent. Yet Leach (1974) has reviewed the landscapes of Roman and Pompeian wall painting with care: Vergil's scenery follows in a tradition. It is not unusual, for example, to find a tomb standing in a pastoral background. For Leach, and more radically for Alpers, the pastoral landscape is not to be seen as objective or in any way prior to the interchanges which it frames; it is instead a creation virtually parallel with the music of the rustic singers. It is the poet who makes a world (Alpers); without his voice and those of his friends no echoes structure the void. The *Bucolics* are, first of all, about people (Galinsky opposes the substantial nature of friendship, in Eclogue 10, to the fruitless song of Corydon in 2). The ending of Eclogue 9 (Leach), so far from intensifying in gloom, reminds us of Vergil's optimism: however barren the terrain through which he walks, each man has the choice, like Lycidas, to hold music on his lips: *Hic, Moeri, canamus* (9.61 "Here, Moeris, let us sing").

IV. The *Georgics*

The decade of the 1920s, as we have observed, engaged the community of American classical scholars in Vergilian studies as never before. After the flurry of publications and Master's theses devoted to the authenticity of the *Appendix*, two books appeared which set out to place the totality of Vergil's output in perspective. H.W. PRESCOTT (1927) and E.K. RAND (1931) detailed Vergil's early attempts at lighter verse in the *Catalepton* and in perhaps other poems of the *Appendix*; his effort, in the *Bucolics*, to forge a new pastoral poetry; the perfected craft and extended vision which made the *Georgics* for Dryden "the best poem of the best poet" and led Vergil to embark on the even more ambitious undertaking which would occupy his remaining years. Prescott was credited by reviewers with having introduced American readers to Heinze by paraphrase,[18] and the lengthiest discussion in his book was given to the *Aeneid*; Rand's account of the "magic" of Vergil's art apportions 170 pages to the *Georgics*, less than 100 to selected passages in the *Aeneid*. A more rural America was quick to respond. In a eulogy which seems to have culled a host of separate appraisals from numerous other similar papers of the day, A.L. KEITH (1937-38) addressed with fervor Vergil's feeling for the practical, for land held as a permanent possession. Vergil, he wrote, places "a halo of glory and beauty upon the soil" and celebrates the "triumph of reason over nature" (p. 530); he "ascribes soul to the earth" (p. 531), and he has considered the "dignity of the soil and its relation to the sturdy qualities of manhood" (p. 532).

"Soul" the soil may have; before all else, the *Georgics* are replete with their poet's careful research. It is hardly surprising that a work so various continues to afford diverse occasions for learned comment. Occasional studies run a range of topics: notes on caesuras, sound effects, rhythm (L.J. RICHARDSON, 1912); the influence of Vergil on Tennyson (W.P. MUSTARD, 1899); the *tinus* in Vergil's flora (H.R. FAIRCLOUGH, 1915); the *Georgics* and British poets (MUSTARD, 1908); astronomical cruces (R.J. GETTY, 1948, 1951); astronomy and neo-Pythagorean numbers (E.L. BROWN, 1963); the plants in Vergil's *Georgics* (E. ABBE, 1965).

The major line of investigation which has taken shape in the United States—once more as with the *Aeneid* and *Bucolics*—seeks first the "architecture" of the poem, then the meaning of that structure for the *Georgics* as a work of Augustan literature. L. Richardson, Jr., argued impressively for balance and interconnection within the four books of the *Georgics*: each book contains a digression which sets forth one of four great ordinances that govern the natural world: *Labor* (book 1), *Growth and Life* (book 2), *Love* (book 3), *Law* (book 4). Special sections are incorporated in each book in which Vergil directs our attention first to the heavens and cosmic order; next to Italy, placed in the temperate center of the earth and rich with all goods; then to the limits of Rome's empire in the frozen north and burning south; and at last to a private garden tended by one old man. The collocations are evocative: the *Georgics* place Rome and her power at the heart of the universe, but geography and even natural bounty only receive definition in the last book in the simple human who enjoys sufficiency in one cottage garden.

A vexed question had been the conclusion of the fourth Georgic: did Vergil really remove a passage praising Cornelius Gallus, when the famous elegist fell into political disfavor? S.P. BOVIE (1956) documented the way in which Vergil's descriptions of natural features were drawn to animate his narrative with vertical suggestion: there is movement upward from below in nature—this itself is a great law. Once we understand this assumption in Vergil, the received conclusion of the fourth Georgic, in which Eurydice dies and Orpheus descends to bring her back up to the sunlight, seems indeed to have been what Vergil originally intended as a final statement. We need not think that Vergil truly wrote anything dedicated to Gallus which he later excised. G.E. DUCKWORTH (1959) bolstered Bovie; and Otis, in a masterful analysis of the *Georgics*, developed a clear demonstration of how Vergil poises moments of increase and tranquil calm against others in which all rushes toward collapse. The stories of Orpheus, who cannot control his passion to see Eurydice, and Aristaeus, who follows the gods' instructions and thus regains what he has lost, clearly are central to the meaning of the entire work. In 1966, C.P. SEGAL argued that Vergil, so far from condemning Orpheus, sympathizes with him, finding him a more complex and suggestive character by far than the dutiful Aristaeus. Segal showed how Vergil, at the end of the *Georgics*, not only sets man at the center of everything (this Richardson had revealed), but specifically poses the problem which the *Aeneid* would elaborate: self-undoing brought on precisely by the capacity for feeling and for poetry which distinguishes man from all other beings. W.R. NETHERCUT (1972) compared the structure of Lucretius' *De Rerum Natura* with that of the *Georgics* (an exercise desiderated by Richardson): Vergil reverses the dynamic of Lucretius, making growth and enhancement come forth from dissolution (in Lucretius, the coming of Venus in the first poem is answered by the coming of the plague at the conclusion of book 6). However, it is the *natural world* which presents this example; unlike Lucretius, Vergil stresses that to be human does not mean to live on the simple physiological level but, as Orpheus does, with an intensity of feeling that makes it possible to transcend, but impossible ever to live within, natural cycles.

This meditation on the labile tenor of *homo furens* (exactly the issue at the conclusion of the *Aeneid*) makes a complete reading of the *Georgics* arrive finally at the kind of "suspension" between contraries of which we spoke in the *Bucolics*. Aristaeus performs the sacrifice he has been instructed to offer, and a new swarm of bees circles around him. The bees are, above all, a society in the fourth Georgic; Aristaeus' example speaks of social health. Orpheus, the individual as poet and artist, fulfills his destiny by suffering. This and many other antinomies have drawn the attention of PUTNAM (1975, 1979), who feels that Vergil raises more questions about Rome and her present than others have acknowledged.

Proponents of the more traditional interpretation of the *Georgics*—that it is inspired by genuine enthusiasm for Italy's future in a new Golden Age, or that it at least engages the Augustan present in a positive way—are still to be found. P.A. JOHNSTON (1980) writes that Vergil provided a cultural program feasible for his day by changing the mythology of the Golden Age from a metallic one of decline (Gold, succeeded by Silver, then Bronze, and Iron) to an agricultural mythology: natural wealth can come in abundance for the farmer, *as if* spontaneously, once he has mastered his skills; by working in concert with the cycles of nature, he can bear some responsibility for bringing about a new Age of Gold for himself and for Rome (pp. 49–50). R.M. WILHELM (1976) has compared Cicero's *De Re Publica* and other republican sources to show that Vergil, in book 2 of the *Georgics*, uses the principle of ingrafting and combining the best qualities from different lines of descent as a metaphor for nurturing the empire. Most recently (1982), WILHELM has traced the image of the *currus* (chariot, plough) throughout the *Georgics* and into the *Aeneid*. Skill and control are needed in the *moderator rei publicae*; sane statecraft is a natural analogue to agricultural expertise. For those who entertain ambiguity over Turnus' death in the *Aeneid*, it is noteworthy, in Wilhelm's study, that the simile in which Turnus is compared to a boulder caroming blindly out of control down a mountain to crush land, animals, men below (*Aen.* 12.684–9) is preceded directly by his leaping wildly out of his chariot (*e curru*, 12.681). One more symbol of Turnus' *furor*, this abdication of the reins.

It seems possible to grant Vergil's vision of a unified Italy and to applaud his analysis of political restraint and control or its abandonment; to do so, however, only causes us to question whether Vergil's confidence in different passages extends to the wider context provided by the entire work. G.B. MILES (1980), in a fresh and provocative reading, emphasized first that the *Georgics* show us Vergil in search of answers. To farm was not understood as an escape from the world; it was, rather, a challenge for man to confront the most difficult hindrances to existence. To farm is to pursue solutions. Miles next observes that neither the harsh realities which check human endeavor in book 1 (nature's law is diminution; wars sow the land with armor and bones), nor, in book 2, the too kindly environment which seduces the fantasy at harvest time to withdraw from the present, allows a future for the imagination. Books 1 and 2 represent different misconceptions of man's life as farmer and, ultimately, as citizen. The proem to book 3 contrasts the present (triumphs, temples) with the outmoded past at the end of book 2: in book 3 we survey what man has to take with him into life. We learn that energy and passion are all too easily withdrawn, even from the most hardy. Book 4 has two halves: in the first part on the bees, three divisions recapitulate books 1, 2, and 3. We read first of natural hazards to the hive and its community; this corresponds with book 1. The interlude on the old man and his garden matches the peaceful rustic world of book 2. Death comes to the bees, finally, just as it has done, in book 3, to the horses and cows. The last half of book 4, as we know, explores human control and its loss.

It has been easy to agree that Orpheus commands our interest, and to relegate Aristaeus to the background. But if, as Miles argues, the *Georgics* (Vergil's confrontation with life and nature) seek final points to make, we must look anew at Aristaeus, for he survives. This survival, in a world in which all verges downward, bespeaks on Vergil's part some measure of confidence. It is possible to put together a "formula" for human life. Aristaeus reminds us, first, that man has it in his power to *act* and to draw strength for his life (as Orpheus did not) from participation in the yearly miracles of nature (D.S. WENDER, 1969). After this, man has acquired creative skill (*ars*); Jupiter debarred mortals from the Golden Age so that each might come to refine for himself his own talent and efficacy (A. PARRY, 1972). Aristaeus, thirdly, is to show respect for Orpheus and Eurydice, to respect human mortality; Miles has noted that the ritual which Aristaeus prolongs over nine days recalls the Parentalia with its sacrifices for one's predecessors and acknowledgement of one's nature and origin.

It is not to be overlooked, further, that Aristaeus is to reverence the dead *whom he himself has injured*. This is to compose the past, in sorrow. If we compare Lucretius' account of the plague at Athens with Vergil's narration of that at Noricum, we notice an interesting difference: in Vergil, the plague educates men; it teaches them to bury the dead (3.558—Nethercut). For Vergil releasing the past must be taught as an art of survival not natural to men. It is relevant here that Aristaeus is to include poppies in his offering: Miles has admirably elucidated the whole scene by underscoring their gift of forgetfulness. To live in any future, man must have release from the prior loss that has made life not worth living.

In this way the *Georgics* end with an implied prayer that their reader lay bitterness and remorse to rest. Vergil seems here to have hoped it possible. His concern for this greater freedom is significant also in the *Aeneid*. W.W. DE GRUMMOND (1981) has made a strong case that Vergil had in mind Juno's *saevi dolores* (*Aen.* 1.25) when Aeneas sees Pallas' buckler and kills Turnus (12.945). What links the passages in question, however, is precisely the failure of Juno and, at the end, of Aeneas, to relinquish pain.

V. Reflections

It is worthwhile, in conclusion, once more briefly to set the vitality and appeal of Vergil studies during the past twenty years beside the investigation of the *Appendix* with which the century began, and then to consider our lately-found interest in the *Georgics* in relation to the discovery of "the other *Aeneid*" (D. ARMSTRONG, 1967) in the 1960s and of the *Bucolics* soon after.

It is of note that the arguments over the minor poems attributed to Vergil—many, if not all, of them spurious—prepared in an important way for subsequent essays in the interpretation of his recognized works. Such arguments, by their attention to sometimes minute physical features of the text and by their examination, ultimately, of structure, laid a foundation for that kind of literary and critical analysis of classical letters which Basil L. Gildersleeve once hoped would become America's special contribution.[19] These earlier discussions, no less than the contemporary debate over the

Aeneid, exhibit by their energy a motivation central to an American reading of classical authors: the pursuit of meaning, of affirmation. Thus, the poems in the *Appendix* must be by Ovid, if not by Vergil, or even Statius; we would prefer them least of all to have been written by an author of whose identity we must simply remain in doubt. We ought, similarly, to be able to identify at least the marvelous child in Vergil's shadowy pastorals; what we cannot know with certainty does little for us. When the *Georgics* were appreciated, this happened because they could be thought to elevate morally and esthetically our own farmers and the land which granted us so much. Living ourselves in greater blessing, a people of destiny, we once read the *Aeneid* as hagiography and found in it the sanctification of a glorious destiny; we held it close as a treatise on the rewards of hard effort, sacrifice, patriotism—a celebration of nationhood.

Whether we understand this insistence upon the "sense" or deeper significance of a work to result from an intellectual confidence that some meaning is there to be revealed, from a certain boldness mixed with impatience at suspending judgment, or from an emotional and more romantic faith (all three qualities play their part in the American temperament), it is clear that the search for "relevance" began well before the proliferation, in the 1950s, of the Humanities and Classical Civilization courses which have progressively required classicists to present the major writers in a manner that addresses the broad concerns of educated men and women in all fields of study—i.e. as documents which most of all appraise man as he confronts circumstances that hinder or support his decision to live. But since the 1950s we cannot underestimate the importance for the profession of classics of this development in the university curriculum; it seems almost directly tied to the many interpretative essays on antiquity to come from the past two decades. The *Appendix*, in such a context, has had little to offer and has dropped from sight; the *Aeneid*, by contrast, has invited, as a natural battleground, a gathering of clans under a host of banners called forth according to the great natural division among men: Aristotelians (the world as Process) and Platonists (the world as Form); partisans of Democritus (who, seeing life mentally, laugh) and of Heraclitus (for whom to live is to feel, and thus to weep); aficionados of the *Odyssey* or of Comedy, and, on the other hand, of the *Iliad* or Tragedy; champions of the Future and of Possibility, and witnesses to the path traveled to reach the goal and to Fact.

M.C.J. PUTNAM (1972) has observed that in his three great *opera*, the *Bucolics*, the *Georgics*, and the *Aeneid*, Vergil moved by stages from the abstract to the more concrete. The *Aeneid*, Putnam urges, completes this sequence by opposing *res*—the actual facts and events which lead to Rome and her empire—and *imago*—the shining scenes which suggest to Aeneas the illustrious men whose names and battles will belong to the future state. In America, our reading of Vergil has expanded in a contrary order: we have proceeded from the "factual" reporting of idiosyncrasies in the *Appendix*, and a semi-factual exegesis of the *Aeneid* (factual in part, because specific patterns of resonance and reversal have been charted; non-factual in part, because we have pressed for interpretation where the presence of patterns may not disclose the poet's purpose quite so easily) to an increasingly abstract and difficult description of the *Bucolics*. How can we explain our inversion of Vergil's own development, and how can it be appropriate that it is only at the close of the 1970s that books began to appear on Vergil's *Georgics*, his own intermediate masterpiece? How can we say that the *Georgics* offers a satisfying conclusion for America's reconstitution of Vergil? Taking Putnam's analysis as our guide, we may seek an explanation in our changing sense of the relative weights to be assigned, at different periods of our history, to the inner and more openly subjective side of life, and again to the intrusion upon such inner freedom by external exigencies or compulsion. The 1960s, much like Putnam's *Aeneid*, confronted *imago* with *res*: both abroad and at home one preached peace and practiced violence. W.R. Johnson has laid mainly to the account of the "Harvard School" the revaluation of the *Aeneid* during this era; the generation of classicists which responded to the issues of the time, however, was formed during the preceding decade. It is perhaps piquant to learn that Vergil was one of the authors least offered at Harvard during the 1950s, with no full course given to the *Aeneid* and only the mandatory samplings of books 1, 2, 4, and 6 available at the third-semester level. It is instead two scholars in Greek, Cedric H. Whitman and John H. Finley, Jr., who seem especially—the first in courses in Homer's *Iliad* and Sophocles, the second in presenting Aeschylus' tragedies—to have been formative in conceptualizing the tensions which also animate the *Aeneid*: the ambiguous position of the hero in passage, caught between two worlds external to him, the society he has left behind and that to which he will come; the conflict between natural beauty and the harsh creativity of newly-held power.

The events of the 1960s and the philosophic vantage of a new group of critics, therefore, combined to raise for study the relationship between ideals and actions, between actions and the social context external to them against which they might be measured, between subject and object. The first important discussions of the *Bucolics* drew similar distinctions, separating Vergil's "subjective" or empathetic characterizations from Theocritus' or Homer's more externally oriented narration (Otis, 1964), exploring the creation of poetry in a disturbing world (Segal, 1965), setting out clearly the contrast between favored and dispossessed citizens, between the natural goodness of Italy and the ominous landscapes Vergil associates with Rome (Putnam, 1970). Since that time, as we saw in reviewing the more recent work on the *Bucolics*, scholars have been less interested in schematic divisions: Van Sickle (1978) conceives the book as joining, separating, and recombining different thematic registers as the poet attempts to define for himself a new style of bucolic song—the emphasis here is more on the poet's reverie with himself, less upon any part of his work as it opposes an external and objective world to a pastoral dream; and we have seen that Alpers makes the presence of the singer the point of creation of rustic fantasy—this is a fully "subjective" reading of the *Bucolics*. This criticism, in sum, shows us contrasting reactions from two different decades: the latter of these, the 1970s, is far less agonistic; Vergil's poetry and the scholar's mind seem to flow with greater leisure.

The *Aeneid* and the *Bucolics* represent opposite ends of Vergil's poetic career, differing clearly in the degree to which the dynamics of either are generated by the confrontation of independent and equally viable societies, i.e. by the creation of context. For Vergil it was necessary to work through the *Georgics* to arrive at epic; but in human interchange, in adjacent periods of history, nothing is more likely than the law of reaction from whatever has gone before. In this way, the literature of Germany from the years just after World War Two, the Athenian comedy in the decade following the Peloponnesian Wars, and the popular music of the 1970s in the United States reflect a disengagement from the more frenetic years now past. The recent flurry of books on the *Georgics* can be understood in the light of what we have just said: the *Georgics* precisely return us to action within context, within the objective limits set upon man by the earth, the seasons of the sun, his own mortality.

The three works of Vergil, as American scholarship has grown close to them, become a kind of heroic curriculum: first, rebellion and differentiation at a time when fellow citizens took arms against each other (the years: the 1960s; the book: the *Aeneid*); then, a more subjective experience, removed and private, apart from personal and national fragmentation (the 1970s; the *Bucolics*); lastly, as Achilles discovers with Priam, an occasion on which other men no longer appear as the context which delimits one's desire, but instead become one's own with whom to mourn in the greater world which is not ours. The last moments of the *Georgics*, if we leave the postscript aside, are the most hopeful conclusion Vergil was to offer; Aristaeus is a fine analogue for us. Knowing whom we have hurt, we carry the past, with its strength, in tenderness into the future.

Notes

1. Throughout this article names of American scholars under review will appear in upper case followed by the date of publication when each book or article is first cited. These

names are listed alphabetically in the Bibliography at the end of the book. Subsequent citations will include the date when more than one item is mentioned by a given author. Other authors cited will not be listed in the Bibliography but their publications will be identified in the notes to this article.

2. See, from 1940-1973, *The Classical World Bibliography of Vergil*, introduced by W. Donlan, Garland Reference Library of the Humanities, vol. 96 (New York and London, 1978), which contains within one binding the surveys of Duckworth and McKay. Annual reviews by McKay appear in *Vergilius* after 1973. See also W.W. Briggs, Jr., "A Bibliography of Vergil's 'Eclogues' (1927-1977)", *ANRW* II.31.2 (Berlin-New York, 1981), pp. 1267-1357.

3. *Aus Vergils Frühzeit* (Leipzig: Teubner, 1901).

4. F. Leo, "Vergil und die Ciris," *Hermes* 37 (1902): 14-55; "Nochmals die Ciris und Vergil," *Hermes* 42 (1907): 35-77.

5. W.R. Hardie, "A Criticism of Criteria," *CQ* 10 (1916): 32-48.

6. R.E.H. Westendorp-Boerma, "Où en est aujourd'hui l'énigme de l'Appendix Vergiliana?" in *Vergiliana: Recherches sur Virgile*, ed. H. Bardon and R. Verdière (Leiden: Brill, 1971): 386-421.

7. "The Praise of Country Life in the *Culex*", *PP* 134 (1970): 323-7.

8. *Ciris: A Poem Attributed to Vergil* (Cambridge: Cambridge University Press, 1978).

9. "The Dating of the *Ciris*," *CQ* n.s. 21 (1971): 233-53.

10. "Praise of Country Life" (note 7) and "The Authorship of the *Culex*: An Evaluation of the Evidence," *Latomus* 29 (1970): 348-62.

11. E. Fraenkel, "The *Culex*," *JRS* 42 (1952): 1-8.

12. See V. Pöschl, *Die Dichtkunst Virgils* (Wiesbaden: Rohrer, 1950), p. 158.

13. Mention must be made at the last of G. Highet's anatomy of the speeches in Vergil's *Aeneid* (1972). Though it does not, like American Vergilian works, aim at unfolding a deeper meaning of the story, its detailed exposition of dramatic technique is indispensable.

14. P. Grimal, "Les intentions de Properce et la composition du livre IV des 'Elégies'," *Latomus* 11 (1952): 183-97, 315-26, 437-50. Most famous as an inspiration to Grimal and others was P. Maury, "Le Secret de Virgile et l'architecture des 'Bucoliques'," *Lettres d'Humanité* 3 (1944): 71-147, in which the paired compositions which frame Eclogue 5 form the columns of a "bucolic chapel" with the deified Daphnis enshrined in its center. Maury argued for numerological principles in the verses given to the different parts of the book. Recent surveys of the interpretation of the arrangement of the *Bucolics* include E. de Saint-Denis, "Encore l'architecture des 'Bucoliques' Virgiliennes," *RPh* 50 (1976): 7-21, written with a lively and incisive pen; and N. Rudd, "Architecture: Theories about Virgil's *Eclogues*," in *Lines of Enquiry* (Cambridge: Cambridge University Press, 1976), pp. 119-44.

15. "Observations on the Fourth Eclogue of Vergil," *HSCP* 14 (1903): 17-35.

16. L. Herrmann, *Les Masques et les Visages dans les Bucoliques de Virgile* (Brussels, 1930).

17. H.J. Rose, *The Eclogues of Vergil* (Berkeley: University of California Press, 1942).

18. R. Heinze, *Virgils epische Technik* (Leipzig: Teubner, 1903). Heinze's work for the first time brought together the evidence upon which a fair distinction between Homer's *oral* style and Vergil's *literary* style could be drawn. Prescott's adaptation of Heinze made it possible for Americans to begin to read the *Aeneid* in its own right.

19 B.L. Gildersleeve, "University Work in America and Classical Philology," *Princeton Review* 55 (1879): 511-36.

BIBLIOGRAPHY

Abbe, E. *The Plants of Virgil's Georgics.* Ithaca, N.Y.: Cornell University Press, 1965.

Alpers, P. *The Singer of the Eclogues.* Berkeley: University of California Press, 1979.

Anderson, W.S. "Vergil's Second *Iliad.*" *TAPA* 88 (1957): 17–30.

———— *"Pastor Aeneas.* On Pastoral Themes in the *Aeneid.*" *TAPA* 99 (1968): 1–17.

———— *The Art of the Aeneid.* Englewood Cliffs, N.J.: Prentice-Hall, 1969.

Armstrong, D. "The Other *Aeneid.*" *Arion* 6 (1967): 143–68.

Bellinger, A.R. "Catullus and the *Ciris.*" *TAPA* 53 (1922): 73–82.

Boltwood, R.M. "Turnus and Satan as Epic Villains." *CJ* 47 (1951–52): 183–6.

Bovie, S. P. "The Imagery of Ascent–Descent in Vergil's *Georgics.*" *AJP* 77 (1956): 337–58.

Bowersock, G.W. "A Date in the *Eighth Eclogue.*" *HSCP* 75 (1971): 73–80.

Brooks, R.A. *"Discolor Aura:* Reflections on the Golden Bough." *AJP* 74 (1953): 260–80.

Brown, E.L. *Numeri Vergiliani.* Brussels: Latomus, 1963.

Clausen, W.V. "On Editing the *Ciris.*" *CP* 59 (1964): 90–101.

———— "The Textual Tradition of the *Culex.*" *HSCP* 68 (1964): 119–38.

———— "The Date of the *First Eclogue.*" *HSCP* 76 (1972): 201–5.

De Grummond, W.W. *"Saevus Dolor:* The Opening and the Closing of the *Aeneid.*" *Vergilius* 27 (1981): 48–52.

Di Cesare, M.A. *The Altar and the City. A Reading of Vergil's Aeneid.* New York: Columbia University Press, 1974.

Duckworth, G.E. "Turnus as a Tragic Character." *Vergilius* 4 (1940): 5–17.

———— "The Architecture of the *Aeneid.*" *AJP* 75 (1954): 1–15.

———— "Fate and Free Will in Vergil's *Aeneid.*" *CJ* 51 (1955–56): 357–64.

———— "The *Aeneid* as a Trilogy." *TAPA* 88 (1957): 1–10.

———— "Vergil's *Georgics* and the *Laudes Galli.*" *AJP* 80 (1959): 225–37.

———— "Mathematical Symmetry in Vergil's *Aeneid.*" *TAPA* 91 (1960): 184–220.

———— *Structural Patterns and Proportions in Vergil's Aeneid.* Ann Arbor: University of Michigan Press, 1962.

———— "Studies in Latin Hexameter Poetry." *TAPA* 97 (1966): 67–113.

Elder, J.P. *"Non Iniussa Cano:* Virgil's Sixth Eclogue." *HSCP* 65 (1961): 109–25.

Fairclough, H.R. "The *Tinus* in Virgil's Flora." *CP* 10 (1915): 405–10.

———— "On the Virgilian Catalepton II." *TAPA* 47 (1916): 43–50.

Fenik, B. "Parallelism of Theme and Imagery in *Aeneid* II and IV." *AJP* 80 (1959): 1–24.

Frank, T. "Vergil's Apprenticeship. I, II, III." *CP* 15 (1920): 23–38, 103–19, 230–44.

———— *Vergil. A Biography.* New York: H. Holt, 1922.

Galinsky, G.K. "Vergil's Second Eclogue. Its Theme and Relation to the Whole Book." *C&M* 26 (1965): 161–91.

———— "The Hercules-Cacus Episode in *Aeneid* VIII." *AJP* 87 (1966): 18–51.

———— *"Aeneid* V and the *Aeneid.*" *AJP* 89 (1968): 157–85.

———— "Vergil's Romanitas and his Adaptation of the Greek Heroes." *ANRW* II.31.2 (Berlin-New York 1981): 985–1010.

Getty, R.J. "Some Astronomical Cruces in the *Georgics.*" *TAPA* 79 (1948): 24–45.

———— *"Liber et alma Ceres* in Vergil, *Georgics* I, 7." *Phoenix* 5 (1951): 96–107.

Hadas, M. "The Tradition of the National Hero." *AJP* 69 (1948): 408–14.

Hahn, E.A. "Vergil and the Under-Dog." *TAPA* 56 (1925): 185–212.

———— "The Characters in the *Eclogues.*" *TAPA* 75 (1944): 196–241.

Hornsby, R.A. *Patterns of Action in the Aeneid.* Iowa City: University of Iowa Press, 1970.

Hritzu, J.N. "A New and Broader Interpretation of the Ideality of Aeneas." *CW* 39 (1945-46): 98-103, 106-110.
Jackson, C.N. "Molle Atque Facetum." *HSCP* 25 (1914): 117-37.
Johnson, W.R. *Darkness Visible*. Berkeley, Los Angeles, London: University of California Press, 1976.
Johnston, P.A. *Vergil's Agricultural Golden Age*. Leiden: Brill, 1980.
Keith, A.L. "Vergil and the Soil." *CJ* 33 (1937-38): 523-36.
Kent, R.G. "Likes and Dislikes in Elision, and the Vergilian Appendix." *TAPA* 54 (1923): 86-97.
Knapp, C. "Some Remarks on the Character of Aeneas." *CJ* 26 (1930-31): 99-111.
Knox, B.M.W. "The Serpent and the Flame: The Imagery of the Second Book of the *Aeneid*." *AJP* 71 (1950): 379-400.
Leach, E.W. "Nature and Art in Vergil's Second *Eclogue*." *AJP* 87 (1966): 427-45.
_____ *Vergil's Eclogues: Landscapes of Experience*. Ithaca, N.Y.: Cornell University Press, 1974.
Linforth, I.M. "Notes on the Pseudo-Vergilian Ciris." *AJP* 27 (1906): 438-46.
Lloyd, R.B. "*Aeneid* III: A New Approach." *AJP* 78 (1957): 133-51.
Miles, G.B. *Virgil's Georgics: A New Interpretation*. Berkeley: University of California Press, 1980.
Miller, F.J. "Vergil's Motivation of the *Aeneid*." *CJ* 24 (1928): 28-45.
Murphy, M.G. "Vergil as a Propagandist." *CW* 19 (1926): 169-74.
Murphy, P.R. "Emotional Echoes of *Aeneis* One in *Aeneis* Four." *CB* 33 (1956): 20-21.
Mustard, W.P. "Tennyson and Virgil." *AJP* 20 (1899): 186-94.
_____ "Virgil's Georgics and the British Poets." *AJP* 29 (1908): 1-32.
Nethercut, W.R. "Trees and Identity in *Aeneid* 8 and *Bucolic* 2." *Vergilius* 13 (1967): 16-27.
_____ "The Imagery of the *Aeneid*." *CJ* 67 (1971-72): 123-43.
_____ "Three Mysteries in the *Aeneid*." *Vergilius* 19 (1973): 28-32.
_____ "Vergil's *De Rerum Natura*." *Ramus* 2 (1973): 41-52.
Newton, F.L. "Recurrent Imagery in *Aeneid* IV." *TAPA* 88 (1957): 31-43.
Otis, B. *Virgil. A Study in Civilized Poetry*. Oxford: Clarendon Press, 1964.
_____ "Propertius' Single Book." *HSCP* 70 (1965): 1-44.
Parry, A. "The Two Voices of Virgil's *Aeneid*." *Arion* 2.4 (1963): 66-80.
_____ "The Idea of Art in Virgil's *Georgics*." *Arethusa* 5 (1972): 35-52.
Powell, B.B. "Poeta Ludens: Thrust and Counter-Thrust in *Eclogue* 3." *ICS* 1 (1976): 113-21.
Prescott, H.W. *The Development of Virgil's Art*. Chicago: University of Chicago Press, 1927.
_____ "The Present State of the Vergilian *Appendix*." *CJ* 26 (1930-31): 49-62.
Putnam, M.C.J. "Unity and Design in *Aeneid* V." *HSCP* 66 (1962): 205-39.
_____ *The Poetry of the Aeneid*. Cambridge: Harvard University Press, 1965.
_____ *Virgil's Pastoral Art. Studies in the Eclogues*. Princeton: Princeton University Press, 1970.
_____ "The Virgilian Achievement." *Arethusa* 5 (1972): 53-70.
_____ "Italian Vergil and the Idea of Rome." In *Janus: Essays in Ancient and Modern Studies*. Ann Arbor: University of Michigan Press, 1975, pp. 171-99.
_____ *Virgil's Poem of the Earth*. Princeton: Princeton University Press, 1979.
_____ "*Pius* Aeneas and the Metamorphosis of Lausus." *Arethusa* 14 (1981): 139-56.
Radford, R.S. "The Juvenile Works of Ovid and the Spondaic Period of his Metrical Art." *TAPA* 51 (1920): 146-71.
_____ "The Priapea and the Vergilian Appendix." *TAPA* 52 (1921): 148-77.
_____ "The Language of the Pseudo-Vergilian *Catalepton* with special reference to its Ovidian Characteristics." *TAPA* 54 (1923): 168-86.
_____ "The Culex and Ovid." *Ph* N.F. 40 (1931): 68-117.
Rand, E.K. "Young Virgil's Poetry." *HSCP* 30 (1919): 103-85.

_____ *The Magical Art of Virgil.* Cambridge: Harvard University Press, 1931.

Reckford, K.J. "Latent Tragedy in *Aeneid* VII, 1–285." *AJP* 82 (1961): 252–69.

Richardson, L., Jr. *Poetical Theory in Republican Rome.* New Haven: Yale University Pres, 1944.

Richardson, L.J. "Some Observations on Vergil's *Georgics.*" *TAPA* 43 (1912): lxxiv–lxxvi.

Ross, D.O., Jr. "The *Culex* and *Moretum* as Post-Augustan Literary Parodies." *HSCP* 79 (1975): 235–63.

Rowland, R.J., Jr. "Books of Lists; Observations on Vergil's *Aeneid*, Books VI–VIII." *The Augustan Age* 1 (1981–82): 20–25.

Salmon, E.T. "The Fourth Eclogue Once More." *CP* 34 (1939): 66–8.

Savage, J.J.H. "The Art of the Third *Eclogue* of Vergil (55–111)." *TAPA* 89 (1958): 142–58.

_____ "The Art of the Second *Eclogue* of Vergil." *TAPA* 91 (1960): 353–75.

Segal, C.P. "*Tamen Cantabitis, Arcades.* Exile and Arcadia in *Eclogues One* and *Nine.*" *Arion* 4 (1965): 237–66.

_____ "*Aeternum Per Saecula Nomen.* The Golden Bough and the Tragedy of History." *Arion* 4 (1965): 617–57; *Arion* 5 (1966): 34–72.

_____ "Orpheus and the Fourth *Georgic*: Vergil on Nature and Civilization." *AJP* 87 (1966): 307–25.

_____ "Vergil's *Caelatum Opus.* An Interpretation of the Third *Eclogue.*" *AJP* 88 (1967): 279–308.

_____ "Vergil's Sixth *Eclogue* and the Problem of Evil." *TAPA* 100 (1969): 407–35.

Shipley, F.W. "Ovidian Vocabulary and the *Culex* Question." *TAPA* 57 (1926): 261–74.

Stahl, H.-P. "Aeneas—An 'Unheroic' Hero?" *Arethusa* 14 (1981): 157–77.

Steele, R.B. "Non-Recurrence in Vocabulary as a Test of Authorship." *PQ* 4 (1925): 267–80.

_____ "Authorship of the *Ciris.*" *AJP* 51 (1930): 148–84.

_____ "The Authorship of the *Moretum.*" *TAPA* 61 (1930): 195–216.

Stewart, Z. "The Song of Silenus." *HSCP* 64 (1959): 179–205.

Sturtevant, E.H. "Harmony and Clash of Accent and Ictus in the Latin Hexameter." *TAPA* 54 (1923): 51–73.

Thomason, R.F. "The *Ciris* and Ovid. A Study of the Language of the Poem." *CP* 18 (1923): 239–62, 334–44.

Van Sickle, J.B. "The Unity of the *Eclogues.* Arcadian Forest, Theocritean Trees." *TAPA* 98 (1967): 491–508.

_____ *The Design of Virgil's Bucolics.* Rome: Edizioni dell'Ateneo & Rizzari, 1978.

Wender, D.S. "Resurrection in the Fourth *Georgic.*" *AJP* 90 (1969): 424–36.

Wilhelm, R.M. "The Second *Georgic*: The Sowing of a Republic." *ZAnt* 26 (1976): 63–72.

_____ "The Plough-Chariot: Symbol of Order in the *Georgics.*" *CJ* 77 (1981–82): 213–30.

INDEX